HUMAN SERVICE ORGANIZATIONS

YEHESKEL HASENFELD
University of Michigan

Prentice-Hall, Inc., Englewood Cliffs, New Jersey 07632

Library of Congress Cataloging in Publication Data

Hasenfeld, Yeheskel.
  Human service organizations.

  Bibliography: p.
  Includes index.
  1.–Social service. I.–Title.
HV40.H334   361.3   82-7500
ISBN 0-13-447490-2   AACR2

Prentice-Hall Series in Social Work Practice
Neil Gilbert and Harry Specht, eds.

Editorial/production supervision
  by Virginia Cavanagh Neri
Cover design by Ray Lundgren
Manufacturing buyer: John Hall

Printed in the United States of America

10 9 8

ISBN 0-13-447490-2

Prentice-Hall International, Inc., *London*
Prentice-Hall of Australia Pty. Limited, *Sydney*
Prentice-Hall of Canada Inc., *Toronto*
Prentice-Hall of India Private Limited, *New Delhi*
Prentice-Hall of Japan, Inc., *Tokyo*
Prentice-Hall of Southeast Asia Pte. Ltd., *Singapore*
Whitehall Books Limited, *Wellington, New Zealand*

למשפחתי

CONTENTS

8 ASSESSMENT OF ORGANIZATIONAL PERFORMANCE 204

9 CHANGING HUMAN SERVICE ORGANIZATIONS 218

REFERENCES 248

AUTHOR INDEX 266

SUBJECT INDEX 270

PREFACE

As a social worker and sociologist, my interest in human service organizations is motivated both by my desire to make them more responsive to their clients and by my quest to understand the social processes that shape their character. It is my conviction that human service practitioners can make their organizations more responsive only if they understand the variables that shape service delivery systems. At the same time, social scientists cannot fully comprehend these organizations unless they interact with and study both the practitioners and their clients. The purpose of this book is to facilitate the dialogue between them.

My interest in human service organizations is also rooted in personal experiences. Reflecting on my encounters with them, I cannot fail to acknowledge my ambivalent attitudes. I am grateful for the services they have provided me, without which I could not have attained many of the things I value. In many instances, their staff have left a deep, positive imprint on me. At the same time, I also remember many unpleasant experiences, especially those that showed a lack of care and competence or outright inhumanity. And so I interact with human services with a feeling of trepidation—hoping for the best but fearing the worst.

My sense is that these ambivalent attitudes are replicated whenever citizens interact with human services, as is amply documented in numerous scientific and popular accounts. I suspect that my chief reason for studying them is to explain this paradox, and particularly to comprehend the conditions that enhance or hamper their ability to uphold, protect, and promote the welfare of their clients. That is the theme of this book.

The task has proven to be most challenging because the universe of human services is vast, complex, and ever-changing. I have tried to formulate a theoretical perspective that applies to all human services, and yet explains their diverse service delivery patterns. To do so, I have relied on several intellectual approaches, the foremost being the political economy perspective as explicated by Mayer Zald. Zald has proven to be more than an intellectual mentor. He has read many of the chapters and offered cogent and often devastating criticism that sent me back to the drawing board. While I ultimately charted my own course, I am greatly indebted to him as a colleague and friend. The writings of Charles Perrow on organizations, in general, and human services, in particular, have also provided me with an important analytical perspective. Specifically, they have enabled me to "demystify" human service organizations and avoid being entrapped by their rhetoric. The studies by Freidson of the medical care system are eloquent examples of such a mode of inquiry—one that I have tried to emulate. I have used all these works liberally as references.

The approach I have adopted in my analysis has its origins in the seminars on human service organizations conducted by Robert D. Vinter and Rosemary C. Sarri. They first introduced me to this field, and more than anyone else, taught me most of what I know about these organizations. Their ideas and writings, and the opportunities they provided me to work with them, have benefitted me greatly. This book could not have been written without them. Along with them, Albert J. Reiss Jr. has sharpened my sociological view of these organizations, and William Gamson has helped me to understand the importance of power in shaping social relations, particularly those between clients and organizations. David Street, whose untimely death has deprived me of a dear colleague, critiqued my earlier work and taught me the value of "sociological imagination."

Many of the ideas in this book germinated when I collaborated with my close friend, Richard A. English, on a reader on human service organizations. The surprising receptivity of that volume by the field has given me the impetus to undertake this project. Yet it took the prodding of Harry Specht, the consulting editor, and Ed Stanford of Prentice-Hall to get me going. The reactions and responses of my students to earlier versions of this book have been invaluable, and I am gratefully indebted to them.

The production of this book was immeasurably enhanced through the able hands of my editor, Rhea Kish. Not only has she edited the book with meticulous care, but in the process she has taught me how to express my ideas more succinctly and clearly. I have also attempted to avoid the use of language that may be gender biased. I have used the plural pronoun or the phrase "he or she" when appropriate. I have used sex-specific terms only when they truly represented the population under study. Pam Engelhaupt typed most of the manuscript with great care. Finally and most important, this book could not have been written without the love, affection, and understanding of my family—Helen, Rena, and Rachel. I dedicate it to them.

Yeheskel Hasenfeld

1

THE UBIQUITY
OF HUMAN SERVICE
ORGANIZATIONS

The hallmark of modern society, particularly of its advanced industrial states, is the pervasiveness of bureaucratic organizations explicitly designed to manage and promote the personal welfare of its citizens. Our entire life cycle, from birth to death, is mediated by formal organizations that define, shape, and alter our personal status and behavior. We are born and die in hospitals; socialized and trained in schools; marry (and later perhaps divorce) in churches or courts; seek all sorts of aid and assistance from a vast array of welfare organizations; protect ourselves and our properties through law enforcement agencies; and find solace and enjoyment in cultural and recreational organizations. I denote that set of organizations whose principal function is to protect, maintain, or enhance the personal well-being of individuals by defining, shaping, or altering their personal attributes as "human service organizations." These organizations are distinguished from other bureaucracies by two key characteristics. First, they work directly with and on people whose attributes they attempt to shape. People are, in a sense, their "raw material." Second, they are mandated—and thus justify their existence—to protect and to promote the welfare of the people they serve.

The proliferation and dominance of human service organizations in our lives is an outgrowth of the modern welfare state. The welfare state is based on the principle of governmental guarantee of "minimum standards

of income, nutrition, health, housing, and education, assured to every citizen as a political right, not as charity" (Wilensky, 1975: 1). The relationships
between citizens and the welfare state are mediated by human service organizations, which register and respond to citizens' claims. The magnitude
of these claims has increased dramatically over the last few decades. As
noted in Table 1.1, expenditures for social welfare from private and public
agencies, expressed as a percent of the Gross National Product, rose from
13.4 percent in 1950 to 27.1 percent in 1977. Approximately 12 percent of all
employed persons in the United States work in human service industries,
either providing direct services or administering them (U.S. Department of
Commerce, 1980),[1] with the majority employed in health or educational
industries.

Several factors have contributed to the bureaucratization of the welfare state. First, the welfare state needed to establish mechanisms to ensure
that individuals demonstrate their eligibility for services and then obtain

TABLE 1.1   Public and Private Expenditures for Social Welfare: 1950 and 1977ᵃ (in billions of dollars, except percent)

TYPE OF EXPENDITURE	1950	1977
Public	23.5	361.6
Private	12.2	146.8
Total	35.4	497.7
Income maintenance	10.7	194.4
Public	9.8	166.6
Private	1.0	27.8
Health	12.0	164.5
Public	3.1	67.3
Private	9.0	97.2
Education	11.0	116.2
Public	9.4	98.3
Private	1.6	17.9
Welfare and other services	2.0	33.2
Public	1.3	29.3
Private	.7	3.9
PERCENT OF GNP		
Income maintenance	4.0	10.6
Health	4.5	9.0
Education	4.1	6.3
Welfare and other services	.8	1.8
Total	13.4	27.1

ᵃ"Public" refers to federal, state, and local governments; "private" to nongovernmental agencies.
Source: U.S. Bureau of the Census, *Statistical Abstracts of the U.S. 1980*, p. 331.

[1]This figure does not include support personnel such as clerical or maintenance staff.

them fairly and equitably. Human service bureaucracies accomplish both aims via their formal rules, procedures, and systems of accountability. These are supposed to ensure that universalistic criteria are applied to verify citizens' claims for benefits, and that the provision of these benefits is not prejudicial. In short, they are designed to "purge particularism" (Perrow, 1972). Second, the complexity of human needs in industrialized society and the ever-increasing sophistication of the services to meet them exceed the capacity of traditional social units and individuals to respond to them. Consequently, the welfare state has had to establish specialized units in which the necessary knowledge, skills, and expertise are concentrated and in which an efficient division of labor can be instituted. Third, the welfare state has sought to establish new forms of social control when the household ceased to serve as a place of work and thus could no longer fully control the behavior of its members (Janowitz, 1978). Human service organizations have come to assume this control function in a variety of ways. They take major responsibilities in socializing individuals for future roles (examples include schools, social and recreation centers, universities, and other youth service agencies). They serve to identify individuals who fail to conform to their prescribed roles and attempt to resocialize them (for example, police, hospitals, correctional programs, or mental health agencies). They provide the means and resources for individuals to become socially integrated (for example, financial assistance or therapy and counselling agencies).

THE INDIVIDUAL AND HUMAN SERVICE ORGANIZATIONS

For the individual, the bureaucratization of the welfare state has resulted in the transformation of private welfare into public welfare. That is, concerns about personal welfare and well-being, which in the past were handled within the private domain, have now become a public responsibility to be dealt with through public human service organizations. When parents enroll their child in school, they have delegated their parental responsibility for the child's education to a bureaucracy. The child has acquired the formal status of "student" by virtue of his or her affiliation with the school. When a person is admitted to a hospital, his or her illness is no longer a private affair, but becomes a public concern duly recorded in an official dossier. The person has acquired the formal status of "patient."

Such transformations have profound consequences for individuals. Making their needs and problems public enables them to gain access to human services that are essential to the improvement, maintenance, and restoration of their well-being and personal welfare. The ability to obtain welfare services is no longer determined strictly by one's ascriptive affiliations (i.e., the social group they are born into). However, at the same time, individuals are required to expose significant aspects of their private lives to public scrutiny and control. They acquire a public identity on the basis of official interpretations of their personal needs and circumstances. These identities influence an individual's social position and status. Being a "university student" confers a positive social status, while being designated a "welfare recipient" confers a negative status. Hence, individuals' transactions with human service organizations profoundly affect their social status.

By turning to human service organizations to meet their welfare needs, individuals increase their dependence on them, and the organizations acquire considerable power to shape their lives. On the one hand, officials control the welfare resources they need; on the other hand, the individual has little influence over the organization's policies. The individual's loss of power vis-à-vis human service organizations is a fundamental characteristic of the welfare state (Coleman, 1973). In very many instances the individual is *coerced* or has no choice but to deal with these organizations: children are required to attend school; the mentally ill may be committed involuntarily to the mental hospital; and the destitute have no choice but to apply to the welfare department.

A CLASSIFICATION OF HUMAN SERVICE ORGANIZATIONS[2]

Considering the vast variety of human service organizations, it is useful to classify them along some key dimensions that highlight their distinctive functions and characteristics and that also differentiate them from other types of organizations. Human service organizations, as was pointed out earlier, are distinguished from other bureaucracies by the fact that their "raw material" consists of people; and they can be differentiated by the transformations they seek in their clients. Therefore, they can be classified according to these two dimensions: the types of clients they serve and their transformation technologies (i.e., the procedures and techniques they use to bring about changes in their clients).

The types of clients an organization is mandated to serve influences not only its domain and functions, but also society's expectations and evaluations. It makes a dramatic difference whether the school serves predominantly gifted children or slow learners. Similarly, the clients served by the Social Security Administration are viewed quite differently from those served by welfare departments. Thus, organizations whose primary mandate is to maintain and enhance the well-being of persons judged to be functioning adequately in society lie at one end of the continuum. At the other end lie those organizations mandated to control, ameliorate, and remedy the ill or deviant state of persons judged to be malfunctioning in society. Human

[2]This section is adapted from Hasenfeld and English (1974: 4–7).

service organizations experience serious difficulties in establishing consensus about what constitutes the adequate or inadequate functioning of their clients. Disagreements erupt both within the organization and among community groups as to the degree of "normalcy" of the clients. The demands by parent groups to "mainstream" their developmentally disabled children into regular classrooms reflect such a controversy: the parents attempt to minimize the degree of "abnormality" of their children; school officials and teachers tend to maximize it. Similarly, treating the mentally ill or offenders in community-based facilities typically evokes disagreements between advocates and opponents of such programs about the degree of danger these clients pose to the community.

The second dimension refers to the type of services provided by the organization, or more generally to the nature of its *transformation technologies*. These technologies will determine what the organization does with and to its clients and what its product will be. I distinguish between three types of transformation technologies (see Chapter 5).

1. People-processing technologies. These attempt to transform clients not by altering their personal attributes, but rather by conferring upon them a social label and a public status that evoke desirable reactions from other social units (Hasenfeld, 1972). This is accomplished through a system of classification and disposition that is used to identify and define clients as, for example, "mentally ill," "gifted child," or "cancer patient." By means of such labels, other human service organizations are expected to respond to clients in a predetermined manner, such as providing psychotherapy to the mentally ill or placing the gifted child in an accelerated class.

2. People-sustaining technologies. These attempt to prevent, maintain, and retard the deterioration of the personal welfare or well-being of clients; they do not, however, attempt to change directly their personal attributes. Custodial care of the severely disabled, nursing-home care for the elderly, and income maintenance programs (e.g., SSI and AFDC) well illustrate these technologies.

3. People-changing technologies. These aim directly at altering the personal attributes of clients in order to improve their well-being. These technologies include, for example, psychotherapy, education, and medical treatment. As with the other dimension, human service organizations are frequently plagued with ambiguities about the objectives of their transformation technologies, for the distinctions between them are ill-defined. For example, while the welfare department may claim that its primary purpose is to alter its clients' attributes so they can become productive members of society, its critics argue that it essentially employs people-processing and people-sustaining technologies. Similarly, while the advocates of the juvenile court reaffirm its aim to change the behavior of juvenile offenders, its critics point to the court's preoccupation with processing rather than treatment. The cross-classification of these two dimensions produces six types of human service organizations (see Table 1.2). It should be kept in mind that, like all typologies, this one presents ideal types. Empirically, human service organizations may encompass several types within their boundaries. For example, it is obvious that a hospital is both a people-processing and a people-changing organization.

Table 1.2   A Typology of Human Service Organizations

TYPE OF CLIENT	PEOPLE PROCESSING	PEOPLE SUSTAINING	PEOPLE CHANGING
Normal functioning	*Type I* College admissions Office Credit rating bureau	*Type III* Social Security Retirement home	*Type V* Public school YMCA
Malfunctioning	*Type II* Juvenile court Diagnostic clinic	*Type IV* Public assistance Nursing home	*Type VI* Hospital Residential treatment center

Each type of organization encounters some unique dilemmas as it attempts to meet its mandates. Type I organizations must demonstrate that their processing technologies are sufficiently discriminating in identifying client attributes and matching them with appropriate dispositions. For example, a credit-rating bureau must convince financial institutions that it is able to differentiate between "good" and "bad" credit risks. The college admissions office must assure university officials that it can identify potentially successful students. At the same time, these organizations must convince their publics that their classification-disposition schemes are not capricious or biased to favor certain clients. Employment placement services are typically criticized for favoring job seekers who can be easily placed, and college admissions officers are challenged to demonstrate that they do not discriminate against ethnic minorities. However, offering their classification-disposition schemes to public scrutiny makes these organizations more susceptible to manipulations by prospective clients and increases the potential for controversy over the validity and reliability of their technologies.

While it is advantageous for Type I organizations, when in doubt, to exclude clients from certain designations, the obverse is true for Type II organizations. Because they have jurisdiction over deviant clients, they must demonstrate that they can effectively identify all of them. For these organizations, the penalty for designating a deviant client as normal is greater than for labeling a normal client as deviant, because societal disapproval is greater in the former than in the latter instance. It is for this reason, for example, that physicians prefer to commit the error of diagnosing a person as ill when he or she is in fact well, rather than to diagnose an ill person as well (Scheff, 1966). The decision rule of "when in doubt assume deviance," however, can severely tax organizational and personal resources, and increase the service demands on those organizations that must respond to such diagnoses. Hence, Type II organizations are caught in the cross-pressures between their mandate and the limited resources of those who must take up the responsibility for their clients.

To meet their mandates, both Type III and Type IV organizations must demonstrate that their clients are "entitled" to their care and sustenance. They must develop criteria of eligibility to distinguish between those entitled to their services and those who are not, despite the fact that such distinctions may, in reality, be quite arbitrary. For example, persons denied public assistance because they reside with relatives may, nonetheless, experience the same needs as persons living alone.

Both types of organizations, but particularly Type IVs, encounter the issue of determining an acceptable and adequate level of care and sustenance. Both ideological and fiscal factors enter into such a decision and pull the organization in opposite directions. This is most evident regarding malfunctioning clients about whom there is little agreement on what constitutes an adequate level of care. Witness, for example, the debate about the desirable level of support welfare recipients deserve.

The problems of distinguishing between normal and malfunctioning clients also plagues Type V and VI organizations. In addition, they must operate with change technologies that produce uncertain outcomes. For example, the effectiveness of various modes of psychotherapy is questionable (Orlinsky and Howard, 1978), as is the effectiveness of numerous educational technologies. Furthermore, there is not always consensus about the desired outcomes themselves. Schools are embroiled in controversies about their educational mission, while correctional institutions are pushed and pulled between a punishment and a rehabilitation goal.

THE DISTINCTIVENESS
OF HUMAN SERVICE
ORGANIZATIONS

In many respects human service organizations share the characteristics of other bureaucracies. They are contrived, goal-directed, social units that import resources from their environment to produce a specified set of products and to maintain themselves (Katz and Kahn, 1978). As goal-directed social units, they are founded to produce products needed by other social units who, in turn, will provide these organizations with future resources. In the same way that a manufacturing firm is established to generate products desired by potential consumers, so do human service organizations develop programs and services that will be supported by potential beneficiaries. Should the programs fail to win the support of key resource providers, the organization is in danger of being eliminated. To obtain the necessary resources from its environment and to market its products, every organization must develop boundary roles and exchange relations with appropriate external units. The department store has its buyers and sales persons. The mental hospital has its intake and discharge staff. Both organizations deal with various external units to obtain the necessary fiscal resources to finance their operations, and both seek social support and legitimation for their activities. To produce their respective products, the bank, the welfare department, or the hospital must rely on a series of specified tasks carried out by people and machines, each trained or programmed with a certain skill. These tasks constitute the technology of the organization. To achieve proficiency, the organization develops a plan for a division of labor that defines the tasks of each person in the organization, and the manner in which they are to be carried out.

To ensure that the various organizational activities are carried out appropriately and in accordance with its aims, every organization establishes an internal structure. This defines the authority of each person and the mechanisms of coordination among them. Authority is defined by Simon (1976: 125) as "the power to make decisions which guide the actions of others." Through the distribution of authority the organization controls and coordinates the activities of its members. In the business corporation, for example, strategic decisions are made by the president and the various executive officers. They delegate authority to middle management to ensure that the policies are being implemented and coordinated among the various divisions and departments. The middle managers, as heads of their respective departments, allocate supervisory authority within each department and define the responsibilities of the other staff persons in them. Similarly, in the hospital, strategic decisions are made by the medical directors and hospital administrators. Their policies are implemented by the heads of the various units, such as the chiefs of the medical departments and the administrators of the nonmedical units. Within each department, lines of responsibility are established to define and coordinate the activities of the various staff members. In short, all organizations, including the human services, develop a bureaucratic structure that has many of the elements defined by Weber (see Chapter 2). That is, authority is legally and rationally based and is distributed hierarchically; responsibilities for operating decisions are delegated to the various work units; roles and positions are specialized; many activities are formalized and standardized; and the rules governing the behavior of staff are applied universally. Of course, how much or how well organizations follow the Weberian model varies enormously, but all at least adhere to some of its elements.

Human services, as a class of organizations, share a unique set of characteristics because they all work with and on people (Hasenfeld and English, 1974: 8–23). First, the fact that the "raw material" consists of people vested with moral values affects most of their activities. The service technologies must be morally justified because every activity related to clients has significant moral consequences. The seemingly simple decision of evaluating a student's performance and assigning a grade has important moral consequences to the student, which the teacher and the school as a whole cannot ignore. Furthermore, the organization and its staff are limited by what they can do *to* their clients and how they carry out their work with them; and, because clients are self-activating entities, the organization must develop acceptable mechanisms to attain their compliance. These themes are discussed in Chapters 5 and 7.

Second, and related to the above, the goals of human service organizations are vague, ambiguous, and problematic—namely because it is far more difficult to agree about achieving the desired welfare and well-being needs of people than it is to transform inanimate objects. While consensus may exist at the abstract level, implementation necessitates that human service organizations make normative choices in a society that is characterized by interest groups upholding competing values and norms. Recall, for example, the ever-present debate about the objectives of public assistance, or about the educational mission of public schools, or how hospitals should treat the terminally ill, and so on. These issues are explored in Chapter 4.

Third, the moral ambiguity surrounding human services also implies that they operate in a turbulent environment. That is, their environment is composed of many interest groups, each attempting to achieve its values and aims through the organization. For example, the juvenile court encounters: the police who are interested in removing troublesome youth from the community; child advocacy groups who want the court to provide treatment services; judicial interest groups who stress the need for due process; and county officials who want to curtail the costs of operating the court and its services. Moreover, these groups and their interests change over time. With shifting social conditions, new groups may arise, such as advocates on behalf of minority youth; or attitudes may change from leniency toward juvenile offenders to a demand for harsh punishment. Because human service organizations are dependent on external donors to finance their operations, they are highly dependent on their environment, and, consequently, readily affected by changes in it. This topic is discussed in Chapter 3.

Fourth, human service organizations must operate with indeterminate technologies that do not provide complete knowledge about how to attain desired outcomes. The lack of a determinate technology that could inform staff what to do when and how to achieve appropriate outcomes results from three interrelated factors. (1) People represent extremely complex systems; their attributes are highly interrelated and yet vary from person to person. Hence, as "raw material" they are variable and unstable. (2) The knowledge about how people function and how to change them is partial and incomplete. (3) Many of the attributes human service organizations are asked to transform cannot be observed or measured. As a result, human service organizations must operate with service technologies that lack clarity, are riddled with unknown elements, and are unpredictable in their consequences. An analysis of these technologies and their operationalization is the theme of Chapter 5.

Fifth, the core activities in human service organizations consist of relations between staff and clients. These relations serve as the vehicle and the tools through which the organization takes jurisdiction over the clients, assesses and determines their needs, works to transform them, and accomplishes some desired results. That is, all the essential tasks of human service organizations are carried out by a series of transactions between clients and staff. Indeed, the "career" of clients and their fate in the organization are influenced by the structure and content of these transactions, and particularly by the information and attributes they present and staff reactions and responses to them. The nature and quality of staff-client relations, therefore, is a critical determinant of the success or failure of the organization. When patients, for example, distrust their physicians, they are less likely to heed their advice or follow their directions. When students dislike their teachers, their motivation to learn suffers. Yet the quality of these relations is not readily controlled by the organization because it is affected by the personal attributes of both staff and clients. These issues are explored in Chapter 7.

Because of the primacy of staff-client relations, the position and role of line staff is of particular importance in human service organizations. Lipsky (1980) has characterized these organizations as "street-level bureaucracies" because their essential services are provided by lower status staff who, as a result, exercise considerable discretion in performing their duties. That is, while the mandate of the organization is implemented through the relations and transactions between staff and clients, these cannot be readily monitored and supervised. Numerous legal, ethical, ideological, technical, and economic reasons limit the ability of the organization to monitor these relations. Therefore, lower status staff exercise more autonomy than they might be formally granted. Similarly, because the service technologies tend to be indeterminate and the organizational goals ambiguous, the capacity of the organization to coordinate the work of its various units is limited. It is for this reason that human service organizations are often described as "loosely coupled" systems (Weick, 1976). These themes are explicated in Chapter 6.

Finally, human service organizations lack reliable and valid measures of effectiveness, and, therefore, may be more resistant to change and innovation. The multiplicity and ambiguity of organizational goals, the indeterminancy of the service technologies, and the inherent difficulties in observing and measuring human attributes together contribute to the difficulties in evaluating service outcomes and assessing organizational effectiveness. Being deprived of such feedback enables the organization to reify its claims of success and to reinforce its dominant service ideologies. These issues are discussed in Chapter 8. Moreover, the absence of reliable and valid measures of performance diminishes the capacity of the organization to innovate, because it lacks a reliable yardstick by which to compare its performance to new developments in its field of service. The lack, for example, of valid and reliable measures of the effectiveness of psychotherapy may actually lead practitioners to ignore new technological developments. For these and other reasons, human service organizations experience many difficulties in adopting innovations and implementing change, a theme that is explored in Chapter 9.

Both the similarity and the distinctiveness of human service organizations to other bureaucracies create a question about which organizational theory is appropriate for the study of these organizations. Most theories of organizations have been formulated with industrial organizations or governmental agencies as their empirical referents. Do these theories adequately apply to human service organizations? This issue is examined next in Chapter 2.

2

THEORETICAL APPROACHES TO HUMAN SERVICE ORGANIZATIONS

The literature on human service organizations is characterized by multiple and incompatible theories, leading to incongruous and conflicting findings and conclusions. This state of affairs is not peculiar to the study of human service organizations. It is characteristic of the study of organizations in general and results from the wide variety of theoretical orientations to the subject matter. The proliferation of organizational theories reflects the indeterminacy, the ambiguity, and the complexity of both the theoretical and the empirical construct of an organization. First, the very concept of organization encompasses multiple meanings. Stogdill (1971), for example, identifies eighteen different theoretical meanings, ranging from the organization as a cultural product to the organization as an input-output system. Second, the concept of organization intersects different units of analysis—individuals, groups, large work units, and networks—all of which are critical to an understanding of the organization itself. Third, numerous processes occur in organizations: face-to-face interaction, formal and informal communication, exercise of authority, decision making, consumption of resources, production of goods and services, to name a few. Analyzing and understanding these and other processes requires conceptual tools from a variety of disciplines, such as social psychology, economics, sociology, engineering, and political science. Fourth, the concept of organization encompasses many different empirical examples. In the case of human service organizations, these range from a megabureaucracy, such as a welfare department, to a small, voluntary, highly specialized agency, such as a marital counselling center.

Viewed historically, in each era specific organizational forms and structures arise that reflect the cultural and socioeconomic conditions of that period (Stinchcombe, 1965). Likewise, theories of organizations arise in response to the issues and concerns facing these organizations. Bendix (1956), in his seminal study tracing the rise of different organizational and managerial theories from the late nineteenth century to the mid-1930s, has demonstrated how the movement from Social Darwinism to scientific management and then to the human relations theory of organizations was in response to structural changes in the relations between workers and managers over that period.

One could similarly argue that the different theories about human service organizations that have emerged reflect changes over time in their functions, their service technologies, and their clients. This is exemplified by the major transformations in organizational perspectives on the mental hospital over the last fifty years (Perrow, 1965). Until World War II the mental hospital was primarily a custodial institution aimed at protecting society from the insane. The analogy by Deutsch (1948) of the state mental hospital to a concentration camp, while an obvious exaggeration, nevertheless conveys something of the image it suggested to an outside observer. Much of the rationale for the custodial hospital derived from the Social Darwinist ideology prevalent at the turn of the century. After World War II, however, the psychiatric care needed by many returning soldiers, among other social changes, generated enough pressure to improve conditions in mental hospitals, and the ideology soon changed.

The demand for reform precipitated a rash of critical studies of the mental hospital based on a "goal model" for organizations. Such a model assumed that organizations existed to achieve official goals through a series of rational procedures, and that organizational effectiveness was measured on the basis of the attainment of these goals. In short, it was assumed that if the nonrational aspects of the hospital could be identified, exposed, and replaced by more rational internal work structures, the therapeutic aims of the hospital would be enhanced. The studies by Dunham and Weinberg (1960) and by Belknap (1956) reflect this perspective.

The 1950s also saw the introduction to psychoactive drugs and a greater commitment by the federal government to the welfare of the mentally ill. This led to a decrease in the number of patients in mental hospitals and an increase in the availability of financial resources for community care. The rise of the community mental health ideology generated a new organizational perspective on mental hospitals known as the "therapeutic community," in which the interpersonal relationship between patient and therapist was the key determinant of a mental hospital's effectiveness (Greenblatt, Levinson, and Williams, 1957; Rapoport, 1960).

In the 1960s and 70s further changes took place. Mental hospitals became more open to environmental influences through increased governmental intervention; greater emphasis was placed on patient rights; and an array of mental health programs proliferated. Not surprisingly, an "open systems" approach to the study of mental hospitals came into vogue. The emphasis here was on improving the smooth flow of patients in and out of the hospital, efficiently integrating multiple treatment technologies, and improving links between the hospital and other service providers—all assumed to enhance the effectiveness of the hospital (Schulberg and Baker, 1975).

From this illustration, it is clear that each theoretical perspective does not simply determine what aspects of the organization will be studied with which conceptual tools. Each theory also embraces a set of assumptions, often implicit, about the role of organizations in society and about the relations between individuals and organizations; such assumptions shape the thrust of the research, the findings, and the remedies offered to improve human service organizations. This chapter will highlight some of the major theoretical approaches to organizations and their applications to human service organizations; it will examine some of their underlying assumptions and subject them all to critical appraisal. The purpose is not to be exhaustive, but to give a succinct review of the theories most relevant to our study of human service organizations.

THE THEORY OF BUREAUCRACY

The proliferation of human service organizations is but one instance of the increasing bureaucratization of modern society, a development that has produced major transformations in the organization of work, the patterns of authority relations, and the position of individuals in society. These themes were the focus of the major writings of Max Weber (1946; 1947; 1962), the founder of sociological analysis of organizations.

Weber was not interested merely in defining the attributes of bureaucracy, but rather in articulating the societal processes that generate such an organizational form and the impact it has, in turn, on society itself. Hence, Weber saw an intimate connection between the rise of an industrial market economy and the emergence of bureaucratic organizations, which were seen as the most efficient tool to mobilize resources and power in such a social system (McNeil, 1978). To quote Weber, "The decisive reason for the advance of bureaucratic organization has always been its purely technical superiority over any other form of organization. The fully developed bureaucratic mechanism compares with other organizations exactly as does the machine with the nonmechanical modes of production" (Weber, 1946: 214). For Weber the essential characteristic of modern society was the predominance of *legal authority* as the basis of the power relationship between the ruler and the ruled. That is, people accept authority because they believe it is exercised through procedures appropriate and acceptable to the ruler and the ruled—"resting on a belief in the 'legality' of patterns of formative rules and the right of those elevated to authority under such rules to issue commands" (Weber, 1947: 328). Moreover, the rulers achieve their superior position by legal means through election, appointment, and promotion. This contrasts with *traditional authority* based on "an established belief in the sanctity of immemorial traditions and the legitimacy of those exercising authority under them," or *charismatic authority* "resting on devotion to the specific and exceptional sanctity, heroism, or exemplary character of an individual person" (Weber, 1947: 328).

Bureaucracy, then, is the manifestation of legal-rational authority. Its attributes are derived from legal-rational rules and the pursuit of maximum efficiency. In the ideal type of bureaucracy, staff are appointed and function according to the following criteria (Weber, 1947: 333-34):

1. They are personally free and subject to authority only with respect to their impersonal official obligations.
2. They are organized in a clearly defined hierarchy of offices.
3. Each office has a clearly defined sphere of competence in the legal sense.
4. The office is filled by a free contractual relationship. Thus, in principle, there is free selection.
5. Candidates are selected on the basis of technical qualifications. In the most rational case, this is tested by examination or guaranteed by diplomas certifying technical training, or both. They are *appointed*, not elected.
6. They are remunerated by fixed salaries in money, for the most part with a right to pensions. Only under certain circumstances does the employing authority, especially in private organizations, have a right to terminate the appointment, but the official is always free to resign. The salary scale is primarily graded according to rank in the hierarchy; but in addition to this criterion, the responsibility of the position and the requirements of the incumbent's social status may be taken into account.
7. The office is treated as the sole, or at least the primary, occupation of the incumbent.
8. It constitutes a career. There is a system of "promotion" according to seniority or to achievement, or both. Promotion is dependent on the judgment of superiors.
9. The official works entirely separated from the ownership of the means of administration and without appropriation of his position.
10. He is subject to strict and systematic discipline and control in the conduct of the office.*

*Reprinted by permission of Macmillan Publishing Co., Inc. from *The Theory of Social and Economic Organization* by M. Weber, edited and translated by A. M. Henderson and Talcott Parsons. Copyright ©1947 renewed 1975 by Talcott Parsons.

Mouzelis succinctly captures the underlying logic of the ideal type of bureaucracy by suggesting that it is "a system of control based on rational rules, rules which try to regulate the whole organizational structure and process on the basis of technical knowledge and with the aim of maximum efficiency" (1968: 39).

It can be readily seen why such a model of bureaucracy would come under severe criticism, both for failing to reflect the true nature of organizations (which it was not intended to do) and for generating many dysfunctions and unanticipated consequences that actually hamper rather than enhance rationality. For example, Merton (1940) suggested that strict adherence to rules and regulations by line staff and their inability to respond to the multiple needs of their clients were likely to reinforce rigidity as a defense against client demands and lead to the formation of a "bureaucratic personality." Practitioners in human service organizations are particularly likely to decry what they consider excessive reliance on rules and regulations, the dehumanization of both staff and clients in the service delivery process, the lack of flexibility so essential for effectively serving clients, and the reliance on performance measures that are impersonal and insensitive to the quality of the staff. Moreover, the model of bureaucracy depicted by Weber does not take into consideration the importance of the role of the professional in the organization—a role that inherently calls for freedom from hierarchical authority, from rigid rules, and from regulations.

Thus, substantive critique of Weber has centered on two interrelated themes. First, the ideal type of bureaucracy does not take into consideration the variations in the tasks that organizations have to perform, which may range from routine to highly nonroutine. Second, exclusive reliance on hierarchical authority and formal rules and regulations may not be the most effective means to maintain control in the organization and ensure staff compliance.

The revisionists of Weber have pointed out that the model of bureaucracy is indeed most efficient and rational for *routine tasks* (Litwak, 1978; Perrow, 1972; Dornbusch and Scott, 1975). When the tasks facing the organization are nonroutine and nonuniform, which is the case in many human service organizations, its structure needs to be modified. To quote Litwak, "where the organizations deal with nonuniform events, a model of bureaucracy may be more efficient which differs in degree from Weber's in at least six characteristics: horizontal patterns of authority, minimal specialization, mixture of decisions on policy and on administration, little a priori limitation of duty and privileges to a given office, personal rather than impersonal relations, and a minimum of general rules" (1961: 179).

Similarly, alternative patterns of control in the organization may be more effective under such circumstances. Professionals who perform nonroutine tasks rely on professional norms rather than a set of rules and regulations to guide their behavior. Goss (1963), in studying patterns of bureaucracy among hospital physicians, noted that they were subjected to a dual control system. In making decisions about patient treatment, physicians relied on their own professional norms and standards: their superiors exercised only *advisory* authority, giving suggestions they had to consider seriously but need not follow. However, in making administrative decisions, such as scheduling and record keeping, the physicians were subjected to hierarchical authority and explicit rules and regulations.

Organizations can employ other control mechanisms that are far less visible or apparent. March and Simon (1958) have proposed that organizations control staff by shaping the content of the decisions each has to make—for example, by controlling the flow of information each staff person receives; by defining the range of alternatives they can consider; and by organizational training, indoctrination, and socialization.

Even with these revisions, the essential logic of Weber's conception of bureaucracy remains intact; and the empirical study of organizations, including human services, seems to confirm it. For example, the empirical studies by Dornbusch and Scott (1975) on the exercise of authority in such diverse organizations as schools, hospitals, research facilities, and football teams confirm the Weberian conception of authority and its function in organizations. Briefly, these studies suggest that staff indeed perceive authority to be proper when it is based on legal-rational grounds—that is, it is explicit, formal, and directly related to the evaluation of work. Line staff perceive evaluation as soundly based when it corresponds to their definition of good performance (that is, something they can bring about by their own efforts). Hence, when the evaluation is perceived as soundly based, staff efforts are more likely to be controlled by it. Moreover, when the evaluation is perceived as bringing about a more fair distribution of organizational sanctions, it has greater control over staff. In short, as expected, legal and rational authority promotes efficiency.

Weber's concern with bureaucracy extended beyond the elaboration of its internal structure. He was equally concerned with the impact of bureaucracy on the distribution of power in society and its consequences on individual freedom and liberty—issues that have been neglected by the revisionists, but which, nonetheless, should be of critical import to students of organizations in general and of human service organizations in particular. As noted by Mouzelis (1968) and McNeil (1978), Weber foresaw the possibility that the very efficiency of a bureaucracy would lead to the concentration of immense power in the hands of bureaucrats and managerial elites, power that would be buttressed by their control over a highly complex technology. Such concentration of power and technical expertise tends to isolate the organization from political influences and public opinion, and constitutes a threat to individual freedom and democratic processes. Indeed, the bureaucratization of such human services as health, education, and welfare has been accompanied by the concentration of power and control of service delivery—reinforced by state regulations—in the hands of bureaucrats, and it has often made them immune to pressures for reform by their clients. In particular, clients have become increasingly powerless vis-à-vis human service organizations and less capable of affecting changes in them (see also Coleman, 1973). The account by Rogers (1969) of the failure to bring the New York school system under local control is a case in point. Thus, while the bureaucratization of human services has brought with it greater rationalization of services, increased efficiency, and, in many instances, improved service technology, it has also resulted in the greater isolation of such organizations from the publics they are mandated to serve. How to achieve an acceptable balance between these two opposing forces remains a major challenge.

SCIENTIFIC MANAGEMENT

While the theory of bureaucracy attempts to *explain* the determinants of the structure and the processes in formal organizations, scientific management focuses on *prescriptions* for the efficient management of organizations; such a focus makes it a normative theory of organizations. Scientific management theorists are primarily concerned with ways to optimize the efficiency and productivity of the organization. Not unlike Weber, Taylor, the father of scientific management, perceived the organization as a rational and efficient tool for the production of goods and services *provided* it is structured and controlled by scientifically based principles.

The essential argument of scientific management can be summarized as follows. The organization must be based on a principle of cooperation between line staff and managers; without this the organization cannot achieve maximum productivity. Such cooperation can be obtained if the organization adopts principles of management based on scientific analysis, experiments, and measurement of the best ways to improve its efficiency and productivity. Adherence to these scientific principles is in the best interest of both workers and managers. Since workers are primarily motivated by monetary incentives, increased productivity based on scientific management will enable them to earn maximum wages, while at the same time it maximizes the profitability of the organization (Mouzelis, 1968: 79–84).

The scientific approach to increased efficiency may emcompass several steps. First, some objective criteria and goals that the organization wants to optimize are defined. Second, a model is developed that identifies the organizational processes required to achieve these goals. This model is based on careful analysis and measurement of worker-machine activities in the organization. Third, the model is analyzed by mathematical tools to determine which combination of worker-machine activities will produce the optimal level of goal attainment. Finally, and most important, the organization's activities are restructured to accord with the best solution generated by the model (see, for example, Ackoff and Rivett, 1963). While the "time and motion study" inaugurated by Taylor is still with us, far more sophisticated mathematical and engineering tools have been developed to resolve numerous organizational management problems related to efficiency and productivity. These tools include linear programming, program evaluation and review technique (PERT), statistical decision theory, inventory analysis, and queing theory, to name a few.[1]

To illustrate the application of management science tools to human services, I shall turn to an example from education: school integration. School systems facing court-ordered desegregation encounter the problem of devising a busing program that achieves maximum racial balance at minimal costs and distances. From a management science perspective, this problem is analogous to a transportation and allocation problem of the most efficient and economic way to ship goods from a set of origin points to a set of destination points. Several mathematical models have been developed to solve such a problem. Lee and Moore (1977) developed a model to determine how many children from each race in a given area should be assigned to each school under the following objectives: (1) Each child is entitled to a space in the school system; (2) racial balance must be achieved in each school corresponding to the racial proportions in the entire district; (3) transportation time should be minimized; (4) transportation costs should be within reasonable bounds; and (5) overcrowding and underutilization of schools should be minimized. They then formulated a mathematical model that takes these objectives into account and finds the best solution for allocating the children among the schools in the district, depending on the relative priority assigned to each objective. For example, if the school system gives priority to providing an education to each child, fully utilizing the schools, and minimizing transportation costs, the allocation solution produced by the model will indeed achieve these objectives, but will not achieve racial balance or avoid overcrowding. If the school system gives priority to racial balance, providing an education for each child, and fully utilizing the schools, the allocation solution will accomplish these goals but with very high transportation costs. In short, based on the goals the school system wants to maximize, the model will produce the best allocation of pupils to the various schools. Note that all these goals must be expressed in quantitative terms so that they can be treated in the mathematical model.

Concentrating less on the technical aspects of the organization's activities, management and administration theorists have also been preoccupied with identifying the principles of "good administration"—namely, how to structure the organization to promote rationality. As exemplified in

---

[1]It is not my intention to discuss specifically any of these tools, but rather to identify their underlying logic and the explicit and implicit assumptions they make about organizations.

the work of Urwick (1943), Mooney and Reiley (1939), Koontz and O'Donnell (1959), and Drucker (1954), such principles include the ideas that: (1) authority and accountability should flow in a clear and unbroken hierarchical order; (2) no member of the organization should receive orders from more than one superior; (3) no superior should directly supervise the work of more than six subordinates; and (4) work should be divided into units with specialized activities (Massie, 1965). These principles have evoked considerable controversy in the field of administration and have been criticized for lacking empirical validity, for contradicting each other, and for failing to consider variations among organizations. Nonetheless, they should be viewed for what they are intended to be: a set of pragmatic tools to help managers solve organizational problems (Mouzelis, 1968: 92).

Although much of management science has been developed in the industrial context, in recent years these tools have been increasingly applied to human service organizations with the same objectives in mind: increasing efficiency by reducing waste and minimizing costs. The stimulus to apply management science tools to human services can be attributed, in part, to the escalating costs of human services at a time of shrinking resources and the corresponding demands for accountability, tangible service outcomes, and maximum return for each dollar invested. Moreover, the vast proliferation of publicly funded human service organizations, which touch the life of everyone, has brought in its wake charges of governmental inefficiency, duplication of services, and waste and abuse of services. It has been argued, with some justification, that the typical governmental response to inept human service organizations has not been to replace them but to establish new, equally ineffective organizations. In light of the seeming success of management science in solving problems in industrial organizations, the military, and the space program, it was not unreasonable to expect that it could "clean up the mess" in human services (Hoos, 1972: 2–3).

Cyert (1975), a chief proponent of the application of management science to human service organizations, argues that the inefficiency of such organizations stems from their insulation from market mechanisms (i.e., supply and demand, price, profit), which enables them to indulge in allocation and utilization of resources without a set of explicit goals or objective measures of performance. Following this line of reasoning, the use of management science tools would force human service organizations to define a clear set of organizational goals and to develop explicit performance measures for each unit in the organization. Resource allocations could then be made on the basis of the goal priorities, and the efficiency of each unit could be evaluated in terms of its contribution to the attainment of these goals. This would introduce an objective control system in the organization to ensure efficient utilization of resources. Based on performance evaluation feedback, the organization could reallocate resources among more efficient units as well as help faltering units improve their productivity.

In assessing the relevance of scientific management to human service organizations, we need to identify some of the implicit assumptions about organizations that underly this perspective. First, it treats organizations as closed systems; namely, it ignores their many external influences and their need to relate to other organizations and publics. The environment is viewed as a constant, and, at best, as a constraint that organizations must take into account. Second, scientific management assumes that organizations have an explicit set of goals that are relatively constant over time and can be ordered in terms of importance. The theory cannot accept or handle conflicting and ambiguous goals. Moreover, the theory assumes that the goals are equally shared by all members of an organization and that the subgoals of subunits are congruent with the official goals. Third, the theory is elitist in that only the executive cadre is given the responsibility for defining organizational goals. Fourth, management science views organizations as nonpolitical and ignores external and internal political processes that affect the distribution of power among members. In this respect, the theory views organizations as cooperative systems devoid of conflict and dissension. Fifth, the theory offers a dismal and mechanistic view of the members of an organization by assuming that they have no other motives and interests except money.

The empirical study of organizations, particularly human service organizations, clearly demonstrates the dubious validity of these assumptions and their lack of empirical grounding. Therefore, the normative solutions presented by management science to various organizational problems are based on assumptions that often ignore some of the most crucial factors underlying these problems. Stimson and Thompson (1975) argue that mathematical models for school desegregation have ignored the complex social issues involved in school integration by simplifying the issue to that of busing of children to achieve racial balance. Thus, they have failed to deal with many of the concerns and problems seen by teachers and parents; ignored the political complexity of the educational establishment; opted to view the issue as school desegregation rather than school integration; and failed to deal with the value implications of their proposed plans. Similarly, in reviewing the application of management science and operations research in hospitals, Stimson and Stimson (1972) note that most of the applications were directed toward (1) improved scheduling in outpatient clinics, (2) efficient deployment of nursing staff, (3) improved utilization of facilities, (4) inventory control of blood banks, and (5) development of management information systems. Assessing the results of the models developed in these areas, the authors conclude that they had little impact on the actual operations of the hospitals because they failed to take into account the needs of the patients, the interests and power of the physicians, the complex relations between the hospitals and their environment, and ignored many variables that could not be quantified and measured.

The "trap" of scientific management for human service organizations lies exactly in the implicit value choices required by the normative models but made without consideration of the ethical issues involved in such choices. I have suggested that every action by a human service organization in relation to its clients involves normative choices. The adoption of scientific management tools obscures these normative choices by surrounding them with a "scientific cloak."

THE HUMAN RELATIONS PERSPECTIVE

The simplistic and mechanistic view of human nature in the scientific management model of organizations has limited its validity and applicability to the enhancement of organizational effectiveness. The famous Hawthorne studies, which began in the Taylorian tradition—identifying the relationship between working conditions and workers' performance—have led researchers to the conclusion that workers' attitudes and sentiments, their patterns of interaction, and the structure and culture of the work group might influence workers' performance much more than the physical attributes of their work (Roethlisberger and Dickson, 1939). The behavior of people in organizations and the quality of the interaction between them and their work organizations has been the focus of the human relations perspective ever since the Hawthorne experiments.

The underlying assumption of the human relations school is that "man is basically good, infinitely malleable, capable of perfectability, and therefore organizational goals and individual interests should be compatible" (Kaplan and Tausky, 1977: 171). Similarly, McGregor (1960) argues that the classical management theory, which he labels as "Theory X," views people as inherently disliking work and therefore they must be directed and coerced to achieve organizational goals. In contrast, the human relations perspective, "Theory Y," assumes that people have an inherent desire to work and can exercise self-control and self-direction if they are committed to the goals of the organization. Such commitment can be elicited if people are encouraged to exercise their imagination and creativity and realize their potential in the organization. It follows, therefore, that organizational effectiveness and productivity will be maximized when organizational structure and processes enable members to achieve self-actualization. To quote Likert (1961: 103), "The leadership and other processes of the organization must be such as to ensure a maximum probability that in all interactions and in all relationships within the organization, each member, in light of his background, values, desires and expectations, will view the experience as supportive and one which builds and maintains his sense of personal growth and importance." Much human relations research has tried to prove the validity of the assumed causal relationship between such processes and organizational effectiveness and productivity.

The Hawthorne experiments have further established the proposition that a worker's performance is determined by relationship patterns that emerge in the face-to-face work group. Porter, Lawler, and Hackman (1975) suggest that the group has a pervasive impact on the behavior and attitudes of individuals in the organization because it controls many of the stimuli to which the individual is exposed in performing organizational tasks. In particular, the work group will influence a worker's motivation, level of effort, and ways of carrying out the job. Therefore, the human relations school is very concerned with group processes that enhance work productivity. According to these studies, the ability of the group to facilitate worker effectiveness is based on two fundamental and highly interrelated strategies:

1. The use of group participation in making decisions about work practices. It is assumed that this facilitates the congruency between group goals and organizational goals and enhances the motivation and commitment of the workers to the organization (Coch and French, 1948). It is on the basis of this strategy that Likert formulated his linking pin concept of organizational structure, in which "each work group is linked to the rest of the organization by means of persons who are members of more than one group" (Likert, 1967: 50).

2. The use of a leadership style that is democratic, permissive, follower-oriented, participative, and considerate. This conclusion was derived from several studies examining the impact of leadership style on group cohesion, member satisfaction, and productivity (e.g., White and Lippitt, 1960; Indik, 1965; Likert, 1961; and Blake and Mouton, 1964). It was assumed that because such a leadership style enhances group cohesion and member satisfaction it leads to productivity.

The organizational model that embodies all these principles is labeled by Likert (1967) as "System 4" and is contrasted with the Weberian model of organization, labeled "System 1." System 4 includes such structural attributes as total confidence of leaders in their subordinates; full participation of subordinates in job problem solving; full vertical and horizontal communication patterns; group participation in goal setting; psychological closeness of superiors to subordinates; and diffusion of control functions in the organization.

Like scientific management, the human relations approach is a prescriptive theory that has generated a complex inventory of planned change strategies to enable organizations to achieve the ideals of System 4. These strategies, which fall under the rubric of "organizational development" (or OD), include such planned change programs as T-groups or sensitivity training, survey feedback, grid organizational development, and the sociotechnical systems approach.[2] Common to most of these approaches is the attempt to alter attitudes and to improve interpersonal relations in the organization in order to move it closer to Likert's System 4 or to McGregor's "Theory Y" (Strauss, 1976).

The human relations perspective has greatly appealed to practitioners and managers of human services and has stimulated a number of prescriptive models for restructuring such organizations. There are several reasons for this appeal. First, the effectiveness of human service technologies, such as psychotherapy, teaching, and counseling, depends on the use of self by the practitioners and therefore depends on their level of commitment, motivation, attitudes toward the organization and fellow workers, and their attitudes and sentiments toward the clients. The improvement of such attitudes and commitments, a central preoccupation of the human relations school, is of key importance to human service organizations.

Second, the effectiveness of most human service technologies is also predicated on the motivation, attitudes, and commitment of the clients to the goals of the organization. A basic axiom of the helping professions is that the helping process can commence only if the client is motivated and committed to the treatment goals. Since clients occupy a quasi-membership role in human service organizations, it can be assumed, by logical extension, that the human relations that enhance the motivation and commitment of staff will do the same for the clients. For example, educators have long pointed out the importance of classroom climate—students' attitudes toward teachers and peers—as a major determinant of students' behavior, work, and commitment to the learning process. To improve classroom climate, teachers are trained to use human relations techniques such as small-group problem solving, use of groups to provide feedback, and improved horizontal communication in the classroom (Bigelow, 1971).

Third, because the use of self is so critical in the helping process, it has been argued that staff-staff relations will have direct impact on staff-client relations. Cressey (1965), in his study of prison organizations, notes that in a punitive-custodial prison, the patterns of authority among the employees are based on strict hierarchical relations, close adherence to rules and regulations, and full compliance with the authority of rank. In the treatment oriented prison, however, lines of authority are based on technical competence; relations among staff are based on professional norms rather than bureaucratic rules; and staff has considerable professional autonomy. Similarly, studies of mental hospitals have shown that conflict among staff, lack of effective staff-staff communication channels, and disagreements about the treatment of patients are likely to result in collective disturbances among the patients (Caudill, 1958). Hence it is believed that the establish-

---

[2]For a review of these approaches the reader is referred to A. R. Beckhard (1969) and French and Bell (1973).

ment of a System 4-type structure in human service organizations will not only improve the relations among staff but will also enhance staff-client relations.

I will examine the strengths and weaknesses of this theory by looking at two specific examples of its application to human service organizations. The first example concerns the rise of the "therapeutic milieu" in mental hospitals. It was based on the central assumption that the social structure of the institution (i.e., distribution of authority, division of labor, patterns of staff interaction, communication patterns, and relations between staff and patients) is a key determinant of the effectiveness of patient treatment. Schwartz (1975) argued that a therapeutic milieu emerges when the division of labor (1) minimizes status differentials and provides for personal growth and creativity by subordinates and patients; (2) provides for democratic participation in the decision-making processes; (3) has a leadership style that provides guidance, support, security, and satisfaction to subordinates; (4) has a communication system that is free flowing; and (5) generates high morale among staff. The parallel between the therapeutic milieu and Likert's System 4 is unmistakable. Rapoport (1960), in an intensive study of the therapeutic milieu unit developed by Maxwell Jones, identified four ideological components underlying its treatment orientation: (1) democratization: everyone in the unit, including patients, to have equal voice in decision making, both therapeutic and administrative; (2) permissiveness: maximum tolerance of behaviors that may deviate from conventional norms and minimal use of discipline and rules; (3) communalism: staff and patients to share all facilities without distinction and to have close relations and free communication; and (4) reality confrontation: patients to be continuously confronted with the meaning of their behavior as perceived by others.

The findings by Rapoport indicate that the unit fell far short of meeting these ideologies. Nurses, for example, were extremely confused about their roles, particularly about how they should relate to the physicians, how much the patients should be permitted to exhibit disruptive behavior, and the extent to which patient problems were to be shared with others. The physicians found that patients expected them to be therapists, to exercise their professional authority, and not to use community meetings as a mode of therapy. Staff also found it necessary to have meetings from which patients were excluded to devise procedures for maintaining order and control in the unit. It is revealing that twenty years after the original study, Manning (1976) replicated it and found that the unit has moved even further away from the ideal of the therapeutic community.

Several conclusions arise from this and other experiences in the implementations of the therapeutic milieu. First, organizational effectiveness depends on a service technology that has a clear set of procedures, an explicit division of labor, and well-defined role expectations. Human relations cannot substitute for the lack of such a technology (Perrow, 1965).

Second, the organization cannot function effectively without differential allocation of authority among its members. Power equalization among staff and between staff and patients is not tenable when decisions call for different expertise and responsibilities. Third, despite the emphasis on democratization and communalism, tension and conflict among staff and between staff and patients are inevitable. Fourth, there is no evidence that the reliance on human relations did, in fact, enhance the effectiveness of the treatment personnel or improve the treatment outcomes for the patients.

The second example involves the use of organizatinal development techniques to improve the educational effectiveness of schools. The underlying value assumption here is that an effective school is a community in which students, teachers, and administrators can establish a "more meaningful base from which to explore themselves and the world as it is, more awareness of themselves as controlling their own fate ..., and more competence at the sort of self-initiated learning that can serve them for the rest of their lives" (Schmuck and Miles, 1971: 18). It is assumed that such a community can be created by decreasing formal and hierarchial relations in the school, equalizing power among all school participants, opening up communication, inviting multigroup participation in problem solving, and improving interpersonal relations.

In this vein, Schmuck, Runkel, and Langmeyer (1971) attempted in one school to improve communication among teachers, increase the staff's ability to resolve interpersonal and interrole problems, and use more group problem-solving procedures. It was hoped that by so doing, the school would become more open to educational innovations and have an improved classroom atmosphere. All faculty members took a six-day laboratory course where they learned and practiced communication skills, awareness of interpersonal processes, and small-group problem-solving techniques. The laboratory was followed by two additional one-and-one-half-day training sessions. The impact of this intervention was later measured through questionnaires given to the faculty of the experimental school and to some other control schools. The results indicated that, indeed, in the experimental school teachers reported greater participation in problem solving, improved communication, and more managerial support by the principal. Yet, in comparison to the other schools, the experimental school did not show greater innovations in such areas as curricular changes, establishment of new jobs or duties, or new methods of evaluating educational programs. No measures of impact on classroom instruction were available. Other similar experiments also generated mixed and inconclusive results.

Undoubtedly, the human relations school has made a major contribution toward our understanding of the behavior of individuals in organizations. Its emphasis on the organizational structure and processes that influence the attitudes, morale, interpersonal relations, and general psychological well-being of staff is of particular importance in human service organizations where the ego involvement of staff with clients is a key component of the service delivery. Moreover, the normative commitment toward a humane organization in which the social and psychological well-being of both staff and clients is highly valued should be lauded by human service practitioners. However, there is only inconclusive evidence to support the theoretical assertions relating group participation, democratic leadership, full vertical and horizontal communication, and harmonious interpersonal relations to organizational effectiveness. It is indeed questionable whether these variables are the most important in fostering a humane organization, let alone one that effectively services its clients.

The empirical evidence in support of Likert's System 4 and of most of the assumptions made by the human relations school is quite weak. Perrow (1972), in his review of such research, concludes that it fails to demonstrate that group processes contribute much to organizational effectiveness. Stogdill (1974), in his extensive review of the empirical research on leadership style, also concludes that "the relationship of democratic, permissive, follower-oriented, participative, and considerate patterns of behavior to productivity is zero or negative as often as it is positive" (p. 418). Similarly, there is weak and inconclusive evidence that organizational development activities lead to effective resolution of organizational problems and improved organizational functioning (Strauss, 1976). The coup de grace has been delivered recently by Franke and Kaul (1978) in their reanalysis of the data from the original Hawthorne experiments. They found that managerial discipline, the economic hardship of the Depression, and time set aside for rest explained most of the variance in the productivity of the work groups and individual workers. Therefore, the quality of the human relations among workers and between them and management could hardly contribute to productivity. The studies from human service organizations, as noted above, also fail to lend convincing evidence for the validity of the theory.

The assumption that the human relations model is universally applicable and thus beneficial to all types of organizations may be the reason for the conflicting and contradictory evidence. Litwak (1961), among others, suggests that the human relations model is only applicable to organizations that pursue nonuniform tasks. Examples of such tasks might be intensive psychotherapy, treatment of abusive parents, and group counselling of alcoholics. Under these circumstances, it is argued, an organizational structure that minimizes hierarchical differentiation, maximizes communication, and promotes group problem solving would be required to carry out such tasks effectively.

The most serious deficiency of the theory is its failure to consider organizational variables, other than social psychological ones. Other variables that may be far more important would include: environmental exigencies, resources, organizational goals, size, client needs and attributes, service technology, staff competencies, and wages and salaries (Strauss, 1968). For example, transforming the welfare department to a System 4-type organization may improve the politeness and empathy between staff and clients, but it is unlikely to have any significant effect on the welfare benefits clients receive, nor will it alter the conditions attached to the provision of these benefits. One also suspects that humane treatment of patients in a mental hospital or inmates in a correctional institution is more likely to be advanced by reducing the size of the facility, improving the staff-client ratio, using better-trained and better-paid personnel, increasing supervision, instituting more effective treatment technology, and employing active external watchdog agencies to monitor the activities of the institution.

In this context, the theory tends to ignore the political and economic processes within and without the organization that influence its performance. For example, the attainment of power equalization, so central to the theory, will be determined by the willingness of those who control power in the organization to share it with the powerless. The extent to which such sharing will take place is not likely to depend on human relations, but rather on the negotiations, bargaining, and compromises among the various interest groups that control resources needed by the organization. Similarly, conflict, which is assumed by the theory to be pathological to the organization, may often be a more effective way to get positive changes in service delivery patterns than organizational development techniques. To quote Mouzelis, "the theory fails to make the fundamental distinction between interpersonal frictions and social conflict which has its basis in the structure of organizations and the society in which groups and individuals are embedded" (1968: 115).

In human service organizations the use of human relations techniques may degenerate into mere manipulation of the practitioners. It may lead line staff to believe that indeed they have an important voice in the management of the organization when in fact their participation in decision making is largely symbolic. Moreover, group processes may be used to socialize and indoctrinate staff toward a set of ideologies that justify the service patterns of the organization, thus reducing the capacity of staff to consider alternative service goals or to examine the validity of such ideologies. This, in turn, can lead to conservative responses to client needs.

Finally, the emphasis on human relations as a cure for organizational ills may divert the attention of human service practitioners and analysts away from other real factors that generate organizational problems. Lack of an effective treatment technology may be misapprehended as the inability of various professionals to work together as a team. Lack of resources to provide decent services may be misjudged as poor staff motivation to invest themselves in the clients; and political barriers to interorganizational cooperation may be misinterpreted as poor interpersonal relations. As a conseqence, members of the organization may make numerous relational changes, such as establishing different work teams, new patterns of communication, and small-group decision-making processes, without producing any real organizational changes.

DECISION-MAKING THEORY

While the classical theory of bureaucracy overemphasized the principle of rationality in organizational design, the human relations perspective underplayed its significance. Herbert A. Simon (1976) attempted to bridge these two extremes through his decision-making model of organizational behavior. To quote Simon, *"the central concern of administrative theory is with the boundary between the rational and the nonrational aspects of human social behavior.* Administrative theory is peculiarly the theory of intended and bounded rationality—of the behavior of human beings who *satisfice* because they have not the wits to maximize" (1976: 28).

The rationality of people is limited and bounded because they lack complete knowledge of all the possible alternative choices, all the consequences that will follow each choice, and the future value of each anticipated consequence. As a result, decision makers search for a satisfying solution by constructing a simplified model of reality that is based on past experiences, selective perception of existing stimuli, and familiar alternatives. When decisions are made in the organizational context, it is the organization that defines the parameters of the decision. Specifically, the division of labor, authority, standard operating procedures, and patterns of communication set the limits and shape the boundaries of the decisions individuals in the organization can make: by controlling the occasions for decisions, by determining the information inputs into the decision, by defining the range of acceptable outcomes and available alternatives, and by influencing the values considered to be desirable (March and Simon, 1958).

We can observe the impact of these mechanisms of control, for example, in the behavior of intake workers at a child guidance clinic. First, standard operating procedures define the relevant stimuli for intake decisions; in this case it is information about difficulties between parents and children. In fact, these may specified on the intake form. Other types of information concerning, for example, health and financial problems or marital difficulties may be perceived to be of secondary importance, and could indeed elicit a rejection of the child for treatment if they seem primary in the parents' eyes. Second, the interpretation of the information is shaped by the service technology of the agency, which generates a certain vocabulary, and often a classification scheme to interpret and communicate information. A psychoanalytic orientation may generate such categories as "school phobia," "passive-aggressive," and "self-rejection." Third, the service programs offered by the agency will define for the workers the range of alternatives available to them in making an intake decision. These may include: rejection and referral to other agencies, scheduling additional diagnostic interviews, or admittance to treatment. Finally, the choice made by the workers will be influenced by organizational definitions of "approriate" clients, which are also derived from the service technology and the programs developed by the agency. Thus, children defined as suffering from "school phobia" or "unresolved Oedipus complex" might be more likely to be accepted for treatment than children classified as "sociopaths" or "delinquents." In short, the behavior of the intake workers is not controlled solely by explicit directives and rules and exercises of authority. Rather, they are controlled by the *parameters* that influence their decision-making processes, which are far less visible and emanate from the organizational structure itself.

Such a perspective is particularly important for an understanding of patterns of service delivery in human service organizations, for it shatters the myth of what I have termed elsewhere the "clinical decision-making model" (Hasenfeld, 1974). The espoused model of the professional helping process, as in psychotherapy or social casework, assumes that clinical decision-making processes are governed by: (1) the information elicited from the client, (2) the body of knowledge against which such information is evaluated, and (3) the prescribed treatment procedures derived from that body of knowledge. Such a model ignores the fundamental fact that the entire helping process is anchored in an organizational context and that every decision made by the professional is influenced by such organizational variables as program content and structure, client eligibility criteria, organizational vocabulary, standard operating procedures, communication patterns, and the interdependencies of units within the organization. By focusing on the orgnizational determinants of the practitioner's decision-making processes, the March and Simon model of organizational behavior provides us with the analytical tools to comprehend and explain the decisions human service workers make regarding their clients.

Nevertheless, the model is not without significant limitations. Being social psychological, it takes the organizational context as given and fails to provide explanations about the determinants of organizational structure, standard operating procedures, patterns of communication, and the like. The theory is essentially silent about the factors that give rise to different types of organizations. Also, it is a closed system model in that it treats the environment of organizations as a constant and does not consider the impact of environmental conditions on organizational structure and processes. As a result, critical issues concerning differential access and allocation of power and resources within the organization and conflict of interests among organizational units are ignored.

Cyert and March (1963) attempted to extend the decision-making model to the organization as a whole by suggesting that the organization could be viewed as a coalition of participants with different values and personal goals. Through a process of bargaining, decisions about commitments of resources are made, thus defining the operative goals of the organization. (See Chapter 4.) These multiple goals are such that they provide sufficient benefits to members of the coalition to keep them in the organization. Conflict is managed through the bargaining process, and the emerging goals define the range of acceptable decision rules in the organization.

Another organizational dynamic is *uncertainty avoidance*, whereby the organization attempts to reduce uncertainty from the environment by trying to establish stable contractual relations with elements in the environment, by developing standard operating procedures, and by formulating fairly fixed plans. When the organization confronts problems for which existing solutions are not adequate, it will engage in search behavior. Yet, the search will be characterized as simple-minded and biased by past organizational experiences, members' expectations, and unresolved conflicts. Organizational adaptation (learning) occurs on the basis of the experiences gained in finding solutions to problems.

Finally, in the evolution of decision-making theory, March and his associates (Cohen, March, and Olsen, 1972; March and Olsen, 1976) present a decision-making model of organizations, which they label the "garbage can model," that is particularly apt for many human service organizations. Previous decision-making models have assumed that organizations attempt to avoid uncertainty by buffering themselves from the sources of ambiguity and by setting up organizational mechanisms, such as division of labor and standard operating procedures, to maintain stability and predictability. Nevertheless, in many situations organizations face great uncertainties. In particular, this situation arises when the organization's goals are ambiguous and its technology is uncertain and indeterminant. One can think of numerous examples of human service organizations that fit such a description, including universities (the favorite example of March and his associates), experimental schools, therapeutic communities, innovative delinquency treatment programs, and community-based treatment programs. How are major programmatic decisions made in these types of organizations? Using the garbage-can metaphor, they propose that four relatively independent streams are poured into the can: problems, solutions, participants, and choice opportunities (situations that call for a decision). Decisions result from the particular mixtures of all these streams, rather than from any rational connections between them. The "can" is "a meeting place for issues and feelings looking for decision situations in which they may be aired, solutions looking for issues to which they may be an answer, and participants looking for problems or pleasure" (March and Olsen, 1976: 25). Several factors influence these streams and the decision outcomes. First, the structure of the organization affects the arrival and departure times of each stream, the energy that each participant will give to the decision, and the links among the various streams. Second, the cultural and normative context of the organization will create a bias toward certain problems, solutions, styles of participation, and choice opportunities. Third, the personal attributes of the individuals in the organization, their beliefs, hopes, available time, and attention span also influence the shape and content of the garbage can.

Three styles of decisions are identified: (1) oversight: a choice is made without attention to existing problems; (2) flight: a choice is made after it has been disassociated from a problem and thus does not resolve any problem; and (3) resolution: a choice is made which resolves the problem.

Several propositions can be derived from such a model: (1) Most decisions are made through oversight or flight; (2) as the energy required to solve problems increases, problems are less likely to be resolved, decision-makers will shift from one problem to another more frequently, and choices will take longer to make but will less likely resolve problems; (3) important problems are more likely to be solved than unimportant ones; and (4) important choices are less likely to resolve problems than are unimportant choices.

A case study of an experimental school that had both very broad, vague goals and an unclear, indeterminate technology provides a good illustration of the garbage-can model (March and Olsen, 1976: Chapter 16). During a six-month observation period, different groups in the school raised problems ranging from enlarging the school building to replacing teachers to designing a new educational plan. These problems attracted different participants partly on the basis of the interests, values, and time each was willing to devote to the issues. The issues themselves exposed still other problems: the need to define the school's goals, how to involve teachers in the decisions about a new educational plan, conflict between teachers and parents, and poor relations among several teachers. Participants proposed solutions without reference to specific problems, and these solutions became included in discussions of problems. Among these solutions were proposals about the goals of the school, new educational structures, mergers of certain grades, and hiring of teachers. Not surprisingly, several decisions were made that were never implemented because, for some participants, raising a problem or proposing a solution was an end in itself. Some choices that were made could not be traced back to any particular problem or proposed solution.

What this model seems to suggest is that many program features of human service organizations, particularly with reference to service delivery patterns, cannot be rationally explained since they do not represent choices based on clear definitions of problems and careful searches for potential solutions. Rather, they are the end result of several relatively independent processes thrown together precisely because these organizations embrace ambiguous goals and lack a clear technology to implement them.

Nevertheless, it would be a mistake to generalize this model to all human service organizations, even those with ambiguous goals and technologies, for most operate under a set of constraints that substantially reduce choices and that introduce considerable predictability in their daily operations. Even Cohen and March (in March and Olsen, 1976), in an analysis of the decisions of university presidents, clearly point to these limiting factors that made their behavior more predictable. These determinants include the operating budget (enrollment, fund raising, and research activities); departmental autonomy in setting academic policies; and the tenure system. That is, the detailed description of the micro-social-psychological processes of decision making may indeed resemble a garbage-can model; but actual organizational outcomes may well be better predicted by structural variables like the availability and distribution of resources and power, the service needs of the population, and the dominant values in the organization.

CONTINGENCY THEORY

Most of the organizational theories reviewed thus far have not addressed, in any systematic way, the structural variations among organizations. What explains the fact that in some organizations staff work at highly specialized tasks while in others the same kind of staff perform numerous and varied tasks? And what accounts for the hierarchical structure of authority and centralization of one organization and the horizontal structure and decentralization of another? These and similar issues about the *design* of organizations have become a predominant concern of contemporary theorists of organizations (e.g., Lawrence and Lorsch, 1967; Perrow, 1967; Thompson, 1967) whose aim is to identify the conditions that determine organizational structure. Although most of the studies in this vein are carried out on industrial organizations, some have been applied specifically to human service organizations.

The contingency theory of organizations essentially revolves around two interrelated propositions: First, environmental demands and contingencies will determine patterns of internal differentiation in the organization (Lawrence and Lorsch, 1967). Second, the attributes of the technologies adopted by the organization will determine the structure of the work units that implement them (Perrow, 1967; Thompson, 1967).

Lawrence and Lorsch (1967) have argued that the organization must interact with different elements in the environment. For example, a community mental health center must interact with the discharge unit of the state mental hospital, with clients facing mental health crises, and with community agencies seeking consultation. Each of these segments of the environment varies in terms of the *degree of uncertainty* they present to the organization, namely the extent to which their relevant operations are changeable and unpredictable. The discharge unit presents little uncertainty to the organization because it provides information about discharged patients on a regular basis, makes clear who they are, and identifies their service needs. In contrast, walk-in clients in crisis present a great deal of uncertainty because they can come at any time, provide information that is difficult to comprehend, and do not offer feedback about the consequences of the staff intervention. Such varied environmental conditions require the agency to differentiate itself internally in order to respond effectively to them; the competencies, timing and scheduling, and staff supervision needed to handle clients in crisis are quite different from those needed to interact with the discharge unit. In short, the greater the variation in uncertainty presented by the environment, the greater the internal differentiation needed. Yet, increased differentiation also requires that the organization develop effective mechanisms of integration and coordination among the different work units.

Similarly, Thompson (1967: 72–73) proposes the followng relationship between the environment and the internal structure of the organization.

	STABLE ENVIRONMENT	SHIFTING ENVIRONMENT
HOMOGENEOUS ENVIRONMENT	Few functional units; standardized rules	Limited differentiation; decentralized decision making
HETEROGENEOUS ENVIRONMENT	Variety of functional units; standardized rules	High differentiation; decentralized decision making

By implication, then, the efficient organization is one that improves the goodness of fit between the environmental contingencies and its internal structure.

A similar logic is applied to the relationship between technology and organizational structure. Perrow (1970), for example, proposes that in the case of human service organizations, technologies (i.e., the tasks performed vis-à-vis the clients) can be classified according to whether (a) the clients are perceived to be stable and uniform or unstable and nonuniform; and (b) the knowledge of the intervention procedures is complete or incomplete. Four types of technology are therefore identified: (1) routine (clients stable, knowledge complete); (2) craft (clients stable, knowledge incomplete); (3) engineering (clients unstable, knowledge complete); and (4) nonroutine (clients unstable, knowledge incomplete). Each technology calls for a different internal structure. A routine technology— for example, the determination of Social Security benefits—requires essentially a classical bureaucratic structure in which line staff have little discretion, management has considerable authority, and work is regulated through rules and standard procedures. In contrast, a nonroutine technology, like psychotherapy, requires that line staff have considerable discretion, that authority be shared, and that coordination be based on feedback (see also Litwak, 1961; Thompson, 1967).[3]

While contingency theory makes a great deal of intuitive sense and potentially offers important guidelines for appropriate organizational design, its empirical validation is far from satisfactory. First, serious measurement problems are encountered in operationalizing the concepts of environmental uncertainty and the dimensions of technology, particularly as measures independent of other organizational attributes (see for example, Downey, Hellriegel, and Slocum, 1975; Lynch, 1974). Second, findings from human service organizations are contradictory. Hage and Aiken (1969), in a study of welfare organizations, found that those with routine technologies were more likely to have centralized decision making and to emphasize written rules and procedures. In contrast, Mohr (1971), in a study of health agencies, found little relationship between technology and the structure of work units. Third, the contingency theory of organizations postulates direct causal relationships between environment, technology, and structure. Yet, as Child (1972) cogently argues, these relationshps are mitigated by the key decision makers in the organization. They can choose to interact with certain environments and ignore others. Decisions about technologies and structure may be determined by complex configurations of available resources, environmental demands, and existing organizational values and traditions. Nonetheless, as contingency models become more refined and incorporate other variables, such as the interests of key decision makers, they may prove to be fruitful in predicting the structure of organizations. While cognizant of the limitations of contingency theory, I shall refer to its underlying logic to explain variations in the division of labor among and within human service organizations.

THE NATURAL SYSTEM
PERSPECTIVE

Critics of the rational model of organizations, which views the organization as a tool deliberately designed to achieve specific goals, have pointed to the many unanticipated consequences emanating from such a model, thus undermining its validity. Merton (1957) noted that the emphasis on formal rules and regulations to control the behavior of members of the organization leads to rigid staff behavior and consequent increased difficulty with clients. Such difficulty prompts staff to defend their actions by ever-greater reliance on formal rules and regulations. Hence the emergence of the "bureaucratic personality." Selznick (1948) has shown that the delegation

---

[3]See also Chapters 5 and 6.

of authority, central to the bureaucratic model, results in departmentalization and increased bifurcation of interests among the subunits in the organization. Each unit, then, tries to protect its interests, which leads to increased commitment to the subunit's goals over and above the general organizational goals. The bifurcation increases the conflict among units; the conflict reinforces the internalization of the unit's goals by its participants and leads ultimately to displacement of the organization's goals.

The natural system theorists view the organization as analogous to a biological system. The organization is perceived as an "organic whole," composed of interdependent units each of which contributes to the maintenance and survival of the organization in its ever-changing environment. The organization, therefore, is more than a formal set of relationships through which resources are manipulated to achieve a set of specific goals efficiently and effectively. Instead, it is a social system that is an end in itself; it has needs for survival and adaptability that transcend goal attainment. As Selznick put it, the organization "is deemed to have basic needs, essentially related to self-maintenance; the system develops repetitive means for self-defense; and day-to-day activity is interpreted in terms of the function served by that activity for the maintenance and defense of the system" (Selznick, 1948: 29). Such a perspective is also termed "structural-functional" to denote the underlying assumption that the structure of the organization reflects its basic needs or functions, and emerges in response to them.

Parsons (1957), for example, classified the basic organizational needs of the mental hospital along an external-internal dimension. The external needs were classified as: attaining legitimation from the community; dealing with the recipients of its services; acquiring the facilities to carry out its functions; and integrating itself into the community. The internal needs were identified as: socialization of personnel to the values of the hospital; fulfillment of routine technical functions; and integration between the administrative and operative systems.

When the organization responds effectively to these basic needs it is transformed over time into a "social institution." That is, it becomes valued in and of itself; it acquires a distinct character; it is adaptive to the values of the external environment and responsive to internal interest groups (Selznick, 1957). Clark (1970) demonstrated this process in his study of three distinctive colleges: Antioch, Reed, and Swarthmore. At a critical stage in the development of each college, a leader emerged who, guided by a unique sense of mission, seized the opportunity to carve a distinctive niche for the college. The success of these leaders to achieve and sustain such a distinctive character was based on their ability to recruit faculty and gain internal power to protect their ideals; develop a curriculum that expressed these ideals; enlist an external base of support to provide the necessary resources; develop in the student body a strong subculture that supports these ideals; and create an image strong enough to gather momentum.

As suggested by Perrow (1972), the natural-system perspective is also firmly anchored in an exposé tradition. Thus it is argued that organizations are not what they claim to be because "the explanation for organizational behavior is not primarily in goals and purposes, the output of goods and services. It lies also in the myriad of subterranean processes of informal groups, conflicts between groups, recruitment policies, dependencies upon outside groups and constituencies, the striving for prestige, community values, the local community power structure, and legal institutions" (Perrow, 1972: 180). My study of employment placement services for the inner-city poor (Hasenfeld, 1975) has shown that these agencies lacked any significant influence or power with potential employers or the more established state employment services. They therefore had to find job opportunities that could not be easily filled by the employers or were perceived as undesirable by the established agencies. As a result, these job opportunities came predominantly from industries belonging to the "secondary labor market"— industries characterized by low profit rate, high labor turnover, low wages, marginal job security, and lack of advancement opportunities. These were the very same jobs that had contributed to the poverty of the applicants and which they had hoped to escape. By referring them back to these jobs, I suggested that the agencies actually perpetuated the cycle of poverty.

Dickson (1968) has shown how the U.S. Bureau of Narcotics has consistently pursued an aggressive campaign to expand its domain and thus ensure its survival and growth. After the passage of the Harrison Act in 1914, the Narcotics Division (the forerunner of the Bureau) launched a systematic campaign to broaden and enhance its domain through reports and newspaper articles about the dangers of narcotics, and by court cases against all previously legal uses of narcotics by physicians in treating addicts. The success of such a campaign, not surprisingly, greatly increased the activities of the division, and its budget increased from $325,000 in 1918 to $1,329,000 in 1925. However, since 1932 the bureau has experienced a steady decline in its budget appropriations. Dickson argues that in response to the declining resources, the bureau tried to drum up more business for itself by launching a campaign to outlaw marijuana, and it succeeded in persuading Congress to pass the Marijuana Tax Act of 1937. As a result, the number of federal convictions under the new act increased significantly, and the bureau could pressure Congress to increase its budget appropriations, which rose slowly but steadily until the early 1940s when the country began diverting nonmilitary resources to the war effort.

There are numerous other studies of human service organizations in this exposé tradition, including Goffman's (1961) seminal study of the mental hospital, the study by Scott (1969) of agencies for the blind, and Street, Vinter and Perrow's study (1966) on juvenile correctional institutions.

At this juncture it seems appropriate to take a critical look at the natural-system perspective and particularly at its utility for the study of human service organizations. The natural-system perspective views the organization as a whole and is thus sensitive to variations among organizations. Furthermore, it focuses on the interdependent relations between the various units within the organization that form and define its "character." Emphasis on the critical role of the environment in shaping the nature of the organization is probably its most significant contribution. The organization is viewed as an open system whose inputs are obtained from the environment and whose outputs are aimed at enhancing its survival in the environment. The concomitant focus on the adaptive processes of the organization as the key determinants of its structural attributes and processes is equally important in explaining how organizations develop and change over time and why they deviate from formal and rational plans. Such a perspective also highlights the importance of such variables as resources, power, and values in explaining the emerging character of the organization.

Despite the importance of these concepts and variables, they have remained highly abstract, vaguely defined, and difficult to measure. Most of the research has been based on case studies, which are difficult to replicate or generalize from. The conclusions from such studies are often based on problematic measures and are thus susceptible to alternative and contradictory interpretations.

As a theory, the natural-system perspective tends to deemphasize the role of rationality in organizations (Gouldner, 1959) and the fact that many processes in the organization are rationally designed to achieve specific objectives. Moreover, concepts such as "natural development" and "organization as institution" lend the organization an unwarranted mystique—of being an entity with a life all of its own. By evoking such an image, it overlooks the fact that the organization is a tool used to advance the interests of various social groups, and that its fate is determined through the political maneuverings of these interest groups. Similarly, the structural-functional notion that the organization has a set of "basic needs" obscures the fact that each organization may satisfy these "needs" quite differently and drastic differences in key patterns of services may result.

Despite these limitations, the natural-system perspective is well suited to the study of human service organizations. First, since most human service organizations are nonprofit and must rely on external donors for resources, they are highly dependent on their environment and are far less able than industrial organizations, for example, to control their environment. Consequently, processes of adaptation to environmental exigencies play a critical role in shaping the character of the organization and its patterns of service. At the same time, human service organizations are infused with values because they must make normative choices about human needs and their responses to them. These choices are equally important in defining the central mission of the organization. They must be selected from competing value systems, and they move the organization to align itself with social and political groups upholding a given set of values. Much of what the natural-system perspective defines as the transformation of the organization into an institution reflects such value commitments. Also, because human service organizations lack determinate technologies, norms of rationality are less likely to be pursued in the design of the organization. Consequently, the internal structure and processes of the organization are likely to display inconsistencies, conflicting service-delivery patterns, and lack of rational connectedness, much as would be predicted by the natural-system perspective.

THE NEO-MARXIAN PERSPECTIVE

For Weber the rise of bureaucracy as a keystone of modern society manifested the transformation of the power relations between the rulers and the ruled from traditional and charismatic authority to legal-rational authority. For Marx, however, the rational-legal foundation of bureaucracy was merely a facade used to hide the true function of bureaucracy: protecting the interests of the dominant class. Specifically, bureaucracy is seen as an instrument of the dominant class to perpetuate its domination and control over the means of production, and to serve as a buffer between the exploiter and the exploited (Mouzelis, 1968: 9). Furthermore, bureaucracy itself is a mirror image of the patterns of domination and exploitation in society. The hierarchical structure within bureaucracy and the reliance on rigid rules and regulations are mechanisms used by the organizational elite to control the behavior of lower-status staff and to minimize their ability to exercise any control over the tools of their work. At the same time, these mechanisms are also used to mask from the bureaucrat the true nature and purpose of the organization. The consequences to the bureaucrat are alienation, loss of individuality, and petty competition for the symbols of power.

The neo-Marxians (e.g., Benson, 1977; Bowles and Gintis, 1976) expanding on these ideas do not purport to develop a theory about bureaucracy per se. Rather they aim to explain its functions in the larger social system. With particular reference to human service organizations, they attempt to demonstrate how these functions are shaped by the interests of the capitalist system (Galper. 1975). Several themes underlie such a perspective. First, human service organizations can be understood only with reference to the social processes emanating from a capitalist economy, which is characterized by the expropriation of the means of production from the workers and their control by a business elite. It is assumed that the aim of the elite is to expropriate the surplus value produced by workers—namely, the difference between the value of the goods they produce by their labor and the wages they receive. The social system is so organized as to enhance the accumulation of the surplus value by the elite while maintaining control over the working class. Second, although the capitalist system generates economic inequality, human service organizations are not necessarily designed to reduce them. Rather, they perpetuate inequality by legitimating the class system. They do so in several ways. They reinforce the ideologies that justify the capitalist system through their own service technologies and through the treatment of their recipients. By providing limited and largely symbolic services, they generate the aura of a humanitarian and caring society. And, they divert the attention of the oppressed classes from the real causes of their oppression. Third, human service organizations serve a social control function in such a system. Through their control of needed human services they force those in need to conform to the norms of the capitalist system; and by focusing their services on individuals rather than on collectivities, they prevent the development of class consciousness. Fourth, human service organizations serving the lower classes reflect in their own structure and processes the overall patterns of domination in society. Clients are powerless, subject to rigid mechanisms of compliance, and lack any significant voice in the decisions about their own fate. Lower-status staff, similarly, must follow rigid bureaucratic rules and regulations and lack autonomy in carrying out their jobs. Inhumanity, alienation, ritualistic compliance, and lack of self-fulfillment are the results for both staff and clients. Fifth, human service organizations, like other social institutions, are subject to dialectical forces that result in their own transformation and dissolution (Benson, 1977). For example, the increasing use of prisons to contain and control rebellious ethnic minorities has intensified racial and ethnic conflicts within them; this has led to the political radicalization of inmates and thus undermined the potency of prisons as social control agents. Moreover, the more ethnic minorities are subjected to incarceration, the less the prisons' efficacy as a deterrent.

Piven and Cloward (1971) analyzed the functions of public welfare from this perspective. They argued that the relief system is ancillary to the capitalist economic system and is designed to control the flow of labor in and out of the economy. The control function of relief is expressed in two ways. "First, when mass unemployment leads to outbreak or turmoil, relief programs are ordinarily initiated or expanded to absorb and control enough of the unemployed to restore order; then, as the turbulence subsides, the relief system contracts, expelling those who are needed to populate the labor market" (p. 3). Note that this thesis is diametrically opposite to the liberal interpretation of welfare, which views welfare expansion as a demonstration of humanitarian concern for the poor.

Because a capitalist economic system is marked by constant change and fluctuation—cycles of expansion and contraction—public welfare serves as a "safety valve" for the capitalist elite: Welfare is provided at times of massive unemployment to minimize the workers' revolt against the economic system. To maintain the legitimacy of the capitalist system, welfare is always attached to a market incentive to work, either by forcing welfare recipients to accept work as a condition of continued support, or by setting such a low level of relief that it forces people back to the labor market (the "less eligibility" principle). Thus, welfare serves also as a deterrent to not-working. Piven and Cloward marshal support for their basic thesis by an historical analysis of the emergence of the English Poor Laws, and more recently by the welfare explosion in the 1960s. In the latter instance, they attribute the rapid expansion of welfare and the Great Society programs to attempts by the federal government to cope with civil disorders and urban riots by appeasing and coopting urban blacks.

Central to the argument of Piven and Cloward is a need to demonstrate that the organization of public welfare departments is directly influenced by the functions they serve. Because welfare departments are constantly pressured to reduce their rolls and to discourage requests for aid, they develop harsh and inhumane procedures for handling actual and potential welfare recipients. Not surprisingly, welfare workers are likely to be highly demoralized and develop a cynical attitude about their work; departments thus experience high staff turnover, which further reinforces the oppressiveness of these organizations.

Bowles and Gintis (1976) use a neo-Marxian perspective to explain the functions of public schools in American society. They argue that the failure of schools to reduce social inequality is a direct result of their role in upholding the capitalist system. They start their analysis by suggesting that social inequality derives from the class exploitation in a capitalist economy. They then proceed to demonstrate, by extensive use of empirical data, that schools are designed to serve the needs of the capitalist economy. Schools do so in several ways. First, the school curriculum reflects the range of skills needed by employers. Second, discriminatory patterns in hiring workers on the basis of sex, race, and class are reinforced by the allocation of educational resources: Regardless of their cognitive potential, white upper-class students receive a better education. Third, while IQ and other cognitive tests do not predict educational success, they are used extensively to reinforce the ideology of "meritocracy" (i.e., a society in which social status is acquired strictly on the basis of merit) and to mask the perpetuation of class differences in the school. Fourth, success in school is closely related to the development by students of those personality traits that are highly desired by employers, such as dependability, submission to authority, internalized control, and noncreativity. Finally, the structure of the schools themselves reflects patterns of domination in the work place. Schools are organized along hierarchical lines of authority, and students lack measurable control over their own educational process. Grades and other external means of rewards and sanctions closely resemble the role of wages in maintaining conformity.

Other examples of a neo-Marxian perspective on human service organizations include an analysis of the health care system by Krause (1977) and of the community treatment of deviants by Scull (1977).

Undeniably, a central thesis that links human service organizations to the larger economic system and that connects the implications of their supportive role in such a system to their internal functioning is highly appealing and persuasive. The contribution of the neo-Marxian perspective is in its focus on human services not as single organizations but as industries—a class of organizations engaging in similar activities—and their relations to other major social institutions. This focus allows the structural position of human service organizations in the larger society and their articulation with other components of the social system to be more effectively studied and understood. This helps avoid the trap of viewing human service organizations from a myopic and parochial perspective. Specifically, the neo-Marxians make us more aware that the processes and structure of human service organizations can only be understood through their functional interrelationships with other institutions and in the context of the larger social system, most notably the economy. Consequently, the interplay between the social stratification system and human service organizations becomes of paramount importance in the analysis of such organizations. On one hand, the attributes and characteristics of the people being served are highly influenced by their social class position, which in turn affects the organizational response to them. On the other hand, human service organizations, when processing people, directly and indirectly affect their social location and status. Therefore, the study of human service organizations and their effects on people must be anchored in the broader context of the dynamics of social stratification processes in society.

The ultimate validity of the neo-Marxian perspective, however, is dependent on the accuracy of its depiction of the social system as a whole and the assumed primacy of the capitalist economy as they conceive it. However, such a model of society has come under considerable criticism for lacking sufficient empirical validity—particularly with regard to the assumed existence of a monolithic and dominant capitalist class.

As for human service organizations, studies from this perspective fail to demonstrate convincingly how the interests of the capitalist class, assumed to be cohesive and unified, are articulated through the political system and come to control the activities of human service organizations. For example, the politics of welfare in the 1960s, which resulted in its expansion, demonstrated vividly the political interplay between different social groups including militant blacks, the white middle class, labor unions, and ethnic politicians. The power plays and bargainings among these groups that shaped the Great Society programs reflect anything but the workings of a ruling class (Muraskin, 1975). Durman (1973) also challenges the findings of Piven and Cloward by demonstrating that the explosion of welfare cannot be attributed only to governmental relaxation of rules in the face of urban unrest; it was also a consequence of changing demographic patterns that resulted in dramatic increases in the number of persons eligible for welfare.

In the final analysis, such a perspective tends to trivialize the impact of human service organizations in reducing misery, in improving well-being, and in redistributing income. The argument that human services are a device by the elite to pacify the middle and working classes does indeed acknowledge the fact that the majority of people do perceive human services as a way to promote social justice, humanitarian values, and social equity, and therefore lend them political support. This is not to deny that human service organizations experience serious deficiencies and limitations in meeting such objectives, some of which clearly reflect economic and political inequalities. But to cast them as only tools of economic exploitation is to ignore both the complex societal processes that shape human service organizations and the multiple effects they have on society.

THE POLITICAL ECONOMY PERSPECTIVE: A CONVERGING FRAMEWORK

This odyssey through the various perspectives on human service organizations cogently demonstrates that we indeed lack a coherent and comprehensive theory of organizations in general and of human service organizations in particular. But some prerequisites for such a theory should have become more evident from our brief critical appraisal. First, we are looking for a theory that focuses on the organization as a whole and at the same time explains its internal structure and processes. Second, the theory needs to address itself systematically to the relations between the organization and its environment. Third, the theory needs to explain the processes by which major decisions are made about allocation of resources and determination of domain. Fourth, the theory must explain the processes that define and shape its service technologies. Fifth, the theory should explain how the organization changes over time. Lastly, the theory should address itself to the relations between the organization and its clients.

I believe that the political economy perspective as articulated by Zald (1970a) and Benson (1975), among others, begins to address itself to these requirements. In a significant way, it is an attempt to synthesize some of the themes developed in other theoretical perspectives, particularly the natural-system perspective, decision-making theory, contingency theory, and the neo-Marxian perspective. This synthesis is still in its infancy and provides only a broad conceptual scheme for organizational analysis.

The political economy perspective, to quote Zald, "is the study of the interplay of power, the goals of the powerwielders, and the productive exchange systems" (1970a: 223). It focuses on the interaction between the political and economic forces both within and without the organization that shape its basic structure and processes. "Political" refers to the processes through which power and legitimation (i.e., social support) are acquired by the organization and distributed internally, operative goals are determined, and major tasks of the organization are defined and controlled by the dominant elite. "Economic" refers to the processes by which resources needed for the service technologies of the organization (i.e., clients, manpower, money) are acquired and distributed in the organization, divisions of labor are specified and operationalized, and production of the organizational outputs is maintained (Wamsley and Zald, 1976).

From this perspective, the organization is viewed as an arena in which various interest groups, external and internal, possessing resources needed by the organization, compete to optimize their values through it. These values are expressed in the *organizational constitution*, which Zald (1970a) defines as a set of norms governing: (1) the system of incentives for its members; (2) the discretion and decision-making responsibilities of different positions; (3) the persons or groups to whom the organization is responsible; and (4) its operative goals and service technologies.

The organizational constitution arises and changes through the power relations between the various external and internal interest groups in the organization. These relations involve pooling resources controlled by each group to produce a set of outputs no single group could produce on its own. For example, a family service agency can be conceptualized as an organized resource pool of different interest groups with a variety of output goals: benefits to families in the community, prestige to certain community groups, professional reputation and status, and services to other human service organizations. These outputs are desired by interest groups such as civic and business associations, social workers, the juvenile court, schools, and mental health advocates. The relative power of each group in shaping the organizational constitution varies directly with the importance of the resources it controls and varies inversely with the availability of such resources elsewhere (Emerson, 1962). Hence, although families provide a critical resource to the family service agency in the form of clients, their power to shape the organizational constitution is limited because so many families are available who need the agency's services. In contrast, the United Fund may assume a major power position in shaping agency policies because it controls key financial resources that cannot be obtained elsewhere. However, the United Fund may exercise such power judicially and allow the agency's professional staff to set major policies because its own reputation in the community is based, in part, on the professional prestige of the agencies it supports.

In short, organizational processes are based on exchange relations established between the different interest groups that compose the organization and the power each exercises in controlling and influencing these relations.

The mobilization of resources, particularly legitimation, is in part a function of the relations developed between the organization and its political environment. This environment may include superordinate and authoritative executive and legislative agencies, judicial bodies, other organizations, social action groups, political parties, professional associations, and other interest groups. These elements may set conditions for lending their legitimation to the organization and may favor and strengthen the power of certain groups in the organization. For example, the power of the judge to define the goals of the juvenile court stems mostly from the judge's exclusive access to judicial legitimation. Others may challenge the legitimation of the organization, and if powerful enough may force changes in its constitution. The dominant elite as well as others in the organization may seek to reach an accommodation with certain political elements or enlist their support in order to strengthen their position and influence in the organization. This in turn will affect the organizational constitution.

The organizational constitution will also be influenced by the economic environment of the organization, and the opportunities and limitations it presents to the decision makers. The economic environment includes the availability and cost of resources like clients, manpower, technology, and facilities; the demand for the organization's services and how that is made known; the structure of the local human services network; and general economic conditions affecting availability of fiscal resources. Economic conditions may enhance and support the values of some interest groups while reducing the attractiveness of the values of others. For example, the amendments to the Social Security Act introducing Medicare, Medicaid, and SSI have provided an economic incentive to those promoting the value of community placement of mental patients (Segal and Aviram, 1978).

It can be readily seen that factors in both the political and economic environments may interact to affect the power of different interest groups in the organization. Lack of demand for the organization's services may lead to withdrawal of legitimation by legislative agencies and thus reduce the power of the dominant elite. In contrast, organizational elites enjoying a broad base of support and legitimation may find it feasible to shift services to new areas of demand and thus maintain organizational viability as well as their own power.

The organizational constitution, once formed, filters stimuli from the political and economic environment by selecting those likely to enhance the position of the dominant elite and rejecting those challenging its position. Therefore, only when the ability of the dominant elite to mobilize resources for the organization or maintain its competitive position is seriously threatened does it fear loss of power sufficiently to change the organizational constitution.

The internal distribution of power and authority is similarly a function of (a) the contribution and importance of different units to the attainment of the operative goals of the organization, and (b) the resources each unit can mobilize from the external environment. Thus, psychiatrists occupy a central position in the mental health center, not only because their expertise and skills are vital to the goals of the center, but also because they control major sources of legitimation. This example further demonstrates the links between the external and internal polity of the organization. That is, access to external sources of power enhances one's power position inside the organization and vice versa.

The political and economic processes that determine the distribution of power in the organization also influence the choice of service technologies, since their "products" reinforce the values and interests of the organizational elite. For example, the choice of psychotherapy over environmental support strengthens the position of the psychotherapists over the social workers in the mental health agency. Yet, this choice is also affected by economic conditions, which may override the interests of the power holders.

As service technologies are operationalized, they shape the internal division of labor, and various work units acquire power depending on the centrality and irreplaceability of their tasks. Thus, the custodial staff may acquire considerable power in an institution where the service technology is geared mostly toward the physical maintenance of patients. Finally, service technologies also affect an organization's incentive system to ensure staff compliance with its work requirements. In this context, internal cooperation and conflict among units will also be affected by the degree of competition for scarce resources, and the congruency of values held by members of each unit.

The major components of the political economy of a public human service organization are depicted in Table 2.1. Zald (1970a) used a political economy perspective to explain the transformation of the YMCA from an evangelical organization to a broadly aimed socialization agency. A major source for the change was the shift in the demand for YMCA programs from different segments of the population, which ranged from twelve-to-seventeen-year-old youth to adults. The YMCA also needed to stabilize its financial resources, for which it had originally competed with other churches. Physical recreation facilities and residences were thus established in order to diversify its economy and stabilize its income.

The YMCA's economic changes interacted with important changes in its polity as well. In the battle between those who stressed evangelism and those who stressed general services, the latter ultimately won because the local associations found that their survival depended on adopting more flexible goals. At the local level, the associations stressed the importance of lay control over the organization—particularly the role of the lay board—while they resisted developing a professional staff. As a result, the goals of the association were more sensitive to the wishes of the members, most of whom were of middle-class background. The combination of these eco-

Table 2.1 Major Components of Political Economy for Public Human Service Organizations

	ENVIRONMENT STRUCTURE AND PROCESS	INTERNAL STRUCTURE AND PROCESS
P		Institutionalized distribution of authority and power
O	Authoritative governmental agencies	
L	Authoritative legislative bodies	Dominant coalition or elite
I		Opposition factions
T		Succession system for executive personnel
I	Accreditation and independent review bodies, professional associations	
C		Recruitment and socialization system for executive cadre
A	Civic and professional interest groups	
L		Constitution
	Competing and complementary human services	Ethos, myths, norms, and values reflecting institutional purpose
	Moral entrepreneurs	
		Patterns for aggregation and pressing demands for change by lower personnel
	Clients (actual and potential)	
E		Allocation rules
C	Input characteristics: clients, expertise technology, facilities, supply and cost factors	Accounting and information systems
O		
N	Output characteristics: service demands and knowledge thereof	Task and technology related unit differentiation
O		
M	Network of human services	Incentive system
I		Pay, promotion, tenure, and fringes
C	Macroeconomic effects on supply-demand for services	Authority structure for task accomplishment

Source: Adapted from Wamsley and Zald (1976: 20).

nomic and political factors moved the YMCA toward being a general service organization supported mostly by membership enrollments.

The political economy perspective, then, articulates more specifically the external and internal economic and political processes that shape the character of a whole organization as well as its components. It pays particular attention to dynamic relationships between an organization and the environment. This is of special importance to the study of human service organizations since they are highly dependent on the environment for legitimation and money. By focusing on the power relations among the various interest groups comprising the organization, we gain a better understanding of how critical decisions are made about the allocation of resources and how the organizational constitution is defined. Understanding these decisions enables us to trace the processes influencing the selection of the service technologies of the organization. Recognizing that this selection is linked to both external and internal political and economic factors sheds new light on how the core activities in human service organizations are established. We are able to get beyond the ideologies that justify and rationalize their existence and begin to realize that these technologies actually reflect power relations among contending interest groups. In most human service organizations, the service technologies are not simply derived from a clear-cut definition of a desired product—as may be the case in industrial organizations. While there may be only one way to produce an automobile, there are infinite ways to educate a child, rehabilitate the mentally ill, or assist the poor. Here, the choice is political, reflecting competing values, and economic, reflecting fiscal constraints and opportunities.

Finally, such a perspective enables us to analyze the role of clients. Clearly, it suggests that the ability of clients to influence the organization and the patterns of relations between them and staff will be a function of the needed resources they control, both political and economic. When clients possess few resources, the organization's responsiveness to their needs will depend on the relative power of those interest groups championing their cause. In subsequent chapters I shall use the political economy perspective to identify key processes that shape the character of human service organizations.

Nevertheless, this approach has its shortcomings. It obviously casts its net very broadly; and like the natural-system perspective, its variables lack specificity and clarity. In particular, the concept of power, central to the theory, is defined too broadly and cannot be readily operationalized. As a result, the distinction between political and economic variables becomes blurred. Furthermore, it is difficult to measure the importance and strength of various political and economic variables independently of the organizational phenomena they are supposed to explain. Only by observing certain organizational changes, one can often infer the relative power of various groups in the organization. Therefore, the explanation of organizational change may become tautological. The political economy perspective, then, provides a framework, but not yet a causal model that can be empirically tested.

CONCLUSION

This chapter has appraised the relevance and adequacy of several organizational theories for the study of human service organizations. The relative utility of each theory is partly a function of the issues selected for study and partly a function of its empirical validation. For example, the Weberian theory of bureaucracy as revised by contemporary theorists has considerable empirical validation, but that such revisions have sidestepped some of the major issues originally raised by Weber about the impact of bureaucracy on individuals and society. In contrast, the assumptions underlying scientific management are highly questionable, and the range of issues it addresses presents a myopic view of the human service organization. Similarly, the human relations approach, while centering on the important issues of individual behavior in organizations, ignores many others, and its empirical validation is still problematic. Decision-making theory attempts to synthesize the rational and nonrational approaches to organizations with significant empirical grounding. Nevertheless, it fails to address macrolevel issues such as organization-environment relations, the determination of operative goals, and resource allocation.

It is only when we move to contingency theory that there is a shift toward viewing the organization as an open (rather than closed) system. Yet the emphasis is still limited to the effects of the environment on elements in the organization, rather than on the organization as a whole. And the empirical findings are contradictory. The organization as a whole receives full attention in the natural-system, neo-Marxian, and political economy perspectives. These theories are truly sociological in scope since they articulate the relations between the human service organizations and the larger social system. These theories address themselves directly to such issues as the societal processes that shape the character of the organization, the impact of the organization on society, and the specific consequences of organizational activities on the welfare of various social groups. It is partly because of the complexity of these issues that these theories are abstract and difficult to operationalize and validate empirically.

For human service practitioners, the choice of theory has important policy implications, since it defines the range of strategies to be used to bring about improvements in organizational functioning. Based on its underlying theoretical orientation, each theory will offer its own diagnosis and remedy for organizational problems, which may well contradict those offered by others. The practitioner should be able to assess the theoretical and empirical validity of such strategies, and the first step is to identify the underlying organizational theory.

3

ORGANIZATION-ENVIRONMENT RELATIONS

A key characteristic of human service organizations is their dependence on donors (e.g., federal and state funding agencies, United Funds, and private charities) for a steady flow of resources and support. As a result, they are vulnerable to external influences and to the potential loss of autonomy. Public schools, welfare departments, community-based treatment centers, and county hospitals exemplify such organizations, which are often described as "captives" of their environment (Carlson, 1964). Yet, despite their openness to environmental influences—and perhaps because of it—human service organizations typically resist establishing effective links and coordination with other agencies (Aiken et al., 1975; Warren, Rose, and Bergunder, 1974). This is often expressed by a fierce defense of organizational domain, by an indifference to cooperating, and by symbolic rather than substantive coordination.

Human service organizations are also said to be influenced by the norms and sociocultural characteristics of the local community since they are dependent on it for legitimation and clients. At the same time, these organizations are accused of being insensitive to their clients' ethnic and cultural backgrounds and thus to their values and norms. Moreover, despite the need of human service organizations to articulate closely with the community, they frequently fail to meet community needs (Scott, 1967a; Rogers, 1969).

To understand these paradoxes, we need to explore more fully the relations between human service organizations and their environments. The environment is both a set of resources that the organization must mobilize to survive and carry out its activities and a set of constraints to which it must adapt when operationalizing service objectives. The patterns of service delivery reflect the organization's strategies to manage its relations with the environment. Put another way: How the organization copes with environmental exigencies and secures external resources will have direct consequences on how it serves clients.

THE GENERAL ENVIRONMENT

Following Hall (1977), I distinguish between the *general environment* and the *task environment* of the organization. The general environment denotes those conditions in the environment—economic, demographic, cultural, political-legal, and technological—that affect all organizations and must be assumed as given. Except in rare instances, no single organization can significantly alter these general environmental attributes. For example, the catchment area of a community mental health center may be characterized by a population predominantly of a certain ethnic origin and particular age distribution—factors the center cannot change.

The task environment refers to a specific set of organizations and groups with which the organization exchanges resources and services and with whom it establishes specific modes of interaction. These may include funding agencies, referral sources, and providers of complementary services. The characteristics of the task environment are also influenced by the general environment. For example, the choice of funding sources available to a family service agency is influenced by the wealth of the environment, its economic complexity and differentiation, and the proportion of resources allocated to health, welfare, and education. Similarly, the range and type of clients and agencies that a community mental health center can select to interact with is a function of the sociodemographic, cultural, and religious factors associated with mental illness, the level of urbanization and industrialization of the community, the availability and distribution of medical resources, and the organizational richness and differentiation of human services in the community.

At the most general level, the environment—as characterized by resources, population, technology, and culture—determines the range and type of human service organizations it can sustain. Therefore, the environment differentially supports the emergence of organizations and differentially selects those that will survive on the basis of the fit between their structure and activities and the environment's characteristics (Aldrich and Pfeffer, 1976; Hannan and Freeman, 1977a). Wilensky, in his study of welfare expenditures in sixty-four countries (1975), provides a good example of such an ecological process. He found that the determinants of the social security effort made by each country (measured by the proportion of the GNP expended on social security) are: (1) the per capita GNP, which measures the level of economic growth in each country; (2) the percentage of people aged sixty-five and over; (3) the age of the social security system; and (4) the political regime (democratic or totalitarian). The higher the economic development of the country, the greater the surplus it can commit to welfare. At the same time, high economic development reduces the birth rate and increases the proportion of aged in the population. A large proportion of older people generates a need and a political force that motivates the country to commit resources to social security. As the social security systems mature, they move toward wider coverage and higher benefits because "more of the covered people either reach retirement age or experience disability or the death of a working spouse; the mass of citizens press for higher benefits and expanded coverage for themselves and their dependent relatives; political elites see a greater need for programs; bureaucrats entrench, cultivate budgets, personnel, and clientele . . . " (Wilensky, 1975: 25).

To recognize and better understand the differential effects of general environmental conditions on the development and continuance of human service organizations, I will focus on the following conditions: economic, sociodemographic, cultural, political-legal, and technological.

Economic Conditions

The state of the general economy directly influences and constrains the state of the economy inside the organization. This is amply demonstrated by the differential allocation and utilization of public assistance within the United States. Tropman (1975), for example, notes that the levels of public assistance grants are directly related to the wealth of each state, as measured by per capita income. Zeigler and Johnson (1972) provide data to show that the ability of public schools to obtain fiscal resources (as measured by expenditures per pupil) is determined by the median family income, per capita state and local taxes, and the median age of the state's residents. Wealthier communities also support better health care systems and United Fund social services.

To a large extent, the relationship between the community's economic affluence and the solvency of its human service organizations is a function of the community's capacity to invest in such services. For example, Klatsky (1970) found that state employment agencies in wealthier states not only pay higher salaries to their employees, but also provide employment insurance to a larger proportion of the unemployed and therefore obtain a disproportionately larger share of federal funds than less affluent states. As a result, employment agencies in wealthier states place disproportionate emphasis on employment compensation tasks, whereas those in poorer states emphasize placement services. Similarly, Turk (1977) presents data to show that the ability of urban communities to mobilize themselves for collective action in such areas as developing antipoverty programs, model cities, and coordinated health services was in part a function of the level of economic activity and wealth in each community.

While economic conditions determine the supply of resources to human service organizations, they also affect the demand for human services. That is, economic conditions influence the type, range, and magnitude of human problems and needs that human service organizations will be asked to respond to. For example, massive unemployment—particularly in industrial communities—tends to produce immense social and personal dislocations that create a heavy demand for the intervention of such organizations as welfare departments, mental health agencies, and child and family service agencies. Human service organizations in poor communities are likely to face service demands that reflect the consequences of chronic unemployment, family dislocation, high rates of disease and malnutrition, mental illness, and mental retardation (Tussing, 1975). In fact, Brenner has demonstrated that a persistent relationship exists between economic changes and mental illness. As he puts it, "adverse economic changes usually bring about severe social and personal disorganization for a considerable number of persons in the society. This process is so marked and thorough that, as a result, individuals are defined and treated by society as being mentally ill" (1973: 201). Thus, during economic downturns, human service organizations encounter an increasing number of clients having problems and needs associated with social and personal disorganization.

The interaction between the severity of human needs and availability of resources to respond to them puts human service organizations in a double-bind situation: The economic conditions that produce a high-risk population also adversely affect the capacity of human service organizations to mobilize resources to respond to their needs. This is most poignantly shown in the study of the Detroit public schools by Sexton (1961). First, she documented the well-known relationship between family income and performance on achievement tests. In fact, this relationship was accentuated as children moved through school, and the gap between rich and poor on the achievement tests increased. Second, she noted that schools in lower income areas were significantly more inferior than those in higher income areas: They had larger classes, fewer qualified teachers, and poorer facilities. Thus, while children of poor families experienced greater educational deficiencies, the schools they attended were less likely to have the resources necessary to respond to their needs.

Sociodemographic Conditions

Age and sex distribution, family composition, race and ethnic composition, residential location, and social class are highly correlated with the incidence and frequency of a variety of human problems and needs. For example, poverty is highest among female heads of households, the aged, the nonwhite, and residents of rural areas. Similarly, studies have shown that the prevalence of various psychiatric disorders is closely related to sex, rural versus urban location, and social class (Dohrenwend, 1975). Rates of neurosis are consistently higher for women, while rates of personality disorders are consistently higher for men. Both types of psychiatric disorders are more prevalent in urban settings, and the highest overall rate of psychiatric disorders is consistently found in the lowest social class. Whatever the specific explanations for such relationships, the demand for mental health services is influenced by these variables.

Therefore, the characteristics of the population served have profound effects on an organization—for example, the attributes of its clients, the range of service demands it confronts, the effectiveness of its service technology, and the receptivity of the environment to its services.

Nowhere is an organization's sensitivity to the characteristics of a population more apparent than in how it determines who its clients will be and the nature of their needs. As I will show in Chapter 7, the clients' attributes are a major factor in determining an organization's service effectiveness; but an organization's ability to obtain desired clients is restricted by the attributes of the population in its geographic location. This is aptly demonstrated in a study of school effectiveness by Herriott and Hodgkins (1973). Measuring the success of schooling by the percentage of former tenth-graders who did not complete the twelfth grade, or by the percentage of twelfth-grade graduates going to college, they showed that the social class composition of the school neighborhood (as measured by percentage of males in white-collar occupations) had a significant impact on each of these success measures. In my study of rates of referral to the juvenile court (1976), I showed that such rates are determined not only by the overall crime rates in the community, but also by the rate of net migration, level of education, and rate of unemployment in the community.

Piven and Cloward make a cogent argument that much of the welfare explosion during the 1960s had its roots in the changing sociodemographic characteristics of the inner-city population. As they put it, "A large mass of economically obsolete rural poor were redistributed to the cities, particularly to northern cities. A very large number of these newcomers (especially blacks) were not absorbed into the urban economy but were left to subsist on incomes well below established welfare payment levels" (1971: 222). Such a massive migration, coupled with exclusion from the urban economy, also caused an erosion of the family as an agent of social control, an increase in the number of female-headed families, and a very high concentration of unemployed volatile youth. Such a population presented heavy service demands on the welfare system, which, according to Piven and Cloward, ultimately had to respond because of the civil disorders that developed in the cities.

Correspondingly, the effectiveness of an organization's services often depends on its sensitivity to the sociodemographic characteristics of the target population. For example, McKinlay and McKinlay (1972) have shown that free prenatal health services were underutilized by women of low socioeconomic status, primarily because their needs for housing, minimal income, and marital stability took precedence over their health care needs.

Because the sociodemographic attributes of its clients are so important, it is not surprising that human service organizations seek out "hospitable" populations whenever possible. Private social service agencies are a case in point. Being less restricted than public agencies, they can locate among a "favorable" population. Such agencies have moved steadily from the central cities toward the suburbs in pursuit of middle-class clients. The findings of Cloward and Epstein (1965) about the disengagement of private, family service agencies from the poor is an example of such a trend. Similarly, Elesh and Schollaert, in a study of the distribution of physicians in Chicago, found that "substantial differences in the number of physicians exist between white and black tracts. On the average, there are over three times as many physicians of all types, more than two and one-half times as many general practitioners, and five times as many specialists in white as in black tracts. Nor is there evidence of a compensating difference in the number of hospitals, since black tracts average one third as many as white tracts" (1972: 241). The authors noted that it would take a very substantial increase in the income of the black tracts to establish equity in the distribution of physicians.

Cultural Conditions

Human service organizations are particularly sensitive to the dominant cultural and value systems in the community. A close relationship has always existed between the predominant social and cultural beliefs of a period and the particular form and direction human services have adopted. The characteristics and goals of human service organizations, then, have reflected the ideologies of dominant elites about the causes of human problems and needs, the values that must be upheld in responding to them, and the means of responding. The very idea of the welfare state itself, as Janowitz (1976) points out, was rooted in the emergence of Western political theory that emphasized: the separation of church and state, popular participation in the governmental process and utilitarianism, socialism, and the betterment of human existence through scientific rationalism.

The rise of various organizational forms of human service delivery is thus predicated on the existence of a cultural and ideological system that is reified and maintained by these organizations. This proposition is demonstrated in Rothman's (1971) insightful study of the emergence of the asylum as an institution in American society. During the colonial era, the poor, destitute, and insane were supported in community households, not in separate institutions. There was no reason to punish the needy since poverty itself was seen as painful. Almshouses were created to provide only for those incapable of caring for themselves, or without relatives, or too disabled to be cared for by kinsfolk or neighbors. Moreover, the almshouse was organized to emulate the family structure. These organizational arrangements emanated from the religious beliefs of the colonists—namely, that poverty was natural and just and its relief necessary and appropriate. The social order was seen as having divine sanction, and wealth and poverty were a reflection of it. Poverty, therefore, provided an occasion and obligation for charity, which in turn justified wealth.

During the nineteenth century, however, American society went through major social transformations caused mainly by accelerated population growth, industrialization, and urbanization. According to Rothman, Americans in the Jacksonian period began to learn that "men were born innocent, not depraved, that the sources of corruption were external, not internal, to the human condition" (1971: 69). Deviancy was, therefore, perceived to be a product of the environment, specifically the result of community and family disorganization. To combat it, the value of social order, stability, the sanctity of the family, obedience to authority, and respect for rules had to be reinforced. The invention of the penitentiary and the asylum "represented both an attempt to compensate for public disorder in a particular setting and to demonstrate the correct rules of social organization" (p. 154). The deviants were thus removed from their disorganized environment and put into an isolated, contrived environment in which order, respect for authority, regimentation, regularity, and uniformity could be imposed. In the same vein, the almshouse also underwent a major transformation. No longer a remedy of last resort, it became the major organizational response to poverty. The poor were to be institutionalized in order to remove them from the corruption and vice in the community, and instill in them order, discipline, and rigid routines. Institutions for the poor, together with insane asylums and penitentiaries, proliferated rapidly through the first half of the nineteenth century.

The relationship between dominant moralistic beliefs, perceptions of deviance, and organizational responses to them is further exemplified in the study by Gusfield (1967) on changing societal reactions to alcoholism. In the evangelical revivalism of the early nineteenth century, abstinence and sobriety were elevated to high moral virtues, while drunkenness was seen as a sin that required repentance. The organizational responses to alcoholism were primarily religious, and evangelical groups used their religious meetings as a tool for "saving" alcoholics, providing food and shelter only if they repented. Toward the end of the nineteenth century, middle-class evangelical Protestants were threatened by the tremendous influx of lower-class immigrants, mostly Catholics and Lutherans, who did not uphold the virtue of abstinence. This threat gave impetus to a political movement to outlaw alcohol and to define alcoholism as a crime. The passage of the Prohibition Amendment signified a symbolic victory for those groups who defined alcoholism as a crime, even though enforcement of Prohibition was, at best, limited and a whole new criminal group arose. Nevertheless, the drunkard was subjected to imprisonment, a practice that still goes on. It was only after Repeal (1933) that alcoholism came to be defined as an illness, leading to the establishment of social service agencies that emphasized treatment and rehabilitation.

These examples illustrate how, at any given period, human service organizations manifest the dominant cultural and moral systems in society and promote, strengthen, and uphold these systems. The rise of various organizations as responses to human problems and needs was usually determined by the existing normative system from which they received legitimation.

Political-Legal Conditions

The human service organizations' permeability to the influences of political and legal conditions in the community can be expressed in two ways. First, a significant proportion of the resources available to them are publicly controlled, and access is governed by political processes. Second, a large array of legal constraints defines and controls many conditions that the organization must meet and conform to in serving its clients.

Both at the national and local level, political processes, which often culminate in legislative enactments, determine not only the resources available for social welfare programs, but also the conditions under which they are to be expended. The history of such legislative acts as the Social Security Act and its various amendments, the Community Mental Health Centers Act, and the Economic Opportunity Act provides vivid examples of the enormous impact of legislative processes on the establishment and transformation of human service organizations. As suggested by Gilbert and Specht (1974), social welfare policies define and control the eligible clientele, the services to be offered, acceptable organizational forms for delivering services, and methods of financing services. This political-legal environment has a direct bearing on each organization's options for making crucial decisions about its goals, use of resources, service technologies, and clients to be served. Gilbert (1977), for example, in his analysis of the impact of Title XX of the Social Security Act, which provided the largest single source of social services funds, suggests at least four consequences. First, Title XX created the opportunity to provide social services to a broader category of clients including the nonpoor. Second, it broadly defined social services so that each state was free to support a very wide range of social services. Third, it provided for purchase-of-services arrangements with voluntary agencies, thus encouraging more types of service delivery. Fourth, it provided federal grants on the basis of population size rather than on grantsmanship. The political-legal opportunities created by Title XX have, therefore, encouraged a proliferation of human service organizations with diverse service delivery modalities covering a broad range of human needs, a development not feasible before such legislation.

The political climate of the environment additionally influences the opportunities open to human service organizations. Downs (1976), for example, found that the development of innovative correctional programs for juvenile offenders was influenced by the liberality of the state as measured by the percent Democratic vote in the 1968 and 1972 presidential elections. Wirt and Kirst (1972) also suggest that the political culture of the state influences the level of financial support given to public education. States having a "localist" political culture (New England) are less likely to provide financial support for local public education than states with a "centrist" political culture (the South). They also cite a study conducted by Johns and Kimbrough (1968) in which 122 school districts were classified according to four types of community power structure: monopolistic elite, multigroup noncompetitive, competitive elite, and segmented pluralism. They found that the financial efforts for education occurred less often in noncompetitive power structures than in more "open" structures.

The structure of community power also influences the degree of political "hospitality" to human service organizations. The account by Marris and Rein (1967) on the development of antipoverty programs in various cities suggests such a relationship. For example, in Chicago the almost absolute control of city politics by the mayor's office precluded the emergence of any program independent of that office, or active citizen participation in shaping the nature of the program. In Cleveland, which was beset by political conflict and racial divisions, the program itself became an object of competing political interests and was stalemated by disunity. In contrast, the community action program in New Haven was highly successful because it could build on a broad-based consensus among political groups in the city and enjoyed the support of a powerful progressive coalition under the leadership of city hall.

The legal system, by defining and specifying conditions that human service organizations must meet in serving clients, sets important constraints on such decisions as location, programs, service technologies, and personnel. A child-care center, for example, must comply with a myriad of regulations including: zoning laws; fire, safety, and health regulations; professional staffing and licensing standards; legal rights of parents and children; and the like. The environment's "hospitality" can be assessed, in part, by the extent to which the legal system enhances or restricts the establishment of human services. The struggle to establish halfway houses for the mentally ill or ex-offenders in the community is a case in point. Communities hostile to such services are likely to enact numerous ordinances and regulations that almost exclude the possibility of establishing such facilities (Aviram and Segal, 1973).

Technological Conditions

The range of services available to human service organizations will be determined by the environment's level of technological development in such areas as medicine, mental health, education, and community and social planning. Any single organization is highly dependent on the environment for acquiring its service technology. The level of technological sophistication and innovation exhibited by each will be, in part, determined by the general level of technological progress in society, and the commitments made to the pursuit of knowledge through research and training.

The apparent simplistic and indeterminate service technologies deployed by many human service organizations thus reflect the overall technological progress made in responding to human problems and needs. For example, many recent developments in community mental health have been made possible with the discovery of psychoactive drugs. As suggested by Segal and Aviram (1978), these drugs provided a chemical means to control the mentally ill and allowed the unlocking of hospital wards, the early release of patients, and the use of community care. In the same vein, organizational responses to heroin addiction have changed radically with the discovery of methadone.

The surge in behavior modification technologies has also been an important factor in changing the responses of human service organizations to the mentally retarded and to autistic children. The new technology provides human service organizations with intervention techniques that offer the promise of treatment and rehabilitation, rather than reliance on custodial care.

At the same time, these and other behavioral and social intervention technologies raise momentous moral and ethical issues that may seriously constrain the ability and willingness of human service organizations to use them. Thus, even though it may be technologically feasible to eradicate certain human problems, it may not be morally acceptable to do so. Furthermore, the existence of advanced human service technologies does not ensure their adoption. Rather, the rate of adoption is determined by a number of organizational factors, financial and social costs, return on investment, communicability of the innovation, and the like (Zaltman et al, 1973). These will be discussed in greater detail in Chapter 9.

THE TASK ENVIRONMENT

Environmental Resources and Organizational Domain

As indicated, the general environment defines the range of opportunities, constraints, and options available to the organization as it attempts to carve a niche for itself and, to paraphrase Selznick, transform itself into an institution. "Institutionalization is a *process*. It is something that happens to an organization over time, reflecting the organization's own distinctive history, the people who have been in it, the groups it embodies and the vested interests they have created, and the way it has adapted to its environment" (Selznick, 1957: 16). More specifically, the organizational leadership must involve itself in at least five critical decision-making areas: (1) formulation of the service mission of the organization within the context of the opportunities, constraints, and contingencies presented by the environment; (2) negotiations and mediation between the organization and external interest groups to gain legitimation and procure resources; (3) selection of the service technologies to carry out the mission of the organization; (4) establishment of the internal divisions of labor in the organization; (5) initiation and implementation of changes in the organization in response to environmental exigencies and changing intraorganizational configurations (Hasenfeld and English, 1974: 153).

Organizational actions and choices in relation to these decisions will both reflect and define the organization's domain. Following Levine and White (1961), organizational domain refers to the claims that the organization stakes out for itself in terms of human problems or needs covered, population served, and services rendered. Thus, a child guidance clinic may define its domain as treating psychodevelopmental problems of young children in a certain geographic area by clinical casework. Many of the variations among human service organizations having similar service objectives can be attributed to differences in domain. For example, one community mental health center may concentrate on a low-income population, another on middle- and upper-income clients; one may offer extensive consultation to other agencies, another none; and one may offer family crisis intervention services while another provides a suicide prevention program.

It is crucial to recognize that the determination of the organizational domain defines the relevant task environment for the organization. To quote Thompson (1967: 26–27), "the organization's domain identifies the points at which the organization is dependent on inputs from the environment. The composition of that environment, the location within it of capacities, in turn determines upon whom the organization is dependent." Put differently, the choices presented to the organization in defining and pursuing its domain are a function of the potential and actual resources available to it and the conditions attached to their mobilization. Resources include: money, authority and legitimation, clients, manpower and expertise, and products and services. The access to these resources is controlled by external groups and organizations and can be secured only through transactions and exchanges with them. The set of all external groups and organizations controlling access to potential and actual resources for the organizations will be defined as its *task environment* (Thompson, 1967).

The Composition of the Task Environment

The task environment can be conceptualized as consisting of at least six major sectors.

1. Providers of fiscal resources. These may include federal, state, and local agencies from whom an organization obtains grants, the United Fund, private donors, and fee-paying clients. For example, the providers of fiscal resources to a local community mental health center may include the NIMH, a state department of mental health, a county commission, or health insurance companies.

2. Providers of legitimation and authority. These include organizations and groups that delegate some of their vested authority to an organization, or who lend social support based on their prestige and status. Publicly controlled human service organizations, like welfare departments and public schools, derive much of their authority from specific legislative acts, whose enforcement is monitored by various federal, state, and local executive agencies. Privately controlled human service organizations derive their authority mainly through the legitimation they receive from other prestigious organizations and groups such as churches, civic associations, professional associations, community leaders, and business elites.

An important function of legitimating and authority-granting agencies is to monitor and evaluate the organization, thus linking the legitimation and authority to continuing performance according to explicit or implicit evaluative criteria.

3. Providers of clients. These include not only groups and organizations that refer clients to an organization, but also individuals and families who may directly seek out the services of an organization. For example, the public school is not dependent on other organizations for pupils, but rather on families and their residential choices. In contrast, the community hospital is very dependent on physicians for most of its patients. Human service organizations have a variety of providers ranging from the clients themselves to other organizations.

4. Providers of complementary services. These include other human service organizations whose activities are needed by an organization to assure successful client services. For example, a drug treatment center may depend on a local hospital for the detoxification of its clients; and a juvenile court may rely on the diagnostic facilities of a community mental health center for its cases. Similarly, social service agencies that serve as field placement sites provide a complementary service to schools of social work.

5. Consumers and recipients of an organization's products. These include all the external units upon which an organization depends for the disposal of its "product." For human service organizations, the product consists of clients with altered social status and public identity, or with changed physical or personal attributes. The consumers of such a product are the clients themselves—voluntarily or involuntarily—and their social networks; for example, graduates of a public school, treated patients and their families, ex-offenders, and the disabled aged in a nursing home. However, the most important consumers of the product may be other organizations that require clients or manpower for their own purposes and without which the organization may not be able to justify its existence. For example, the most important consumers of the product of many high schools are colleges and universities: By admitting high school graduates they reaffirm the basic mission of high schools and ensure their continued social support and flow of resources. For the vocational rehabilitation program, key recipients are potential employers willing to hire the disabled. And for the neighborhood service center, the critical recipients are other human service organizations willing to provide services for the clients referred to them (Perlman, 1975). These external units play a pivotal role in confirming an organization's mandate and thus legitimating its claims for resources.

6. Competing organizations. These include organizations that may be competing with an organization for clients or other resources and can, therefore, influence the organization's access to them. A family service agency may be in competition with private therapists. Two or more organizations may be in competition when they seek money from the same source. Social service agencies funded by the United Fund potentially compete with each other for a greater share of these resources.

Any specific organization or group in the task environment may represent several of these sectors at the same time—for example, by being the provider of fiscal resources, legitimation, and clients. An industrial organization that supports a drug treatment center for its employees is such an example. If one element in the task environment controls access to several different resources, it will, of course, be that much more important to an organization; and as I will describe later, it can have a significant impact on an organization's structuring of service delivery systems.

Mapping the task environment is a crucial first step in identifying the choices an organization has to make in transforming itself into an institution. These choices result from both the interests the organizational leadership wishes to optimize and the need of the organization to adapt to and cope with the "rules of the game" imposed by potential resources providers. Based on a national study of juvenile courts (Hasenfeld, 1976), Figure 3.1 presents the mapping of the task environment of a typical court.

Forming Domain Consensus

The ability of an organization to obtain necessary resources from the task environment depends upon its having achieved some degree of consensus about its domain from those elements that control access to the resources. Without such domain consensus, controlling elements are likely to challenge the legitimation of the organization and withhold critical resources. Therefore, in forming its domain, an organization must convince key elements in the task environment that they will directly or indirectly benefit from its activities, and that it will not encroach on their own domain. In short, forming a domain consensus encompasses a process of negotiations, compromises, and exchange agreements between an organization and elements in its task environment that reflects their respective calculations

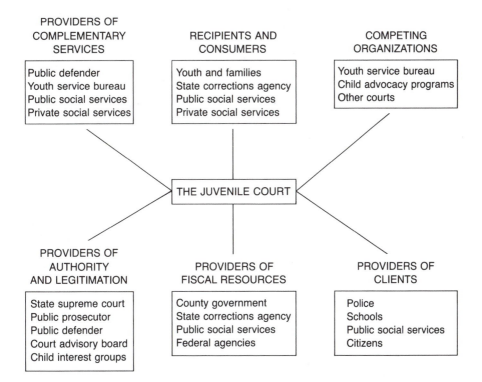

FIGURE 3.1   The task environment of the juvenile court

of the costs and payoffs to be derived from an organization. Thus, the domain of an organization is not static, but is subject to political and economic changes in the task environment.

For human service organizations forming a domain consensus is particularly complicated because it cannot be negotiated via market mechanisms, and organizational activities cannot be subjected to the relatively simple criterion of profitability. Rather, the negotiations might be subjected to considerations that include: (1) the ideological compatibility of the domain with those of key elements in the task environment; (2) the support for the organization by important political and professional elites; (3) the potential threat of the domain to the flow of clients and resources of other organizations; and (4) the benefits that may accrue to other organizations (e.g., reinforcement of their own domain, facilitation of their service delivery system, disposal of undesirable clients, reduction in competition, access to new resources, and the like).

By implication, a domain consensus may be formed with minimal consideration of the needs of clients, particularly if they do not control access to key resources. This is borne out by the example of the juvenile court, where for clients' needs to have influence on the court's domain they must be represented by important elements in the task environment such as child interest groups, the public defender, or public social services. Unfortunately, as our study of juvenile courts indicates, those most likely to be youth advocates, such as the public defender and child interest groups, are least likely to have any influence on the juvenile court (Hasenfeld, 1976).

The problems associated with establishing a domain consensus and their consequences on client services are demonstrated in a case study by Alford (1975: 152–58) of a hospital's effort to establish a neighborhood health care center. The hospital, located in a high poverty area with very few private practitioners, applied for an OEO grant and Title II funds from the Children's Bureau of HEW to establish a neighborhood health care center. Approval of the plan was sought and received from the health and hospital planning council of the city. However, concern was raised about the proximity of the center to others that were either proposed or already in existence under the sponsorship of other hospitals in the area. In particular, another hospital objected vigorously because the proposed center was to be located two blocks from it. Although the grant applications were approved by OEO and HEW, no agreement could be reached on the site, and the funding agencies refused to allocate additional funds to cover the costs of locating the center elsewhere. While no one denied the substantial health needs that were evident in the area, the conflict between the two hospitals, as reflected in the deliberations of the various planning organizations whose approval was necessary, caused considerable delay. The center was finally opened in a temporary store-front facility, but a permanent location was never funded. The center was never developed in accordance with the original plans, and its operations remained precarious because of the territorial controversy. Lack of domain consensus denied the area of an effective health care center.

Graziano (1969) offers another example of the difficulty of forming a domain consensus when a threat is perceived by elements in the task environment. A group of parents of autistic children, disenchanted with the traditional psychoanalytic services given by a local child guidance clinic, organized a program based on behavioral modification principles. This program was objected to, not only by the clinic itself, but by other community mental health agencies who feared the threat of its new treatment technology. An attempt was made to locate the program at a local university, which could then use it for research and teaching purposes. But, the university administration, sensitive to the controversy in the local mental health network, did not wish to jeopardize its own relations with them and refused to participate. Similarly, the request for funds from the Community Chest agency was delayed for about three years because the agency itself depended on local professional and business leaders to maintain its domain, and these leaders were more likely to represent the interests of the threatened mental health agencies. A further attempt by the program to secure funds by expanding its domain to include services to poor children was turned down because the required approval of the local mental health association was not forthcoming. As a result, the program subsisted on tuition fees and cake sales by a few determined parents. It was only after the program was able to demonstrate its effectiveness that it succeeded in securing funds from the state department of mental health, whose decisions were less swayed by the hostility of the local mental health agencies.

Domain consensus can reduce uncertainty and ensure a steady flow of resources from the environment to an organization. Resource certainty fundamentally determines the existence and survival of the organization and thus is a central concern for its executive leadership. The ability of the organization to achieve domain consensus is dependent partly on the characteristics of the task environment and partly on the strategies employed by the organization to relate to its elements. Following Aldrich (1972), several dimensions that have bearing on the ease or difficulty of forming domain consensus may be used to characterize the task environment.

1. *Stability or instability:* The degree of turnover of elements in the environment
2. *Homogeneity or heterogeneity:* The degree of similarity of elements in the task environment
3. *Concentration or dispersion:* The degree to which resources are evenly distributed among the elements
4. *Richness or paucity:* The level of resources in the environment potentially available to the organization
5. *Turbulence or placidity:* The degree to which the environment is disturbed or changed by other external activities

It could be hypothesized that under conditions of stability, homogeneity, and concentration of resources a new organization would have to conform closely to the preexisting domain agreements among the elements of the task environment. Environmental turbulence coupled with paucity of resources is also a barrier to forming domain consensus because it is likely to produce more turnover in the elements of the task environment and fierce competition for the limited resources. In contrast, when the environment is rich in resources, resources are more dispersed, and the environment is heterogeneous, it is then easier to achieve domain consensus because the environment will support and tolerate different organizational forms.

POWER-DEPENDENCE RELATIONS

To secure the resources controlled by elements of the task environment, an organization must engage in various exchange relations, the terms of which will be determined by the degree of the organization's dependence on each element. An *exchange relation* consists of transactions involving the transfer of resources between two or more organizations for the benefit of each (Cook, 1977). We can analyze these relations within the framework of the social exchange theory (e.g., Emerson, 1962, 1975; Blau, 1964). As explicated by the theory: The dependence of the organization is directly proportional to its need for the resource controlled by the element and inversely proportional to the availability of the resource elsewhere (see also Thompson, 1967; Jacobs, 1974). For example, the dependence of a family service agency on the United Fund is proportional to its need for the funds controlled by United Fund and inversely proportional to its ability to obtain such funds from other sources (e.g., client fees, other donors, contracts with other agencies). Similarly, although a welfare department needs many clients, its dependence on *each* client is minimal since it can easily find access to as many clients as it wishes. In contrast, agencies for the blind have a high need for young blind clients through whom an effective fund campaign can be launched. Yet, there is a limited number of such clients among the blind, and therefore organizational dependence on the young blind is high (Scott, 1967a).

If we denote the dependence *(D)* of organization *A* on element *B* in the task environment as *Dab*, then the power *(P)* of that element over the organization is *Pba* and is equal to *Dab (Dab = Pba)*. That is, the power of *B* over *A* is equal to the dependence of *A* on *B*. The power of *B* over *A* means that *B* is able to decrease the amount of resources it must provide *A* in exchange for the resources controlled by *A* (Cook, 1977). The element itself may need the services or resources controlled by the organization, and its dependence on it will be measured in the same manner. A balanced exchange will be:

Dab = Dba, which is equivalent to Pba = Pab.

It means that both the organization and the element equally influence each other. For example, while the Boy Scouts organization is dependent on the United Fund for its funds, the latter is equally dependent on the large constituency of the Boy Scouts for contributions. Therefore, there is a rough balance of power between them. However, when the element in the task environment is less dependent on the organization, an imbalanced exchange will result, and we can say that the element *B* has a *power advantage*. This is denoted as:

Dab > *Dba*, which is equivalent to *Pba* > *Pab*.

For example, while a vocational rehabilitation center is dependent on potential employers to hire its graduates, the employers are not dependent on the center for job applicants. So the employers have a power advantage and can dictate the terms of the exchange.

Some distinctive conditions may increase the dependence of the human service organization on external units (Hasenfeld, 1972):

1. Legal statutes, governmental policies, parent organizations, and other regulatory groups have imposed an enforced dependence on external units. For example, because of statutes a welfare department may be dependent on the state employment security office for job counselling and placement of its clients.
2. An external unit has discretion over the utilization of an organization's services. For example, private schools are much more dependent on their students' parents than are public schools since these parents have considerable discretion over the use of school services.
3. The organization has a high need for the client services controlled by the external unit, as exemplified by the dependence of employment security offices on potential employers for jobs for their clients.
4. The external unit is a major legitimator and validator of the organizational goals. For example, a child guidance clinic may be dependent on key psychiatrists and other helping professionals to legitimate its claim to competence.
5. The organization lacks effective ways to find out about alternative units that could provide the needed resources.

On the other hand, some distinctive conditions may increase the power of the human service organizations in relation to the external unit:

1. The policy regulations of the organization allow it freedom and latitude to interact with elements in the environment. For example, the organization is free to decide from which external units it can purchase services for its clients.

2. The organization possesses essential resources that are sorely needed by the external unit. For example, the organization may be the key or only provider of clients to the unit whose services it needs.

3. The organization can obtain the needed services from a variety of alternative sources. For example, the community mental health center may not depend on any specific community agency for clients if it receives referrals from numerous agencies.

4. The organization develops self-validating organizational ideologies to justify its goals. For example, a self-help group like Alcoholics Anonymous does not accept the validity of external evaluation of its efforts but instead relies on its own member to validate its goals.

5. The organization develops effective means for identifying alternative external units as suppliers of needed resources.

All these conditions are summarized in Table 3.1.

The central dynamic that governs organization-environment relations can be stated in the following proposition: The greater the dependence of the organization on any given element in the task environment and the less its countervailing power, the greater the influence of that element on the organization and the greater its ability to dictate the terms of the exchange. For example, Pfeffer and Long (1977), in their study of resource allocations by the United Fund, found that agencies that had greater power (as measured by their ability to obtain outside resources) received a larger proportion of the United Fund allocation. That is, an organization will use its power advantage to dictate the terms of the exchange in its favor.

In general, organizational policies and service delivery patterns will reflect the contingencies and constraints set by those external units upon whom the organization is most dependent for resources. For example, it is impossible to understand the myriad of internal policies and regulations established by welfare departments without recognizing that they are aimed at satisfying rules and restrictions imposed by the major providers of fiscal

TABLE 3.1   Conditions Increasing Dependence vs. Countervailing Powers

CONDITIONS OF DEPENDENCE	COUNTERVAILING POWERS
External imposition of policies	Freedom permitted by external powers
External discretion on use of organization's services	Possession of essential resources
High need for services of external unit	Availability of alternative services
External validation of goals needed	Development of self-validating organizational ideologies
Ineffective intelligence about alternatives	Effective intelligence about alternatives

Source: Adapted from Hasenfeld (1972: 259).

resources. Similarly, the domination of psychiatry in community mental health centers usually reflects dependence on the psychiatric profession for legitimation and authority. In both instances, powerful organizations impose certain policies and directions on the organization to protect and advance their own domains and interests.

This domination by powerful external units becomes most visible when an organization attempts to pursue policies that run counter to such interests and collide with the countervailing powers. This is dramatically demonstrated in the case study of the Oakland Economic Development Council, Inc., as reported by Warren, Rose, and Bergunder (1974: 131–47). The OEDC was a fairly typical community action agency designed to develop a variety of service programs for the poor. It was very dependent for fiscal resources and legitimation on the OEO and city hall, and needed the cooperation of such organizations as the board of education and the welfare department to carry out many of its programs. As long as the OEDC concentrated on developing programs that emphasized the need to change poor people rather than the need to change the structure of the social services delivery system, it enjoyed the flow of critical resources from these external units. However, when OEDC, through a change of leadership, became more politically aggressive, and attempted to mobilize the poor for political action to alter the basic political and economic structure controlling the distribution of social services in the city, these resources were withdrawn to a point where the agency lost its autonomy. As OEDC attempted to gain control over services for the poor and politicize social problems, organizations like the board of education and the welfare department withdrew their cooperation for several joint programs. The city council waged a full-fledged political battle for control of the board of OEDC and successfully mobilized the OEO to withhold funds from the agency. These actions, coupled with the governor's veto of a federal grant to the agency, led rapidly to the decline of OEDC and the takeover of the antipoverty program by the city council.

Strategies for Changing Power-Dependence Relations

Although human service organizations vary widely in the degree to which they depend on their task environments, all are motivated to enhance and preserve their autonomy and acquire some measure of control over their environments. Strong dependence on external units with no countervailing powers generates much uncertainty for an organization, makes it vulnerable to external pressures, and jeopardizes its internal integrity and survival.

To reduce such vulnerability, organizations often employ various strategies to improve their power-dependence relations. The choice of strategies will be determined by: (a) the concentration or dispersion of the resources needed by the organization, and (b) by the amount of strategic resources it controls. In general, the greater the concentration of resources in the environment and the fewer strategic resources in the organization, the poorer its ability to negotiate favorable relations with the environment. Four major types of strategies can be identified: authoritative, competitive, cooperative, and disruptive (Thompson, 1967; Benson, 1975).

Authoritative strategies. When the organization occupies a dominant position in the social service network because of its control of money and authority, it can use that position to dictate the terms of its own exchange relations and those of other elements in the network. Such a strategy, to quote Benson, is "authoritative in the sense that the directing agent uses its power to mandate precise activities and not merely to encourage or reward these activities. This implies, too, that the directing agent is sufficiently powerful in relation to a network to permit a precise specification" (1975: 244). We should add that its success in applying such a strategy will also be contingent on its ability to monitor the activities of the other organizations and apply effective sanctions to ensure compliance.

Governmental agencies, controlling both the money and authority for various social service programs, frequently use such a strategy in relation to local units. For example, the Department of Labor uses its authority to define the major specifications of the local CETA programs it legitimates and funds. Similarly, from 1936 to 1967 the Bureau of Family Services used its authority very effectively to regulate all the service activities of state departments of welfare by specifying what social work services each department was allowed to provide its clients (Derthick, 1975). The tortuous relations between antipoverty programs and local government units is another example of the use of authority to control programs. City halls have been able to exert highly effective control over some programs and blunt or repel their political action efforts.

The use of authority as a strategy has a high payoff for an organization because it forces the external units to comply with the terms of the exchange without significantly affecting the organization's autonomy. Such a strategy may have either beneficial or deleterious effects on client services. If the organization uses its authority to force external units to provide services to clients who might otherwise be ignored or rejected, or to force them to establish joint programs for more effective service delivery, authority can then be a powerful weapon for better client services. Such a strategy by the Labor Department, for example, forced state employment security offices to shift their service emphasis to the hard-to-employ and to the disadvantaged. The use of authority to enforce school desegregation gained momentum only after the passage of the Civil Rights Act of 1964, which empowered HEW to withhold federal funds from school systems that practiced racial discrimination. Similarly, authority was used through federal legislation to force cooperative relationships between welfare departments and employment security offices to establish WIN—the Work Incentives Program, which encouraged welfare recipients to find jobs.

But authority can have deleterious effects on client services. As suggested earlier, authority may be used to thwart innovations in the delivery of social services. Many new delinquency prevention programs have been terminated because their innovations have been perceived as threats by law enforcement agencies, state juvenile corrections agencies, and other control agencies (Empey and Erickson, 1972). Freidson (1970) points out how the authority of the medical profession has been instrumental in getting vast resources allocated to medical research on mental deficiency, only a small proportion of which is genetically or biologically caused, while educational facilities for training the mentally disabled remain severely underfinanced.

Use of authority is obviously limited to a small number of organizations who have a clear dominant position in the social service network. Moreover, important costs accrue in deploying such a strategy. First, it requires that the organization expend considerable resources to monitor compliance with its directives. That is, the effectiveness of authority is directly related to the efficiency of the monitoring system. Note, for example, the inability of state regulatory agencies to monitor effectively the compliance of the nursing home industry with various health, safety, and welfare regulations. Second, compliance may be symbolic rather than substantive. This is exemplified in the protracted process of school desegregation in the South. After a period of "massive resistance" to federal court orders, local school boards devised insidious ways to limit desegregation to tokenism by reliance on such tactics as "pupil placement laws." Legal actions then had to be taken against each school board to challenge the legality of its policies and enforce real compliance with the law (Crain, 1968).

Competitive strategies.   An organization can increase its power by using competition to make its services more desirable and attractive in the social service network. Competition is possible when the resources the organization seeks are dispersed in the environment, and it has sufficient internal resources to maintain a power balance with its competitors. Therefore, the organization knows that alternative sources of support are available and that the costs of competing with other organizations will not undermine its own resource base. Under these conditions, competition to increase organizational power is a highly desirable strategy, since the potential payoff is increased organizational independence and freedom to negotiate exchange relations (Thompson, 1967: 32–33). The successfully competitive organization can, hence, avoid having to accommodate to pressures from units in the task environment that may be incongruent with its desired goals. Rather, it has the freedom to enter into exchange relations with those units that do support its organizational goals.

"Solo practice" in medicine is a case in point. Typically it involves physicians who work by themselves in offices set up with their personal resources, and who treat patients who have freely selected them. Such physicians compete with other health care providers for patients and rely on their reputation, prestige, affiliation with prestigious hospitals, convenient location, and the like to attract them. The payoff is a high degree of freedom and autonomy the physicians enjoy in structuring their work environment (Friedson, 1970). Physicians can use competition as a strategy in attracting patients because the supply of patients is dispersed and the number of physicians is usually small enough to assure sufficient demand for their services, thus muting imbalances of power among them.

Competition among industrial organizations centers around product characteristics, quality, and price; this is not generally the case for human service organizations, where the characteristics, quality, and price of the products are not immediately measurable. Hence, the competition revolves more around the public image that an organization can create. To quote Elesh, "it is through these images that the relevant publics are able to match their 'wants' (to use the economists' term) with organizational characteristics to make desired choices" (1973: 373). Such images are likely to be shaped by accruing reputation and prestige. Hospitals, for example, may do so by affiliating with medical schools, purchasing expensive equipment, contracting the services of eminent physicians, and engaging in well-publicized medical research. Mental health clinics may enhance their reputation and prestige by employing a high ratio of psychiatrists and clinical psychologists, establishing highly visible demonstration projects, and getting testimonials from selected clients and other agencies. While none of these activities speaks directly to the products of these organizations, they help create an image of high-quality service, by which the organization hopes to compete successfully for resources and clients.

Use of competition as a strategy can have major consequences for service delivery patterns, particularly if these are shaped to support the organization's competitive posture. As noted earlier, Scott, in his study of agencies for the blind, found that they concentrated on serving young and employable blind persons because this enabled them to compete more successfully for public funds. As Scott puts it, "the success of fund-raising campaigns depends upon strong emotional appeals on behalf of the needy. In their fund-raising campaigns, agencies for the blind exploit a certain number of cultural strategies in our society. These strategies concern blindness, youth, work, and hope" (1967a: 254).

Since prestige and reputation are major ingredients for enhancing a competitive position, they too are likely to become important considerations in the development of an organization's service delivery system. For example, the organization may attempt to select only clients who can be successfully serviced or avoid serving clients from low socioeconomic groups.

Teele and Levine (1968), in their study of intake patterns in child guidance clinics, found that children accepted for treatment were likely to come from middle- and upper-class families and have mild psychiatric symptoms. Older children from lower socioeconomic groups defined as delinquent or as having serious psychiatric symptoms were least likely to be accepted. One could speculate that these selection processes ensured a high rate of success and buttressed the clinics' prestige and professional reputations.

The pursuit of prestige and reputation may also divert critical organizational resources from direct client services to image-enhancing activities that may not have any intrinsic value for the quality of client services. A nursing home that boasts attractive physical facilities may have neglected staff-patient activities to enhance its image.

It has been argued that competition among human service organizations fosters duplication of services and wastes resources, and is therefore undesirable. Yet, duplication of services, in itself, is not necessarily harmful since it offers clients options and encourages organizational innovation. In fact, one could make a cogent argument that lack of competition among human service organizations, which is often the case, results in organizational insensitivity and lack of adjustment to changing client needs and wishes. Warren (1970), for example, advocates the introduction of competition into the human services by making a large part of each agency's income dependent on the consumers it can attract. This, he argues, will motivate agencies to close gaps in services and be more adaptable to clients' needs. The proposal for a system of educational vouchers attempts to accomplish this objective for public education. However, for this approach to become workable, major changes must occur in income redistribution and other social patterns, otherwise such a market system will only reinforce social and economic inequities (Mayer, Moroney, and Morris, 1974: 135-57).

Cooperative strategies. Cooperation is the strategy most used by human service organizations since the conditions necessary for competition—dispersion of needed resources and possession of strategic resources—are rare. By *cooperation* we mean that the organization is willing to make a commitment to supply an element in the task environment with a service it needs, thus reducing the element's uncertainty about getting such a service (Thompson, 1967: 34). The organization increases its power over the element since in exchange for such a commitment, the latter is now obligated to provide the resources sought by the organization. For example, a cooperative relationship between a welfare department and a day care facility ensures the department of the needed service for its clients and guarantees the day care facility a steady source of income.

Three forms of cooperative strategies will be distinguished: contracting, coalition, and cooptation. I will explore the occasions for using each of the strategies, the costs and payoffs associated with each, and the consequences of each on service delivery systems.

Contracting. A *contract* is a negotiated agreement, formal or informal, between two oganizations for the exchange of resources or services. It is likely to be used when the resource sought by an organization is concentrated in the task environment and the organization controls a highly needed service, which gives it some measure of power against other organizations. For example, a welfare department may contract with a shelter care facility to provide care for disabled adults. The shelter care facility faces a concentration of fiscal resources in its environment since most of the funds to operate the facility are controlled by the department of welfare. But it provides a highly needed service and is therefore in a position to bargain with the department. Similarly, the relationship between a public school and a local child guidance clinic may be contractual in the sense that the school is a vital source of referrals to the clinic which, in turn, provides an important service to the school by treating children with school-related problems. In both instances, the parties to the contract reduce their dependence on the task environment because of the commitments they secure to receive the needed service or resource.

Sarason and associates (1977) describe an exchange agreement between a residential educational center for disadvantaged youth and two colleges that provided work-study arrangements and supervised internships for teachers at the center who were attending college. The center obtained highly needed manpower as well as opportunities for its own staff to develop professionally, and the colleges got important research projects. Contracts were sought by the center to validate its educational objectives and by the colleges to support the research interests of their faculties.

Because human service organizations tend to operate in a network in which both services and resources are controlled by a few organizations, contracting is the predominant form of interorganizational transaction. Moreover, this form is likely to be reinforced or even to be required by legislative and administrative regulatory acts. For example, the Economic Opportunity Act of 1964 authorized the contracting of public and private nonprofit agencies to provide services funded by the act. Title XX authorizes state agencies to rely on contractual arrangements with various agencies to provide services to target groups.

While the payoff from contractual arrangements is a reduction of uncertainty and a secure flow of resources and services to an organization, some serious costs are incurred. First, an organization, by accepting the terms of the contract, reduces its options and thus gives up some of its flexibility and autonomy. Second, the terms of the agreement may commit an organization to a set of activities perhaps not consonant with its major interests. For example, the shelter care facility may have to accept clients with more severe disabilities than it wishes to serve. Third, contractual arrangements with government agencies typically necessitate compliance with a complex set of regulations, accountability and reporting procedures, and constraints on service provisions that can severely limit organizational autonomy (Wedel, 1976; Manser, 1974).

Contracting is a key mechanism for coordinating and integrating the social service network. Agreements among organizations for the exchange of services and resources establish necessary links among them and ensure that clients will receive needed services, thus facilitating continuity of care. An agreement between a community mental health center and a public school to provide teachers wth consultations about the mental health of their students sets up a flow of mental health services to school children who otherwise might be deprived of them. In short, such contractual arrangements relieve the client of the burden of connecting disparate components of the service delivery network.

Contracts permit agencies to specialize and increase their effectiveness while enabling them to rely on other organizations to provide the necessary complementary services to their clients. At the same time, however, such contracts may create very complicated interorganizational arrangements that impede the smoothness and comprehensiveness of the service delivery system. For example, a community treatment program for high-risk adolescents may have contracts with the department of mental health, the welfare department, and the department of education to provide comprehensive services to these youth. Yet the program may face problems because of the restrictions attached to the funds from each department. For example, only youth who are wards of the state and under the jurisdiction of the welfare department might be eligible for various financial and medical assistance allowances; only youth discharged from state mental health facilities might be eligible for psychiatric counselling; specialized educational services might be permitted only for youth who meet the criteria set by the department of education; and the department of mental health might refuse to pay for mental health services for a youth adjudicated as delinquent.

Service contracts also raise serious problems of accountability—that is, determining whether clients are actually receiving the services for which the contract has been established. Since it is ultimately the client, not the organization, that receives the contracted service, only by noting the effects of these services on the client can the organization determine whether the spirit of the contract has been met. A vocational rehabilitation agency contracting a training program for its clients cannot easily assess whether the program has effectively delivered the contracted training services. Unless the organization develops very elaborate monitoring procedures, it must rely primarily on client feedback. Yet clients may be totally incapable of providing such feedback, particularly if they are very young, incapacitated, labeled as deviant, or very old. Indeed, in the hands of unscrupulous service providers, contracts may be abused and subverted to serve the providers' vested interests instead of the clients', as is so aptly demonstrated in the case of nursing homes for the aged (Townsend, 1971).

Coalition. A *coalition* is the pooling together of resources by several organizations for a joint venture. It provides a structure through which decisions related to a common set of interests are made via explicit mutual agreement among the member organizations (Wilson, 1973). Coalition as a strategy is likely to emerge under the following conditions: (1) each organization on its own is relatively powerless against those who control the resource it desires (e.g., money, legitimation, clients, favorable legislation, service programs); (2) there is the right amount of complementariness and compatibility of interests among the organizations; and (3) each organization perceives a payoff that exceeds the costs of joining the coalition. By pooling their resources, the members of the coalition form an "organization of organizations" that then acquires power to negotiate more effectively with elements of the task environment. For example, several social service agencies may join in a coalition with the objective of obtaining federal funds for a program aimed at a certain target population. Each agency realizes that it cannot obtain these funds on its own, but by joining with others it stands to gain additional resources, legitimation, and reaffirmation of its service objectives. Organizations may join a coalition not only to exploit new opportunities and maximize payoff, but also to overcome an environmental threat. The formation of the United Fund as a coalition of voluntary social service agencies was prompted by the threat by large corporate donors—the principal source of their funds—to withdraw their contributions unless such a coalition were established (Seeley et al., 1957).

Coalitions are difficult to form because of the preconditions just mentioned and are likely to be unstable since they require each member to relinquish some autonomy and abide by decisions of the coalition. To quote Wilson, "associations almost never allow another association to speak for them, and when they do, it is typically on the understanding that unanimous consent is necessary for the coalition to act, or that the coalition will have a sharply limited scope of action, or that it is an ad hoc arrangement with a brief life expectancy" (1973: 271). Numerous other organizational costs are associated with coalition formation besides the general loss of autonomy (Adrian and Press, 1968). First, there are communication costs: The success of the coalition is dependent on active interaction among members and the sharing of sufficient information to stimulate joint action. Second, there are responsibility costs: Each member of the coalition must divert resources to fulfill tasks assigned to it by the coalition. Third, actions by the coalition may generate dissonance within individual organizations. The coalition of civil rights organizations in 1963 forced militant organizations, like SNCC and CORE, to consent to political action through relatively conventional channels, much to the chagrin of their members (Barker and Jansiewicz, 1970). Fourth, members of the coalition may face serious disagreements on how to divide up the benefits obtained from the coalition.

It is not surprising, then, that coalitions are formed for specific time-limited objectives and are dissolved soon after the objectives have been met. The coalition of civil rights organizations, which included such organizations as the Urban League, NAACP, SCLC, SNCC, CORE, and the Negro American Labor Council, lasted only from 1963 to 1965. These organizations were able to bury their differences long enough to organize the August 1963 March on Washington, which culminated in the passage by Congress of landmark civil rights legislation. The very passage of the Voting Rights Act of 1963 and the Civil Rights Act of 1964 led to the disintegration of the coalition. Once the legal battle had been won, major differences among the organizations erupted over strategies to improve the economic, social, and political conditions of blacks in America. Ideological differences surfaced rapidly and could no longer be bridged, particularly since organizations were attempting to define and protect their domains and were competing for constituencies (Barker and Jansiewicz, 1970).

Successful coalitions can produce significant payoffs. A coalition of child-serving agencies, for example, was successful in obtaining large grants from the OEO to provide child and family services to inner-city poor (Manser, Jones, and Ortof, 1967). Murphy (1971), in his study of the antipoverty program in New Haven, Connecticut, attributes its unusual success to its ability to forge a coalition of public and private agencies that were committed to participate in antipoverty projects. These agencies were chosen, rather than grass-roots organizations, so as to draw on their "staying power" in the city, thus lending the program legitimation and stability. The costs of joining the coalition were minimized because the agencies were expected to expand their services in the inner city, rather than undergo major program changes. The payoff was explicit: access to significant funds from the Ford Foundation and the federal government. The coalition, which numbered over twenty-five public and private agencies, was in an exceptionally strong position to bargain with the grantors and to compete with other cities for funds.

Nevertheless, the success of the New Haven antipoverty program cannot be measured simply by the magnitude of the resources it was able to mobilize and the number of projects it launched. The evidence seems to suggest that, to achieve success, the program did not encourage citizen participation and avoided any attempts to push for radical changes in the city's social welfare delivery system. There were even hints that the program engaged in "creaming" off desirable clients in order to demonstrate success. The program suffered irreparable damage to its reputation when racial riots broke out in the city.

Effective coalitions, then, can be potent instruments of social change. The aggregation of resources—each organization being relatively weak against power holders—creates an organization of organizations that has considerably more power than its constituents and that can therefore bargain effectively with power holders. Pearl and Barr (1976) describe a coalition of eleven member agencies in the family and children services area that has been highly successful in expanding welfare benefits to adolescents and male sole-support parents. It was only by pooling the resources from each agency that a common social action campaign was possible. Nevertheless, as the previous case study demonstrates, the compromises necessary to organize and maintain a coalition may impede its ability to engage in innovative social service.

Cooptation.   *Cooptation* is a process whereby representatives of key elements in the task environment are absorbed into the leadership or policy-making structure of an organization in order to avert threats to its stability or existence (Selznick, 1949). By inviting participation from these elements into its policy-making structure, the organization hopes that, in return, these elements will be won over and will lend support (or will at least stop threatening) its legitimacy.

Cooptation as a strategy is likely to be used when the resources needed by an organization are concentrated, and it lacks strategic resources of its own, or when it encounters threats it cannot easily neutralize by resources it already controls. In cooptation the organization is exchanging, in effect, a significant amount of its autonomy for support from the external elements. It is not surprising, therefore, that this strategy is used by human service organizations mostly at their founding stages. Inviting representatives of key influential groups and organizations in the environment onto its board of directors illustrates the strategic use of cooptation to acquire power (Zald, 1969; Allen, 1974). As members of the board they are willing to provide the organization with resources they control—legitimation, money, knowledge—in return for influence on the goals and mission of the organization. Successful cooptation is measured by the willingness of the external elements to define interorganizational issues from the perspective of the organization (Warren, Rose, and Bergunder, 1974).

Some evidence suggests that many human service organizations have responded with cooptation to threats by citizen action groups. Some universities, for example, have allowed students to have formal representatives on various academic committees but have not given them any significant power to affect their decisons. Warren, Rose, and Bergunder (1974) argue that cooptation was the most predominant strategy used by antipoverty programs in response to the demands for participation by residents in poverty areas. This was accomplished by allowing residents some form of policy and program review and by employing them in the programs ("personnel" cooptation). Yet in very few of the programs they studied did these forms of participation result in changes in the organization's activity that were initiated by the poverty area residents.

While the payoff from cooptation is mobilization of support and dilution of threats to the organization, the costs to organizational autonomy are high. Participation by external units in organizational decision making implies that the organization may have to modify and adapt its objectives and activities in direct proportion to the power of the external representatives. The cooptation of key legislators to support a delinquency prevention program might necessitate that it be located in one of their districts or provide employment opportunities to their constituents.

To the extent that their disruptive power can be neutralized, the cooptation of client groups may effectively serve the vested interests of the organization's leadership and maintain organizational stability. For example, when Congress enacted the Work Incentive Program for AFDC recipients as part of the 1967 amendment to the Social Security Act, the Labor Department feared a great deal of trouble from recipients if state employment agencies began forcing women off welfare and into the labor market. To thwart such an eventuality, it reached an agreement with the National Welfare Rights Organization in which the organization received $400,000 from the Labor Department to monitor local state employment agencies and ensure that the rights of welfare recipients were not violated. At least from the Labor Department's perspective, it is not difficult to see such an arrangement as a form of cooptation (Piven and Cloward, 1977).

This is not to deny that the cooptation of clients may stimulate change in the organization, opening it up to client input and making it more responsive to their needs. But many of these changes are only cosmetic since they do not alter significantly the distribution of power and resources in the organization. In short, the costs to the organization in loss of autonomy are minimized in relation to the payoffs in client acquiescence.

Disruptive strategies.   According to Benson, *disruptive strategies* refer to "the purposive conduct of activities which threaten the resource-generating capacities of the target economy" (1975: 242). In so doing, the disruptive organization hopes to extract concessions from the target agency and thus alter the power-dependence relations between them. Disruptive strategies are likely to be selected under the following conditions: (1) an organization is powerless against its task environment, so that the powerful elements it wishes to influence can ignore its nondisruptive requests; (2) the organization perceives it has little to lose should the disruption fail; (3) the organization does not have sustained interaction with the external element that could provide common ground rules for conflict management; and (4) substantial ideological conflict exists between the organization and the external element.

Within the general aim of gaining power in the task environment, the organization may have multiple objectives for using disruption and protest as a strategy. It may do so (1) to acquire sufficient power to move toward bargaining; (2) to increase the credibility of its dedication in pursuit of its goals; (3) to generate public visibility that will attract supporters; or (4) to activate the intervention of third parties (Wilson, 1973: 282–83).

The success of disruption as a strategy depends on several factors. First, the element in the task environment to be disrupted must already be experiencing vulnerability in an important aspect of its operations so that any disruption will cause major strain on its resources. Second, the disruptive organization must be able to mobilize sufficient resources to maintain the disruption long enough for it to be effective. Third, counterattacks by the element will not jeopardize the disruptive orgnization's existence. This may be possible only when the resource base of the disruptive organization is well insulated from the influence of the element. Fourth, the disruption and protest should mobilize others to the cause championed by the disruptive organization.

Small-scale or temporary use of disruptive strategies is not uncommon in the human services arena. Such strategies are used by organizations to register displeasure with actions of other organizations in the network, with the aim of forcing them to readjust their interorganizational relations. For example, a police department might be displeased with what it perceives as lenient processing of juveniles by the court. It might resort to flooding the court with formal petitions, which seriously disrupts court intake, thus forcing court officials to take note of police sentiments and attempt to reach some accommodation. Similarly, a department of mental health may threaten to withdraw or withhold funds from operators of shelter care facilities in order to correct deficiencies in the services. However, disruption and protests are most likely to be used by the powerless (e.g., clients) against powerful human service organizations and are aimed at producing major structural changes in the relationships between them. This can be illustrated by two well-known forms of protest: tenants' rent strikes and welfare rights movements.

One of the most famous rent strikes occurred in Harlem in 1963–1964 under the auspices of the Community Council on Housing led by Jesse Gray. By organizing a rent strike on several city blocks, Gray and his organization were hoping to dramatize the squalid conditions of these tenement houses and to force the intervention of third parties—city agencies—on behalf of the striking tenants. Indeed, as the strike gathered momentum, several organizations joined ranks to criticize various city agencies for not enforcing housing regulations and failing to prosecute slum landlords for violating housing codes. These included numerous local politicians, representatives of civil rights organizations, local community organization agencies, and two unions (Lipsky, 1970). A court decision ordering tenants to pay all rent due the landlords to the court and stipulating that landlords could apply to the courts for these funds to repair their buildings was a major victory for the strikers. In addition, several city agencies, in response to the strike, mobilized to enforce the city housing codes more rigorously.

In his analysis of the effectiveness of the rent strike, Lipsky (1970) suggests that it provided the needed impetus to mobilize housing reform programs that were already in existence, but lacked saliency and commitment of resources. Two specific programs were of particular importance: pest control and emergency repairs of buildings. At the same time, Lipsky presents data to suggest that the outcome was mixed for the actual buildings in which tenants struck; approximately half the buildings remained in poor condition.

The movement of welfare recipients to protest and disrupt welfare departments gained momentum with the establishment of various community action programs under the federal government's War on Poverty. In 1965, through the organizing efforts of Mobilization for Youth in the Lower East Side of New York, the Committee of Welfare Families was formed. The committee's first action was to launch a winter clothing campaign on behalf of welfare recipients. This was later followed by a campaign to increase the amount of special grants recipients could receive; such grants, although under the control of the Welfare Department, were discretionary and therefore easier to dispense (Jackson and Johnson, 1974). The emphasis on special grants, rather than the regular grant that was fixed by law, became the major focus of the welfare rights organizations that sprung up in the 1960s.

The most articulate rationale for the use of disruption as a strategy to end poverty was offered by Piven and Cloward (1977). They argued that a huge pool of eligible poor families in cities were not receiving welfare grants. By inducing them to apply for welfare, a significant decline in poverty would occur; and the welfare system would experience a monumental crisis that would ultimately result in the establishment of a national minimum income standard. Therefore, they advocated a massive campaign to enroll all eligible nonrecipients, to educate recipients to obtain maximum benefits, and to disrupt welfare centers.

While the Piven and Cloward plan was not adopted by the National Welfare Rights Organization, it suggested that welfare recipients mobilize for action through benefit campaigns. As Piven and Cloward put it, "welfare rights organizing throughout the country relied primarily on solving the grievances of existing recipients as an organizing technique" (1977: 297). Demonstrations, sit-ins, and threats of disruption proved to be effective tactics in getting welfare officials to meet the demands of welfare recipients. In both New York and Massachusetts, for example, millions of dollars were poured into special grants because of the direct pressures of welfare rights organizations. Moreover, these disruptive tactics ultimately resulted, at the local level, in a formalized system of negotiations between such organizations and welfare officials. Welfare rights organizations were often granted official representation in local welfare offices and were accepted as legitimate advocates for recipients.

Undoubtedly, the impact of the welfare rights organizations has been significant in several aspects. First, they greatly increased the number of eligible poor families applying for and receiving welfare grants. Second, they ensured that recipients received the grants they were entitled to. Third, they reduced the blatant harassment and humiliation of recipients by welfare officials. Yet, as Piven and Cloward (1977) in their assessment of the movement point out, the long-term consequences have been less favorable. As part of the backlash against the rising costs of welfare, special grants have been abolished, and states have enforced more rigid eligibility requirements.

As these examples demonstrate, disruptive strategies may be effective in extracting concessions from human service organizations on behalf of the disenfranchised, the poor, and the disadvantaged. But they also generate counterattacks that in the long run may negate short-term gains. Moreover, while concessions to disruptive organizations may appease their constituencies, they are often small and only serve to divert attention from more basic inequities in the structure of social services.

CONCLUSION

One cannot underestimate the impact of the environment on the service delivery patterns of human service organizations. The general environment, encompassing economic, sociodemographic, cultural, political-legal, and technological conditions, defines for an organization the range of resources available to it, the range and types of human problems and needs it will face, the value system within which it will have to function, the political and legal constraints it will need to adapt to, and the human service technologies available to it.

Within this environment, a human service organization must achieve a domain consensus by making strategic choices about the units in the environment with which it will interact. These choices will determine the characteristics of the resources an organization will be able to mobilize and the nature of its output. Thus, the formulation and maintenance of the domain consensus will define in very specific terms the service delivery system to be developed by an organization.

Mobilizing resources from the environment necessitates that an organization enter into various exchange relations with the task environment. The attributes of these transactions are determined by the power-dependence relations between an organization and each of the elements in the task environment. The greater the dependence of an organization on a given element, the greater the influence of that element on an organization's service delivery system. An organization may use several strategies to gain power over elements in the task environment: authority, competition, cooperation, and disruption. Each of these strategies produces certain payoffs as well as costs to the organization and has direct consequences for its client services.

Interorganizational relations reflect the interaction modes that each organization adopts to secure resources, reduce uncertainty, and gain some mastery over its environment. Patterns of interorganizational relations are, therefore, a consequence of the various strategies that organizations employ to achieve these objectives. These relations may be highly rational and adaptive from each organization's viewpoint; but when they are examined in their totality, they are often seen to be loosely connected systems with limited coordination. The network of services is likely to be characterized by redundancy together with major service gaps; limited cooperation and contradictory or inconsistent service delivery patterns; and multiple interorganizational links and contacts but no overall rational and effective service network.

4

ORGANIZATIONAL GOALS

Much contemporary criticism of human service organizations centers around the apparent discrepancies between their stated goals and their actual performance. For example, public schools are under attack for failing to educate children properly. Welfare departments are accused of perpetuating poverty and dependency and of not helping people to become self-sufficient, contributing members of society (Mandell, 1971). And correctional institutions are told to abandon their rehabilitation goals since they are unable to demonstrate any success in rehabilitating offenders (Martinson, 1974). However, some students of human service organizations point out that these organizations were not really established to fully meet their purported goals, but rather to fulfill functions that are not or cannot be acknowledged publicly. Piven and Cloward (1971) thus argue that the real purpose of public welfare is to regulate the flow of unskilled labor in and out of the labor market depending on the fluctuations in the business cycle. Kassenbaum, Ward, and Wilner (1971) have shown that the use of rehabilitation in prison is nothing more than another device to maintain and support the primary goals of the institution: custody and control.

These examples also point to the lack of agreement on what the goals of human service organizations should be. This is so because the activities of such organizations touch upon and reflect choices among competing values about human welfare. When the goals of a psychiatric hospital emphasize short-term care and community-based rehabilitation for its patients, it, in effect, adopts certain values about human welfare: that the mentally ill are not a danger to the community; that the mentally ill should become an integral part of the community as much as possible; and that mental illness should be viewed as a situational crisis rather than a serious form of deviance. Clearly, many other social groups in the community uphold opposing values and beliefs about the mentally ill (Cumming and Cumming, 1957). In short, the goals adopted by human service organizations reinforce a certain set of values and beliefs over which there is no clear consensus in a pluralistic society, and thus they are likely to be challenged by those social groups who hold opposing or different belief systems.

In the same vein, human service organizations experience continuing pressures to adopt goals that satisfy the interests of diverse social groups, and, therefore, they may be forced to pursue multiple and conflicting goals. The simultaneous pursuit of custody and rehabilitation by correctional institutions provides one clear example.

These issues, which will be the major focus of this chapter, are not unique to human service organizations, and are likely to be experienced by industrial and commercial organizations as well (Perrow, 1970). Nevertheless, the issue of goals is substantively more problematic in human service organizations.

The purpose here will be to review some of the theoretical issues involved in defining organizational goals; to explore the characteristics of goals in human service organizations; to identify the processes by which they are formulated and changed; and to indicate some of their effects on the delivery of services.

OFFICIAL AND OPERATIVE GOALS

Since organizations are social units purposely constructed to achieve various aims, organizational analysis is often preoccupied with identifying the dynamics by which such aims are determined and the processes by which they are realized. At the most general level, organizations may be viewed as having goals that fulfill some basic societal functions. For Parsons (1957), who follows a functional-structural perspective (see Chapter 2), organizational goals reflect the type of functions the organization performs for the larger social system. In the case of the mental hospital, Parsons defines its goal thus: "to cope with the consequences for the individual patient and for the patients as a social group, of a condition of mental illness" (1957: 108). He elaborates this goal in terms of a set of specific social responsibilities of the hospital: custody, protection, socialization, and therapy. In other words, the existence of the organization is justified only to the extent to which its goals articulate with societal values and norms.

This approach, however, has been criticized for failing to recognize that organizations may pay only lip service to societal needs, and that in reality they pursue aims and objectives that serve the interests of certain individuals or groups at the expense of others. Certainly, there is an ample body of research on mental hospitals to demonstrate that many hospitals hardly meet the four social responsibilities and yet they continue to survive. Moreover, when organizational goals are defined from such a perspective, they are likely to be so abstract as to become simple truisms that no one is likely to dispute, and they thus reveal very little about the organization. No one will argue, for example, with the goal of juvenile courts to serve "the best interests of the child," yet much of the current controversy over the functioning of juvenile courts has to do with their methods of handling juvenile offenders. Therefore, a distinction must be made between the "official" and the "operative" goals of an organization. As Perrow defines them (1961: 856), "official goals are the general purposes of the organization as put forth in the charter, annual reports, public statements by key officials and other authoritative pronouncements .... Operative goals des· ignate the ends sought through the actual operating policies of the organization: They tell us what the organization actually is trying to do, regardless of what the official goals say are the aims."

The distinction between the two types of goals, and their implications to the actual services of an organization, are best illustrated in the following study of the daily activities of the Community Action Centers established through the Economic Opportunity Act of 1964 (Hasenfeld, 1971). The official goals of the CAC were:

1. To link low-income people to critical resources, such as education, manpower training, counselling, housing, and health.
2. To increase the accessibility of available critical services often beyond the reach of the poor or blocked off by erroneous definitions of their real needs.
3. To create competent communities by developing in and among the poor the capacity for leadership, problem solving, and participation in the decision-making bodies that affect their lives.
4. To restructure community service institutions to assure flexibility, responsiveness, and respect toward the problems faced by the poor.

To study the actual operationalization of these goals I employed several research strategies, which included: (1) participant observation of the centers for approximately one year; (2) analysis of data from a random sample of client case files; (3) systematic observations of a sample of client-staff transactions; (4) formal interviewing with all the staff in the centers. The findings indicated that in reality the centers functioned in a fashion similar to that of a welfare department. Low-income clients were actually linked to very few new resources, usually only medical services and the state employment security commission; their access to critical services did not improve significantly; staff-client relations were characterized by a high degree of bureaucratization and inflexibility; and the emerging indigenous leadership in the community was coopted by the existing political system. In fact, one could have concluded that the operative goals of the CAC were to provide jobs to the poverty workers themselves rather than to their clients.

What this and other such studies indicate is that official goals mostly serve as an organizational mechanism to elicit legitimation and support from a broad range of social groups. These goals are, therefore, stated in abstract and vague terms that appeal to widely shared values and norms. In human service organizations they also serve a specific purpose essential to organizational survival: to provide post facto justification and rationale for organizational activities that might be challenged or questioned. As already noted, every action taken by a human service organization in relation to its clients involves value choices and moral decisions about which there may be no consensus. A decision to admit a child to a correctional program, to deny a welfare recipient certain benefits, to reward certain students in school are all examples of moral decisions that occur daily in human service organizations. They need to be readily justified when or if challenged. References and appeals to official goals are devices to provide such justifications, since the vagueness, generality, and truisms of these goals enable the interpretation of events and actions to conform with their occurrence. In short, official goals serve as a buffer between the organization and its environment. Yet, as I shall note later, official goals can also be used against an organization if it can be demonstrated that it has not fulfilled its public promises.

Operative goals reflect the organization's actual commitment of resources. That is, allocation decisions of available resources indicate what members of the organization intend, in fact, to accomplish. Thus, in the case of a mental hospital, if most of the money, personnel, and time are committed to the hiring of attendants, the physical care of patients, and the prescription of drugs, and minimal amounts go for psychotherapy by professional staff, it is not difficult to deduce the operative goals of the hospital—i.e., custody and control of patients. A close look at operative goals and the processes by which they are defined enables us, then, to identify the preferences and choices made by those who control the organizational resources. Moreover, the operative goals can predict the type of human service technologies that the organization is likely to adopt to achieve its goals.

Nevertheless, the study of official goals should not be discarded even though they may predict little about actual organizational behavior. The *relationship* between official and operative goals in human service organizations is of major importance, if not to the organizational theorist, then to the social policy analyst and certainly to the human service practitioner. This is so for several reasons. First, the official goals of human service organizations are frequently determined by complex legislative processes that, in turn, have important consequences for the future characteristics of the organization. That is, many human service organizations represent the programmatic manifestation of social welfare legislation and policies. The directives aimed at implementing these policies become their official goals. Therefore, the gaps and incongruities between official and operative goals allow for a critical assessment of the effectiveness of the policy or legislation. The Community Mental Health Centers Act is a case in point. To qualify for federal funds, each center had to provide five essential services: inpatient services, outpatient services, partial hospitalization services, emergency services, and consultation and educational services. In addition, each center had to provide a reasonable volume of services to the indigent, assure continuity of care for each patient, effect maximum coordination with other public and private agencies, and develop adequate community involvement (Chu and Trotter, 1974). Studies of community mental health centers (e.g., Connery, 1968; Chu and Trotter, 1974) indicate that many of these goals were not operationalized for a variety of reasons, including the domination of the psychiatric profession, the attachment of the centers to existing psychiatric facilities, and discrimination against the poor. What is important to note is that these failures resulted either from environmental and organizational forces not anticipated by the policy makers or from the purposefully designed vagueness of the official goals themselves. The study of such discrepancies provides an important tool for the evaluation of social programs.

Second, official goals often indicate the value choices and normative commitments made by the organization. These, in turn, shape its approach to human needs or problems. Such goals are likely to be based on some normative theory of human and social behavior and its definitions of morality and deviance. For example, it is impossible to understand the goals of AFDC and the controversies connected with it without recognizing that they are based on what Handler terms a "pathological theory of poverty." As he points out (1972: 138):

> The pathological theory of poverty is "played out" in different ways in welfare policies. Work tests, of course, have been ubiquitous in the history of welfare. One can hardly overstate the ability to earn one's way as a measure of non-deviant behavior. Other manifestations of this viewpoint include: the various rules and practices that govern support obligations; criminal and civil sanctions for desertion and abandonment; responsible relative laws; man-in-the-house rules; budgetary controls; fit and proper home requirements; and required social services.

In a similar fashion, most of the manpower training programs aimed at the poor have been based on the assumption that poverty and unemployment are a consequence of "marginal productivity" or "social and personal disabilities." The inability of the poor to earn decent wages is attributed to lack of education and training, poor work motivation, or physical and psychological disabilities. Against this ideology is the view that unemployment and poverty are caused by structural factors inherent in the labor market itself, such as the existence of a "dual labor market," discrimination in hiring, and the entrapment of the poor in marginal industries (Hasenfeld, 1975). Nevertheless, the goals of the manpower training programs are mostly guided by the social-and-personal-disabilities ideology.

Thus, one cannot fully apprehend the forces that determine actual delivery patterns of social services without seeing how they are shaped by official goals, which reflect an adherence to a moral theory about the individual and society, a theory based on values and norms not necessarily shared by all.

Finally, for the social reformer, official goals may serve as a way of calling the organization to task for not measuring up to them. It is exactly because these goals enjoy broad support that social reformers can challenge an organization's legitimacy by pointing to its failures to implement them. This enables the mobilization of constituencies who are aggrieved by an organization's failure to meet its commitments. The rise of various client advocacy groups may be explained from this perspective.

DEFINING ORGANIZATIONAL GOALS

Distinguishing between official and operative goals helps reduce one source of ambiguity, but it does not resolve many other difficulties in defining and identifying organizational goals. These conceptual and empirical problems, general to all organizations, are particularly acute for human service organizations, and emanate from their special characteristics.

Difficulties in Defining Goals

From individual to organizational goals. Probably the most serious difficulty with the concept of organizational goals arises from having to ascribe to organizations attributes that are typically reserved for individuals; in so doing we imply that organizations have a "personality" or "character." But an organization is essentially a collectivity of individuals and while we might be able to identify the personal goals of each, how can we aggregate them intelligibly into organizational goals, particularly if the personal goals are highly diverse or even conflicting? In short, we need to identify the processes by which such multiple and different interests become translated into a set of collective goals. Agreements about goals may be more readily attained among members of a firm producing inanimate objects than among members of most human service organizations.

First, since their mandate calls for a response to human needs or problems, agreements about goals among the members of such organizations involve choices from among competing moral theories and belief systems. Each member of the organization has a belief system and a preferred set of normative commitments that are then perceived as desirable guides for organizational action. Such belief systems or personal ideologies emanate from the social affiliations, cultural background, and the personal and professional socialization of each member. For example, in a psychiatric hospital each physician may have a preferred set of goals for the hospital based on professional training and socialization. Those who view mental illness from a somatic perspective expect the hospital to return patients to the outside world as quickly as possible without trying to change their personalities. In contrast, those who adopt a psychoanalytic perspective of mental illness expect the hospital to provide for intensive exploration and change of the patients' personalities. Nurses and attendants also bring their own moral assessment of mental illness. Some expect the hospital to protect the larger society from the disruptive behavior of patients. Others may ascribe to the mentally ill a status of moral inferiority that calls for minimal interaction and maximum isolation (Strauss et al., 1964). Similar differences in values and expectations can be found among teachers in public schools, social workers at family service agencies, and workers in welfare departments. Thus, human service organizations encounter serious problems when they have to synthesize such competing personal belief systems and goals.

Second, human service organizations also have to respond to and cope with the personal goals of the clients they serve. The diversity of clients' personal goals will also reflect differences in personal experiences, socioeconomic status, cultural and ethnic background, and affiliation. And yet, as clients interact with the organization, they attempt to influence its staff to accept and respond to their personal goals. It is extremely difficult, if not impossible, for an organization to find a common denominator for clients' personal goals, and it must, therefore, develop mechanisms to reduce such disparities. For example, an organization may select clients who have similar personal goals, ascribe the same goals to all clients, or ignore their personal goals altogether.

Multiplicity of goals. Human service organizations must also respond to multiple goals assigned or ascribed to them by various publics and constituencies. We have already noted how legislative processes may define a series of goals that compete for resources. An organization may face different publics composed of other human service organizations, interest groups, legislative bodies, and professional associations, all having some stake in the organization and its services. An organization, in turn, may be dependent on these publics for resources, legitimation, and social support, and must, therefore, take their interests into account—interests that may be incompatible or in conflict with each other. In the juvenile court, for example, child advocacy groups may pressure the court to adopt social rehabilitation goals, law enforcement agencies may push for "law and order" goals, and the legal profession may demand adherence to due process and fair-justice goals.

Moreover, as Scott (1977) points out, the goals adopted by members of an organization to motivate and guide their activities may be quite different from the goals used by external units to evaluate the organization's performance. While the staff in a vocational rehabilitation agency may be motivated by the goal of personal and social rehabilitation for their clients, the agency may be evaluated by its success in placing clients in jobs.

It is thus apparent that in response to these conflicting demands from within and without, the organization will adopt multiple and often conflicting goals. These pose serious administrative problems in setting priorities, achieving some internal integration, and settling competing claims for resources.

Specificity and stability of goals.   An inherent problem in defining goals is to distinguish between ends and means. As Simon (1964) points out, what may be seen as an end at one level of the organization may be seen as a means at another level. And yet, if a distinction is not maintained, serious misjudgments and misplaced internal emphases can result. When a subunit in the organization functions as if its activities were an end in themselves, rather than a means to a more comprehensive organizational goal, it may in fact subvert the latter.

This problem is closely related to the issue of *goal specification.* An almost infinite number of specifications can be derived from a general and broad goal. This problem is intensified in human service organizations exactly because their mandates are defined in broad terms and because their products are intangible. Much of the controversy that often surrounds them results from disputes over what their specific goals should be. As I will note later, the lack of a determinate service technology further contributes to the ambiguity. Therefore, much of the diversity seen among human service organizations pursuing the same general goals may be attributed in part to the disparate ways each attempts to define more specific goals.

In addition, there is also the issue of *goal stability* in time and substance. Distinctions are often made between short-range and long-range goals. In reality, however, an organization that achieves its short-range goals may not be any closer to achieving its long-range goals than one that performs more poorly in the short range. In the same vein, the values to which the organization commits its resources may become obsolete or undesirable as the values of social groups in the environment change. Human service organizations are particularly sensitive to such value changes and, therefore, cannot assume that goal commitments to a particular set of values will remain stable. Consider, for example, the effects on adoption agencies of changing attitudes toward single-parent families. Similarly, changing attitudes toward developmentally disabled children have forced school systems to pay more attention to their educational needs and to integrate them into the schools. In fact, much of the indeterminancy of organizational goals can be attributed to the continual processes of changes in values and norms about human problems and needs. These, in turn, create pressures and tensions for the organizations who find it difficult to shift already committed resources to accommodate such changes.

One can, therefore, summarize the foregoing discussion by concluding that organizational goals are multidimensional, difficult to specify, unstable, and often indeterminate (Hannan and Freeman, 1977b).

Alternative Solutions

Several organizational theorists (Yuchtman and Seashore, 1967; White, 1974; Georgiou, 1973) have argued that the concept of organizational goals should be abandoned altogether. White (1974), in the most eloquent statement of this position, offers the following image of an organization: Individuals with differential control over resources join together in a collectivity for the purpose of sharing these resources to further or fulfill their own personal goals. An organization then is nothing more than a "formally constituted collectivity which utilizes resources." What emerges in an organization are not goals, but rather agreements on the allocation and utilization of resources that each individual commits to the collectivity. As White puts it, "A statement of organizational goals, therefore, is nothing more than an agreement on the range of allocations that will be tolerated by members participating in its formulation" (1974: 369).

While White's formulation makes an important contribution to our understanding of the processes by which decisions about resource allocations are made in an organization, his conclusions about organizational goals are debatable on several grounds, particularly as they apply to human service organizations. First, as noted earlier, human service organizations may be mandated to pursue certain goals by other organizations (i.e., their representatives) and not by individuals. Legislative bodies or federal and state executive agencies may, in fact, define the critical goals of an organization. Thus, one must recognize that organizations as well as individuals have interests they may wish to ascribe to any organization over which they have influence. Second, in human service organizations agreements on resource-allocation decisions involve commitments to values and norms concerning the organization's response to human needs and problems. These, in turn, serve as guides for organizational actions that transcend the agreements themselves because they provide meaning and moral justification to organizational activities. Thus, an agreement to allocate resources to develop a milieu therapy program in a psychiatric hospital also involves certain normative commitments to the patients and staff as well as to a certain ideology about mental illness and the mentally ill. These provide major guidance and direction to the behavior of members of an organization far beyond the mere agreement on resource allocation. Moreover, these commitments generate a momentum of their own by competing with other values and commitments in the organization and by recruiting supporters for the cause. Third, agreements about resource allocations in an organization are expressed in certain service delivery patterns. These are viewed as the organizational goals by various external constituencies such as clients, other organizations, and other interest groups. That is, judged by its activities, these external constituencies assume the existence of certain organizational goals which they then expect the organization to fulfill. The organization has to respond to such expectations since it is going to be evaluated on the basis of its adherence to these goals. Hence, when through a resource-allocation agreement, the hospital develops a family care program for low-income families, key constituencies in the community, such as the families themselves, community action groups, or state and federal agencies providing funds for the program, see it as one of the goals of the hospital, and they are likely to evaluate the hospital, in part, on how well it maintains its commitment to such a program. In this context, White's model also fails to consider the question of organizational effectiveness, and its measurement in relation to a set of standards, either internal or external, which can also be construed as goals.

I concur with the position taken by Mohr (1973) and his conceptualization of organizational goals, since it is particularly adaptable to human service organizations. Mohr distinguishes between two types of goals: transitive and reflexive. The *transitive goal* refers to the primary projected impact of the organizational outputs upon the environment. The projected impact can be deduced from the programs set out by the organization. Each program is designed to produce a product or a service and transfer it to the environment, thus generating some desired impact upon it. For example, a school may develop a vocational education program, an athletic program, a program for the physically disabled—all of which are intended to produce some impact on the environment, such as meeting the needs of industry for skilled workers, promoting recreation and sports in the community, and meeting the educational needs of a specific group of children. It should not, therefore, be difficult to determine the transitive goals associated with a program as long as we recognize the following: (1) the transitive goal refers either to changing or maintaining some condition in the environment and not simply to a set of activities (i.e., reference to their intended consequence); (2) the intended impact includes only results that are connected to the service or to organizational activities in a reasonable cause-and-effect relationship. Thus, having a vocational education program does not define a goal of inculcating children with a work ethic or preventing immoral behavior. The intended impact must be concrete and directly related to the program outputs. (This, in part, resolves the ends-means issue.)

This definition of transitive goals acknowledges that the organization may have multiple goals as reflected in its various programs; and the relative emphasis given to each goal could probably be measured by the amount of resources committed to each program. Such a definition does not assume any kind of consensus about the intended impact of each program.

Mohr further proposes that every organization also has a general *reflexive goal*—namely, "that inducements will be sufficient to evoke adequate contributions from all members of the organizational coalition" (1973: 476). That is, each organization must establish targets and procedures for the internal allocation of resources in order to induce members to make the necessary contributions to carry out the organizational activities. The reflexive goal, then, is akin to White's definition of organizational goals in that it focuses on setting up a working agreement among members of the organization so that each will be motivated to contribute to the collectivity in return for the fulfillment of personal goals. Inducements may be related to salaries and wages, working conditions, status, power, and privileges. For example, the willingness of professional social workers to work for a given agency may be predicated upon the willingness of the agency to give them the freedom to work independently, the opportunity to supervise others, and the opportunity to advance their professional training.

Mohr concludes that, from a social policy perspective, the transitive goals are of greater importance in the assessment of the organization. Yet, for the organization itself, both types of goals may be coequal since they constrain each other. Nevertheless, for human service organizations, when reflexive goals command greater amounts of resources than transitive goals, the phenomenon of *goal displacement* arises. We shall return to this issue later.

The major contribution of Mohr's formulation lies in its resolution of some of the conceptual problems we have already discussed. The reflexive goal addresses the translation of personal goals of organization members into a system of inducements and contributions that ensures the survival of the organization. The concept of the transitive goal indicates that organizations are designed to pursue more than personal goals: Their activities and programs are supposed to have an impact on the environment. Yet, the formulation fully acknowledges the organization's multiple and even conflicting goals. Finally, the model suggests that transitive goals can be specific enough to identify the cause-effect relations between programs and intended impact, and yet general enough to transcend the activities and programs themselves.

DETERMINING ORGANIZATIONAL GOALS

The process by which organizational goals are shaped and determined can best be described from a political economy perspective, which focuses on the interplay of power, the goals of the power wielders, and the interactions between the demand and supply of organizational services (see Chapter 2). It will be recalled that the polity refers to "the whole web of groups and individuals, internal or external to the organization, that possess resources to sanction decisions" (Zald, 1970a: 229). The term economy focuses on "the internal allocation of men, money, and facilities and on the external supply of resources and clients" (p. 224). Both sets of variables are the key determinants of organizational goals since the latter reflect decisions about the allocation of critical resources with reference both to those who control such resources and to the demand for organizational services. Such a perspective, therefore, suggests that the processes of establishing organizational goals are complex; that they involve a number of different groups and individuals; that they embody negotiations among these actors; that they attempt to satisfy multiple interests; and that they change as political and economic configurations within and without the organization alter.

As suggested earlier, organizational goals, both transitive and reflexive, mean a set of commitments to the allocation and utilization of resources for various functions and activities. The transitive goals reflect commitments of resources to certain programs, while the reflexive goals reflect resource commitments to the personal needs and interests of members of the organization. These resources, which include authority, money, manpower, expertise, clients, and facilities, are controlled by various organizations, associations, and individuals who represent one or more constituencies. By *constituency*, I mean a social group whose members share a common set of interests, norms, or values by virtue of their similar location, position, or status in the social system. The constituency may be very loosely organized and express its interests only through periodic voting on social issues; or it may be highly organized into social, political or professional associations. Each constituency has its representatives use the resources it controls to maintain or advance the constituency's interests, position, and status. I will call a constituency and its representatives an "interest group." Each interest group, thus, formulates a set of transitive and reflexive goals *for* the organization that reflects its interests, norms and values. What brings interest groups together is the common realization that the organization either may offer an opportunity to advance their interests or may become a threat. Each group further recognizes that it alone cannot achieve its goals through the organization. Yet all would gain more strength from the organization by pooling their resources and thus optimizing their own goals. That is, each interest group, through its analysis of the supply and demand for the services of the organization, calculates that it may be worthwhile to invest its resources in the organization in the hope of obtaining a desirable return on its investment—i.e., buttressing its constituency's interests.

Following the paradigm proposed by Cyert and March (1963), the determination of organizational goals results from the processes of negotiations among these interest groups. Typically, these negotiations are marked by the emergence of various coalitions whose members can agree on a common set of goals for the organization, and thus can pool their resources to influence the organizational decision making in their direction. The relative power of each coalition is determined by the total amount of resources needed by the organization that it can control and mobilize. The most powerful among them will be the *dominant coalition*. The negotiations and compromises among the members of the dominant coalition will determine the nature of the organizational goals as agreements emerge about the allocation and distribution of the resources controlled by its members. Thus, the transitive and reflexive goals of the organization reflect the collective intents of the dominant coalition.

Such political and economic processes inevitably give rise to multiple and often conflicting goals, generate ambiguous operational definitions of these goals, and are only as stable as the dominant coalition. Perrow (1961), for example, in his study of the goals of a voluntary general hospital, describes how shifts in the dominant coalition altered its operative goals. At the founding stage, the hospital was highly dependent on financial contributions from the board of trustees. In turn, the trustees controlled all appointments in the hospital and the allocation of resources. The medical services developed by the hospital reflected the interests and values of the social groups from which the trustees were drawn. Yet, as the needs of the hospital shifted away from fiscal resources to medical technology, physicians emerged as a powerful interest group and gradually became the dominant coalition in the hospital. The operative goals were therefore defined in strictly medical terms, and most of the critical activities in the hospital were aimed at strengthening the interests of the medical group. With the increased complexity of the hospital, the increased dependence on medical insurance systems, competition from other hospitals, and pressures from various community agencies, hospital needs shifted again to include administrative and managerial skills not available to the medical group. As a result, the dominant coalition absorbed the hospital administrators, and new goals were added that reflected the interests of the administrators.

Ohlin, Miller, and Coates (1977) provide an excellent example of the goal determination process as formulated here. They traced the changes in the transitive goals of the Massachusetts Department of Youth Services (DYS) from institutional, punitive, and custodial care to deinstitutionalized, community-based rehabilitation of juvenile offenders. The reform of DYS was initiated after a series of studies and newspaper exposés about the mistreatment of children in institutions, a decline in the legitimation of the department, the election of a governor committed to reform of the department, and the appointment of a reform-minded commissioner. The interest groups that supported the new goals included a number of child advocacy groups, several liberal legislators, and the commissioner and some of his staff. They formed a loosely coordinated coalition to promote reforms through the resources they controlled, which were primarily legitimation, authority, and political influence. The interest groups that opposed the reforms included many DYS staff who benefited from the old correctional system, some legislators whose constituencies pushed for a law-and-order posture, and some juvenile court judges who firmly believed in protecting society from juvenile offenders. They formed an antireform coalition that controlled some critical resources, mainly the existing correctional programs in the institutions, plus some political influence. In addition, other interest groups controlled most of the budget of DYS and much of its formal authority. These included the relevant legislative appropriation committee, the governor's office, and the governor's Committee on Law Enforcement and Administration of Justice. Their interests were primarily reflexive—i.e., the support of those groups that would strengthen their own political power. They were likely to support a coalition that could promise favorable public opinion and increased political strength.

The proreform coalition was able to initiate the reform by closing down the state institutions through the authority vested in the commissioner and the tacit support of the governor's office, which perceived a gain in favorable public opinion from its support of reform (although not at any political costs). The move toward deinstitutionalization was also supported by critical fiscal resources mobilized by the proreform coalition from the federal Law Enforcement Assistance Administration and the governor's Committee on Law Enforcement and Administration of Justice. The closing of the institutions robbed the antireform coalition of one of its primary resources, the correctional institutions, and, at least temporarily, weakened its position. The proreform coalition clearly emerged as the dominant group. The reform itself, which involved the development of community-based treatment programs, the decentralization of the department, and the establishment of regions, required considerably more resources and administrative skills than the coalition was able to mobilize. As a result, numerous problems emerged that tarnished the image of the proreform coalition, particularly that of the commissioner and his staff, and weakened its support from the governor's office and key legislators. The antireform coalition capitalized on this and initiated a series of investigations and had the department audited, which ultimately led to the resignation of the commissioner. While the proreform goals were not abandoned, they were subjected to several constraints by the governor's office and the legislature, which began to assume a more important position within the dominant coalition. This resulted, for example, in the establishment of small secure state facilities for juvenile offenders considered to be dangerous and in greater fiscal control of the department by the legislature and the governor's office. Although the antireform coalition has remained weak, it still presents a potential threat to reforms, particularly since the proreform coalition lost some of its power in the dominant coalition. Interestingly, while the department continues to stress deinstitutionalization and community-based rehabilitation, it has also become quite concerned with "dangerous" youth and has committed some of its resources to control and custody goals.

This example also highlights the powerless role that clients are likely to play in the determination of organizational goals. In general, clients are not organized and do not possess critical resources to enable them to enter the process of negotiations. This is particularly true when clients are defined as dependent, weak, or deviant, and lack political representation. In such instances, the dominant coalition in human service organizations is unlikely to represent client interests. At best these interests will be defined and represented by a proxy interest alliance such as a child advocacy group, a professional association, or other moral entrepreneurs. Thus, for example, the needs and interests of the mentally ill are defined by such organizations as the American Psychiatric Association and the National Association for Mental Health, while the needs of children have historically been defined by various child-saving movements (Platt, 1969). These organizations, however, are likely to be dominated by various professionals and ideologies committed to the enhancement of professional interests and the preservation of dominant social values and morality. Hence, their definitions of client needs may be considerably at variance with those that clients might have expressed if they were organized. It is in this context that one can appreciate the rise of client organizations of the disabled, ex-offenders, welfare recipients, and the aged in order to provide direct input into the goal determination process of human service organizations.

The clients' ability to influence organizational goals increases significantly when they control important resources needed by the organization. Zald's study of the YMCA (1970b) clearly demonstrates how the dependence of the organization on membership fees and contributions has shaped the nature of the programs offered by the YMCA to reflect the members' wishes. A similar example is reported by Clark (1956) in his study of the adult education program. The advocates of a voucher system in education are suggesting that the increased dependence of public schools on resources directly controlled by parents will make them more responsive to the educational needs and wishes of the voucher holders. These and other similar proposals are attempts to increase the power of the clients against organizations and thus to strengthen their ability to shape organizational goals.

EFFECTS OF GOALS ON
SERVICE DELIVERY

The previous discussion has already hinted at some of the consequences that the goal determination process and its outcome have on service delivery patterns in human service organizations. It is important to identify these more clearly if we are to understand the forces shaping service delivery.

Services and Programs as
Expressions of Goals

We must reiterate that the goal commitments of an organization serve as guides for the formulation of programs and services. Decisions about allocation and utilization of resources for transitive and reflexive goals set major constraints on the definition and structure of activities in each unit of the organization. Specifically, the goals define the range of human problems and needs legitimately within the domain of an organization and the strategies to be used in responding to them. Each unit in an organization is thus constrained in the use of its resources by these definitions. For example, a family service agency is unlikely to develop a client outreach program if client problems are defined as intrapsychic, and the strategies to respond to them are primarily psychoanalytic (Cloward and Epstein, 1965). Similarly, the same agency will not hire indigenous workers for counselling positions when its reflexive goals are to protect the dominance of the professional social workers. A nursing home for the aged will commit minimal resources for social rehabilitation services if its primary transitive goals are custodial, and commit even less if its reflexive goals are to make profit. In contrast, a health care organization committed to serve low-income clients normally not reached by the health care system is likely to develop several different programs to reach out to clients (Berkanovic and Reeder, 1974).

Goals as Measures of Organizational
Accountability

As indicated earlier, once an organization makes a commitment to a set of goals, it is held accountable to them by those organizations and interest groups that monitor it and provide legitimation. The goals become criteria by which an organization is evaluated, and thus they pose additional constraints on the ability of different units in the organization to shape service delivery patterns. In general, each unit will have to structure its service delivery patterns in order to score well on the evaluative criteria used by the monitoring and legitimating groups. Blau (1955), in a classical study of a public employment placement agency, noted how the goal of successfully placing applicants in jobs became the major evaluative criterion of the effectiveness of the agency, and therefore resulted in highly discriminatory service delivery patterns inside the agency. Staff who wanted to score well on this criterion tended to reject applicants from minority and disadvantaged groups because they might not be successful on a job.

Similarly, Polk and Schafer (1972) argue that promoting academic excellence has become one of the major criteria by which the effectiveness of high schools is measured. Schools that produce a high proportion of college-bound graduates are defined as more effective than those that do not and are endowed with prestige and reputation. The emphasis on academic success generates within the school a tracking system whereby those deemed unable to meet this organizational goal are routed into a "non-college" track. The effects of such tracking on those locked into it are further deterioration of their educational achievement, reduced educational opportunities, limited access to educational resources, and higher dropout rates even when controlling for IQ differences.

Organizational Goals
as the Ideology
of the Dominant Coalition

A central aspect of organizational goals in human service organizations is that they encompass a moral theory about human needs and problems. I denote that aspect of the organizational goals "ideology": a belief system about the causes of human needs and problems, the desired moral values to be upheld and achieved when responding to these needs and problems, and the acceptable modes of response. It is clear that organizational goals will reflect the ideologies of the dominant coalition, and patterns of service delivery will conform to these ideologies. This is eloquently illustrated by a case study of hospital wards by Coser (1963). The hospital, for long-term chronically ill patients, contained regular wards as well as a rehabilitation center. According to Coser, the patients' physical capacities considerably overlapped. Yet, the dominant ideologies in the center and the wards were radically different and resulted in contrasting treatment of patients. In the wards, the ideology was essentially custodial: Physicians and nurses believed that the patients were incapable of improving and had low social worth. In the rehabilitation center, the prevailing belief system was that patients were capable of improving, and that they had high social worth. The nurses on the ward emphasized orderly housekeeping and routinized records. Interaction with patients was minimal and mostly dealt with physical management. Nurses discharged their roles in a highly bureaucratic fashion. In contrast, in the rehabilitation center, there was a great deal of social interaction between staff and patients, and emphasis was put on keeping patients active and involved. Not surprising, staff-patient ratio was low on the wards and high in the rehabilitation center.

In a comparative study of six juvenile correctional institutions, Street, Vinter, and Perrow (1966) also point to the contrasting effects of different ideologies on the programs and staff-inmate relations in each institution. They identify three predominant ideologies: obedience/conformity, reeducation/development, and treatment. In the obedience/conformity institutions, the predominant assumption was that "the orientations of the inmates could not be altered basically but inmates could be conditioned to behave properly" (p.63). The programs in such institutions were therefore custodial and punitive, emphasizing control, regimentation, and the coercive use of authority. In the reeducation/development institutions, it was assumed that inmates had the potential to develop and acquire useful skills, and that appropriate training and education was the remedy to delinquent behavior. Consequently, the major programmatic emphasis in such institutions was on schooling and vocational training. Inmates were required to spend considerable time in classrooms and vocational workshops. In the treatment institutions, it was assumed that "deviance could be corrected only by a thoroughgoing reorientation or reconstitution of the inmate; otherwise, his unconscious identifications and other intrapersonal forces would probably lead toward continued delinquent behavior" (p. 64). Much of the program, then, concentrated on the development of therapeutic relations between staff and inmates either through one-to-one consultations or group sessions.

Organizational Goals and Service Incongruencies

The negotiations and compromises reached within the dominant coalition generate multiple goals for an organization that must satisfy different constituencies. These goals may not be complementary, and each may be associated with a set of activities incompatible with others in the organization. Through its division of labor, the organization may attempt to reduce the conflict among these goals by segregating them into different units and roles. However, the organization cannot segregate their impact on the clients. Thus, clients in human service organizations are likely to experience incongruencies and disjunctures in the service patterns that reflect the organization's multiple goals. As they interact with different staff members, clients may well experience conflicting expectations about appropriate behavior and action, and discontinuities in the services given to them—the actions of one staff member will not necessarily resemble the actions of others. Duff and Hollingshead (1968) demonstrate the consequences of multiple goals on patient care in a hospital that pursued three goals: treatment, teaching, and research. Patient care, particularly for those who could not afford sponsorship by a private physician, was characterized by confusion and inconsistency. Patients found the attention they received varied according to the teaching and research interests of the house staff, residents, and interns. Definitions of illness and level of care were subject to change as these interests changed. Continuity of care was hampered because of the rotation of residents and interns, and occasionally patients were subjected to diagnostic and treatment procedures not fully justified or necessary. Patients were often viewed as "clinical material" and as tools of research and learning, rather than as human beings in need of care.

As another example, the multiplicity of goals in a welfare department may subject clients to conflicting and inconsistent responses from staff. On the one hand, the goal of income maintenance subjects clients to highly bureaucratic procedures as their eligibility to public assistance is determined and monitored. On the other hand, the goal of rehabilitation through social services subjects the clients to a casework ideology, to counselling, and to the exploration of personal problems and needs. Clients, therefore, must learn to display different behavioral responses depending on the particular goal that is being emphasized during their encounter with welfare officials.

Organizational goals are often marked by vagueness, ambivalence, and indeterminacy because of the multiple interests the organization is attempting to satisfy. The lack of goal specification, therefore, enables the organization to justify conflicting courses of action and to accommodate the multiple demands made on its resources. While such a strategy helps organizational survival, it subjects clients to incongruous and unintegrated modes of service delivery. As different units in the organization develop their own goal definitions, clients may experience radically different responses to their needs as they move from unit to unit. For example, patients in a psychiatric hospital may be encouraged by ward attendants to remain docile and passive; in group sessions conducted by social workers they may be expected to express feelings and ventilate hostility and aggression; and their predominant psychiatric treatment, as determined by physicians, may be based on medication. Yet, all these activities are justified in the name of the vague goal of treatment and rehabilitation. In their own professional training, social workers may experience the same conflicting expectations because of the vagueness and indeterminacy of the goals of schools of social work. One segment of a training program may emphasize research and analytic skills, while another may emphasize the development of effective interpersonal skills. Some segments of the curriculum will advocate the dominance of a macrolevel perspective on social work practice; others will dismiss that in favor of a microlevel perspective. Students thus experience the pulls and pushes of conflicting goals and ideologies, together with vague educational goals. One can hypothesize that the greater the vagueness and indeterminacy of the organizational goals, the greater the number of multiple organizational expectations from clients, and the greater the clients' sense of frustration.

TRANSFORMATION OF ORGANIZATIONAL GOALS

Changes in organizational goals may emanate from several sources. First, changes in the membership of the dominant coalition or in the relative power of its members may bring about renegotiations of the organization's goals. Similarly, new interest groups may arise that control resources needed by the organization, and who press for alterations in the goals. Second, the needs of the organization may change over time, requiring the input of different resources. This necessitates interaction with new groups who have access to these resources and accommodation to their interests and demands. Third, changes in the availability of resources to the organization may necessitate reexamination of current decisions about resource allocation and utilization, and this can lead to changes in goals. The process may be a result of either shrinkage of resources in the environment or expansion of potential resource opportunities. Finally, environmental changes may alter the importance of an organization's transitive goals.

Throughout the history of human services, one can find numerous examples of organizations whose goals become obsolete and irrelevant in the face of changing environmental conditions, be they demographic, sociocultural, economic, political, or technological. Many of the charity organizations that flourished at the turn of the century disappeared with the rise of the New Deal, when federally funded social services replaced private charity as the modal institution for assisting the poor. Similarly one can note the decline of such organizations as orphanages and the social service exchange. These organizations failed to survive because they were unable to adapt to the changing environment and assume new, viable goals. Such failure may be attributable to several factors: (1) The organizational leadership was unable to forecast changes and lacked the skills to identify potential arenas for the organization to enter. (2) The goals of the organization were so narrowly defined that they excluded consideration of other possible goals; excessive commitment to narrow and specialized goals resulted in organizational rigidity and dogmatism. (3) The resources of the organization were invested in such a way that they could not be extricated and mobilized for other purposes. (4) The dominant coalition that provided the critical resources to the organization was dissolved, and the organization selected goals that failed to attract new powerful interest groups (see also Chapter 9).

In contrast, organizations that can successfully change their goals and maintain their viability are said to undergo *goal succession* (Sills, 1957). The example most frequently cited is that of the National Foundation for Infantile Paralysis. With the discovery of polio vaccine, the original goals of the foundation were successfully accomplished. Rather than wither away, the organization adopted new goals: the prevention, detection, and combating of birth and genetic defects among infants. Sills attributes the successful change in the organizational goals to the broad legitimation that the foundation enjoyed in the community, and to the control of local chapters by the national headquarters. The latter could introduce the change without significant resistance from within the organization, and it was reinforced by the organization's high degree of legitimation, reflected by the support of key interest groups in the community. The Red Cross went through a similar process of goal succession. Shortly after World War I the organization experienced a decline in membership interest and increased apathy. It desperately needed new goals to justify its existence and thus adopted a new program to preserve and improve public health. The organization experienced a similar crisis after World War II and again successfully added new goals by establishing a national blood donor program. Again, it seems that the Red Cross succeeded because it was able to capitalize on its broadly based legitimation, and because its national leadership had the foresight to predict and identify programs perceived as highly desirable by the community. The YMCA, even though it lacked a strong centralized leadership, underwent goal succession effectively as it shifted from religious proselytizing to character development and socialization. Zald and Denton (1963) attribute the success of the organization's transformation to a variety of factors: (1) its broadly stated goals provided it with flexibility and permitted diverse programs; (2) its dependence on membership fees forced it to adapt to the needs of its clientele; (3) its federated structure increased local autonomy and reinforced its adaptation to membership needs; and (4) its goal of character development also permitted the establishment of a broad range of programs appealing to multiple constituencies.

These and other examples suggest that the ability of human service organizations to undergo goal succession effectively is based on three factors. First, the organization must enjoy broad community support. This can be accomplished either through enlisting the help of various influential groups or appealing to a wide range of clientele. Second, the organization must have broadly defined goals. These will enable it to shift from one program to another without having to undergo a major ideological transformation. Entrenched narrow ideologies are likely to generate conflict within and without an organization as it attempts to move into new areas. Third, the organization must have an internal structure that sets few constraints on its ability to launch new programs. An organization saddled by a complex, unwieldy decision-making system, or by personnel too narrowly trained, or by a heavy investment of resources that cannot be reinvested, is likely to experience considerable difficulties in changing its goals. Similarly, an organization must possess a service technology that can be transformed to meet new service objectives, or it must be able to import new technologies not radically incongruous with the existing ones.

In sum, goal succession means that the organization has successfully accomplished its original transitive goals and has been able to select new transitive goals, primarily on the basis of identifiable community needs and only secondarily on the basis of its self-maintenance needs.

More typically, human service organizations undergo processes of *goal adaptation*, whereby the transitive goals are modified not because they have been successfully accomplished, but rather because changes in environmental exigencies render the attainability of the original goals improbable. Thus, the impetus for changing organizational goals is based on both the need of the organization to respond to changing demands from the environment and its needs for self-preservation.

Bernard, Kurtagh, and Johnson (1968), in their study of the transformation of a social service agency, provide an example of such a process. The agency, the Neighborhood Service Organization, was formed in 1955 through a merger of three traditional settlement houses with the purpose of providing more effective delinquency prevention services to low-income neighborhoods. The services included "therapeutic group services" to maladjusted children in a public school, a detached worker program for delinquent youth, and a community organization service in a public housing project. The agency expanded rapidly and in the mid-1960s tripled its budget and personnel; it was highly recognized for the quality of its services. Nevertheless, the agency came to recognize that the impact of its direct services on the target population was limited at best. Moreover, with the onset of national attention to the problems of poverty and the increased availability of funds for various demonstration projects, the agency decided to change its goals again, both in order to become more effective and to sustain its viability. Its executive leadership decided to move away from direct services and initiate various demonstration projects involving the police, schools, housing authorities, and the public welfare department and their primary clientele. The agency conceived its role as being an advocate for low-income clients, and an assistant to existing agencies, through demonstration projects, for developing more effective programs for their clients. Such projects included setting up social work services for maladjusted students in the schools; getting the housing authority to establish a position of social services coordinator; and helping the police develop a special project to enhance police-youth cooperation.

Often the goal adaptation process begins as a result of the community's changing needs for services. Adoption agencies are a case in point. With the dramatic decline in the number of desirable babies available for adoption—as a result of changing attitudes toward birth control and single-parent families—the agencies faced a crisis. Although they did not contribute to these changes, they recognized that adoption needs changed and that they too must change if they were to survive. Many therefore shifted their programs to focus on "hard-to-adopt" children and on the provision of services to unwed adolescent mothers.

Finally, human service organizations may undergo a process of *goal displacement,* in which the organization abandons its commitment to its transitive goals in favor of its reflexive goals. This situation is most likely to occur when the organization experiences threats to its resourses and can maintain their steady flow by reducing its commitment to its original service objectives. Helfgot (1974) has studied the process of goal displacement in Mobilization for Youth (MFY) as manifested in the program changes undertaken by the agency from the early 1960s to the 1970s. The agency was initiated with a service ideology emphasizing the structural causes of poverty, while rejecting the notion that poverty was a consequence of individual pathology. Thus its goals were to modify the institutional structure of the human services in order to eradicate poverty. Its original programs were aimed at reducing discrimination in hiring, changing the traditional educational technologies of the schools, and forcing public agencies to become more responsive to the needs of the poor. Yet, from the mid-1960s the original goals were gradually displaced, and by the 1970s the agency adopted the very culture-of-poverty ideology it had initially rejected. As a result, its programs emphasized vocational training almost exclusively and it shunned any community action (see Table 4.1).

Much goal displacement can be explained by changes in the larger political and social environment that were expressed by shifts in funding patterns. The original funding sources for the agency, which included the Ford Foundation and the National Institute of Mental Health, accepted the emphasis on institutional change. Yet, in the later phases of the agency's transformation, the funding sources shifted to the Department of Labor and the city's Human Resources Agency, because the latter could offer much greater resource stability. Yet, to achieve such stability, the agency had to abandon its institutional change goals since they were not supported by these funding sources. In short, goal displacement occurred because the agency's need to survive and maintain resource stability took precedence over its original mission.

Scott (1967b), in his study of sheltered workshops for the blind, offers another example of goal displacement. The original goals of the workshops were, first, to train the blind in occupational skills that would enable them to obtain full-time employment in commercial industry and, second, to provide an appropriate workplace for those blind persons too disabled to compete in the labor market. Yet, from their inception, the workshops experienced considerable financial difficulties, particularly since the goods they manufactured were in small demand, and the costs of production were high. The Depression threatened the very existence of the sheltered workshops as demand for their products declined even further, and the deficits could not be covered by charity drives. It was only through extensive lobbying in Congress that a bill was enacted which required federal agencies to buy goods produced by the workshops as long as they met the agencies' specifications. This bill ensured the survival of the workshops, but led to goal displacement. The workshops were transformed and resembled commercial enterprises because the managers had to ensure delivery of the quantity and quality of goods specified by the various federal agencies. Thus, rather than training the blind to assume full-time employment in commercial industry, able and competent blind persons were kept in the sheltered workshops so that production goals could be met efficiently. In fact, as the need for manpower expanded dramatically during World War II and many opportunities to place the blind in commercial industry became available, the workshops did everything possible to retain their best workers.

Interestingly, even after the sheltered workshops managed to become financially secure, there was no return to the original goals. Scott points to

TABLE 4.1. Goal Transformation of Mobilization for Youth

	PHASE I PLANNING 1958–1962	PHASE II MILITANT CA 1962–1965	PHASE III TRANSITIONAL 1966–1968	PHASE IV MANPOWER TRAINING 1969–1972
I. *Organization Ideology*				
a. Primary ideology	Structural interpretation of poverty	Structural interpretation of poverty	Structural to culture of poverty	Culture of poverty (individual defect)
b. Ideology of indigenous involvement	Interpreters, consumers and subjects	Consumers and subjects	From consumers to minority group involvement	Minority group involvement
II. *Program Emphases*				
a. Dominant activities	Inapplicable	Vocational training; service; community action	Training; service; decreasing community action	Vocation training; decreasing service
b. Extent of militant community action	Inapplicable	Great deal	Small amount	None

Source: Adapted from Helfgot (1974: 478).

the particular role that ideologies play in sustaining goal displacement. He notes that the displacement of goals was justified through a shift in ideology toward rehabilitation of the blind. Emphasis was no longer on social integration of the blind, but rather on shielding them from having to confront their handicap when in the company of sighted workers, and protecting them from public stereotypes of blindness. In more general terms, this study demonstrates that in human service organizations ideologies about the service mission of an organization may arise from considerations having little to do with the welfare and well-being of the clients. Yet, the public may accept them as an honest expression of organizational commitment to its clients.

To summarize our discussion of the transformation of organizational goals, Table 4.2 indicates the differences between the three types of goal transformation: goal succession, goal adaptation, and goal displacement. They are distinguished from each other along three dimensions: the relative emphasis on reflexive goals, the past achievement of the original transitive goals, and the organizational basis for the selection of new goals.

TABLE 4.2 Patterns of Goal Transformation

GOAL TRANSFORMATION	EMPHASIS ON REFLEXIVE GOALS	ACHIEVEMENT OF TRANSITIVE GOALS	BASIS FOR SELECTION OF NEW GOALS
Goal succession	Balanced	High	Community needs
Goal adaptation	Balanced	Moderate	Community and organizational needs
Goal displacement	High	Low	Organizational needs

CONCLUSION

Human service organizations are characterized by broad, indeterminate, multiple, and often conflicting goals. Nevertheless, these goals have major consequences on the patterns of service delivery. At the more general level, these goals reflect ideological commitments and belief systems about human welfare, morality, and deviance. Thus, in one respect, human service organizations can be seen as a vehicle aimed at strengthening and enforcing a certain system of morality in society.

The discrepancies between official and operative goals in human service organizations point to the fact that like other bureaucracies, these organizations are beset by problems of survival, pressures to accommodate multiple interests, resource constraints, and lack of viable service technologies—all of which render the official goals into statements of ideals directed mostly at eliciting social support and legitimation. Nonetheless, these discrepancies should not be ignored since they enable the social policy analyst and reformer to identify some of the barriers to organizational effectiveness.

The operative goals of the organization, which are expressed through the actual allocation of resources in the organization, include: (1) transitive goals, which refer to the intended impact of the organization's product on its environment; and (2) reflexive goals, which focus on the self-mainte-nance and survival of the organization. These goals are determined through a negotiation process among interest groups who control key resources needed by organizations. These goals ultimately reflect the negotiations and compromises of the dominant coalition.

As a result, service delivery patterns will reflect the efforts of the organization to achieve these multiple interests, often at the cost of ignoring client interests, generating service incongruities, and limiting service options. These are manifested most dramatically when the organization displaces its goals in order to buttress its survival. Goal succession, in contrast, enables the organization to be sensitive to service needs and is likely to be achieved when the organization displays flexibility, has broad-based legitimation, and effective executive leadership.

5

ORGANIZATIONAL TECHNOLOGY

The technology a human service organization uses to bring about some predetermined change in its clients is a key determinant of its service delivery patterns in general, and its staff-client relations in particular. Put simply, an organization's technology defines its core activities vis-à-vis clients.

No other variable so clearly distinguishes a human service organization (whose "raw materials" are human beings, not inanimate objects) from other bureaucracies as does the nature of its technology. Working on *people* to transform them from a given status to a prescribed new status requires a wide knowledge of human functioning and behavior, knowledge that is inherently complex, incomplete, ever-changing, and often contradictory and inconsistent. Furthermore, such organizations must confront not only a multitude of factors from biological to cultural that affect human behavior, but also the moral implications of intervening in people's lives. This heavy burden has major consequences for both organizations and their clients.

For these reasons, human service organizations are more likely than other bureaucracies to be beset by dilemmas and uncertainties concerning the selection, implementation, and operation of their service technologies. First and foremost, there is frequent discord about the desired end product. For example, should rehabilitation programs for the blind concentrate on restoring their independent functioning or on developing an environment that accommodates a state of dependency (Scott, 1969)? Similarly, diversity of opinion exists about what correctional programs should achieve, ranging from deterrence and development of vocational skills, to personality and attitude change (Lipton, Martinson, and Wilks, 1975).

Second, there is the dilemma of selecting a desirable and effective technology. Witness, for example, the continuing debate about which is the most effective teaching technology: the behavior-control model, the discovery-learning model, or the rational model (Nuthall and Snook, 1973)? A similar controversy has raged over the appropriateness and effectiveness of various psychotherapeutic technologies (Orlinsky and Howard, 1978).

Third, there is the dilemma of matching clients with an appropriate technology in the face of ambiguous and uncertain assessment criteria. Rosenbaum (1976) found that subjective and inconsistent criteria were used to track students into ability groupings in schools. Roth and Eddy (1967) noted much subjectivity in the selection of patients for rehabilitation programs. These and other examples raise the issue of equity in clients' access to human services.

Finally, in contrast to other organizations, the attainment of "quality control" is particularly problematic for human service organizations. Because the technology relies so heavily on the relationships between staff and clients, its success is predicated on the organization's ability to elicit appropriate behavioral responses and interaction patterns from both. Hence, it cannot rely soley on nonpersonal means, such as equipment and tangible goods, to control staff-client relations. It must resort to personal means, such as persuasion, appeals to common values, or behavioral sanctions, to achieve compliance of staff and clients. Consequently, the selection of effective compliance mechanisms for staff and clients is a major concern of human service organizations.

In this chapter I will explore the characteristics of human service technologies that generate these and other dilemmas. I will analyze how human service organizations operationalize their technologies, and discuss the impact of these technologies on the structure of work and on staff-client relations.

A DEFINITION OF HUMAN SERVICE TECHNOLOGY

A *human service technology* can be defined as a set of institutionalized procedures aimed at changing the physical, psychological, social, or cultural attributes of people in order to transform them from a given status to a new prescribed status. The term "institutionalized" denotes that the procedures are legitimated and sanctioned by the organization. Accordingly, social casework, as an example of a human service technology, has been characterized as "an enabling process through which one individual (the caseworker) helps another (client) to take steps toward achieving some personal or social goals by utilizing the resources available to the client" (Taber and Taber, 1978: 137).

Similarly, Bidwell defines educational technology as "a series of inter-actions between someone in the role of teacher and someone in the role of learner with the explicit goal of changing one or more of the learner's cognitive states (what he knows or believes, or his skill in performing cognitive tasks) or affective states (his attitudes, values, or motives)" (1973: 414).

Organizational theorists have tended to limit the definition of technology to only those procedures that are scientifically based or anchored in a demonstrated knowledge of cause-effect relations. Greenwood views technology as a discipline that aims "to achieve controlled changes in natural relationships by means of procedures that are scientifically based" (1960: 2). Perrow delineates five minimal attributes of techhology:

1. Some knowledge of a nonrandom cause-and-effect relationship is required; that is, the techniques lead to the performance of acts which, for known or unknown reasons, cause a change under specified conditions.
2. There is some system of feedback, such that the consequences of the acts can be assessed in an objective manner.
3. It is possible to secure repeated demonstrations of the efficacy of the acts.
4. There is an acceptable, reasonable, and determinate range of tolerance; that is, the proportion of success can be estimated, and even though the proportion might be small, it is judged high enough to continue the activity.
5. Finally, the techniques can be communicated sufficiently that most persons with appropriate preliminary training can be expected to master the techniques and perform them under acceptable limits of tolerance (1965: 915–16).

This delineation is too delimiting since much of the work done in these organizations is not based on a knowledge of cause-effect relations. Nonetheless, it would be misleading to suggest that these organizations lack a technology. Their staffs *do* employ various procedures, mandated and legitimated by the organizations. Human service technologies are not only based on scientific knowledge but also on experiences and belief systems. In contrast to organizations processing inanimate raw material, human service organizations encounter human problems and needs for which responses cannot be delayed or ignored for lack of scientifically based knowledge. The social worker facing a suicidal client, for example, must respond immediately to the client's distress and will resort, therefore, to any set of intervention techniques, approved by the agency, to assist the client, even though such techniques may have little scientific grounding. This point is well articulated by Freidson (1970) in his discussion of medical technology. He suggests that since the focus of medical practice is on the practical solutions of concrete problems, physicians are obligated to carry on even when they lack a scientific foundation for their activities. Medicine is "oriented toward intervention irrespective of the existence of reliable knowledge" (Freidson, 1970: 163).

Most human service technologies encompass several components that correspond to the phases through which clients are processed by the organization.

1. Recruitment and selection.   This phase consists of a set of procedures to recruit and select clients deemed appropriate for the services of the organization. These procedures confer upon those who are brought in contact with an organization a status of "eligibility" or "ineligibility." This component is typically embodied in a hospital's admission office or a social service agency's intake unit. These procedures define the population over which an organization seeks to assume jurisdiction that permits it to intervene in their lives. Hence, they determine the attributes of the "raw material" to be processed by an organization. An organization's and a lay person's definitions of eligibility may conflict, since the former emanate from the organization's choice of technology while the latter result from individual perceptions of needs and problems.

2. Assessment and classification.   This phase consists of a set of procedures to evaluate client attributes, which leads toward classification and labeling. Labeling, in turn, prescribes the nature of the client transformation that the organization will aim for. In the jargon of the helping professions, this process is typically termed "diagnosis." This process directs service providers to focus selectively on particular aspects of the client's biography, recasting and ordering them to fit any of the organizationally determined diagnostic categories (Scheff, 1965). As a result of this labeling, the organization ascribes a distinct meaning to the client's attributes that is likely to differ significantly from the meaning the client and the lay public would give to them. Such a classification process pigeon-holes clients into artificial categories and creates distinctions and demarcations that are much sharper than those existing in everyday life (Freidson, 1965).

3. Status transformation.   This phase consists of a battery of techniques designed to bring about a predetermined change in the physical, psychological, social, or cultural status of the client. These techniques are the "core" technology of the organization in the sense that they are most directly responsible for the service outcomes. As such, they involve purposeful manipulation of clients' attributes or environments. Because the successful application of these techniques necessitates client compliance, mechanisms of control and client monitoring are embedded in the core technology. Such mechanisms may include periodic testing and evaluation of a client's progress, as well as the selective use of incentives and sanctions to reinforce compliance.

4. Termination and certification. This phase consists of a set of procedures that define and control the exit of the client from the organization, and provide public confirmation of the client's altered status. Through these procedures, the organization differentiates among various categories of *processed* clients by assigning exit labels that attest to the new public status the clients have acquired as a result of the organizational intervention in their lives. This new status, be it "graduated with honors," "chronically mentally ill," "certified as a welder," or "ex-offender," will influence the response of other organizations and social units to clients upon their exit (Hasenfeld, 1972). The exit label may not necessarily be acceptable to the client. Braginsky and associates (1969), for example, have shown that patients who enter a mental hospital to escape the stresses of daily living tend to shun therapeutic help, which might determine their readiness to be discharged. Moreover, the exit label, while linked to status transformation efforts, may not accurately reflect the results of such efforts because of its stereotypic nature. A youth certified as a high school graduate may still have failed to acquire basic reading and writing skills.

Each phase of the human service technology necessitates moral judgments and evaluations as decisions about a client's fate are being made. Therefore, clients acquire a "moral career" as they pass through the organization (Goffman, 1961). This is one of the unique attributes of human service technologies—a topic to which I now turn.

ATTRIBUTES OF HUMAN SERVICE TECHNOLOGIES

The elemental fact that it is self-activating, value-laden people who serve as the "raw material" lends human service technologies characteristics that set them apart from the technologies of other organizations. These characteristics, in turn, require human service organizations to accommodate and adapt to people in ways not utilized by other organizations. Working with human beings creates two fundamental and interrelated problems for human service technologies. First, having people as raw material casts a moral overlay on the technology, which is inescapable and must be coped with by the organization. Second, human service technologies must cope with many uncertainties that emanate directly from the variability and complexity of people and our limited knowledge about them. These uncertainties are reinforced by the need to employ modes of work that necessitate close contact between staff and clients. These two issues shape the unique character of human service technologies.

Human Service Technologies
as Moral Systems

People who are processed by human service organizations are not neutral entities. They are vested with moral and cultural values that determine not only their identity, but also define their moral status in the broader social context. They come to the organization with an identity and status that ascribe a social and, therefore, a moral meaning to their personal characteristics. Age, sex, race, physical features, expressions of attitudes and feelings, and behavior are interpreted and assigned a social meaning consonant with a client's social location and identity. Hence, clients' attributes are not perceived and processed simply as "objective" information, but also as statements about their social and moral status. Therefore, the organization's patterns of intervention, via its technology, are shaped by the staff's moral evaluation of the client. Moreover, as clients are processed through the technology, additional social and moral attributes are being generated and incorporated into their identity.

When a social worker, for example, decides that the client needs to acquire better skills in child rearing, the decision invariably generates a *social* meaning that affects not only the valuation of (and response to) the client by the worker and significant others, but also the client's own identity. Similarly, when a schoolteacher grades a student, he or she makes a moral statement. To quote Freidson, "when a physician diagnoses a human's condition as illness, he changes the man's behavior by diagnosis: a social state is added to a biophysical state by assigning the meaning of illness to disease" (1970: 223). Likewise, as clients are processed through the organizational technology, various aspects of their biographies acquire new social meanings that confirm or alter their moral status. It is in this context that human service technologies can be viewed as moral systems.

It would be a mistake to view the moral system intertwined in the technology as accidental or unintentional. Every human service technology encompasses an explicit or implicit model of human nature that is anchored in a set of social and cultural values which provide moral justification for its use. Therefore, the choice of technology also involves the selection of a moral system to be reinforced and maintained. This moral system is manifested through the criteria used by the practitioners of the technology to determine eligibility; to assess and classify the client; to select the transformation procedure; and to assess the results of the intervention. As an example, Sudnow (1967) found in his study of hospital emergency rooms that the attribution by emergency room personnel of higher social worth to the young over the old resulted in dramatic differences in their efforts to resuscitate young and old patients. On the basis of his observations in an urban ghetto school, Rist (1970) concluded that a teacher gave more attention, greater recognition and, in general, expended more effort to teach children who conformed to her own middle-class cultural and moral values, than she did to those who did not; children who failed to meet her standards were defined as morally inferior. These and similar findings are not surprising once we recognize that organizational decisions regarding the processing of clients involve choices about the commitment and allocation of resources to them—i.e., staff attention and time, concern and empathy, expertise, and quantity and quality of services—choices that are ultimately guided by moral considerations that are not only or necessarily the expression of personal values held by the staff, although they too may play an important role in client processing. More significantly, I refer here to the values underlying *organizationally* prescribed policies and practices that guide the behavior of staff members. The extensive use of tracking in high schools through which students are classified, labeled, and routed to academically "desirable" or "undesirable" tracks, with obvious consequences on their careers, is institutionalized through a complex array of organizationally sanctioned policies and practices (Rosenbaum, 1976). Similarly, the patient selection procedures for various rehabilitation programs are anchored and legitimated by an organizational moral system that individual staff members may or may not share, but are likely to abide by (Roth and Eddy, 1967).

Human Service Technologies as Indeterminate Systems

The successful transformation of human attributes requires a technology grounded in scientific knowledge. However, this knowledge is at best incomplete, highly complex, and frequently equivocal. The immense complexity and variability of human attributes and the difficulty in observing and measuring them, coupled with multiple and often invisible connections and contradictions among them, contribute to a state of indeterminate knowledge about human biophysical, psychological, and social functioning. Even when generalizable knowledge about human attributes is obtained, it may still not inform human service practitioners about ways to change them. Undoubtedly, we are witnessing a tremendous and accelerating explosion in scientific knowledge about human functioning, particularly at the biophysical level; and for numerous human problems and needs the knowledge of how to respond to them seems complete. However, even in those well-understood areas, working with people involves a high degree of uncertainty. This is because human attributes cannot be readily compartmentalized and isolated from each other, many are affected by other attributes that interact with them. Consequently, individual responses and reactions to any particular mode of intervention are not consistent, which thus creates some degree of unpredictability. Moreover, since human beings are self-activating, they can significantly influence the outcome of the intervention technology, further adding to the uncertainty and unpredictability of the results. These reasons also contribute to the difficulties in attaining generalizable knowledge and to the often noted contradictions and ambiguities in practice based on principles derived from such knowledge.

The inability to control for extraneous factors and invisible or unknown processes affecting human behavior often makes it exceedingly difficult to attribute the observed consequences to the effects of a given technology. That is, lack of comparability of cases, lack of equivalent criteria of outcome, variations in the administration of the technology, and variations in the nature of human problems and needs make the evaluation of technological outcomes highly problematic (Bergin and Lambert, 1978). Added to this is the well-known phenomenon of "spontaneous remission," where people improve and get better without the technology. In the case of psychotherapy, for example, it has been shown that the average rate of spontaneous remission is 43 percent (Bergin and Lambert, 1978). The inability to demonstrate causal relationships between a particular set of intervention procedures and outcomes is particularly acute when the focus of intervention and the intended results are invisible and difficult to measure—namely, when human service technologies are aimed at changing human behavior.

The lack of demonstrated causal relationships also raises issues concerning the exclusivity of the professed technology. The lack of a clear and unambiguous relationship between a given set of intervention procedures and outcomes gives rise to the proliferation of numerous variations and practices under the guise of the same technology. This is typified most dramatically in the case of psychotherapy. Orlinsky and Howard, who surveyed the field, concluded that there is an "amazing variety of conceptualizations and procedures that define the clinical practice of psychotherapy. They are, to name a few: psychoanalytic and neoanalytic therapies; behaviorist and neobehaviorist therapies; cognitive, emotive, and body therapies; verbal, activity, and play therapies; individual, group, and family therapies; as well as combinations, permutations, eclectic integrations, and idiosyncratic syntheses. Among them all, there is no standard definition of what occurs in, or is distinctive of, therapeutic *process;* no consensus about the intended effects of therapy, or the criteria of therapeutic outcomes" (1978: 284).

The same conclusion can be readily applied to many of the technologies used by social workers, educators, or other human service practitioners.

It is not possible to go into a detailed discussion of the difficulties of measuring the effectiveness of social programs here (see Chapter 8); however, it is important to recognize that because the technology is practiced in an organizational and social *context,* it will have major influence on the outcome of the technology. Since the organizational technology cannot neutralize the influence of the social context, its effects on the outcome may be significantly more powerful than the effects of the technology itself. For example, the effectiveness of an employment training program in placing the unemployed in jobs may be insignificant in comparison to the effects of general economic conditions prevailing in the community. Socio-economic factors may thus lessen the effectiveness of human service technologies (e.g., Fischer, 1976). Lipton, Martinson, and Wilks (1975), for example, in a survey of correctional treatment evaluation studies, concluded that the various treatment technologies demonstrated minimal effectiveness, if any. However, nowhere has there been an attempt to assess the impact of the larger bureaucratic systems in which the treatment programs were anchored. Yet, studies of these larger systems amply demonstrate that they not only affect the actual implementation of the treatment technologies, but also affect the inmates' institutional adjustment, community adjustment, and recidivism rates (see Lerman, 1975; Kassenbaum, Ward, and Wilner, 1971).

Whatever the reasons, it is abundantly clear that the ability of human service organizations to demonstrate the effectiveness of their technologies is at best precarious, and that therefore, they must rely on other persuasive arguments to justify using them. These may include reliance on professional judgment and prestige, on appeals to moral ideals, and on institutional norms.

Human Service Technologies as Practice Ideologies

The indeterminate nature of most human service technologies *and* their underlying moral values produces serious dilemmas in implementation and practice. First, the organization lacks clear guidelines in selecting an appropriate technology, not only because an explicit technology may not exist, but more likely because several competing technologies are supported to various degrees by scientific knowledge. Second, as indicated earlier, each of these technologies also upholds or assumes certain moral values that must be considered by the organization and may even override considerations about the empirical validity of the technology. The organization has to assess the compatibility between the moral system underlying a given technology and the other values it is mandated to sustain and promote. The use of behavioral modification techniques in the classroom may be scientifically valid, but may clash with the values the school wishes to promote (Stolz et al., 1978). Similarly, while the technology to sustain life may be available, its use may conflict with the individual's right to die or to death with dignity (Fox, 1976). Finally, as suggested earlier, human service practitioners are cast in the role of pragmatic problem solvers; they have to respond to the needs and problems of people requiring their services. They must provide solutions even when scientific knowledge is not available or cannot provide clear guidelines for action.

It is in this sense that psychotherapy, for example, has been described as a practical undertaking that grows out of the clinician's desire to help a suffering human being; and psychotherapeutic techniques, therefore, must be viewed as "free inventions of the human spirit" and not blueprints created in the armchair or laboratory (Strup, 1978: 7). That is, human service practitioners must rely on their own wits, experience, and beliefs, as well as on scientific knowledge in their search for solutions to human problems.

Human service organizations and their practitioners have responded to these dilemmas by adopting *practice ideologies*. Rapoport defines practice ideologies as "formal systems of ideas that are held with great tenacity and emotional investment, that have self-confirming features, and that are resistant to change from objective rational reappraisal . . . . Ideology welds observable aspects of the environment into a kind of unity by filling in gaps in knowledge with various projections that ultimately supply a coherent belief system on which action can be based and justified" (1960: 269). Practice ideologies, then, perform a dual function for the organization: They reduce uncertainty and offer consistent courses of action, and they provide the rationale and justification for staff actions with clients.

Undoubtedly these ideologies are derived in part from the moral posture adopted by the organization, but they also emanate from a model of human nature adopted by its practitioners. For example, psychoanalytically oriented social casework is based on several ideological assumptions, including "an emphasis on the past, a pessimistic view of change, a deemphasis of the importance of social, situational, or interpersonal forces, psychological determinism, a preoccupation with intrapsychic processes, and the assumption that insight is the most powerful therapeutic agent" (Briar and Miller, 1971: 68). In contrast, the functional school of casework based on Rank's theory of personality emphasizes the present, adopts an optimistic view of the possibility of change, assumes that the personality is in a continuous process of becoming, rejects psychological determinism, and perceives the function of therapy as not to induce change, but to free the self so it can develop naturally. Behaviorally oriented social casework views human behavior as learned responses that can be modified through manipulation of stimuli and positive and negative reinforcements. It rejects the psychoanalytic assumption of unconscious conflicts as causes of psychological problems, and views therapy as the specification of distinct behaviors to be changed and the application of behavior modification principles as the means to alter them (Briar and Miller, 1971). Antithetical to these models of social work practice, radical social work assumes that an inherent conflict exists between the welfare of the agencies and the welfare of the clients; it rejects the doctrine that clients' problems emanate from defects in personality development and family relations; and it assumes that the major causes of human misery are rooted in socioeconomic forces arising from the dehumanizing consequences of capitalist economic production (Leonard, 1975). Radical social work practice thus stresses raising clients' consciousness of the conditions of their oppression, linking clients to systems that serve their interests, and building countersystems (Leonard, 1975). One can readily see that dramatically different intervention practices arise from each of these ideological orientations.

Scott (1969) identifies two predominant, yet conflicting, practice ideologies in agencies for the blind. The restorative ideology assumes that the loss of sight is analogous to the experience of death; rehabilitation therefore, involves helping blind persons overcome the grief associated with it and gradually restoring the losses experienced by them. The accommodative ideology assumes that blind persons cannot function in the sighted society; a new environment must therefore be created that accommodates their disability and protects their state of dependency.

The use of ideologies as a basis from which intervention techniques are derived and justified has important consequences for human service organizations. First, because ideologies tend to be abstract belief systems that are often beset by internal inconsistencies and ambiguities, numerous practice principles may be justified under the same ideology. The lack of one-to-one correspondence between ideology and action may permit practitioners to exercise considerable discretion in their interaction with clients. It poses to the organization the problem of controlling staff behavior without clear guides for action. Second, ideologies, because of their self-confirming features, allow practitioners to reify their models of human nature, thus leading to self-fulfilling prophecies. In making assumptions about their clients that are justified by the ideology, practitioners engage in courses of action that elicit effects which indeed enable them to reconfirm the validity of their assumptions. When a teacher assumes that children who do not conform to her middle-class values are intellectually inferior, she responds to them by lowering her expectations and giving them less attention. The resulting poor performance by these children then confirms her assumption (Rist, 1970). When psychotherapists assume that lower-class patients are unable to benefit from individual psychotherapy, they are more likely to display discomfort in treating them, resulting in the premature termination of these clients from psychotherapy, thus confirming the psychotherapists' original assumptions (Lerner and Fisk, 1973).

Finally, and related to the above, ideologies tend to set barriers to innovation, for they act as filters through which only knowledge compatible with them is admissible and acceptable to the organization, while knowledge challenging them is likely to be rejected.

Human Service Technologies as Face-to-Face Interactions

From our definition of human service technology and description of its components, it follows that the core technology (its central elements) is embedded in and manifested through the face-to-face interaction between staff and clients. The form and content of the interaction significantly affects the outcome of the technology, because it is the vehicle through which the intervention procedures are conveyed to the clients.

In the case of educational technology, Bidwell (1973) has proposed that the effectiveness of teaching is mediated by the teacher's influence and is determined by the closeness and positiveness of the sentimental ties between teacher and learner. A similar proposition is advanced by Orlinsky and Howard (1978). After an extensive review of empirical studies, they conclude that the effectiveness of psychotherapy is determined by the positive quality of the bond developed between therapist and patient, irrespective of the particular form of psychotherapy used. Human service technologies, then, posit an optimal mode of interaction as a prerequisite for their successful execution, which may necessitate a particular mix of client and staff attributes, and situational conditions that facilitate the adoption of appropriate roles. However, human service organizations are particularly vulnerable and constrained in their capacity to achieve such a mode of interaction. For example, when clients applying for welfare assume an aggressive and demanding posture, they are undermining the desired mode of interaction, which includes passivity, cooperation, patience, and impersonality. Similarly, when nurses feel rushed and under pressure, they may be unable and unwilling to offer empathy and personal attention to their patients. Even when the organization can control and structure the context of the interaction, it must still contend with the variability and unpredictability of staff and client attributes that may influence its content. This is particularly so when the effectiveness of the technology is highly dependent on the *quality* of the interaction, as in the case of psychotherapy, counselling, and teaching. In these situations, the organization is faced with the difficult task of matching clients with appropriate staff to enhance their mutual compatibility (Parloff, Waskow, and Wolfe, 1978).

The reliance on face-to-face interaction potentially invests considerable discretion in the hands of line staff. Much of the information about clients and their needs is transmitted to the organization by the line staff, and much of the information about organizational policies and services available to the clients is also controlled by them (Prottas, 1979). In calling attention to this phenomenon, Lipsky (1976) has termed these line staff as "street level bureaucrats" whose work is characterized by the following conditions: (1) they are in constant interaction with clients; (2) they have comparative independence and discretion, and their own personal attitudes and behavior may significantly affect the client's treatment; and (3) they can have a marked impact on the clients with whom they deal. The organization's ability to monitor these contacts directly is limited for several reasons. First, such monitoring may be construed as lack of trust in the ability of staff to discharge their duties. Second, it is obtrusive to the development of positive and empathetic relations between the clients and the staff. Third, it may raise, in many instances, ethical issues about confidentiality and the protection of clients' rights to privacy. Fourth, implementation requires considerable expenditure of resources and manpower, thus making it usually impractical.

As a result, human service organizations encounter a special problem in operating their service technologies: how to control the behavior of line staff and reduce the potential misuse or abuse of the discretion they possess. In Chapter 6 I discuss some of the controls used by human service organizations, which include socialization, professionalization, recording, and supervision.

Reliance on personal contact is in many ways contradictory to the bureaucratic principles that govern the structure and processes of these organizations, which promote universalism, affective neutrality, specificity, and restraint. Face-to-face interaction encourages particularism, affective involvement, diffuseness of relations, and discretion. The human service practitioners, hence, experience conflicting role expectations from the organization and from the clients. As will be noted in Chapter 6, professionalization, which provides legitimation of particularism, is one mechanism used by human service organizations to try to reduce such conflict. However, such a solution is available to only a few human services, and the conflict is particularly evident is large public agencies like welfare departments (Street, Martin, and Gordon, 1979).

The conflict between these two sets of norms is further exasperated by two factors. First, the staff have considerable power over the clients because they control the services the clients need. This asymmetry of power encourages staff to use the resources at their disposal to control the face-to-face interaction, and encourages the clients to appeal to particularistic values. Second, the service technology, in promoting the principles of "individualized treatment" and "tailoring the services to the needs of the client," further reinforces the justification for use of discretion and particularism at the expense of fairness and equity (Handler, 1973).

Human Service Technologies as Client Control Systems

The need to minimize clients' ability to negate the organizational efforts to transform their attributes is an inherent problem in human service technologies. As self-activating entities, clients are potentially capable, except in extreme circumstances, of neutralizing these efforts and rendering the organizational technology ineffective. Patients may refuse to comply with a physician's orders; students may ignore their teachers; and clients may resist discussing their interpersonal problems. The need for client compliance and cooperation is particularly heightened when the technology aims at some major changes in the client's behavior, and when it necessitates active client participation and involvement. The reliance on face-to-face interaction furthers the organization's dependency on the client's compliance. Consequently, the control of the client and the need to elicit conformity are critical issues in human service organizations and consume much of the efforts of their practitioners.

Human service technologies thus generally incorporate various mechanisms of client control. Indeed, the distinction between the procedures used to transform clients and those used to control them is highly blurred because the content and form of the relationship between staff and clients simultaneously serve the dual purposes of change and control. The social worker's efforts to establish warm, empathetic relations with the client are aimed, on the one hand, to elicit trust and strengthen the client's motivation to follow the worker's advice, and on the other, to enable the client to explore the interpersonal problems that hamper his or her functioning. The direct manipulation of positive and negative reinforcements in behavioral modification techniques clearly demonstrates the inseparability of client control and change procedures. Even in medical technology, the use of various monitoring devices, and particularly medication, elicits patient compliance while it advances the therapeutic efforts. In psychiatric treatment, medication is often used explicitly to control patients. In short, every human service technology serves also as a system of client control.

Moreover, the technology itself becomes the basis upon which the use of various control mechanisms is justified and rationalized. Milton and Edgerly (1976), for example, noted how seemingly capricious grading practices that were used to elicit respect for the instructor and force students to work harder were justified on the basis of various pedagogical principles. Coe (1970) noted how medical technology, particularly its ideological basis, has justified the extensive use of three patient control mechanisms: First, patients are *stripped of personal identity* by the removal of their personal belongings, by being required to wear hospital gowns, and by being subjected to restricted visitations and rigid daily schedules. Second, staff deliberately *control the resources* provided to the patient, particularly information about diagnosis, mode of treatment, and prognosis. Third, *restriction of mobility* prevents patients from moving about freely or leaving at their own discretion.

Following Gamson (1968), four contrasting modes of client control can be distinguished. First, the technology may regulate the access of clients to various resources. The most subtle form of control is exercised by selectivity at entry, or "cooling out." In this way, an organization rejects clients deemed potentially uncooperative. The selection criteria are built in and derived from the technology, which clearly specifies categories of "appropriate" and inappropriate" clients. The termination of services because the client "resists" treatment is another example of this control mechanism.

Second, clients can be insulated from sources of influence; this form of control is most likely to be used by "total" institutions (e.g., prisons, hospitals). Insulation is accomplished by limiting clients' access to their social networks, by controlling the information available to them, and by stripping them of their social identities. It is typically employed in settings to which clients are committed involuntarily, and where the technology is inherently aversive. Organizations are more likely to use insulation when the ideological basis of their technology assumes clients to be morally inferior (e.g., undeserving, corrupted, or evil), untrustworthy, and not amenable to change.

Third, human service organizations may use *sanctions*—the manipulation of rewards and punishments—to control clients. Sanctions are most typically exercised through the authority invested in officials, which permits the selective allocation of rewards and punishments in accordance with organizational prescriptions. For example, welfare workers can deny requests for aid if clients fail to comply with certain procedures, can terminate aid if clients violate organizational regulations, or can approve additional grants if they perceive clients as cooperative and honest. Sanctions are more likely to be used when the technology views clients as persons whose behavior is controlled by external stimuli, who lack inner motivation, and whose behavior is governed by calculations of personal cost and payoff. Staff are likely to believe that the scope of client change is limited and can be achieved only if it is externally induced and maintained.

Finally, organizations can rely on *persuasion* as a mechanism of client control. Through persuasion, staff attempt to increase clients' identification with them and their norms. Involvement of clients in the treatment process, appeals to common norms, attempts to reduce the social distance between staff and clients, personalized contracts, and, in general, efforts to "humanize" the interaction between staff and clients are illustrations of persuasion. Technologies that require active involvement and cooperation of clients in the transformation process are more likely to rely on persuasion. These technologies also assume that clients are amenable to change, can be self-motivated, are trustworthy, and are inherently moral.

Having specified some of the unique attributes of human service technologies, I turn now to examine the choices organizations make in operationalizing and implementing their technologies, and the resulting effects on staff-client relations.

OPERATIONALIZATION OF HUMAN SERVICE TECHNOLOGIES

The preceding discussion pointed to the immense number of variations and nuances in the technologies used by human service organizations. The concept "human service technology" is in itself complex and multidimensional, consisting of distinct components. Our ability to compare different types of human service technologies, and particularly to identify their differential impact on patterns of relations between staff and clients, hinges, therefore, on the formulation of an appropriate analytic conceptualization of these distinct components. The specific components of human service technologies implemented by an organization will determine how client management and handling tasks are to be performed, how these tasks are organized and carried out, and how they affect the role performances of both staff and clients.

In synthesizing various contemporary concepts of organizational technology, Hickson, Pugh, and Pheysey (1969) have identified three components: (1) operations technology—the equipping and sequencing of activities in the work flow (i.e., the production process); (2) material technology—the characteristics of the materials used in the work flow; and (3) knowledge technology—the characteristics of the knowledge used in the work flow. While these concepts may be adequate to analyze the technologies of industrial and commercial organizations, they do not capture all the characteristics of human service technologies as enunciated above. Specifically, they fail to take into account two core characteristics of human service technologies: the face-to-face interaction between staff and clients and the use of client control mechanisms.

Human services organizations therefore have to operationalize the following technological components:

1. Client attributes technology: The characteristics of the clients worked on in the service delivery process.
2. Knowledge technology: The characteristics of the intervention techniques and knowledge used in the service delivery process.
3. Interaction technology: The characteristics of the interaction patterns used in the service delivery process.
4. Client control technology: The characteristics of the client control procedures used in the service delivery process.
5. Operations technology: The organizing and sequencing of the staff activities in the service delivery process.

Client Attributes Technology

As noted earlier, the raw material for human service technologies is human beings, each of whom is inherently unique and distinct, and all of whom present a vast array of characteristics and attributes. Yet, based on its desired service output, an organization must define and determine: (1) the range of attributes considered relevant and appropriate to the technology; (2) the degree of acceptable variability in these attributes; and (3) the relative stability of these attributes. I will explore the choices an organization must make regarding each of these dimensions.

The extent of organizational interest in client biographies. This includes the type and number of biographical items (biographical space) and the time span (biographical time) of interest to the organization (Lefton and Rosengren, 1966). For example, in an emergency room, an organization's interest in a client's biographical space and time is highly limited to specific biophysical attributes over a short time span. In contrast, in long-term psychotherapy, an organization is interested in many aspects of a client's biographical space over a long time span. In a vocational training program, an organization's interest in a client's biography is limited to a few sets of attributes considered relevant to the program, but over a time period commensurate with the length of the training program.

An organization's interest in a client's biography will influence staff expectations about clients. The greater an organization's interest in a wide range of client attributes, the greater the expectation that clients will permit and cooperate with staff inquiries into them. Similarly, the greater an organization's interest in a client's biographical time, the greater the expectation that the client be committed to the organization's service objectives (Lefton and Rosengren, 1966). Thus, clients in a long-term psychotherapy program are expected and encouraged to reveal as much as possible about themselves and to be committed to and identified with the treatment objectives. In contrast, in processing applicants for job placement, staff may actually discourage clients from offering information not considered relevant to the placement decision, nor would they expect clients to demonstrate a high degree of commitment to the service objectives of the placement agency (Hasenfeld, 1975).

The degree of variability in client attributes.   This refers to the extent of variation among clients' problems, needs, and other attributes considered relevant to the service technology (Perrow, 1967). For example, in a study of nursing units, Overton, Schneck, and Hazlett (1977) found in a rating by nurses of patient variability (e.g., kinds of health problems, need for individualized care) that psychiatric units rated highest and obstetrical and auxiliary units rated lowest.

An organization can control clients' variability through its selection and "tracking" criteria and through its procedures for assessing and measuring clients' attributes. By means of tracking—assigning clients with similar attributes to specific service units—an organization can significantly reduce the variability among clients, as is the case in academic tracking. Similarly, through its assessment procedures, an organization may choose to ignore, minimize, or highlight variability among clients. For example, in a custodial care program, staff may assume that all patients or inmates are alike in their problems and needs. An organization's determination of client variability is, in part, a function of the body of knowledge and ideological system guiding the behavior of its staff.

Client variability will determine the extent to which staff can treat clients uniformly. The greater the variability among clients, the greater the need for staff to individualize service procedures and to engage in nonrepetitive decisions and activities. Client variability will thus result in diversity and heterogeneity in the content and form of the encounters between staff and clients.

The degree of stability in client attributes.   This measures the likely extent of fluctuation in client attributes during the course of the service delivery process. For example, patients in an intensive care unit are likely to be more unstable than patients in a rehabilitation unit (Overton, Schneck and Hazlett, 1977). Here too, an organization can affect staff assessment of stability by its choice of monitoring devices that measure these attributes over time. Teachers are prompted to be more sensitive to fluctuations in student performance in schools that frequently test academic progress than in schools that do so infrequently.

The degree of client stability also affects relations between staff and clients. The greater the degree of client instability, the greater the need for staff to modify or alter the form and content of their interactions with clients and to shift their intervention techniques. It necessitates more frequent communication with clients, as well as with other involved staff members.

Knowledge Technology

Knowledge technology consists of two dimensions: The first refers to the techniques used to bring about change in the clients; the second refers to the knowledge base of these techniques.

The techniques of intervention.   Technologies vary significantly in the battery of techniques they use to achieve the service objectives. In essence, these techniques define and determine both the tasks that staff must perform and how they should be performed. Thus, they have a direct impact on the content and structure of work in human service organizations. In comparing a medical unit with a family service agency or a school, it is obvious that some of the major differences in the content and structure of work are attributable to the different intervention techniques used by each organization. Furthermore, differences in the work content among units within the same organization, such as a nursing unit or classroom, will also be, in part, a function of the differences in the techniques employed.

It would not be feasible to generate an inventory of intervention techniques that covers all types of human service organizations. Rather, what is of particular importance in understanding the effects of these techniques is to see how they define staff skills, how they focus staff attention on certain client attributes, and how they define modes of interaction.

Therefore, I classify the techniques of intervention by the client attributes they manipulate. Four categories of intervention techniques can be identified:

1. Environmental: Techniques that manipulate the ecological, economic, or social environment of clients, such as residential relocation, income maintenance, or social affiliation.

2. Biophysical: Techniques that manipulate the biophysical attributes of clients, such as medication, surgery, or physical therapy.

3. Cognitive: Techniques that manipulate the perception and cognition of clients, such as teaching, training, and dissemination of information.

4. Affective: Techniques that manipulate client affects, feelings, and attitudes, such as counselling and psychotherapy.

Clearly, the battery of techniques used in any given service is likely to include some combinations of these categories, although one form may predominate.

The choice of techniques will determine not only staff skills, but also the differential attention staff will give to various aspects of a client's biography. The often-heard complaint that physicians fail to pay attention to the cognitive and affective needs of their patients is due, in part, to their choice of intervention techniques—in this case, biophysical. Moreover, as will be elaborated below, the choice of techniques will also influence the patterns of relations developed between staff and clients. Environmental and biophysical techniques are less likely to require a close relationship between staff and clients than are cognitive and affective techniques, particularly the latter. Nowhere are these differences more evident than when one compares the effects of different techniques applied to the same human problem or need. For example, contrast the relations between staff and clients in a drug treatment program employing methadone maintenance versus a program employing intensive group and individual therapy. In the former, staff attention is focused primarily on the biophysical manifestations of drug abuse, and relations are centered around administration of the medication. In the latter, staff attention is focused on the behavior, feelings, and attitudes of the patients, and relations are highly interpersonal.

Knowledge of causal relations.   As indicated earlier, an organization may assume that its knowledge of the causal relations underlying its service technology is complete or incomplete (Thompson, 1967; Perrow, 1967). To the extent that staff operates under the assumption of complete knowledge of cause-effect relations, they are able to standardize their intervention techniques by developing explicit guidelines on when and how to use them. In contrast, when they assume incomplete knowledge, they encounter uncertainty, and must, therefore, engage in a great deal of search behavior, experimentation, and intuition. These in turn are likely to affect their relations with the clients. The greater the uncertainty about the consequences of the intervention technology, the greater the need for trusting, cooperative relations between staff and clients, for flexibility and tolerance of failure from both, and for mutual commitment to the service goals.

Interaction Technology

A key attribute of human service technologies is their reliance on face-to-face interaction between staff and clients as the vehicle through which the intervention techniques are conveyed. Consequently, an organization must institute procedures and techniques that define and structure appropriate interaction patterns. This I define as *interaction technology*. It consists of the medium of the interaction, the patterns of the interaction, and the communication structure.

The medium of the interaction. This refers to the extent to which the interaction is channeled through impersonal or personal means. Three modes of interaction occur: (1) Use of equipment such as in medical examinations, administration of medication, computerized instruction, and the like. In these instances the interaction between staff and clients is mediated and controlled by the equipment. (2) Information processing such as eligibility determination, recitation, or testing. In these instances the interaction is controlled by the exchange and processing of information between the staff and the clients. (3) Purposive interpersonal relations such as social casework, some forms of teaching and socialization, or psychotherapy. In these instances the interaction is based on the development of positive personal contacts and bonds between staff and clients. Undoubtedly, in all forms of interaction elements of all these modes might be present; but staff will usually rely on one or two of them.

The choice of a predominant mode of interaction will be largely determined by the techniques of intervention. Biophysical and some environmental techniques necessitate the use of equipment, while affective techniques rely heavily on purposive interpersonal relations. For example, one key difference between behavior modification and psychotherapy is the greater reliance on purposive interpersonal relations by the latter (Gambrill, 1977). Nonetheless, there is not necessarily a one-to-one correspondence between the techniques of intervention and the modes of interaction. Physical relaxation techniques, for example, often rely on information exchange and processing as the medium of interaction, while some cognitive techniques, such as computerized instruction, rely on equipment as the medium.

The mode of interaction, then, will determine the degree to which the relations between staff and clients are personal or impersonal; equipment will elicit the most impersonal relations and purposive interpersonal relations the most personal relations.

The patterns of interaction. Szasz and Hollender (1956) were among the first to propose that different intervention situations prescribe distinct patterns of interaction between staff and clients. Using the medical relationship as a case in point, they identified three distinct patterns:

1. *Activity-passivity.* In this pattern the physician is active while the patient is passive (e.g., a severe medical emergency). In more general terms, the intervention situation is such that the client is in a totally dependent state and the helping agent initiates and performs all the intervention activities.
2. *Guidance-cooperation.* In this model the helping agent assumes major responsibility for the intervention process, but the client is expected to respond actively and to cooperate with the instructions and directions given by the staff (e.g., treatment of an infectious disease).
3. *Mutual participation.* In this pattern both the helping agent and the client assume joint responsibility in the intervention process. The client is not only actively involved in the process, but is expected to participate fully in making decisions about its future course, while the staff serve in a consultative capacity (e.g., treatment of diabetes mellitus).

The pattern of interaction, then, will affect the role expectations of both staff and clients, as dictated by the different intervention situations and techniques used. In particular, it defines the type of participation expected of the client.

Communication pattern. This refers to the characteristics of the communication net that structures the flow of information between staff and

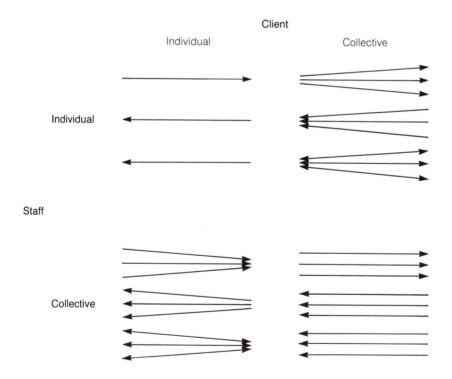

FIGURE 5.1   **Staff-client communication nets**

clients as prescribed by the service technology. As Figure 5.1 indicates, there are four types of communication nets. Casework exemplifies an individual-individual net; classroom instruction an individual-collective net; team treatment a collective-individual net; and milieu therapy a collective-collective net.

In addition, each net can be further differentiated by the direction of the information flow, which may be primarily from clients to staff, from staff to clients, or in both directions. Various models of classroom instruction can be differentiated according to the direction of the information flow. In recitation, the flow is between the teacher and a specific student. In a class task, the flow is mostly from the students to the teacher. And in a multitask class, the information flow is in both directions (Bossert, 1979).

Client Control Technology

In every service technology there are inherent mechanisms for controlling clients so as not to neutralize or undermine the intended effects of the intervention techniques. Therefore, face-to-face interaction between staff and clients serves an important function in influencing clients and eliciting their compliance with requirements of the technology. Building on the previous paradigm suggested by Gamson (1968), modes of client control can be differentiated by (1) the extent to which staff directly mediate reinforcements (rewards and punishments); and (2) the extent to which the control effort is overt and made known to clients (Tedeschi, Schlenker and Lindskold, 1972). Table 5.1 indicates the various types of control mechanisms staff can employ. One can readily note that the control mechanism selected by the staff will have enormous implications to the nature and quality of staff-client relations. Certainly, when staff rely primarily on threats, rather than promises or persuasion, the relationship is likely to be strained and will lack trust. The use of indirect means of control, as in behavior modification, deemphasizes the importance of the relationships developed between staff and clients. In this context, Rosenberg and Pearlin (1962) found that nurses in a psychiatric hospital most preferred to use persuasion and least preferred threats because they felt that not only was persuasion more effective, but it was least likely to generate difficulties with patients. Indirect means of control were considered to be even more effective than persuasion, but more difficult to implement.

TABLE 5.1   Mechanisms of Client Control

		OVERT CONTROL	INDIRECT CONTROL (MANIPULATION)
Staff mediates reinforcements	Yes	Threats and promises	Reinforcement control
	No	Persuasion	Information control

Source: Adapted from Tedeschi, Schlenker, and Lindskold (1972: 292).

Operations Technology

Operations technology refers to the organizing and sequencing of the activities required by a service technology. Specifically, it defines the degree of task interdependence in the work flow (Thompson, 1967; Van de Ven, Delbecq, and Koenig, 1976). Four types of work flow can be identified, ordered from least to most interdependence: (1) Fully independent: No client-directed task is directly contingent on other client-directed tasks. The client's service experience is thus the sum of the discrete tasks performed by the various staff. This pattern is exemplified in college-level instruction, where the mode of instruction in one course is not necessarily contingent on the mode of instruction in any other course taken by the student. (2) Sequential: Each client-directed task is contingent on the completion of another client-directed task. For example, the intake process in a mental health agency may be such that the client must first see a clerk who determines eligibility, then an intake worker who determines the client's problems, and then a referral to the appropriate service worker. (3) Reciprocal: Each client-directed task is contingent upon other client-directed tasks and vice versa. For example, in working with an emotionally impaired child, the teacher depends on the social worker's efforts to help the child accept adult authority, while the social worker depends on the teacher to provide the child with positive learning experiences. (4) Team: Several staff members not only have reciprocal interdependence, but must work together at the same time, as in surgery requiring several specialists. Operations technology, then, determines the working arrangements among the staff involved in a service technology, and in particular the mechanisms for coordination among them. As the technology moves toward more intensive work-flow interdependence, the use of various coordination mechanisms will increase—for example, scheduled and unscheduled meetings, use of horizontal channels of communication, and the like (Van de Ven, Delbecq, and Koenig, 1976).

This specification of the five components of human service technologies (see Table 5.2) enables us to systematically compare similarities and differences between various service technologies and to analyze their resultant effects on the organization of work and the patterns of staff-client relations. This can be demonstrated by comparing two teaching technologies—recitation and multitask—based on a study conducted by Bossert (1979). Recitation "is an activity that involves the whole class or a large group of children in a single task. The children listen to the question the teacher asks, raise their hands, wait to be recognized, and give an answer" (p. 44). In multitask instruction, several different tasks, such as independent reading, small-group projects, artwork and crafts, occur simultaneously in the classroom, and students choose a particular task to perform. I have reanalyzed Bossert's observations of both technologies according to the five components specified above.

In recitation, the teacher's interest in the child's biography is distinctly limited to his or her capacity to learn and interest in given subjects. The teacher assumes some variability among the students, but also assumes that their learning capabilities and interests are reasonably stable. In contrast, in multitask instruction, the teacher's interest in the child's biography is broader and encompasses experiences not directly related to the specific subject matter being taught. The teacher assumes considerable variability among the students and frequent deviations in learning capabilities and interests.

Both modes of instruction rely on cognitive techniques, although multitask instruction also attempts to shape each child's environment to enhance the learning process. In recitation, the teacher assumes complete knowledge of the cause-effect relations in the learning process. In multitask instruction, the teacher assumes incomplete knowledge of cause-effect relations, and hence accepts the need for experimentation in various teaching approaches. In both recitation and multitask instruction, the interaction modes involve the use of equipment and information processing. Yet, in the former, there is greater reliance on information exchange between teacher and students, with limited use of equipment such as books and worksheets. In multitask instruction, there is greater diversity in equipment use. The pattern of interaction in recitation is guidance-cooperation, while in multitask instruction it is based on mutual participation. The communication net in recitation is essentially one-to-one, between the teacher and each student. In multitask instruction, the communication net is more complex and involves one-to-many, from the teacher to groups of students, and many-to-many within and among groups that may include the teacher.

Control of students in recitation is overt, based primarily on the teacher's use of threats and promises. In contrast, in multitask instruction control is indirect and based on reinforcement control through the tasks themselves and through peer relations. In addition, the teacher relies more on persuasion. Finally, teaching tasks in recitation are coordinated sequentially;

TABLE 5.2   Summary of the Components of Human Service Technologies

CLIENT ATTRIBUTES	KNOWLEDGE	INTERACTION	CLIENT CONTROL	OPERATIONS
a. Interest in client biography b. Client variability c. Client stability	a. Techniques of intervention: 1. Environmental 2. Biophysical 3. Cognitive 4. Affective b. Cause-effect relations	a. Medium: 1. Equipment 2. Information 3. Interpersonal b. Pattern: 1. Activity-passivity 2. Guidance-cooperation 3. Mutual participation c. Communication net	a. Reinforcement mediation b. Overtness of control	a. Task inter-dependence 1. Independent 2. Sequential 3. Reciprocal 4. Team

in multitask instruction they are most likely to be independent of each other.

As Bossert (1979) points out, the differences between the two teaching technologies generate quite distinct classroom organizations. In recitation, the teacher assumes the dominant role in the classroom, and the pupils' behavior and teacher's responses are highly visible. There are explicit standards of performance, which are often demonstrated by the top-performing students, who thereby receive additional teacher assistance. Relations between teacher and students are more formal and hierarchical, with little room for individualized handling of students. Relations among students are based on academic performance, producing a competitive status system in the classroom. Children are separated into performance-homogeneous groupings that are fairly stable. In contrast, in multitask instruction, the teacher's role becomes less visible and dominant. Standards of performance are individualized, enabling the teacher to provide assistance to each student according to capability and rate of progress. One pupil's behavior is not readily visible to the others, and the teacher can discretely control the behavior of any particular child. Relations between the teacher and students are informal, more personalized, and do not display hierarchical differentiation. Relations among students are not based on competition, but rather on the various opportunities to work and play together. As a result, peer relations and groupings are ever-changing, more cooperative, and performance-heterogeneous.

FUNCTIONS OF HUMAN
SERVICE TECHNOLOGIES

We have seen that human service organizations have many choices in operationalizing their service technologies. To a significant extent, these choices will be guided by the uses to which an organization wishes to put its service technology. That is, the selection and implementation of any service technology will be governed by the desired products or the projected impact of the organization's outputs upon the environment (see Chapter 4).

Human service technologies serve three functions, based on the nature of their "product." These are: (1) people-processing, as exemplified in the products of juvenile courts, credit-rating bureaus, or testing and diagnosis units; (2) people-sustaining, as exemplified in the products of welfare departments, nursing homes, or hospital chronic wards; (3) people-changing, as exemplified in the products of educational programs, psychotherapy, or physical rehabilitation. Of course, such a typology is based on "ideal types"; in the empirical world technologies seldom serve only one function. In most instances they generate mixed products. For example, a technology based on psychotropic drugs' may be both people-sustaining and people-changing, while most income maintenance programs invariably involve both people-processing and people-sustaining functions. Nonetheless, these ideal types sensitize us to the structural consequences for the organization and its clients that emanate from the predominant function of its technology. Specifically, the function of the technology influences the core activities that staff engage in, the structural location of the technology in the organization, the predominant administrative concerns in managing the technology, the overall staff-client relations, the mechanisms of client control, and the mechanisms of staff compliance.

People-Processing Technologies

People-processing has one central purpose: To confer on people a particular social label, social position, or status that will, in turn, produce a predetermined response from significant social groups or organizations. Hence, the major products are people with changed statuses and positions in various community systems (Hansenfeld, 1972). Instead of directly changing a person's attributes, the organization chooses to alter the *definition* of the attributes, social position, and public identity so that the reactions of others to these new definitions will produce the desired change. For example, when a juvenile court labels a child "delinquent," its intended purpose is to establish a new social status and public identity for the child that alters: (1) the child's social position and its rights, obligations, privileges, and self-esteem; (2) the jurisdiction over the child by various youth-serving agencies; and (3) the responses and reactions to the child by key social groups and organizations. These effects are designed to bring about some significant transformations in the child's attributes, presumably in the direction of reducing antisocial behavior. Similarly, when a psychiatric screening unit makes a diagnosis of a client's mental health problems and needs, it redefines the client's public identity; such a redefinition determines the client's access to a mental health treatment program, the program's jurisdiction over the client, and the anticipated treatment procedures. And, finally, when a client applying for welfare is designated as "destitute," the label enables the client to gain access to needed fiscal resources, but it also redefines the client's rights, privileges, and obligations in a direction presumed to discourage the fostering of a state of dependency.

In all of these instances, the core activities are based on a system of classification-disposition. This system is composed of a set of procedures that guides the staff, interacting with clients, in assigning appropriate labels and linking them to other units, internal or external, whose anticipated responses to the labels are presumably needed for transforming the client's attributes.

Consequently, the locus of the technology is at the boundaries of the organization. Staff activities consist of transactions with clients and their dossiers at input, assignments of classification-disposition labels at output, and exchanges with other units as potential recipients of the clients. Therefore, the management and effectiveness of the technology is highly dependent on interorganizational or interunit exchanges between the processing unit and the potential recipients of the clients. If other units fail to respond as expected to the classification-disposition activities, the very purpose and rationale of the technology is jeopardized. In general, then, the classification-disposition system will reflect the constraints and contingencies emanating from the exchange relations between the processing unit and the potential recipients of the clients (Hasenfeld, 1972). For example, an employment agency is likely to classify and categorize job applicants in accordance with the constraints imposed on it by potential employers, a pattern that reinforces the past employment careers of the applicants (Hasenfeld, 1975). Similarly, a credit bureau rates applicants in accordance with lenders' perceptions about good or bad credit risks, which often results in discrimination against women and minorities.

Disposition—the linking of the client to other units—is a primary managerial concern to an organization employing a people-processing technology. The ability to ensure a smooth flow of people in and out of the processing unit and avoid a backlog is a major factor in shaping the activities of staff. To achieve this objective, an organization may employ several mechanisms that involve manipulation of the client attributes technology. First, as noted earlier, the processing unit uses categorization schemes acceptable to the receiving units. Second, efforts will be made to simplify the processing activities by reducing the range of categories. This has the further effect of limiting the amount of information needed from the client. Third, conceptions of "normal cases" will be developed. These will enable staff to assign clients to typical or likely categories, thus reducing the need for extensive probing or consideration of clients' idiosyncracies (see also Chapter 7). Sudnow (1965) noted how public defenders attempted to make defendants' attributes fit those of a "normal crime" rather than trying to ascertain all the facts of the particular situation. This procedure permitted a rapid and smooth processing of cases through the court. In general, then, the greater the staff workload, the more likely the use of such mechanisms.

The emphasis on staff-client interaction is minimal in this technology, since interaction is used primarily to gather information about the client and is of limited duration. Therefore, organizational concerns about client control are also limited and center mainly on ensuring that clients provide valid and reliable information. Compliance is most often attained by the use of threats. An organization may have acquired the legal authority to force the clients to document their personal biographies (e.g., the welfare department); or it can threaten not to process the client unless access to such information is granted (e.g., the credit bureau).

The organization's main concern is to ensure staff compliance and adherence to the prescribed classification-disposition scheme, and to reduce errors of misclassification. This is, for example, the primary concern in a welfare department, where staff are under strong pressure to reduce the number of "undeserving poor" who receive welfare benefits. In his case studies of people-processing technologies, Prottas (1979) indicates that the ability of an organization to enforce and maintain such compliance is highly problematic. While the organization promulgates numerous rules and regulations for staff to follow, the control staff have over the information received from clients provides them with a measure of discretion that is difficult for the organization to mitigate.

People-Sustaining Technologies

Technologies for people-sustaining aim to prevent, arrest, or delay the deterioration of a person's well-being or social status. They do so by removing or minimizing the effects of conditions that threaten a person's well-being, or by compensating for the deficits in personal resources that cause the deterioration. The "products" are people who have been helped to gain access to resources that will sustain them at their current levels of social functioning. While some efforts may be made to improve social functioning or to change attributes, the major focus is on preventing further deterioration of social functioning. Hence, most income maintenance programs, such as AFDC or SSI, are examples of people-sustaining functions. Similarly, the care of the elderly in nursing homes, or the care of the chronically mentally ill and the severely developmentally disabled in institutions, are instances of these functions.

The underlying assumption of people-sustaining technologies is that the clients have little, if any, potential for change in directions that will significantly improve their social functioning. While these assumptions may be based on empirically valid knowledge (i.e., lack of a known cure to a disease), they are also based on a social and moral evaluation of such persons that casts them into socially marginal categories. As Coser (1963) noted, patients with similar physical conditions may be subject to people-sustaining rather than people-changing technologies because of a staff belief system that ascribes to the patients a low capacity for improvement. Such patients are likely to be subject to what Freidson (1970) terms a "domestic service" pattern of management, which he contrasts with the "therapeutic interaction" pattern of patient management. The former is founded on the assumption that not much can be done for the patients except to keep them in a relatively comfortable and safe environment. In the same vein, offenders having similar attributes may be found in both custodial correctional programs, which assume a low capacity for change and emphasize "doing time," and in treatment-oriented programs, which assume a high capacity for change and emphasize rehabilitation.

It is not surprising to find, therefore, that persons who are socially devalued and occupy a low social status are more likely to be subject to people-sustaining rather than people-changing technologies. Clearly, the organization and its staff are not immune from dominant societal values that ascribe a low capacity for change to such people.

The core activities in this technology are custodial care and sustentation—namely, a set of procedures that prescribes the variety, amount, and frequency of provision, support, and care clients will obtain from the organization. The heart of a public assistance program, after it has established clients' eligibility, is to determine the types and amounts of grants and services clients are entitled to. In a nursing home, for example, the daily regimen regulates bathing and cleaning, the type and schedule of meals, the distribution of medication, and the use of various recreational facilities.

While the organizational locus of people-sustaining technologies is internal and away from its boundaries, it is only partially buffered from the environment. Because it aims to sustain rather than change, it does not need to place boundaries around clients or insulate them from external environmental influences (Thompson, 1967: 43–44). The main objective of the organization is to buffer the sustaining technology sufficiently from environmental influences that may disturb or disrupt its rules. That is, the organization will attempt to neutralize environmental pressures to favor certain clients or to provide them with additional sustenance and care if they are not within its prescribed rules. At the same time, the organization takes its cues from the environment in determining the level of support and care various categories of clients will receive. Put differently, the rules established by the organization are likely to reflect broad societal norms about the level of care and sustenance different people in need deserve. For example, Piven and Cloward (1971) suggest that the grant level in public assistance is fixed to be below the lowest wage scale of unskilled workers, thus reinforcing the work ethic and discouraging unskilled workers from leaving the labor market. Similarly, it has been observed that the level of care the elderly receive in nursing homes correlates with their socioeconomic status (Kosberg, 1973). In short, organizational rules are informed by social stratification processes, specifically by predominant conceptions of the social worth of various clients.

To buffer the technology from undue environmental interferences, an organization will establish a high degree of bureaucratization and standardization of rules. Control of the technology will be anchored in elaborate standard operating procedures aimed at attaining considerable routinization and uniformity of staff activities. Adherence to these rules enables an organization legitimately to ward off claims for support and care that can be shown to violate them.

The need for extensive formalization and standardization of technology is also a function of the nature of the clients served by it. Being highly dependent, with limited capacity to care for themselves, they are at the mercy of their caretakers who, potentially, have substantial control over

their fate. Such control is particularly ominous when demands for sustenance and care are made against highly scarce resources. In most instances,
clients are too disabled or debilitated to counteract the consequences of
such power imbalance. The magnitude of their potential power over clients
may induce the staff to use it for their own personal gain: They may neglect
clients to reduce their workload, manipulate the level of care to control
"troublesome" clients, or favor those they personally like. Invariably such
power will be used to facilitate the smooth functioning of their daily work
(Smith, 1965). There is a high potential for neglect, abuse, and exploitation
of clients, as the numerous exposés of custodial institutions attest. It occurs
not only because of the clients' powerlessness, but also because staff are
seldom expected to demonstrate any improvement in a client's condition.
Moreover, while physical manifestations of maltreatment of clients may be
suspected, they become visible only after extreme and sustained abuse.

The situation is particularly serious when the organization generates
incentives to reduce the amount of client support and care. In publicly
funded custodial care programs, the high volume of clients, the low wages,
the lack of occupational advancement, and the limited resources induce
staff to limit the amount and quality of care to compensate for poor working
conditions. In privately owned care programs, such as sheltered care facilities, the pressure to generate profits also induces staff to economize on the
amount and quality of care (Segal and Aviram, 1978). At the same time,
such facilities are also motivated to prolong the length of care since an
empty bed represents an operating loss to the proprietor.

Enforcement of standard operating procedures and universal criteria
for providing care is the major mechanism an organization uses to minimize
the inherent potential for neglect and abuse of clients in people-sustaining
technologies. This mechanism minimizes staff discretion in services they
control (Handler, 1973). Yet the effectiveness of universal and standard
criteria of performance is obviously dependent on the enforcement capabilities within or without the organization. However, as I have suggested
earlier, the adequacy or quality of care is difficult to assess. Reliance on
bureaucratic procedures for controlling staff behavior, as well as minimizing
environmental interferences, is not without costs. It can lead staff to view
clients as objects rather than subjects and can foster dehumanization. Staff
may be discouraged from responding to clients' individual needs.

In the same vein, people-sustaining technologies will be characterized
by limited staff-client interaction. The focus will be mainly on determining
the type, amount, and frequency of client care that the organization is able
to provide. Hence, interaction patterns will essentially be based on activity-
passivity. Control over the clients will be manifested by manipulation of
reinforcement control and threats and promises. Compliance will be elicited
by withholding sustenance and care from clients who make "unreasonable"
demands, and by granting extra or speedy care to clients who abide by the

rules and facilitate the staff's work. In involuntary settings, such as prisons and state mental hospitals, coercive means will often be used to elicit client compliance.

People-Changing Technologies

People-changing technologies aim at directly altering clients' bio-physical, psychological, or social attributes in order to improve their well-being and social functioning. The emphasis is on the direct manipulation of attributes to achieve a predetermined change. In people-changing technologies, we can distinguish between two subfunctions (Vinter, 1963): (1) Restoration: The emphasis here is on removing or reducing deficiencies, barriers, and incapacities so that the client can function at a socially desirable level. Such technologies include psychotherapy, treatment of diseases, vocational rehabilitation, and resocialization. The clients are judged to be deviant or suffer from incapacities that prevent performance of conventional social roles. (2) Enhancement: The emphasis here is on further improving the social functioning and well-being of persons judged to be moving along normal gradients of development. Examples of such technologies include education, character building, and disease prevention.

In contrast to people-sustaining technologies, people-changing technologies assume that clients have a significant capacity to improve and are amenable to change. These assumptions, too, are based both on empirical knowledge and moral assessment of a person's social worth. For example, in applying medical technology, the young are favored because greater social worth is ascribed to youth (Sudnow, 1967; Roth, 1972). Similarly, there is evidence to suggest that the application of educational technology is a function of the moral evaluation of students by teachers. Those students judged to be of higher social worth are more likely to gain access to effective educational technologies (Rist, 1970; Rosenbaum, 1976).

The greater the amount of change sought by the technology, the greater its complexity and indeterminancy and the greater the organizational need to buffer it from the environment. Two factors account for this: First, the success of the technology is predicated on the capacity of an organization to ensure congruence between the attributes of the persons seeking change and the attributes defined as appropriate by the technology. Roth and Eddy noted that the selection of patients for physcial rehabilitation was based on having the "right" disability, being relatively young, and showing sufficient mental alertness and motivation—factors judged important to successful rehabilitation (1968: 10–18). Second, the organization must insulate these attributes from external influences so that its practitioners can gain as much control over them as possible. This is particularly evident, for example, in the case of surgery, where maximum insulation of the patient from the environment is accomplished.

Buffering the technology from the organizational environment is accomplished in several ways. First, the organization may employ a cadre of professionals whose expertise and prestige serve as a shield against challenges to its technology. Second, the organization, through the support of the state, may obtain numerous legal protections of its boundaries by such devices as licensing, industry-controlled accreditation, peer review, and limited liability and confidentiality of records, which close off the organization from "unauthorized" inspection. Third, the organization may publicize its allegiance to altruistic norms, collective welfare, and codes of ethics as justification for its insulation from the environment. Fourth, the organization may develop elaborate client selection and screening procedures to weed out those who might potentially disrupt the technology. Finally, when the technology requires maximum control over the client, as in the case of hospitalization or commitment to an institution, the clients will be isolated from their social networks.

The need to insulate people-changing technologies to ensure their success is closely related to an organization's need to proclaim its effectiveness. Having committed itself to "producing" persons with improved or restored well-being and social functioning, it is obligated to demonstrate its effectiveness. However, such a demonstration is highly problematic, particularly when the knowledge of cause-effect relations is incomplete, and the attributes to be changed are variable and unstable. Under such circumstances, a close scrutiny of the technology is likely to reveal its precariousness. Consequently, it is in the interest of the organization to shield its technology from external scrutiny and assessment, which may expose its weaknesses and undermine its claims to success. Witness, for example, the persistent resistance by educational institutions to be evaluated by inspection of their outputs and teacher performance (Meyer and Rowan, 1978).

To claim effectiveness while buffering the technology from external inspection is one of the major administrative concerns in organizations employing people-changing technologies. Entrusting the core activities to professionals enables an organization to accomplish both objectives. The professionals, through their recognized exclusive claims to expertise and legitimate autonomy, can buffer the technology and, at the same time, proclaim its effectiveness on the basis of their professional judgment. Concomitantly, the organization is likely to enlist extrinsic measures of success, such as client testimonies, staff reputation, and extensiveness of facilities (Thompson, 1967).

In contrast to the other human service technologies, people-changing technologies require relatively intensive and often extensive relationships between staff and clients, particularly when major changes are sought. These relationships, frequently based on mutual participation, have a dual function. First, they are aimed at creating a social-psychological state that will enhance the client's readiness and receptivity to the change efforts.

Such a state is a necessary precondition for the successful execution of the technology, because the client has the potential to neutralize and counteract staff intervention efforts. As prerequisites to effective treatment, the helping professions invariably underscore the need to: establish trust between the client and the practitioner, elicit the client's recognition of the practitioner's expertise and authority, and obtain the client's cooperation and compliance. These are to be achieved through purposeful staging and management of staff-client relationships. In medical practice, for instance, physicians firmly believe that the effectiveness of treatment is predicated on what they perceive as an appropriate "patient role." Physician-patient relationships are used to train and educate the patient to assume such a role (Balint, 1964). Hence, patients who assume a respectful, uncomplaining, and submissive role are more likely to be perceived as "good" patients (Lorber, 1975); in one study, such patients were found to be more likely to complete the rehabilitation program (Ludwig and Adams, 1968).

Second, in people-changing technologies, staff-client relationships are in themselves one of the important tools for change, particularly for behavioral change. Hence, the core activity in casework is the "casework relationship," which revolves around the "communication of ideas and emotions between caseworker and client" (Briar and Miller, 1971: 124). Similarly, psychotherapy can be readily conceptualized as "an interpersonal process designed to bring about modification of feelings, cognitions, attitudes, and behavior which have proven troublesome to the person seeking help from a trained professional" (Strup, 1978: 3). Not surprisingly, Orlinsky and Howard have found that "effective investment of energy, good personal contact, and mutual affirmation stand out as three aspects of the cohesiveness that seems to mark the beneficial therapeutic bond" (1978: 317).

Because staff-client relationships play such an important role in the battery of change techniques, the organization must create conditions that facilitate their formation and utilization, and particularly must insulate them from external interferences. (This is another reason for buffering the technology from the environment.) Casting the staff in a position of authority and expertise and the client in a position of dependency is one device organizations frequently use to attain these conditions. Asymmetry of power based on expert and referent power is highly effective in influencing the client. We can, therefore, expect that organizations using people-changing technologies are more likely to rely on persuasion as the major mechanism for eliciting client compliance (in addition to reinforcement control) since it is more conducive to the formation of a trusting and cooperative relationship.

In the same vein, an organization is likely to appeal to values and commitments as the primary mechanism for eliciting staff compliance with the requirements of the technology. The requirement of a personal investment in clients cannot be attained simply by the promulgation of rules and procedures or by inducements, because such an investment cannot be ordered or be readily compensated. It must be based on the staff's identification with the aims of the technology. Indeed, one can speculate that when the organization is unable to develop such identification and commitment, the effectiveness of the technology will be seriously threatened.

Table 5.3 summarizes the major distinctions between people-processing, people-sustaining, and people-changing technologies. An organization may employ various combinations of technologies. A drug rehabilitation agency may simultaneously provide a people-processing diagnostic service, a people-sustaining methadone maintenance program, and a people-changing group therapy program. As a result, the units implementing each technology will differ from each other in core activities, organizational locus, managerial concerns, staff-client relations, client control, and staff compliance. Indeed, it is more appropriate to conceptualize human service organizations as multitechnology systems, although one type of technology will often predominate. Thus, although welfare departments attempt to implement a people-changing technology, they commit more resources toward processing applicants and providing basic sustenance.

TABLE 5.3　A Typology of the Functions of Human Services Technologies

	PEOPLE PROCESSING	PEOPLE SUSTAINING	PEOPLE CHANGING
TYPE OF PRODUCT	Altered status	Attribute stabilization	Attribute change
CORE ACTIVITIES	Classification-disposition	Custodial care; sustentation	Planned change
ORGANIZATIONAL LOCUS	Boundaries	Intrapartial insulation	Intramaximal insulation
MANAGERIAL CONCERN	Disposition of product	Acceptable allocation rules	Demonstrated effectiveness
STAFF-CLIENT RELATIONS	Minimal	Modest	Extensive
CLIENT CONTROL	Threats and promises	Threats and promises; Reinforcement control	Persuasion; Reinforcement control
STAFF COMPLIANCE	Bureaucratic	Bureaucratic	Commitment

ORGANIZATIONAL DETERMINANTS OF TECHNOLOGY SELECTION

The choice of technology to be implemented is more ambiguous and problematic for human service organizations than for other organizations because there are no explicit, one-to-one correspondences between desired outcomes and the technological means to attain them. This is not to imply that technological considerations are not important to human service organizations. Surely they are influenced by the existing state of technological development in their particular service domain, and specifically by the technologies used by other trend-setting organizations in the field. Hence, an organization's technological choices will be affected by its boundary-spanning activities and its access to information on technological developments. The saliency of such information to decision-makers in an organization will depend, in part, on the credibility and status of the boundary-spanning staff as "opinion leaders." Such knowledge will limit the alternatives to be considered by an organization. Yet it will not solely determine the actual choice because most human services have not clearly defined their desired outcomes partly because the knowledge for attaining them is so various and indeterminate.

Hence, technology selection is also determined by considerations of political and economic payoffs and costs of alternative technologies. The perceived values of these costs and payoffs to the organizational decision makers will, in turn, be a function of the distribution of power and economic resources both within and without the organization, and the opportunities and constraints associated with their mobilization. Put differently, the leaders of an organization will attempt to select a technology that will be politically and economically feasible, will enhance the survival of the organization, and will strengthen (or at least not undermine) the position of the dominant coalition.

Because the selection is only partially affected by technological considerations, the major factors influencing this choice are the values and interests of the dominant coalition of the organization. That is, a technology will be selected whose ideological underpinnings are congruent with the values and interests of the dominant coalition. This dynamic is particularly observable during a shift in leadership. For example, Astrachan (1978) analyzed the technological changes in a community mental health center from a traditional psychoanalytic mode of treatment to crisis intervention and community organization as a result of a shift in leadership from psychoanalytically trained to community-oriented psychiatrists. Similarly, Strauss and associates (1964) have noted that the ideological orientation of the psychiatrists who control various hospital wards will influence the predominant modes of treatment.

Nonetheless, such a choice is also constrained by several environmental factors. First, community groups upon whom the organization depends for legitimation and support may limit the options open to the decision makers. Scott (1969) argues that the choice of the accommodative rather than the restorative approach to the rehabilitation of the blind is in part based on community resistance to integration of the blind into the mainstream of community life. Likewise, the choice of a certain curriculum as a teaching technology is often affected by the support or resistance of various community groups as communicated through the school board (Hampson, 1975). Second, each technological alternative necessitates a different configuration of resources (e.g., funds, manpower, expertise), whose availability further affects the actual choice. For example, the ability of a hospital to institute a highly sophisticated medical technology will depend on its capacity to secure the necessary funds and to recruit the needed expertise. It is not by chance that manpower programs for the hard-to-employ often opt for "motivation to work" technologies rather than on-the-job training and job placement, because the latter require resources, in the form of job opportunities and subsidies, that are exceedingly difficult to mobilize. In short, the needed investment in money, personnel, expertise, and equipment called for by a given technology vis-à-vis the availability of these resources to the organization will be a key determinant of its adoption. Conversely, an organization may select a particular technology because of the opportunities it affords to mobilize new resources and improve its competitive posture. The availability of public funds to support a given technology may provide a strong inducement for adoption. Third, the interorganizational relations established by the organization and its location in the service network also affect the choice of technology. That is, the organization will choose those technologies that strengthen its competitive position in the environment and facilitate its exchange relations with other organizations. For example, a drug rehabilitation program may opt for methadone maintenance rather than group therapy to increase its number of referred cases, as well as to improve its position against other drug rehabilitation programs.

The internal politics and economics of an organization will also influence the selection of a service technology. First, staff members may resist and reject the introduction of a certain technology if it adversely affects their working conditions. A relatively benign activity therapy program for the institutionalized mentally retarded was effectively resisted by ward attendants because of its perceived negative consequences on their daily work (Bogdan et al., 1974).

Finally, the organization is more likely to choose a service technology congruent with the professional orientation, expertise, and skills of its staff, particularly those who hold important power positions. That is, the workers in the agency, particularly the professional staff, form interest groups to promote their values and the importance of their work. They will, in turn, advocate or resist certain technologies on the basis of perceived payoffs to their interests. An instance of this process can be noted in the persistent and successful advocacy by social workers, both inside and outside public assistance, for the separation of income maintenance from social services; the net effect was to strengthen social casework technology in public welfare. The justification for the separation was based on professional ideologies, citing improved performance by the caseworkers and benefits to the recipients, although one study doubts that clients benefit or otherwise are satisfied by this separation (Piliavin and Gross, 1977).

The operationalization and implementation of the technology selected by an organization will also be affected by political and economic factors. As a result, there may be significant disparities between the task patterns called for by the technology and the actual tasks and activities carried out by the staff. In part, such disparity is a function of the technology's vague and indeterminate attributes, as pointed out so cogently by Perrow (1965). In addition, and because of it, the organization can and will modify the characteristics of the technology in practice for the same reasons noted above. In a study of a juvenile correctional treatment program that used a token economy as a major treatment modality, youth were penalized for "bad" behavior instead of being rewarded for "good" behavior; and the definitions of good and bad behaviors were related mostly to custodial functions—contrary to the prescriptions of the technology (Vinter, Sarri, and Hasenfeld, 1974). These distortions were introduced in order to reduce costs, enable the custodial staff to maintain control over the youth, and simplify the management of the token economy. The overmedication of mental patients to control them and ease their management is another case of misused technology. Similarly, Kassebaum and associates (1971) reported on the effectiveness of group counselling in prison with prison guards as group leaders, which clearly raises serious questions about the appropriate implementation of the technology. Finally, studies of neighborhood service centers noted their inability to develop an effective referral technology for their clients, because of their weak position in the human services network and the limited skills of their staff (Hasenfeld, 1971; Perlman, 1975).

In all these instances, external factors, such as limited resources and pressures from other organizations, and internal factors, such as the interests and power of various staff groups, cause changes in the actual operation of the technology that may deviate significantly from the prescribed blueprint. Therefore, to understand the impact of a technology on an organization and its clients it is essential that one unravel the technology *in practice* by a systematic analysis of how staff actually perform in relation to the clients. In no other type of organization is such an analysis so critical, for, as has been demonstrated repeatedly, few technological imperatives exist to guide the behavior of human service practitioners in meeting human needs. Therefore, the first and most critical step in our efforts to understand human service organizations must be a careful and detailed study of their technologies in practice, as expressed in the realities of staff activities with clients.

CONCLUSION

This chapter has focused on one of the more elusive dimensions in the analysis of human service organizations—namely, their technology. This concept is ambiguous and difficult to define because it tries to capture the meaning of "working on people." Such work lacks clear boundaries and consistency because of the inherent variability of people as raw material and the lack of complete knowledge on how best to serve them. Equally important, working on people involves numerous moral considerations that must be included in conceptualizing human service technologies. As a result, these technologies acquire characteristics not found in those where the raw materials are inanimate objects.

Among the characteristics of human service technologies highlighted in this chapter are: the underlying moral assumptions, the ideological components that serve to close gaps in knowledge, the reliance on face-to-face interaction, and the incorporation of client control mechanisms. These and other characteristics result in a great deal of technological variability among organizations aiming to attain the same service outcomes, because they permit an organization wide discretion in shaping its technology in practice. As a result, the operationalization of a human service technology confronts an organization with multiple choices and options in at least five areas: (1) client attributes, (2) knowledge base, (3) interaction with clients, (4) client control, and (5) modes of operation. The choices made in these areas will determine the nature and organization of work and, particularly, staff-client relations.

Significant determinants of these choices originate in the purposes or functions of the technologies in terms of desired products. Human service technologies have three major functions: (1) people processing, (2) people sustaining, and (3) people changing. The pursuit of each of these functions will have important consequences on the internal structure and processes of an organization.

Finally, political-economic influences will affect the technological choices of an organization. The technology in practice may be quite different from the technology in theory, exactly because of the lack of one-to-one correspondence between the desired outcomes and the required technology.

6

STRUCTURE, POWER, AND CONTROL

An organization's implementation of a human service technology gives rise to distinctive divisions of labor that are manifested in the arrangement of staff activities, the distribution of authority, and the patterns of communication and coordination. In a general sense, this internal structuring of the organization—as reflected in the division of labor, the administrative component, the distribution of power, and the departmentalization of the various work units—represents a series of strategic choices made by the leadership to implement the organizational mandate (Child, 1972; Galbraith, 1977).

In essence, organizational structuring determines both how power is allocated among groups and individuals and who exercises control over individual behavior in the organization (Hall, 1977). Those possessing power determine whose preferences receive attention, how decisions are made and carried out, and how tasks are assigned and work arrangements instituted. Those exercising control determine how performances are to be evaluated and sanctioned, and how much autonomy and discretion individuals have over their work.

Much current theory and research on organizational structure attempts to demonstrate that the arrangement of activities, the distribution of authority, and the control of workflow are guided by a norm of rationality (Thompson, 1967; Hage and Aiken, 1967, 1969; Blau and Schoenherr, 1971). That is, to enhance efficiency and effectiveness, an organization's internal structure is designed to respond to the contingencies presented by the technology, environment, size, and the organization's history (see the discussion of contingency theory in Chapter 2). For example, Lawrence and Lorsch (1967), in a trail-blazing study, attempted to demonstrate that organizational effectiveness increases when the work units are differentiated enough to meet the organization's environmental and technological exigencies, yet are coordinated enough to manage their interdependencies. Similarly, a significant body of research indicates that organizational effectiveness is enhanced when nonroutine technologies are accompanied by high staff discretion and decentralization of power (for a summary of these findings see Zey-Ferrell, 1979). While the validity of these findings is not disputed, their applicability to human service organizations is problematic for several reasons.

First, it has been shown that human service organizations face turbulent environments characterized by multiple and changing interest groups with different and often incompatible values. An organization, responding to these groups, is likely to pursue multiple, often conflicting, goals that severely constrain its ability to design a rational internal structure.

Second, as was made abundantly clear in the previous chapter, human service technologies incorporate many ill-defined tasks and activities; whole definitions and specifications vary widely among organizations and among human service practitioners. Therefore, the internal structure of the agency cannot be readily guided by a technological blueprint when it is subject to these ideological vagaries.

Third, human service technologies create difficulties in monitoring and evaluating staff performance and output. These emanate, in part, from the vagueness of the technologies, the complexity of human attributes, the low visibility of staff activities, and the indeterminancy of output goals. Yet effective control is contingent on the existence of an explicit and acceptable evaluation scheme.

Finally, staff-client encounters, the predominant activity in human service organizations, are not readily subject to organizational control since they are vulnerable to the vicissitudes of both clients and line staff. Consequently, efforts to structure and control these encounters to accord with organizational policies are likely to be wrought with difficulties.

This chapter explores such issues in greater detail, showing how they affect the distribution of power and the exercise of control, and how these in turn influence the service delivery process.

HUMAN SERVICE ORGANIZATIONS
AS LOOSELY COUPLED SYSTEMS

The organizational chart of any community mental health center, school, or hospital conveys an image of rationality, order, and coordination. Units and departments seem to have clear activity domains and rational divisions of labor; lines of authority seem to be clearly designated; and all the various elements of the organization seem to be interconnected and integrated into a functioning whole. Yet, empirical studies of these organizations fail to confirm this image. Quite the contrary. Studies of hospitals (Strauss et al., 1967), schools (Meyer and Rowan, 1978; Lorti, 1975), universities (March and Olsen, 1976), and welfare departments (Prottas, 1979) suggest that "structural elements are only loosely linked to each other and to activities, rules are often violated, decisions are often unimplemented, or if implemented have uncertain consequences, technologies are of problematic efficiency, and evaluation and inspection systems are subverted or rendered so vague as to provide little coordination" (Meyer and Rowan, 1977: 343).

A more appropriate image of the internal structure of human service organizations depicts a "loosely coupled system" in which work units preserve considerable autonomy and identity, and respond to each other in a circumscribed, infrequent, slow, or unimportant manner (Weick, 1976). Such a structure has several characteristic features. First, the various tasks and activities compromising the technological core of the organization are weakly connected and weakly coordinated. They cannot be demonstrated to be logically derived from a clearly defined technology. In the case of the public school, the curriculum content in various classrooms is coordinated only in the most general way, and teachers have considerable latitude in determining the content and method of teaching (Meyer and Rowan, 1978). In the mental hospital, wards are organized in accordance with the particular psychiatric ideologies of the attending physicians, nurses, and aides rather than in terms of some overarching treatment plan (Strauss et al., 1967).

Second, there is a weak system of control over staff activities. For reasons to be noted later, staff exercise considerable discretion in discharging their duties in contexts that lack specific or explicit monitoring and evaluation mechanisms. Social workers are subject to pseudotherapeutic, not task-oriented, supervision; teachers are subject to minimal inspections of classroom performance; and physicians' medical records are seldom subject to careful scrutiny.

Third, a weak and often multiple system of authority exists throughout the organization. Units and individuals in the organization are often quite autonomous and relatively insulated from other units or individuals, particularly from those that may have formal authority over them. For example, school principals have limited authority over the instructional activities of teachers. Hospital administrators have little control over clinical practices. Even when clear formal lines of authority are established, their effective use may be very limited since those with formal authority may be unable to sanction their subordinates because of civil service or tenure provisions, or lack of control over wages, salaries, and other potential rewards or punishments.

Similarly, staff may be subjected to multiple and often conflicting lines of authority, which reduce their effectiveness. Nurses are subject to the authority of both their nursing supervisors and the attending physicians. Teachers are subject to the "administrative" authority of the principal and the "professional" authority of curriculum supervisors. Social workers are often subject to similar dual lines of authority.

Thinking of a human service organization as a loosely coupled system does not imply that all its parts should be characterized this way. In fact, some facets of an organization's activities may be tightly coupled—that is, subject to an explicitly defined technology, operative monitoring and evaluation mechanisms, and effective authority. For example, the service delivery process of basic welfare grants is more tightly coupled than the provision of social services. The certification of students as high school or college graduates is far more tightly coupled than the instructional process itself (Meyer and Rowan, 1978). Admissions and discharge procedures in psychiatric hospitals are more tightly coupled than the treatment process (Strauss et al., 1967).

Undoubtedly, the characteristics of an organization's technologies influence the extent to which activities and tasks are tightly or loosely coupled. Nonetheless, such characteristics are organizationally determined, and hence cannot fully explain the structural choices made by an organization. Instead, human service organizations will develop tightly coupled systems around those activities and tasks that directly affect the enlistment of legitimation and procurement of resources. In particular, those organizational activities and performances selected by key providers of legitimation and resources to evaluate the organization and to determine its future resources are likely to be highly coordinated, controlled, and carefully monitored. In the case of the welfare department, for example, its legitimation and future resources are closely linked to its efficient administration of welfare grants, not to the quality or adequacy of its social services. (Indeed, federal funding is contingent on not exceeding a certain error rate in eligibility determination.) In a study of publicly funded psychiatric hospitals, Ullman (1967) found that because funding was determined by average daily patient load, admissions and discharges, and hence length of stay, were carefully monitored and coordinated to protect the hospital's funding level. Similarly, Meyer and Rowan (1978) have argued that the tight control over the certification of students, class scheduling, and credentialing of teachers contrasts sharply with the lack of control over instructional activities, due to the greater importance of the former in enlisting legitimation and ensuring a steady flow of resources from the community.

What forces operate on human service organizations to generate loosely coupled structures? I shall demonstrate that the determinants of such structures are rooted in the character of the environment, the nature of the technologies, and the patterns of client-official encounters.

Turbulent Environment, Multiple
Interests, and Disparate Goals

Human service organizations are likely to encounter a turbulent task environment that has several distinct features (see Chapter 3). First, it is composed of heterogeneous units and groups with competing claims and interests in the organization. These include providers of resources and legitimation, regulatory agencies, interest groups, potential and actual service beneficiaries, and employees. Second, both the composition of the task environment and the interests of its elements are unstable. That is, an organization will experience frequent uncertainties and changes in its relations with its resource providers and regulators because their interests and demands are influx (reflecting, undoubtedly, the turbulence in *their* environments). Moreover, new interest groups and service beneficiaries are likely to arise, while others alter their demands, because definitions of human services are highly sensitive to social change. Third, and most important, human service organizations increasingly depend on the task environment for resources, which makes them vulnerable to challenges and threats to their domain.

An organization's survival and adaptation to a turbulent environment necessitate that these different interests and demands find expression inside the organization, so that it can demonstrate responsiveness to its multiple constituencies. It does this by pursuing multiple goals and by allocating resources to distinctly bounded clusters of activities that respond to particular interests or demands. Furthermore, the links and ties among these clusters of activities are purposefully made weak and tenuous because of the potential incompatabilities and contradictions among the interests and demands expressed through them. That is, the integrity of the organization and the minimization of conflict among disparate goals is achieved precisely through the loose coupling of the various internal work units.

The impact of a turbulent environment in uncoupling the internal structure of an organization is eloquently demonstrated by Jacobs (1977) in his historical study of Stateville, a large state prison, normally thought of as a highly controlled, tightly monitored organization. From the mid-1930s to the early 1960s the prison functioned in a relatively stable environment. Few outside organizations or groups were concerned or interested in the prison, and those that were were effectively neutralized. The Department of Public Safety, which nominally controlled the prison, was weak because of political cronyism. Prison reform interest groups, such as the John Howard Society, also had weak leadership and little influence. The courts seldom challenged prison administrative practices, and inmates did not have access to the courts. Professionals, such as psychologists, doctors, and chaplains, had no independent bases of power, and their advice and recommendations were routinely ignored. The state legislators and members of the press that occasionally visited the prison were effectively coopted by the warden who controlled all the information disseminated to them. Finally, the inmate population was fairly stable, with low turnover rates due to long sentence terms, and its racial mix had changed little during that time period.

Such a stable and relatively noninterfering environment enabled the prison to attain considerable autonomy and permitted the warden to exercise total dominance over its affairs. Authority was highly concentrated and the prison operated in a militaristic style. All prison activities were carefully monitored; rewards and sanctions were effectively controlled by the organizational elite; and lines of authority were explicit and without challenge. In short, the prison was a model of a tightly coupled system.

All this changed drastically in the 1960s and 1970s, due largely to the onset of considerable turbulence in the prison's environment. Several concomitant developments brought this about. First, the prison population became increasingly black and politicized. The inmate social structure was organized and controlled by active gangs whose members were incarcerated at increasing rates. They persistently challenged prison authority by relying on their access to the legal system. Second, the legal system became actively involved in prison practices through numerous law suits initiated by public interest law groups that sprang up in the 1960s. Particularly active was a group of lawyers who formed the Prison Legal Services, supported by various foundations and governmental agencies. The intrusion of the legal system constrained the old authority patterns in the prison and provided inmates with some minimal rights hitherto not available to them. Third, other interest groups became actively interested in the prison. These included various prison reform groups that had their roots in the civil rights movement; universities and colleges who were brought in by the Department of Corrections (formerly the Department of Public Safety) to assist in improving conditions in the prison; and the press, which through the professionalization of its reporters was less likely to be coopted by prison officials. Fourth, the Department of Corrections, through its own bureaucratization, acquired greater power and control over the prison. It issued a Unified Code of Correction and other administrative regulations, which reduced the discretion of prison wardens. It required the hiring of various professional staff, such as schoolteachers and counselors, who operated outside the hierarchical authority of the prison guard system. Finally, the guards unionized, largely to protect their own interests in the face of the major changes taking place.

These and other similar changes in the prison's environment resulted, first and foremost, in the breakdown of authority lines in the prison. Multiple centers of authority emerged, anchored in the Department of Corrections, the prison warden, the inmate organization, the guards' union, and the professional units. Second, numerous prison activities and tasks became uncoupled from each other. Custodial care was separated from educational activities and from counselling, and the administration of the prison was only weakly tied to the guard system. After a period of internal turbulence, a gradual state of equilibrium emerged as the various spheres of activities in the prison, reflecting the external influences on its goals and functions, became somewhat insulated from each other and controlled by their own specific sets of regulations.

Indeterminate Technology and Ambiguous Evaluation Criteria

The components of any human service technology—client attributes, knowledge base, staff-client interaction, client control, and operations—will determine the staff's perceptions of their service tasks. For example, when interest in client biography is limited, when clients are assumed to be non-variable and stable, when knowledge on which to serve them is viewed as complete, and when the appropriate pattern of interaction is activity-passivity, then the service tasks are likely to be seen as routine, predictable, and efficacious. In contrast, when clients are viewed as variable and unstable, knowledge as incomplete, and the pattern of interaction as requiring mutual participation, then the service tasks are likely to be viewed as nonroutine and unpredictable, and their consequences viewed as uncertain. These task perceptions in turn, relate to the work arrangements developed in the organization. In general, the greater the clarity, predictability, and efficacy of the task perceptions, the greater the ability of the organization to develop tightly coupled work arrangements—that is, standardized and routinized procedures, explicit evaluation and monitoring mechanisms, and hierarchical authority (Dornbusch and Scott, 1975). This is so because such task perceptions enable the formulation of specific outcome measures, clear behavioral directives, and explicit sequencing and coordination of the various task components. In their study of nurses, for example, Dornbusch and Scott (1975) found that in recordkeeping and carrying out doctors' orders, nurses had considerably less autonomy and freedom than in ward management, because the former had clear behavioral directions and could be readily monitored.

A great many human service technologies are characterized by task perceptions that are unclear and unpredictable. Hence, it is not surprising to find that work arrangements are loosely structured in organizations deploying such technologies. Several advantages accrue to the organization from developing loosely structured work arrangements. First, by promoting autonomy, reducing regulations, and limiting the influence of other work units, the organization provides the staff with a working environment consonant with their task perceptions. When staff perceive tasks as nonroutine and their consequences uncertain, they want to be free to rely on their own judgment and to alter tasks on the basis of feedback from their work. Second, the focus of responsibility is shifted to the staff members themselves. Both success and failure can be attributed to the encounters between staff and clients, rather than to overall organizational policies and procedures. Third, the rest of the organization is protected from the technological uncertainties. By uncoupling work units with indeterminate technologies from other parts of the organization, the potential ripple effects of unpredictable consequences of technologies on the rest of the organization are minimized. Fourth, the organization can circumvent the issue of evaluating the achievements of its service technologies since no clear criteria can be formulated. Rather, the organization is likely to rely on extrinsic measures of achievement, which may be based on self or peer appraisals, client testimonies, and reputation (Thompson, 1967).

The relationship between indeterminate technology and the evaluation of performance merits special attention because of its impact on the exercise of authority in the organization and subsequent work arrangements. Undoubtedly, the exercise of authority rests, to a large extent, on the capability of those in authority positions to evaluate the performance of their subordinates, either by monitoring actual behavior or by assessing the outcomes of their activities. When the technology is indeterminate, performance evaluation becomes exceedingly difficult for several reasons (Dornbush and Scott, 1975). First, since outcomes are uncertain, there are serious problems in defining what constitutes success. Second, agreed-upon conceptions of success may not be readily measurable. Third, criteria for assessing task performance are difficult to formulate because knowledge is incomplete and clients are unstable and variable. Fourth, and related to the above, determining an appropriate sampling for monitoring staff activities is difficult. Finally, the content of staff-client encounters is not readily visible, and hence difficult to monitor.

Lack of an adequate performance evaluation system significantly limits the exercise of authority in the organization, because it increases the dependence of those in authority on their subordinates for feedback and information. As I noted earlier, a weak authority structure is one characteristic of a loosely coupled organization. It is through the relationships between indeterminate technology, ambiguous evaluation criteria, and weak authority that one can explain how such a structure evolves.

In a more general way, loose coupling enables human service organizations to accommodate different and often incompatible moral and ideological systems espoused by its various staff members. This is particularly evident when an organization is dependent on the services of several professional groups. Through their training, socialization, work experience, and personal attributes staff develop distinct belief systems about their clients, which influence their perceptions about the goals of the services and about the *means* through which these goals ought to be attained. Although the organization may attempt to limit the ideological variability among its staff through selection and socialization, it can hardly eliminate it, particularly when it employs professionally trained staff with various competencies and expertise. The indeterminacy of the service technology further reinforces such variability and diversity and constrains the ability of the organization to check them. To do so might risk internal strife and conflicts, and publicly expose the vagueness of the organization's service technology. Loose coupling permits the expression of various service ideologies within the organization, thus minimizing potential conflict. Strauss and associates (1967), studying the internal work arrangements in psychiatric hospitals, evoke the image of a "negotiated order." Physicians, social workers, nurses, and attendants—all of whom may hold different psychiatric ideologies—develop, through a series of negotiations, acceptable work arrangements that are compatible with their respective ideologies. Somatically oriented physicians may work together with certain nurses who accommodate their treatment ideology, while social workers may develop close work relations with milieu-therapy physicians and have hardly any contact with the somaticists. In the process of negotiation, formal rules may be ignored or disregarded, and lines of authority may be bypassed.

Front-Line or Street-Level Bureaucrats

Probably the single most important factor contributing to the loose structure in human services organizations is the ubiquitousness of staff-client relations. Several characteristics of these relations limit an organization's ability to control them. First, the primary source of initiative in the agency resides in these relations, not in the formal authority structure (Smith, 1965). That is, organizational activities are initiated through encounters between clients and line staff rather than through directives communicated via the chain of command. Rarely can the organization specify in advance the service processes for each client.

Second, the visibility and observability of these relations, so essential for effective monitoring, is highly limited. With few exceptions, their content is not readily open to inspection for several reasons: (1) numerous legal and ethical restrictions protect the confidentiality of the information exchanged between client and worker; (2) human service practitioners strongly believe that the quality of the relationship and the trust between them and the client will be adversely affected by any external intrusion; (3) the lack of reliable and valid performance evaluation criteria makes the direct observation of staff-client relations a highly volatile supervisory tool that may cause serious conflicts over interpretations of observations; (4) administrative costs of direct monitoring of staff-client relations are exceedingly high because the organization cannot fully anticipate or control their initiation, and because direct monitoring requires a substantial commitment of personnel and time; and (5) in the case of professional staff, direct monitoring is viewed as a serious infringement of professional autonomy and a challenge to professional competence.

Third, and as a result of the above, much of the information generated in these relations is effectively controlled by line staff. That is, the staff controls the client information that is passed on to the organization, as well as the information about the organization that is passed on to the client (Prottas, 1979). In processing welfare applications, for example, the worker has considerable discretion in deciding what client information to accept or ignore, how to record it, and what to tell the applicant about the procedures and services of the agency. Similarly, while line police officers are given commands about what to investigate, they have considerable discretion in conducting the investigation and deciding what to do about it, exactly because they control the acquisition of the information for these decisions (Reiss, 1971: 124–25).

Finally, the relations between the client and various staff members are not readily coordinated because each relationship is highly affected by its context—namely, the attributes and interests of the interacting parties, the reasons and purposes of the interaction, and its location and duration. Thus, there is no assurance that the relations between the patient and the physician will be consonant with the patient's relations with the nurse, or with the social worker, because each relationship is controlled by different factors.

These characteristics of staff-client relations accord line staff considerable discretion. Smith (1965) has proposed that they generate a "frontline" organizational structure (to borrow a military metaphor). In such a structure, line staff function quite autonomously from the rest of the organization; task interdependence is low between work units; and there are significant barriers to effective supervision. Expanding on this notion, Lipsky (1980) conceptualizes lower-level staff who assume the major daily responsibility of interacting with clients in human service organizations as "street-level bureaucrats." Despite their low position in the formal authority structure, street-level bureaucrats exercise considerable discretion because they work in situations too complex to be routinized, they work in situations requiring responses to variable and unpredictable human conditions, and clients come to believe that they hold the key to their welfare.

Street-level bureaucrats use this discretion to maintain their relative autonomy and to promote their own interests, which are likely to differ from those of their superiors. These differences would inevitably arise from the fact that street-level bureaucrats must function in a context and under circumstances seldom covered by agency policies. Street-level bureaucrats deal with vague multiple organizational goals and policies; variable, unpredictable client behavior; service demands that outstrip the available resources; and copious paper work. Furthermore, they feel a need to uphold their own personal and professional ideologies. By using and enhancing their discretion, street-level bureaucrats can resolve these dilemmas by structuring their relations with clients, at least in part, on their *own* terms.

The Consequences of Loose Coupling on the Service Delivery Process

We have seen that loose coupling can serve several functions for the organization. It enables some units to respond to changes and developments in the environment without being constrained by others. It enables the organization to manage and cope with ill-defined service technologies. It protects the rest of the organization from the failures of any given unit. It enables the organization to accommodate opposing service ideologies and reduce conflict, and it promotes professional autonomy (Weick, 1976).

The impact of loose coupling on the service delivery process is less clear. On the one hand, such a structure promotes innovation and experimentation with new ideas that may benefit clients. On the other hand, it can produce a fragmented and disjointed service delivery system. In a loosely coupled structure, control over the quality of the services shifts to the particular staff person or unit with whom the client comes into contact. Consequently, the quality of the services given to a client will vary appreciably with the interests, competence, and skills of the staff person or unit.

Loose coupling can also result in an uncoordinated, disjointed, and even contradictory service delivery process. Clients, of course, cannot readily separate and segregate their experiences with the various parts of the organization. Yet the burden falls on them to integrate and make sense of the diverse practices, directives, and advice they receive from the various units. In a psychiatric hospital, for example, a patient may be rewarded by attendants for being passive and compliant, encouraged by the social worker to be assertive, given psychotropic drugs by nurses, and encouraged by the psychotherapist to reduce his or her dependency on all such drugs. Similarly, the AFDC recipient may receive conflicting directives and advice from various workers: stay home and take care of your children; enroll in a training program; seek employment; reconcile marital discord; press charges for child support; and the like. One can assume that under these circumstances clients will become confused, discouraged, and alienated. Not surprisingly, Smith and King (1975) found, in their nationwide study of mental hospitals, that the quality of care was highly correlated with overall coordination, and that patient discharge was correlated with effective supervision—both of which are characteristics of tightly coupled systems.

SOURCES OF POWER IN
THE ORGANIZATION

In abstract terms, the power of members in an organization is a function of the amount of resources they control. Referring back to Emerson's formulation (1962), the power of a unit (individual or group) varies directly with the organization's need for the resources controlled by that unit and varies inversely with the availability of the resource elsewhere. These resources may be money, legitimation, clients, expertise, or manpower. The organization's relative need for each of these resources and their availability will vary over time, and power will shift among units who control access to them. For example, Perrow (1963), in his case study of the evolution of a general hospital, has shown that as the hospital's need for resources changed from capital and legitimation to medical expertise, the power of the physicians rose and that of the trustees declined. When the hospital's need for managerial expertise became important, the physicians had to share their power with the administrative cadre.

From this perspective, Hinings and associates (1974) have proposed the following steps of power attainment in an organization: (1) the unit (individuals or staff groups) enters an area of high uncertainty for the organization (e.g., procurement of resources, attainment of technical proficiency); (2) the unit effectively copes with the uncertainty; (3) no other unit can substitute for the skills acquired by that unit; (4) the unit activities become central to the performance of other units.

Individuals or groups in the organization can use their initial power to beget more power by seizing control of the organizational activities that meet the above conditions (e.g. budgeting). For example, in their study of the relative power of various departments in a large university, Salancik and Pfeffer (1974) found that the best predictor of departmental power was the outside research funds it mobilized. Using their power, such departments have greater representation on resource allocation committees and obtain a larger proportion of university resources, which further strengthens their ability to obtain research funds. Moreover, those in power may determine areas of high uncertainty and centrality in the organization in order to buttress their own importance. Studying the power relations in a community mental health center, Lorber and Satow (1977) noted that the psychiatrists who dominated the center because of their reputation and prestige defined the preferred treatment technology as psychoanalytically oriented therapy in which they, of course, had the most expertise. Consequently, that form of therapy was accorded the highest prestige in the agency, and clients amenable to it were perceived as most desirable. The least-preferred therapy—provision of concrete services—was delegated to paraprofessionals.

Individuals and groups in an organization may also acquire power as a result of their external links with powerful elements in the environment.

Affiliation with major legitimators, favorable relations with providers of resources, and ability to attract desirable clients are instances of such links. As these external resources become concentrated in fewer elements, those having effective relations with them will be accorded considerable power. It could be hypothesized that as resources become more concentrated, power in the organization will become more centralized (Pfeffer, 1978).

Power may also be acquired through the possession of special skills and expertise essential to the management or control of a core technology that cannot readily be replaced. In a comparative analysis of juvenile correctional institutions, Zald (1962) found that, cottage parents in custodial institutions were perceived as having more power than social workers, while in individual-treatment institutions, the opposite was true. In milieu-treatment institutions, which required a "team" approach, both groups were perceived as having equal power.

If skills can be routinized, they become replaceable. Hence, routinization of tasks reduces the potential power of those assigned to them. Therefore, as the service technology becomes more routinized, power will become concentrated at a higher level. In the same study, Zald (1962) found that in custodial institutions, where the tasks of line staff were quite routinized, power was concentrated in the hands of the superintendent, whereas in the treatment institutions, power was shared among the heads of various programs. Yet, because line staff function as street-level bureaucrats, there are limits to the organization's ability to routinize their activities, even when it is technologically feasible.

Authority

Power is also attained or acknowledged through the possession of formal authority. In recognition of the differential importance of various tasks and their requisite skills and expertise, the organization differentially allocates formal authority to them. In particular, increasing authority is granted to those tasks which direct and coordinate the activities of others in the organization. To recall, Simon (1976: 125) defined authority "as the power to make decisions which guide the actions of others." It is manifested by the fact that a subordinate "permits his behavior to be guided by the decision of a superior without independently examining the merits of that decision" (Simon 1976: 11).

In contrast to other forms of power, authority is based on the recognition of its "legitimacy." In formulating his theory of bureaucracy, Weber (1947) distinguished between three types of authority on the basis of their legitimacy: (1) legal-rational authority, which is based on the legality of the commands; (2) traditional authority, which is attained through inheritance and is sanctified by tradition; and (3) charismatic authority, which is based on the personal appeal and exemplary qualities of a leader. Bureaucratic authority, while it may draw on both tradition and charisma, is fundamentally justified on the basis of accepted laws and social norms. It was Barnard (1938) who pointed out that the effectiveness of authority depends on the willingness of the subordinates to recognize it as legitimate. Therefore, the power inherent in formal authority is a function of the weight of the legal sanctions attached to it *and* its endorsement by subordinates (Dornbusch and Scott, 1975). That is, the amount of authority a position holder in an organization can exercise depends on: the importance and severity of the legal sanctions at his or her disposal; and the acceptance by subordinates of the legitimacy, appropriateness, and fairness of the directives he or she issues. For example, in a university the authority of departmental chairpersons over their faculties is quite limited because the sanctions they can impose are highly circumscribed. Similarly, social workers may attempt to circumvent the authority of their supervisors if they perceive their directives to be unfair or inappropriate.

The distribution of authority in an organization is inherently hierarchical. Tannenbaum (1974) regards this as a universal characteristic of all organizations, and his empirical studies of diverse organizations in different countries support his proposition. The reasons for the universality of hierarchical authority are not difficult to discern. First, it establishes clear lines of responsibility and accountability; it defines who is responsible for the actions of others via the chain of command. Second, it provides for a system of controls to ensure staff compliance. Third, it enables the coordination of various tasks by means of hierarchical centers of responsibility.

The importance of authority in granting power to its holders should not be underestimated. As Zeitz (1980) found, even in professional organizations, those with hierarchical authority were more likely to participate in decision making. This is particularly evident at times of crisis, when the importance of formal authority is magnified as the source of decisions moves up in the hierarchy (Peabody, 1964).

Nonetheless, the congruence between formal authority and the exercise of power is at best partial, because other sources of power in an organization are not necessarily expressed in formal authority. For example, longevity and experience may give a subordinate considerably more influence than a newly arrived supervisor. Put differently, the dynamics of power relations are far too fluid to be effectively expressed in a rigid formal hierarchy. Nor is it always desirable for power wielders to formalize their status; they may be far more effective by operating behind the scenes.

In general, the congruence between formal authority and the exercise of power will be greater in tightly coupled than in loosely coupled organizations. The former, characterized by a stable environment and a determinate technology, can establish an authority structure that is not challenged by change, ambiguity, and uncertainty. In contrast, in loosely coupled organizations the formal authority structure is constantly undermined by environmental uncertainty, goal ambiguity, and technological indeterminacy. In loosely coupled organizations, a substantial incongruence exists between the formal authority system and the actual distribution of power. The same factors which shape the internal structure and the distribution of power in human service organizations, generate considerable divergence between the possession of formal authority and the actual exercise of power. Examples are abundant. School principals find that they can exert much less power over their teachers than indicated by their formal position (Lorti, 1975). Hospital attendants and nurses exercise more power over their patients than indicated by their formal authority (Smith, 1965). And welfare workers exercise more discretion than is permitted officially (Prottas, 1979).

The exercise of power through formal authority depends on the ability of the position holder to monitor and evaluate the performance of his or her subordinates and to sanction them on the basis of such evaluation. Yet, the capacity of human service organizations to do so is highly constrained, thus reducing the effectiveness of formal authority.

Professionalization

Power may also be acquired through professional status, which provides links to external sources of legitimation, prestige, and reputation, as well as control over a body of knowledge and skills that cannot readily be replaced. According to Freidson (1973: 22), *professionalization* can be defined as "a process by which an organized occupation, usually but not always by virtue of making a claim to special esoteric competence and to concern for the quality of its work and its benefits to society, obtains the exclusive right to perform a particular kind of work, control training for and access to it, and control the right of determining and evaluating the way the work is performed."

This definition makes clear that the power of a profession emanates from two sources. First, a profession undertakes a domain of activities that incorporates a high degree of uncertainty, both because of the nature of the activities and the complexity and incompleteness of the body of knowledge (Nilson, 1979). Such uncertainty, coupled with a strong demand for the services of the profession, makes the recipients of its services highly dependent. However, this is a necessary but not sufficient condition for acquiring professional power, since it does not of itself ensure the profession a monopoly on the services and relevant knowledge. Second, then, the profession must be granted exclusive rights to these services and knowledge from the state (Freidson, 1970; Johnson, 1972). It obtains these rights by accommodating the state through control of deviants, maintenance of dominant values and ideologies, and general support of the political system. The state, in turn, delegates some of its power to the profession, permitting it to regulate itself while providing protection from encroachment by other occupational groups.

In the process of professionalization, the organized occupation develops a set of ideologies that defines its values and mission and prescribes appropriate codes of ethics and behavior for its members. These ideologies, which we term "professionalism," are aimed at further enhancing the legitimation of the profession.

Professional power is, then, manifested through the ability of the members of the profession to determine and control the conditions of their work and to attain autonomy from organizational evaluation and administrative authority. Accordingly, human services occupations vary in their degree of professionalization; they range from physicians, who enjoy the highest degree of professional power, to social workers, teachers, and nurses (who are classified as *semiprofessionals*), to hospital attendants, eligibility workers, and prison guards (who are classified as *paraprofessionals*).

Semiprofessionals merit closer scrutiny since clients are most likely to encounter them in their quest for services. They tend to function as buffers between the public and the more prestigious professions; they also control access to professionals. There is a tendency to define a semiprofessional as belonging to an occupation that lacks one or more of the attributes of the "ideal type" profession (Etzioni, 1969). Such a definition is wanting because it is based on professional rhetoric and symbols and fails to address itself to the sources of professional power. The duties of social workers, clinical psychologists, or psychiatrists may be indistinguishable, yet each group enjoys its special professional power. Rather, semiprofessionals are better characterized by their lack of exclusive control over their services and body of knowledge, even though the state acknowledges their unique domain. The acknowledgment is typically in the form of certification based on a specified course of training that is usually controlled by the semiprofessional group. But, the occupational association is not granted the right to police itself, nor is it given exclusive control over the body of knowledge it claims for itself. As a result, semiprofessionals are subject to greater organizational evaluation and administrative authority and have less control over the content and conditions of their work. It is for this reason that Epstein (1970) found, for example, that the attitudes of social workers toward social action were determined by organizational factors rather than by professionalization. Similarly, Coser (1963) noted that the work setting strongly influences how nurses view their professional roles and carry out their duties.

The employment of professionals in the organization poses a potential conflict between professional autonomy and bureaucratic authority (Hall, 1968). However, such a conflict may be more imaginary than real if it is recognized that both bureaucratization and professionalism are alternative mechanisms of control. Through bureaucratization, the organization relies on task specification, routinization, and formalization of procedures to set limits on staff performance. Through professionalism, the organization relies on internalized professional standards and norms to set such limits.

Moreover, the organization develops an internal structure that facilitates the work of the professional, while preserving overall administrative coordination. It does so in several ways. First, it develops what Goss (1963) has termed an "advisory bureaucracy." In such a structure, the professional is subject to hierarchical authority *only* in areas that fall outside the professional sphere, such as scheduling and setting of fees, while the same authority becomes *advisory* with reference to professional matters. Second, the organization formalizes and standardizes *regulative rules*, which pertain to personnel management, requisition of resources and equipment, and reporting, but not *operative rules*, which pertain to the actual work to be done (Zey-Ferrell, 1979). Third, the organization segregates professional from nonprofessional activities by separating their respective work units.

Conflict with semiprofessionals is more likely to arise since they lack the power to back their claims for professional autonomy and control over their working conditions. Their claims for exclusive control over a sphere of activities and knowledge will be challenged both by the administrative authority and by the more prestigious professionals. This conflict is best exemplified in the case of nursing. Nurses occupy a unique and highly ambivalent position in the hospital's social structure. On the one hand, they carry out low-level administrative functions related to patient care delegated to them by management. On the other hand, they perform medical functions under the control and guidance of physicians (Reeder and Mauksch, 1979). Conflict arises when nurses attempt to gain control over their administrative functions in the face of resistance by hospital and medical administrators who are legally responsible for patient care. It also arises when nurses attempt to gain professional autonomy over certain medical procedures, only to face resistance from the physicians who dominate the medical division of labor (Krause, 1977).

Social workers find themselves in a similar predicament. When employed in multiprofessional settings, they are likely to be delegated to perform activities defined as "dirty work" by the more prominent professions. These may include working with less-desirable clients, performing tasks that are not professionally "exciting," or serving as buffers between clients and prestigious professionals. Even when not dominated by other professions, they are still dominated by administrative authority. In contrast to the advisory bureaucracy model, professional and administrative authority tend to blur in social work agencies. Supervisors are often colleagues who have become administrators and blend both administrative and professional criteria in their evaluation and exercise of authority. To quote Ruzek (1973: 233), "social work administrators and supervisors judge and evaluate their 'colleagues' on the basis of agency, rather than purely professional, goals."

Conflict over the appropriate exercise of authority is also manifested in teaching. It is essentially a conflict between the teachers' desire for professional autonomy and the authority of school administrators (Corwin, 1970).

Although teachers may have considerable freedom in classroom instruction, they have much less control over curriculum requirements, certification of students, discipline codes, scheduling, and other decisions that greatly affect their work conditions.

The push for upward mobility by semiprofessionals has significant consequences for the delivery of services. In their efforts to gain professional status and recognition, semiprofessionals attempt to delegate downward what they consider dirty work, resulting in the emergence of a paraprofessional cadre of workers such as nurse's aides, teacher aides, social work technicians, and the like. Not surprisingly, staff for these positions are heavily recruited from the lower social strata; women and oppressed minorities thus become overrepresented. Assigned to the less-desirable jobs in an already dominant professional caste system, they have few opportunities to move up. These factors, coupled with low organizational rewards, foster workers' alienation (Lipsky, 1980). And yet, in many human service organizations such as hospitals, nursing homes, and welfare departments, paraprofessionals carry the major burden of contact with the clients. One can readily conjecture the effects of low organizational status, limited rewards and opportunities, and alienation on the quality of worker-client encounters. Low-level staff are more likely to be motivated to reduce the disagreeable aspects of their work and to minimize their investment in it than to look after the welfare of clients.

In addition, some evidence suggests that aspiring professionals tend to increase their social distance from the poor and other "less-desirable" clients (Walsh and Elling, 1968). That is, prestige may be sought through serving higher-status clients and organizations. In this sense, aspiring professionals are simply following the same path historically taken by some professions now well-established (Johnson, 1972). Moreover, in searching for "desirable" clients, aspiring professionals try to demonstrate their success and effectiveness and to convince the public of their worth and importance. Consequently, those who most need their services may be the least likely to obtain them (Cloward and Epstein, 1965).

Internal Structure and Power

The internal structuring of the organization is, first and foremost, the consequence of power relations among its participants (Pfeffer, 1978). Those having bases of power in the organization use their resources "to recreate the rules, positions, and budgetary allocations which ensure the reproduction of those bases. Thus the structural framework [of the organization] is not some abstract chart but one of the crucial instruments by which groups perpetuate their power and control in organizations" (Ranson, Hinings, and Greenwood, 1980: 8).

Nowhere is this pattern better exemplified than in the division of labor in the hospital. The dominance of the medical profession is pervasive, and the hospital is structured to maintain it (Freidson, 1970; Krause, 1977). This is manifested in several ways. First, more than any other health practitioners, physicians exercise maximal organizational autonomy in structuring their work arrangements. Both patients and other workers in the hospital must comply with a physician's definition of the work to be done, the manner in which it should be carried out, and its scheduling. Second, all other health practitioners in the hospital are subordinate to and under the control of physicians. Whatever they do to serve patients is derived from physician-delegated authority. Third, the structural differentiation of the hospital is designed to protect and enhance the medical specializations of physicians. Finally, much of the physicians' work is not subject to any external scrutiny or evaluation.

In the same vein, the designation and assignment of the dirty work in an organization is a reflection of the distribution of power in it. Powerful members designate as dirty work those activities which they perceive to be burdensome and undignified, and assign them to lower-status members (Hughes, 1971). In human services, this is particularly evident in the division of labor among the various professional groups that reflects their relative prestige. Hence, in mental health settings, for example, dirty work is defined as the handling of chronic and after-care patients, and crisis intervention with persons of lower social status (Emerson and Pollner, 1976). This definition is derived from the practice ideologies and expertise of prestigious professionals (i.e., psychiatrists), who are oriented toward verbal, intelligent, motivated patients. Dirty work is, then, assigned mostly to paraprofessionals or semiprofessionals such as social workers, and is typically avoided by the higher-status professionals such as psychiatrists (Lorber and Satow, 1977).

In short, the stratification of the staff according to their relative power is paralleled by the stratification of work according to its desirability and value to each stratum. Work is, thus, assigned so that it maintains and supports the congruence between its ascribed value and the power and prestige of the worker. In doing so, the division of labor confirms the distribution of power in the organization.

THE EXERCISE OF CONTROL

Power, discretion, and control are, of course, three dimensions of the same organizational dynamic—namely, the ability to protect one's interests in the organization. Thus, the distribution of power determines who exercises how much control over whom.

In general, effective organizational control depends on structuring staff roles in accordance with organizational specifications, on monitoring and evaluating staff performance, and on allocating rewards and sanctions on the basis of such evaluation (Hage, 1974; Dornbush and Scott, 1975). As noted, human service organizations experience considerable difficulty in developing an effective control system. Technological ambiguities make it difficult to specify the appropriate roles various staff members should assume. Second, task visibility and observability is quite low in human service organizations, particularly because the actual provision of services is in the hands of street-level bureaucrats. Third, evaluation criteria are also ambiguous and vague and lack wide acceptance. Finally, as public organizations, many human service organizations are subject to civil service regulations and tenure provisions that reduce their ability to allocate rewards and sanctions consonant with performance evaluation.

According to Ouchi (1977), organizations may focus on two types of control: (1) behavior control: ensuring that tasks are performed in accordance with organizational specifications; and (2) output control: ensuring that the consequences of staff activities meet the organization's output goals. To accomplish both types of control, an organization may deploy indirect means such as recruitment and selection, standard operating procedures, and various forms of coordination, and direct means such as socialization and indoctrination, supervision and evaluation. Table 6.1 lists the means that can be used to achieve each type of control.

Behavior Control

Reliance on behavior control makes it necessary for an organization to develop explicit job specifications and reduce worker discretion. In contrast, output control permits considerable worker discretion as long as the output objectives are met. Therefore, organizations will select behavior control over output control for those workers who have little power in the organization and whose work can be observed, standardized, and formalized.

TABLE 6.1   Types and Means of Organizational Control of Staff

MEANS OF CONTROL	TYPE OF CONTROL	
	BEHAVIOR	OUTPUT
Indirect	Standard operating procedures (e.g., forms, job specialization, and formalization)	Recruitment of experts (e.g., sponsorship)
	Coordination by plan (e.g., schedules)	Coordination by feedback (e.g., teams)
Overt	Sanctions based on behavior monitoring (e.g., bureaucratic review, supervision)	Sanctions based on evaluation of outcome
	Indoctrination to operating norms	Socialization to practice ideologies

The establishment of standard operating procedures to formalize and routinize the work of low-level staff in human service organizations is difficult because of the staff's front-line position. The organization must develop a system that limits the amount and type of information available to the workers, reduces their decision alternatives, and prescribes courses of action for all anticipated events. Circumscribing the amount and types of information transmitted to and from staff is accomplished by the extensive use of forms. Forms structure the encounter between client and worker by setting boundaries around its content, by specifying the relevant information to be collected, and by defining the appropriate transformation of the information into acceptable organizational symbols and labels. Subsequent actions are limited and guided by the information encapsulated in the forms. Moreover, forms serve as critical devices for monitoring workers' behavior. Not surprisingly, attempts by human service organizations to rationalize and control their service delivery process are frequently accompanied by a proliferation of forms.

The effectiveness of forms as a control device is, however, limited because they are vulnerable to manipulation. Unless the organization has independent means of verification, the validity and reliability of the recorded information is subject to both client and staff vagaries. Clients may withold, distort, or fabricate information to improve their chances of obtaining desired services. Workers may record misinformation to enhance and protect their interests and, in general, to improve their work conditions. In this sense, the information recorded on the forms serves to justify decisions already made (Wheeler, 1969).

Forms also have a paradoxical consequence on staff-client relations. On the one hand, by delimiting the content of the encounter, forms protect clients from unneeded encroachment into their private lives. On the other hand, forms force clients to define their problems and needs within a prescribed framework and greatly frustrate their efforts to convey the uniqueness of their situation.

Reduction of decision alternatives is accomplished through job specialization and formalization. This is, of course, the classical notion of the division of labor. It encapsulates the divisions of the service delivery process into a series of specific tasks so that each task can be standardized, requiring a well-defined, highly circumscribed skill. These tasks become formalized through explicit job descriptions. Hence, the core of job specialization and formalization is a reduction in the decision alternatives available to the workers (March and Simon, 1958). That is, each worker is assigned to a programmed decision area having the following characteristics: (1) it is activated only when specific information reaches the worker; (2) it has a set of explicit and delimited decision alternatives; and (3) the worker is provided with a set of rules on how to select the appropriate alternative (see also the discussion on decision-making theory in Chapter 2). For example, the division of labor in a typical employment office is such that the behavior of the placement worker is programmed. The worker assigns an occupational classification code to the applicant on the basis of information about past training and work experience. The job search process is limited to those openings that fall within a range of occupational codes similar to the applicant's, and the decision rule is to find the best match between the occupational codes of the applicant and the job opening (Hasenfeld, 1975).

Reduction of decision alternatives through job specialization and formalization is invariably accompanied by *coordination by plan*, in which the sequence of activities among various workers is determined in advance (Perrow, 1967; Van de Ven, Delbecq, and Koenig, 1976). Workers are controlled by a set of procedures that specify the scheduling and routing of each activity in the service delivery process. These procedures structure the work flow and minimize workers' discretion concerning initiation of a service activity, its sequence in the delivery process, and the involvement of other workers. All these decisions are determined in advance by an overall coordination plan to which the workers are expected to conform. The hospital admission process is a good example of coordination by plan. The patient is first seen by an admissions clerk, who obtains basic demographic and insurance information. From there the patient is routed to a series of medical tests prescribed in a given sequence. Upon completion of the tests, the patient returns to the admissions desk and is assigned a bed. With the exception of emergencies, few deviations occur.

Undoubtedly, the reduction of decision alternatives, coupled with coordination by plan, is one of the most effective indirect control mechanisms in human service organizations because it circumscribes workers' discretion and specifies rules workers must follow in making service decisions. Nonetheless, human service organizations' ability to program line-staff decisions effectively is constrained by the inherent variability and unpredictability of clients' attributes, which force organizations to promulgate more and more rules to cover all possible circumstances. In many instances these rules must be broadly and abstractly stated because clients' attributes and behaviors cannot be anticipated or defined in exact terms. Yet, the greater the proliferation of such rules, the less the capacity of the organization to monitor them and the greater the ability of workers to choose which rules to ignore. Prottas (1979) has argued that the proliferation of rules actually increases workers' discretion, because the applicability of each rule must be determined on a case-by-case basis, which makes monitoring exceedingly costly to the organization. Consequently, decisions by line staff to follow or ignore certain rules, particularly those that are difficult to monitor, may be based on their personal interests rather than on organizational standards.

Furthermore, some rules can be evaded because of the front-line characteristics of most human service organizations. It will be recalled that the ability of supervisors to monitor adherence to the rules depends on the information processed and provided to them by line staff, information which supervisors cannot readily verify independently. Therefore, workers can manipulate information to justify actions that might otherwise violate organizational rules. For example, the employment placement worker may ignore and not record some of the applicant's past work history to justify placement in a readily available job (Hasenfeld, 1975). A welfare worker may fail to explore a client's potential eligibility for certain benefits in order to minimize the work on that case (Prottas, 1979).

Still, by controlling the flow of information and by limiting the decision alternatives available to line staff, the organization can reduce opportunities for (and potential harm from) rule evasion during the service delivery process. Piliavin (1980) reports, for example, that by establishing flat-rate welfare grants (thereby limiting decision alternatives), welfare departments have significantly reduced payment errors. When line staff have few or no choices, the importance of rules as a control device diminishes.

Coordination by plan, while increasing uniformity and consistency in the service delivery process, may result in service fragmentation. Clients' problems and needs cannot be readily compartmentalized and responded to through neatly subdivided sequences of activities. Coordination by plan implicitly assumes that the service delivery process can be linearly ordered and that the effects of each service task on a client are additive rather than interactive. Such an assumption considerably simplifies the organizational view of a client by ignoring the interrelations and interdependencies among a client's attributes and needs. For example, a student's experience in one class clearly influences his or her behavior in other classes, yet school officials act as if a student's experiences are discreet and additive rather than interactive. Multiproblem clients applying for various welfare benefits find that they must compartmentalize their problems to fit each service category, although the justification for each service may depend on the acknowledgment of problems not formally under the jurisdiction of the worker in a particular category. This may result in a "catch-22" situation, where, for example, to qualify for medical benefits, the client must document physical incapacity requiring medical treatment, which the client cannot obtain for lack of medical benefits. Coordination by plan also exacts an additional psychological cost from clients, for it forces them to form a relationship with each successive worker in the service delivery process, and thus must cope anew with the uncertainties posed by each encounter.

The attainment of overt behavior control over line staff in human service organizations is far more difficult and costly; it is also typically less effective than indirect means of control because of the inherent problems in monitoring staff-client encounters. The organizational response to these difficulties is contingent on the relative power of the line staff in the organization. When line staff are relatively powerless, the organization will select and emphasize for monitoring those aspects of behavior that are observable and measurable, regardless of their relevance and importance to the service delivery process. These aspects may include such behaviors as keeping an adequate caseload size, keeping track of the frequency and duration of contacts with clients, maintaining complete and up-to-date records, accounting for the use of tangible resources (money and equipment), and adhering to work schedule requirements. Welfare workers, ward nurses, attendants, child care workers, and probation officers, for example, are most frequently subject to such behavior control, which we term *bureaucratic review.*

The imposition of bureaucratic review is constrained when the line staff exercise significant power in the organization, as in the case of professionals. Using their power, line staff will negotiate to shield their behaviors and encounters with clients from direct monitoring and make it consonant with their values and ideologies. Lacking direct access to the staff behavior, while accepting the legitimacy of its professional values and ideologies, the organization will then monitor line-staff motivation, affect, attitudes, and values. We term such monitoring *supervision,* the purpose of which is to achieve attitudinal and ideological conformity (Toren, 1972). In supervision, then, the information gathered about the attitudes and values of the staff serves as a proxy and an indirect measure of their actual behavior.

Supervisory techniques emulate both teacher-student and therapist-patient relationships. Like the former, supervisors attempt to serve as role models and coach line staff in organizationally acceptable and desirable behaviors. Like the latter, supervisors attempt to uncover feelings, attitudes, and values and use the interpersonal relationship to attain attitudinal and ideological conformity. The mix of both techniques varies with the service technology. Teacher-student type supervision is more prevalent when the technology requires that staff possess and practice specific, concrete technical skills, as in medicine. Therapeutic-type supervision is more prevalent when the technology focuses on cognitive and affective intervention and relies on staff-client interpersonal relations, as in psychotherapy or social casework.

Supervision, while preserving the autonomy of line staff over their work, can be manipulated by both supervisors and subordinates. Line staff can feign attitudinal and ideological compliance by seeming to accept the values espoused by supervisors without changing their behavior. They can also manipulate relations with clients to demonstrate attitudinal compliance. In a study of probation officers, McCleary (1975) found that, in order to protect their clients while supporting the official ideology of the agency, the officers occasionally had to lie to their superiors. In other instances, the officers made decisons about clients that were actually aimed at boosting their own reputations as "good" officers. Supervisors, in turn, also have considerable discretion in interpreting the self-images presented by line staff, and may use them to suit their own purposes. Consequently, supervision, particularly if based on a psychotherapeutic model, harbors the potential for serious conflicts between supervisors and line staff.

Finally, behavior control can be enhanced by indoctrinating line staff to the operating norms of the organization. That is, line staff can be indoctrinated to accept the rules and procedures developed by the organization as if they had intrinsic value and were an integral part of the tradition and reputation of the organization. Socializing of line staff to the merit of these norms, coupled with monitoring compliance with them, is likely to elicit ritualistic adherence to the norms.

Indoctrination to operating norms is more likely to be utilized in hierarchically structured organizations dominated by a small elite, because the norms also serve a latent function: to preserve and support the authority structure, as can be noted in the military. Thus, for example, Jacobs (1977) noted that when a state prison was dominated by a patriarchal authority, it was transformed into a paramilitary organization in which indoctrination of the guards to the operating norms and insistance on ritualistic compliance were the predominant modes of control.

Output Control

As suggested earlier, an organization is more likely to resort to output control when it cannot effectively reduce line-staff discretion. By specifying the desirable outputs and making staff accountable for them, an organization is able to direct staff to engage in tasks necessary to produce these outputs, without having to specify the nature of the tasks themselves. Thus, output control is most often exercised in professionally dominated organizations where the service technology is indeterminate and nonroutine.

Under these conditions, the organization must rely heavily on the recruitment of expertise. The recruitment process has a dual function: (1) to obtain personnel who possess the technical skills needed to achieve the output objectives; and (2) to delimit and constrain the range and type of expertise to reduce potential deviations from the output objectives. However, for many human service programs, the output objectives or goals cannot be readily specified, and thus a one-to-one correspondence does not exist between the goals and the skills required by the staff. Moreover, when *quality* of the output is added, the organization must also consider the competence of prospective employees, and this cannot be readily ascertained. As a result, human service organizations rely heavily on *credentials* as a major tool in assessing the qualifications of prospective staff. Credentials refer both to official certifications of technical skills and, most important, to the reputation and prestige of sponsors. These sponsors include training institutions, previous workplaces, and personal references. The reputation of sponsors becomes a key determinant of competence, substituting for objective criteria. Furthermore, sponsorship becomes even more important to the organization when its core technology is based on a distinctive practice ideology that requires ideological compatibility. Ideological compatibility is a powerful control mechanism because it ensures not only the staff's commitment to the organization's service objectives, but also their acceptance of the legitimacy of the power distribution in the organization (Dornbusch and Scott, 1975). Thus, knowledge of the ideological orientation of a prospective staff person's sponsors is indispensable to an organization.

The emphasis on credentials, particularly sponsorship, as recruitment devices, clearly reinforces the "old boys network" and tends to discriminate against new entrants into the professions, such as women and members of ethnic minorities. Lacking effective sponsors, both their qualifications and ideological compatibility are more readily questioned. (For a general discussion of the discriminatory consequences of sponsorship see Kanter, 1977; Alvarez, Lutterman, and associates, 1979.)

Control over the appropriate use of expertise and adherence to the practice ideology are further facilitated through coordinating work by feedback rather than by advance plan. That is, different staff persons involved in the service delivery process coordinate their activities on the basis of feedback received from the client and coworkers. Such feedback signals the technical skills and expertise required and the changes in their application necessary to achieve the desired outputs based on the client's progress. Various staff experts are called into action as the need arises, and they coordinate their work through mutual adjustment to each other's actions (Van de Ven, Delbecq, and Koenig, 1976; Hage, 1974). Hence, coordination by feedback facilitates the emergence of a consensus on desired output goals. More important, it establishes a system of mutual monitoring and evaluation among the staff involved in the service delivery process. The need for mutual participation and communication with other specialists requires exposure and, thus, review of one's technical skills. At the same time, it preserves staff discretion in the application of these skills. The *team approach* and the *matrix structure* (Galbraith, 1977) are examples of coordination by feedback. These structures acknowledge the relative power of the line staff by fostering decentralization and a flat organizational structure; but at the same time, they increase the visibility of staff activities, at least to other staff members.

The team approach, widely advocated in human services, is nonetheless a weak control mechanism whose effectiveness is obfuscated by the very power relations it tries to manage. First, despite its facilitation of mutual communication, it cannot neutralize status differences among team members; the result is that the more prestigious professionals dominate the team. Dingwall (1980), who studied the relationships between physicians, public health nurses, and social workers in primary care teams, found that the teams were dominated by the physicians despite the pivotal role of the nurses. Such domination was reinforced by the class and sex differences between the physicians and the other team members, and by an ideology of exclusivity and assumed monopoly of medical knowledge. Second, competition, particularly among members of emerging professions, may result in conflict and disagreement over domain and lead to noncooperation. Hence, the effectiveness of coordination by feedback is predicated on some degree of power equality among the members of the work unit.

Overt output control in professionally dominated organizations is achieved through sanctions based on the evaluation of outcomes. That is, staff are made accountable for specific service outputs and are rewarded according to their ability to attain them, while retaining their discretion over the means to achieve them.

However, the vagueness and ambiguity of the output objectives for many human service organizations make it exceedingly difficult to define acceptable measures of service outputs. Witness, for example, the controversy surrounding the definition and measurement of the output objectives of the Head Start Program. When the evaluation of the program's impact on the cognitive and affective development of the children proved negative, supporters argued that the program also included equally important health, nutrition, resource redistribution, cultural, and community goals (Williams and Evans, 1969).

Human service organizations are reluctant to enforce specific criteria for evaluating output outcomes in order to shield its indeterminant and contradictory practices. They are particularly resisted by service practitioners because the criteria may expose their lack of technical expertise as well as reduce their discretion in defining the objectives and content of their work. Patton (1978) describes the intense conflict between teachers and administrators over the implementation of a comprehensive accountability system which stemmed from teachers' perceptions that such a system undermined their professional autonomy. Hence, human service organizations tend to rely on extrinsic measures of outcome that include peer and self-assessment and measures of efficiency (Thompson, 1967).

Measurement of workers' effectiveness through self- and peer evaluation clearly upholds professional autonomy in the organization, but is of dubious validity. Peer ratings, for example, may be less reflective of the quality of performance than of staff relations, professional attitudes, loyalty to the organization, cooperation, and participation in various organizational activities (McNeil and Popham, 1973). Measures of efficiency, such as caseload size, cost of services, and rates of admission and termination of clients, are indirectly far more restrictive of professional autonomy because they divert attention from attaining service effectiveness to scoring well on these efficiency measures. Staff are more likely to concentrate their efforts on reducing costs, processing clients more rapidly, and terminating cases early while compromising their professional standards and the quality of care. Hence, emphasis on these efficiency measures may result in serious goal displacement and signal a decline in professional power. These are more likely to occur when the organization experiences shrinkage and a decline in its resources, which results in greater pressures to demonstrate economy and efficiency (these issues are discussed further in Chapter 8).

Socialization to the practice ideologies of the organization—another form of overt output control—serves the same function as the recruitment of ideologically compatible staff. Much of the socialization occurs through in-house training and supervision. Yet, its effectiveness is based on linking organizational rewards and sanctions with acceptance of the dominant ideologies by staff. Henry (1957), in a classic analysis of the Orthogenic School— a therapeutic residential treatment center—noted that although line staff had considerable autonomy in caring for their patients, they were highly controlled by the director through his in-service training program. This program was used to inculcate staff with the dominant practice ideology, and every action staff took was evaluated and justified in relation to this ideology. Staff were rewarded or sanctioned according to their ability to demonstrate total commitment to the ideology.

The use of organizational ideologies to control staff may result in some serious disfunctions. First, such ideological rigidity may cause the organization to screen out innovative service practices. Second, it may result in the exclusion of a significant number of potential clients who fail to conform ideologically, as was well noted by Scott (1969) in his study of agencies for the blind. The cumulative effect of such ideological hegemony is a serious diminution in the ability of the organization to adapt to a changing environment.

Ideological indoctrination is feasible mostly in small organizations. With an increase in size and a need for various specializations, ideological pluralism is likely to arise as multiple centers of power emerge. As a result, large organizations are likely to deemphasize indoctrination to practice ideology and increase emphasis on evaluation of outcomes.

CONCLUSION

Human service organizations exhibit internal structural and control problems not typically found in other organizations. They resemble loosely coupled systems characterized by weakly connected and poorly coordinated work units. Such a structure arises when an organization faces a turbulent environment, possesses an indeterminate technology, and provides its services through line staff and client encounters.

A key characteristic of loosely coupled organizations is the emergence of multiple centers of power rather than a hierarchical authority structure. They arise partly from the front-line nature of the service delivery system, and partly from the proliferation of professional groups upon whom these organizations depend. For similar reasons, the effective control over staff in these organizations is limited, essentially because staff performance cannot be readily monitored and evaluated.

Loosely coupled systems evoke an image of an organization that is in disarray, inefficient, and unresponsive to the public. Efforts to "reform" human services often center on designing a more centralized and a more tightly coupled structure. Yet such a structure ignores the issues and dilemmas facing human service organizations. It may, indeed, emasculate the service delivery process and reduce its responsiveness to multiple constituencies. This is most apparent when human service organizations, in an effort to control staff and reduce costs, substitute measures of efficiency and productivity for the more elusive and ambiguous measures of effectiveness and quality of care. As Lipsky (1980) points out, this leads to the debasement of services because "there are many ways to save money by eroding the quality of services without appearing to do so. They include offering services on a group rather than individual basis; substituting paraprofessionals, paid from other sources, for regular staff; and conversely, forcing professionals to handle clerical and other routine chores, reducing the time they have to interact with their clients" (p.171).

The ultimate test of a human service organization's efficacy must remain its impact on service delivery to clients. A loosely coupled structure may well serve the interests of various professional groups; it is not clear, however, how well it serves the interests of the clients.

7

CLIENT-ORGANIZATION RELATIONS

Human service organizations can be clearly distinguished from other types of bureaucracies by their primary focus on relations with clients. In contrast to "customer," the role of "client" embraces three interrelated conceptions: First, a client is the recipient and consumer of the organization's services, a role that may be forced upon an individual (e.g., a prisoner or a child in a public school). Second, a client represents raw material to be worked upon and is vested with social values that the organization must consider in its processing and change efforts. Third a client becomes a quasi-member of the organization, in the sense that he or she must cooperate and comply with organizational policies to some degree and conform to certain prescribed behaviors and performances (Parsons, 1970). This is particularly apparent when the organization has both "lateral" and "longitudinal" interests in the client's biography (Lefton, 1970).

Moreover, as indicated in Chapter 5, the role of "client" carries with it a certain social and moral status. As noted by several writers (e.g., Goffman, 1961; Freidson, 1965; Roth, 1972; Prottas, 1979), this is expressed through the imputed diagnosis and prognosis, the attribution of responsibility, and the assessment of social worth. Undoubtedly, an individual's sociocultural attributes also influence the role. Less obvious, but of equal importance, is the influence of the organizational context in which this role is enacted. Being a patient in a state mental hospital is typically more morally degrading than being a patient in a private psychiatric hospital. Hence, the location of the organization in the human services stratification system is also an important factor in the definition of the client role.

Becoming and being a client, while a frequent occurrence for most people, is critically interrelated with social and moral status. Not only does status determine the quantity and quality of services people receive, but a persistent and close relationship exists between one's social status and the particular client roles one is likely to assume. Both tend to be mutually reinforcing.

Who the client is and how that role is enacted are of major importance to the survival and effectiveness of human service organizations. Clients represent critical resources without which they cannot survive, and through whom the demands for their services are registered. The attributes of clients will greatly affect the service technology and, hence, the service outputs of the organization. If we acknowledge that the ability of human service organizations to transform their clients is at best limited, if not marginal, then the attributes clients possess at entry will largely determine their attributes at exit, and thus, the effectiveness of the service technologies. Consequently, the ability of the organization to marshal resources and justify its existence is in no small measure determined by the attributes of its clients and their "careers" in the organization. In this sense, the economic and political status of the organization is affected by the social status of its clients, as manifested in their attributes, and the two are mutually reinforcing.

This chapter presents a framework for analyzing client-organization relations, then analyzes the client and organizational factors that influence the nature of these relations, and finally assesses the effect of these relations on each.

POWER-DEPENDENCE IN CLIENT-ORGANIZATION RELATIONS

The relations between clients and organizations can be conceived as a series of transactions by which resources and services are exchanged. Clients interact with an organization, voluntarily or involuntarily, to obtain its resources and services in a manner that optimizes perceived payoffs and minimizes perceived costs. The organization interacts with clients, by choice or by edict, to obtain the resources they control, in a manner that optimizes the payoffs and minimizes the costs as defined by those who wield power in the organization.[1]

---

[1]There may be instances in which neither the client nor the organization sees any benefit at all from the relationship, which may have been forced upon them. In such cases, the chief aim of the interacting parties will be to minimize their costs.

For example, the relations between applicants for public aid and the welfare department can be seen as a series of encounters in which: (1) the client attempts to obtain the highest level of public assistance with as little "hassle" as possible; and (2) the officials attempt to "weed out" the "undeserving" poor and reduce overpayment errors while maintaining acceptable working conditions. Similarly, the relations between clients and social workers in a family service agency represent a series of transactions through which clients seek help and advice congruent with their interests and values, with the least financial, social, and psychological cost. Workers attempt to provide services in accordance with agency policies (reflecting the interests of the power wielders) and their own professional interests, but with judicious use of the agency's and their own professional resources (hence, the interest, for example, in clients with third-party insurance).

This perspective clearly demonstrates that the interests of the client and the interests of the organization are inherently distinct: The client's interests emanate from the complex set of attributes that determine individual behavior; the organization's interests emanate from the dynamics that shape the roles of its staff. Such a perspective rejects the implicit assumption often held by human service practitioners that their interests are compatible with those of their clients, or that clients' difficulties with an organization are manifestations of their psychological and interpersonal problems.

Four components of these exchange relations can be identified (Katz and Danet, 1973): The first component is the process of *initiation* through which the client and the organization, voluntarily or involuntarily, establish contact. The second component is the *pattern* of the relations, which defines the roles of the client and the service providers and the operating procedures through which services are provided. The third component is the *resource transfer*, which represents the actual service delivery process. The fourth component is the *outcome*, which represents the benefits and costs accrued to the client and the organization from the exchange relations.

The ability of each party to structure the components of the exchange relations to accord with its interests is a function of the power-dependence relations between them. Following the same paradigm articulated in Chapter 3, power can be defined as the ability of A to obtain favorable outcomes from B at B's expense (Cook and Emerson, 1978). That is, the costs to A of obtaining B's resources or services are lower than the costs to B for getting similarly desired resources or services from A. The power of A over B, it will be recalled, is equal to the *dependence* of B on A. Such dependence varies directly with the desirability of the resources or services controlled by A to B, and inversely with the availability of such resources or services from alternative sources. A is said to have a *power advantage* over B when the dependence of B on A is greater than the dependence of A on B. Having a power advantage gives A the potential to use its transactions with B to get additional benefits at B's expense.

Using this framework, we can say that the dependence of the client on the organization, and thus, the power of the organization over the client, is directly proportional to the client's need for the organization's services and inversely proportional to the availability of the services from alternative sources. Similarly, the dependence of the organization on the client is directly proportional to the organization's need for the client's resources and inversely proportional to the availability of such resources elsewhere. It can be readily seen that in many human services the organization has a considerable power advantage over its clients because it monopolizes the services they need. Thus the clients have few or no alternatives, while the organization has many more potential clients than it can serve. This is most apparent, for example, in the area of public assistance. While the welfare department has a virtual monopoly over such aid and an abundance of applicants, the client may be in dire need and has nowhere else to turn.

A central argument advanced in this chapter is that the power advantage of human service organizations enables them to exercise considerable control over the lives of the recipients of their services. Moreover, organizations will use this power advantage to shape staff-client transactions in such a way that the outcomes will enhance their legitimation, flow of resources, and power. Put differently, when the service provision process has important consequences for the political and economic life of the organization, the dominant coalition and other centers of power in it will attempt to use any power advantage over clients in pursuit of their interests. For example, with a power advantage, the organization may attempt to select clients who will enhance its reputation and facilitate the mobilization of legitimation and resources (Greenley and Kirk, 1973). In the case of public assistance, it has been shown that during civil unrest and economic prosperity, it is to the interest of the organization's elite to expand the welfare rolls and to relax application procedures. During economic decline, however, the elite will seek to reduce the rolls and to tighten and restrict application procedures (Ritti and Hyman, 1977). Professional groups within the organization may use the power advantage so that the outcomes of their transactions with clients confirm their professional ideologies and buttress their status (Freidson, 1970; Krebs, 1971). Finally, street-level bureaucrats may use the power advantage to control and improve their working conditions (Prottas, 1979).

Clients who have a power advantage over the organization, as a result of the resources they possess, can similarly use it to control transactions with the organization to optimize their interests. In particular, such clients will be in a better bargaining position to improve the congruency between their personal goals and the organization's output objectives and to control the transfers of resources and the outcomes of the exchanges. For example, both the study by Clark (1956) of the transformation of an adult education program and that by Zald and Denton (1963) of the changes in the YMCA indicate that as the dependence of these organizations on income generated by clients increased, program changes occurred that more closely reflected clients' demands. Rushing (1978) found that resourceful clients are less likely to be committed involuntarily to mental hospitals. Similarly, patients from higher socioeconomic backgrounds tend, in general, to have access to better medical care than lower-class patients (Krauss, 1977). Powerful clients can also influence the patterns of their relations with the service providers. For example, they tend to have access to better-trained staff and receive more prompt attention (Schwartz, 1975).

Gaining a Power Advantage

Clients and organizations each have four basic strategies, directly derived from the exchange paradigm, by which they may increase their respective power. For clients, the following four strategies are possible:

1. They may decrease their need for the organization's services, either by denying the existence of the need or by attempting to respond to it on their own. The development of self-help groups can be viewed as a way of decreasing dependence on human service organizations.
2. They may turn to alternative sources for services, by searching further afield for other sources, or by facilitating the development of alternative service providers. A common tactic of parents resisting school desegregation is to move to another school district or to invest in the establishment of private schools.
3. They may help stimulate the need of the organization for their resources, which may be accomplished by seeking legislation that makes the organization's funding contingent on serving a particular cohort of clients. For example, to qualify for funds, a mental health agency may have to demonstrate that it serves a certain number of after-care patients.
4. They may reduce the alternative sources of clients available to the organization. This has been a long-standing tactic of labor unions, who are often able to prevent employers from hiring nonunion workers. Combining clients into a collective group as, for example, in the case of the National Welfare Rights Organization, is an attempt to force the organization to interact with its clients on a collective rather than an individual basis, and to prevent it from reaching clients outside the control of the collective (Piven and Cloward, 1977).

In the same vein, Hirschman (1970), in a seminal essay, has articulated the effectiveness and the consequences of *exit* and *voice* as strategies to increase organizational responsiveness to the needs of clients. Clients may indicate their displeasure with the quality of the services through exit (i.e., going elsewhere), which leads to a decline in revenues, hence, forcing corrective action by the organization. Alternatively, clients may voice their displeasure through petitions, appeals to higher authorities, or protests to force the organization to engage in corrective measures. Several features of human service organizations, however, affect the success of each strategy. First, many human service organizations are publicly funded, and their revenues are not derived directly from or only from client fees. Second, most human service organizations experience limited competition, if any. Third, distinct disparities exist in the quality of services offered by various human service organizations responding to the same need, as can be noted in the differences between private vs. public schools, university-affiliated hospitals vs. county or city hospitals, or family and child service agencies vs. departments of social services.

Under these conditions, the exit option may not be effective if the existence of the organization is secured through public funding, or if it can easily get new clients because it has a monopoly over the services. Indeed, if it has a monopoly, the organization may encourage the "troublemakers" or dissatisfied clients to exit to avoid protest. Hence, voice is a more effective strategy for influencing organizations whose resources are guaranteed regardless of the quality of their services, as is the case for most publicly funded human services.

Voice will be selected when the exit option is not readily available. However, voice is effective when clients can mobilize sufficient influence and bargaining power against the organization. The selection of voice over exit is more likely when clients have *loyalty* to the organization and its services. Yet, loyalty is important to the organization only when clients can threaten to exit, which is not the case for monopolistic services. Hence, for voice to be effective, the exit option needs to be available to clients, but they should not have easy access to it as soon as the quality begins to decline.

Because of the disparities in quality of similar human service organizations, clients who are concerned with high quality and have the necessary resources will choose high-quality human service organizations, and will rapidly exit those whose quality has deteriorated. They will leave behind other clients who lack the resources to exit, and are at the same time less likely to voice their displeasure. As Hirschman (1970) points out, this is what has happened to public education in the inner cities. As the quality of education began to decline, parents with resources either enrolled their children in private schools or moved to the suburbs. Yet these are the clients who would have been most concerned with the quality of services and most likely to voice their displeasure at deteriorating quality had the exit option not been available to them. Exiting from these organizations, they reduce the probability that the more effective voice strategy will be used. The net result is increased bifurcation in the quality of human services available to resourceful versus unresourceful clients.

The organization may attempt to increase its power advantage over clients through the following four strategies:

1. It may reduce its need for client-controlled resources by divorcing the attainment of resources from the service provision process. For example, in most human service organizations, the mobilization of fiscal resources is only loosely and vaguely dependent on the clients' actual experiences in obtaining the services.
2. It may expand the potential pool of clients by broadening its domain and by relaxing intake selection criteria.
3. It may increase clients' need for its services by developing activities and programs that are in high demand.
4. It may reduce the availability of alternative services through monopolization tactics. It should be noted, in this context, that the move toward consolidating and integrating human services, often under the guise of reducing waste and duplication of services, actually results in the increase of organizational power (Morris and Lescohier, 1978).

One measure of the power advantage of a human service organization over its clients is the extent and amount of *discretion* it has in making decisions about their lives (Gummer, 1979; Handler, 1973). The greater the discretion of the service providers to select courses of action on the basis of their own judgments, the greater their power over clients. Herein lies the essence of professional power. The exercise of discretion permits the service providers, while attending to the needs of clients, to make decisions that promote their own interests, which may not be consonant with those of the client. Glasser (1978) provides the following example:

> . . . the nursing home may have an interest—a legitimate interest—in getting paid for the services it provides, which should disqualify it from being an impartial protector of the aged person's assets. Nonetheless, nursing homes often control the assets of their patients and manipulate those assets to their own ends and to the detriment of their patients. Similarly, the patient may desire the freedom to come and go, to socialize, to have visitors and activities, to retain privacy, while the home's interests may run to more administrative convenience and order. When such conflicts of interest arise, the nearly parental powers of the nursing home can quickly suffocate the basic right of individual patients (p. 109).

Having a power advantage increases the probability that it *will* be used as long as additional benefits can be attained or the costs for attaining them can be reduced. However, internal and external constraints play an important part in the use of power by the exchanging parties. Internal constraints emanate from the *norms* upheld by the organization and the client that govern the exchange relations (Cook and Emerson, 1978). The organization, for example, may uphold norms that stress fairness and equity, commitment to the needs of the client, and respect for the client's rights—norms that are typically embodied in a professional code of ethics. These restrain officials from using their power advantage beyond organizationally prescribed boundaries, and occasionally even encourage suspension of organizational rules in favor of the client. In a study of appeals to Israeli customs authorities, Danet (1973) found that 70 percent of the clients were treated in a universalistic fashion, reflecting the norm of fairness. But 29 percent received a favorable result even though their claims lacked legal justification. These were immigrants whose attributes indicated them to be "underdogs" and powerless, yet the bureaucracy "gave them a break" because of a norm that mandates helping such immigrants integrate into Israeli society.

External constraints, particularly on the organization, are expressed through laws, statutes, and administrative regulations designed to protect the rights of clients. The Mental Health Code for the State of Michigan, for example, contains a patient's bill of rights that is aimed at preventing potential abuse and ensuring that patients receive appropriate and humane care. Nonetheless, a study of the utilization of these mechanisms to protect clients has identified several problems that limit their effectiveness (Handler, 1979). First, to use the legal remedies available to them, clients must be aware of their existence, must have the resources to pursue them, and must anticipate that the benefits will outweigh the possible costs. Meeting these conditions is obviously difficult for many clients. Second, the use of administrative monitoring and supervision requires the formulation of explicit standards for the provision of services and effective information-gathering devices, both of which are highly problematic in human service organizations. Third, the relations between monitoring agencies, human service organizations, and clients are such that organizations have considerably more resources with which to influence the agencies and possibly coopt them.

The importance of organizational norms as restraints on the use of power over clients should not be underestimated, because they may well be the only effective instruments for preventing abuse, particularly when the clients have little power, as in the case of the disabled, the aged, and dependent and neglected children. For example, many of the best nursing homes are operated by religious and ethnic groups. As Vladeck (1980: 126) points out, "the religious responsibility or fraternal solidarity may be important incentives to high-quality services." Such a binding commitment to the welfare of clients will help prevent the staff from using their power advantage to promote their self-interest. Similarly, Kroeger (1975) has noted that the orientation of public assistance workers toward their clients has a significant impact on the level of grants they received. Client-oriented workers were more generous than agency-oriented workers. However, as Zimmerman (1969a) noted, welfare departments, through their control structure, tend to provide disincentives and discouragement to client-oriented workers. The ideologies adopted by the organization that shape its normative and moral stance toward its clients (see Chapter 4) will determine how the staff exercises power. Ideologies that devalue clients' social worth, blame them for the predicaments they face, and are pessimistic about clients' prognoses are unlikely to check the use of the organizational power advantage—to the detriment of the clients.

PATHWAYS TO HUMAN SERVICE ORGANIZATIONS

Organizations not only determine the type and quality of services clients receive but also seriously affect their future welfare and well-being. Differences in the quality of schools have been shown to significantly affect students' future occupational statuses and earnings (Griffin and Alexander, 1978). Differential access to health services has been shown to affect the quality and adequacy of medical care (Dutton, 1978); and commitment to the great variety of juvenile correctional programs results in unequal treatment (Vinter et al., 1976). Similarly, from the organization's perspective, the type of clients it obtains will significantly influence its capacity to demonstrate service effectiveness, because client attributes critically determine the organization's ability to facilitate and improve their welfare and well-being. Hence, if the organization's survival is linked to demonstrated service effectiveness, it will attempt to control the entry of clients.

Entry into human service organizations is predetermined by two critical variables: (1) the amount of control clients have over their choice; and (2) the amount of control the organization has over its admissions (Carlson, 1964). The intersection of the two variables generates four types of entry patterns as depicted in Table 7.1.

The private practice pattern. In the *private practice* pattern, successful entry negotiations require compatibility of interests between clients and the organization, which is achieved, in part, through the clients' knowledge about the organization's services and the ability of the organization to attract "desirable" clients. Clients learn about human services through both lay and professional referral systems (Freidson, 1961). Professional referral systems are more informed about services and are, therefore, more effective in sending clients to high-quality services. Moreover, a professional referral system lends its prestige to the client, facilitating successful negotiations

TABLE 7.1.   Entry Patterns to Human Service Organizations.

ORGANIZATIONAL CONTROL OVER ADMISSION	CLIENT CONTROL OVER CHOICE	
	High	*Low*
High	Private practice	Benevolent
Low	Public access	Domesticated

with the service providers (Mishler and Waxler, 1963). Lay referral systems (i.e., clients' social networks) vary in their knowledge of service providers. As Freidson (1961) found, a "local" social network, whose knowledge of services extends only to the limited personal experiences of its members, is far less effective than a "cosmopolitan" social network that has extensive bureaucratic contacts. Kadushin (1969) noted that pathways to psychoanalysts were mediated by a social network that he termed "the friends of psychotherapy," whose members had extensive knowledge and contact with psychoanalytic therapists.

A client's affiliation with a "cosmopolitan" social network is a necessary, but not sufficient, condition for expanding the range of available alternative human services. A client must also possess personal resources, such as education and income, that will permit absorption of the search costs and other expenses (e.g., transportation, fees) associated with various potential services. Avnet (1962) noted that even among those with comparable insurance coverage, persons with higher incomes and more education were far more likely to gain access to psychiatric services, particularly psychotherapists in solo practice.

Most important, the client must possess attributes that are considered "desirable" by the potential service providers. In the case of psychoanalytic therapy, preferred patients often have a high level of education, are verbal and articulate, are committed to long-term therapy, and have neurotic problems therapists find "interesting" (Kadushin, 1969; Lerner and Fisk, 1973).

However, knowledge and personal resources are not the only determinants of how services are used. McKinlay (1972) reviewed many studies indicating that social psychological factors related to perceptions of need and motivation to seek help will influence the use of services, and that cultural factors, particularly the norms and values of kinship and friendship networks, will shape definitions of problems and acceptable routes to solve them (see also Berkanovic and Reeder, 1974).

In the private practice pattern, the organization's key concern is to attract clients who will enhance its resources and legitimation, particularly by bolstering its reputation and prestige. That is, the organization seeks clients possessing attributes that facilitate and attract resources, are conducive to successful service outcomes, and promote loyalty to the organization. As was mentioned previously, Scott (1967a) found that agencies for the blind considered young blind people to be the most attractive clients because the public responded to them with more contributions. Mechanic (1980) noted that with the establishment of insurance coverage for mental illness, which has greatly expanded access to psychiatric services, mental health agencies prefer insured patients, but tend to "dump" them on state facilities when coverage runs out. Several studies of selection processes in family and child agencies suggest that clients from low socioeconomic backgrounds and those displaying problems defined as not amenable to change by organizational technologies are more likely to be rejected (Cloward and Epstein, 1965; Teele and Levine, 1968).

Private practice organizations rely extensively on reputation, gate-keepers, and intake criteria to attract and select desirable clients. Through reputation, the organization influences the knowledge available to the public about the nature and quality of its services. Reputation is a highly selective form of information dissemination because it invariably overemphasizes the organization's successes and deemphasizes its failures. It, therefore, presents a biased image in order to attract certain types of clients.

Gatekeepers, particularly professional referring agents, who have specialized knowledge and links with the organization, are used to identify potentially desirable clients and route them to the organization. Referring agents become gatekeepers when they and the organization develop mutually beneficial relations. They use the organization's acceptance of their clients in order to demonstrate their resourcefulness to clients and to buttress their own reputations, while the organization relies on them to obtain desirable clients. Duff and Hollingshead (1968), studying the routing of patients to a hospital, noted that patients referred by specialists were far more likely to obtain private or semiprivate rooms than patients who went directly to the hospital. The latter were also more likely to be treated by interns and residents.

Intake criteria, both explicit and implicit, are used to weed out undesirable clients. While most human services are constrained in the use of explicit exclusionary criteria, except for those dealing with the appropriateness of their services to the needs of the clients, implicit criteria are often at work. These may include: (1) classification of client needs as outside the domain of the agency; (2) placement of potential clients on waiting lists; (3) communication barriers with certain client groups, particularly those from cultural and ethnic minorities; or (4) display of negative attitudes by the intake staff (Hasenfeld and Steinmetz, 1981).

The benevolent pattern. The *benevolent* pattern is characteristic of those human service organizations who set their own admission criteria; clients themselves have no real choice in these decisions, because they are deemed incapable or they lack the necessary legal rights. Private residential treatment centers and nursing homes exemplify such a pattern. Juvenile courts, while required by law to process juvenile offenders, have considerable discretion in making admission decisions; on the average, 50 percent of all cases referred to juvenile courts are processed informally (Sarri and Hasenfeld, 1976). With the exception of serious offenders, it is up to the court to extend its benevolence and take jurisdiction of youth.

Under the benevolent pattern, appeals for admission on behalf of clients (or against their wishes) are typically made by other organizations;

the determinants of client entry are thus shaped by the power-dependence relations between the referring agencies and the benevolent organization. When the organization provides critical services that are in short supply, and the clients and other resources are dispersed, it is in a monopolistic position and can set admission criteria that will enhance its dominant interests. When the organization is dependent on referring agencies to "purchase its services," the admission criteria will reflect their mutual negotiations. Still, the benevolent organization is likely to have the power advantage because of the scarcity of its services and the difficulties in monitoring the adequacy or quality of these services (Kramer, 1979). As a result, it can evade criteria or conditions imposed on it by referring agencies, as can be seen in the case of proprietary nursing homes and sheltered care facilities (Vladeck, 1980; Segal and Aviram, 1978).

The client, lacking the exit option, is largely at the mercy of the organization. Should the client fail to meet organizational expectations, it can force his or her exit, as often occurs in private juvenile correctional programs who send their "troublemakers" back to state correctional institutions. Thus, voice by clients is met by forced exit. The benevolent organization exercises considerable discretion in relation to its clients' entry and exit with few checks and restrictions.

The public access pattern.   In the *public access* pattern, the organization faces the dilemma of how to attract and select "desirable" clients, despite its inability to screen out or reject the "undesirables." That is, it must establish mechanisms that, first, dissuade some clients from applying while they reach out for others, and second, encourage unfavorable clients who do cross the organizational boundaries to leave. Hospital emergency rooms, community mental health centers, state employment placement services, and welfare departments exemplify such organizations. When these organizations have an exclusive monopoly, the clients who need them have little discretion over entry, as in the case of welfare departments. Thus, welfare departments more closely resemble the domesticated organizations.

Public access organizations, whose survival and enhancement depend on generating an adequate and sustained demand for their services, will engage in various "reaching-out" tactics to attract clients. These tactics will be used, first, to increase public awareness through advertisements, educational campaigns, and other modes of disseminating information about the availability and importance of the organization's services. Second, reaching-out tactics will include efforts to reduce client costs in accessing and using the services by providing transportation and child care services, employing indigenous "outreach workers," convenient hours and service locations, and the like (Diehr, Jackson, and Boscha, 1975).

In contrast, when the organization attempts to control or reduce the demand for its services, it will increase the access costs to potential clients by use of several tactics (Hasenfeld and Steinmentz, 1981). First, it will increase the waiting time, particularly for undesirable clients. Both Schwartz (1975) and Roth (1972) found in studies of emergency rooms that low-income patients who came for nonemergency services, persons labeled as "welfare cases" or "drunk," and those with unkempt appearances were more likely to wait longer before being treated. Second, such clients may be treated rudely, be degraded, and forced to reveal intimate personal information in offices unshielded from the public (Hall, 1974). Third, clients may be provided with misinformation about their entitlements, or may be routed from worker to worker before they can obtain the needed services (i.e., "getting the run around"). These tactics create a negative reputation, which is directed at discouraging clients, particularly those not in dire need, from applying.

To get rid of unfavorable clients *after* they have entered the organization, the organization may resort to "cooling-out" tactics (Clark, 1960). Diagnoses and labels may be used to exclude clients from the domain of the organization. A juvenile court, for example, finding that a youth is suffering from emotional problems, may refer the case to a psychiatric hospital. The hospital, which may not be interested in treating a youth with a criminal record, can refuse to diagnose the case as "mentally ill" and send the youth back to the court (Emerson, 1969).

In the same vein, clients may be defined as needing the services of other organizations and be steered to them. In contrast to a referral, where the referring agent is actively involved in linking the client with other service providers and maintains primary responsibility for the client's welfare, steering shifts the responsibility and the burden to the client, who must then negotiate successful entry to other service providers. Not infrequently, clients lacking sufficient personal resources and perseverance simply give up. Clients may also be defined as "uncooperative" or as not amenable to the organization's services and be terminated. The organization may also use delay tactics for undesirable clients. In my study of employment placement services (Hasenfeld, 1975), female applicants, for whom the agency had few employment opportunities, were much more likely to be routed to testing and counselling, which meant a delay in referral to jobs. Many women saw little value in the counselling, became discouraged, and terminated their contact with the agency.

Similarly, the organization may route its undesirable clients into unattractive service tracks that will prompt them to drop out. This pattern is particularly evident in high schools, where students from low socioeconomic backgrounds, with learning difficulties, or with discipline problems, are likely to be deprived of many curricular and extracurricular resources and be implicitly encouraged to drop out. While the organization may rightfully recognize that these clients cannot benefit from its services unless it uses up considerable resources at the expense of other clients, it nonetheless sets in motion self-fulfilling prophecies. That is, clients judged as not amenable to change are deprived of the services of the organization; this results in their lack of improvement, which in turn confirms the initial judgment. I will discuss this dynamic more fully below.

The domesticated pattern. In the *domesticated* pattern, neither the clients nor the organization can readily exercise the exit option. Clients are coerced or lack any real choice over their entry, and the organization must accept them irrespective of its interests. Public schools, prisons, state mental hospitals, and welfare departments are examples of domesticated organizations. Consequently, the relations between the client and the organization are potentially stressful and antagonistic; and both parties will concentrate on minimizing the costs of their forced exchanges, rather than on optimizing uncertain and unknown payoffs. Moreover, even when payoffs are available, the relations are open to exploitation. Because the organization has an absolute monopoly over the resources needed by the clients, it may extract an increasingly higher "price" for the same or decreasing amounts of resources (Emerson, 1972). The clients, in turn, will attempt to conceal their own resources (i.e., cheat) or use them to elicit concessions from the organization. For example, with declining economic conditions, welfare departments are likely to tighten eligibility rules and rigidly enforce the conditions of welfare grants. Clients, on the other hand, will be motivated to cheat and feign compliance. The *sub rosa economy* in prisons is another example (Williams and Fish, 1976). A prison uses its basic amenities, such as cell location, work assignments, food, and recreation, to obtain inmate compliance. The greater its need for compliance, the more complying behavior it must extract from inmates to obtain these amenities. Inmates, on the other hand, establish a sub rosa economy in which amenities, hidden from prison officials, are traded, thus reducing some of their extreme dependence. The sub rosa economy also provides some room for bargaining between officials and inmates. Order is maintained by the inmates in exchange for the officials' tacit tolerance of the contraband market.

Because the domesticated organization lacks control over admissions, it relies mostly on cooling-out tactics and internal tracking and segregation mechanisms to minimize the potential disruptiveness of unselected clients (Carlson, 1964). In these organizations, *tracking* refers to an internal system of client stratification whereby those clients accorded a higher status receive preferential services and benefits. As suggested in Chapter 5, clients are stratified on the basis of the social worth ascribed to them by the staff, who are guided by the moral system incorporated in the organizational technology. This ascribed status, in turn, dictates the range and quality of services a client will receive. Tracking can be manifested in several ways. First, clients may be routed into service categories that limit their access to desirable services, as exemplified in the tracking of students into the vocational or general instead of the academic curriculum. Second, clients may be assigned to service units that are ill-staffed, lack expertise, and, hence, offer low-quality services. This can be noted in the assignment of hospital patients to wards rather than to private or semiprivate rooms (Duff and Hollingshead, 1968). Third, clients may be assigned to service categories that are perceived as dumping grounds, in the sense that they offer only minimal resources to sustain clients, as exemplified in mental hospital chronic wards.

The rigidity of the client stratification system depends on the organization's perception and assessment of the degree of incurability, disruptiveness, or risk in lower-status clients. Maximum-security prisons have a highly stratified and segregated system, whereby dangerous inmates are confined to special cell blocks and are deprived of many of the amenities available to less dangerous inmates. In state mental hospitals, patients deemed untreatable are segregated in chronic wards, which lack most of the treatment services available to those in acute wards (Strauss et al., 1964). The tracking system in schools is more fluid and resembles a tournament. Those who advance academically have a chance of entering the better courses, but those who fail to advance lose their chance to do so forever (Rosenbaum, 1976).

Given the organization's value system, tracking is an effective mechanism to improve the benefit-cost ratio of its services. By investing a greater proportion of its resources in highly valued clients, while minimizing its investment in those deemed potential failures, the organization achieves an optimal use of its resources in pursuit of its dominant values and interests. In his study of the high school tracking system, Rosenbaum (1976) found that the administrators defended it on the basis of their need to use school resources efficiently. Accordingly, in their opinion, the early selection of students best qualified for higher education reduced the waste of resources and time and permitted the concentration of efforts to achieve successful outcomes, as measured by college placement. Similarly, when a public hospital with 2,000 chronic patients has a rehabilitation unit for only 100 patients, the selection of those to be admitted is based on staff judgments of who will benefit most. Such judgments, anchored in the broader value system of the community, give preference not only to those with the "right" disability, but also to the young and the "motivated" (Roth and Eddy, 1967).

Lacking the exit option, clients may not accept the organization's tracking criteria and instead perceive them as capricious and discriminatory. These clients may voice protest by becoming rebellious, aggressive, or manipulative. However, such tactics in domesticated organizations are generally ineffective, exactly because voice is not coupled with an exit option.

BECOMING A CLIENT

After entry into the organization, all clients undergo a process of assessment, classification, and categorization that prescribes their access and routes to various services and intervention technologies (see Chapter 5). This process also determines the specific roles the client is expected to play in the organization. Scheff (1965) has proposed that the dynamics of ascribing a diagnostic label, a prognosis, and a treatment plan to clients can be viewed as a process of *typification*. That is, officials assemble, screen, and package the information gathered about the client to fit into a set of working stereotypes, each prescribing a particular plan of action. Clients are thus categorized into typical or "normal" cases having attendant service responses. The importance of this process to both the organization and the clients cannot be underestimated. It is the vehicle through which the organization operationalizes the allocation of its resources to various clients; and it determines the benefits and costs that will be incurred by becoming a client. Consequently, the typing process sets the stage and defines the parameters of transactions and relations between clients and officials.

The Typification Process

Typification is indispensable to the operations of the organizational service technology. From a strictly technological perspective, effective delivery of service hinges on the appropriate typification of clients because the service providers' knowledge is organized by diagnostic units of need, problem, disease, deviance, and the like. These units identify and specify the configurations of client attributes that fit each diagnostic label, which in turn determines the service response. To the practitioners, these diagnostic units are the major tool in directing their inquiry and examination of the client's attributes, in sifting through and interpreting the meaning of the information, and in making decisions about the modes of service appropriate for that client. A failure in the service technology is not infrequently attributed to a "misdiagnosis" of a client. The level of complexity, specificity, and refinement of these diagnostic units and accompanying service plans is, clearly, a function of the "state of the art" of the technology.

However, as indicated in Chapter 5, perceptions of a client's *moral character* are also inherent in the typification process. Four critical and interrelated moral decisions can be identified in this process (Freidson, 1965). The first decision refers to the attribution of responsibility for the client's predicament. Clients perceived to be morally responsible for their difficulties are inevitably viewed as morally deficient; clients judged not responsible are viewed as victims of circumstances beyond their control. For the former, the receipt of services is likely to be contingent on their acceptance of their moral inferiority, which may be denoted by stripping away some of their citizenship rights and demanding repentance. Historically, subjecting welfare recipients to intimate questions, midnight raids, and man-in-the-house rules exemplify the consequences of such a moral decision.

The second decision refers to the client's amenability to change or improvement, and defines the moral responsibility of the staff for the client's fate. For those clients judged not amenable to change the staff is absolved from responsibility for the consequences of the service delivery process, and the inattention accorded them is justified. Hence, the deterioration of the elderly in custodial nursing homes may be justified on the basis of their progressive frailty rather than on staff irresponsibility and lack of attention.

The third decision involves the treatment of clients as subjects or objects. Clients treated as subjects are viewed as having the moral capability of making decisions for themselves and as able to become active participants in the service delivery process. In contrast, clients viewed as objects are perceived as lacking the capability of making appropriate decisions for themselves; staff is thus granted moral superiority over them. Such clients are more likely to experience a dehumanizing relationship with staff, who in turn feel justified in ignoring their wishes and feelings (Howard, 1975).

The fourth decision refers to the attribution of social worth to the client. It provides staff with the moral justification for the differential allocation of services. That is, clients judged to have a higher social worth are also deemed to have a higher priority to services, as can be noted, for example, in the preferential treatment given the young in emergency rooms (Sudnow, 1967).

The parameters of these decisions are largely derived from the cultural and normative context of the organization. To quote Roth (1972: 840), "... those engaged in dispensing professional services (or any other services) will apply the evaluations of social worth common to their culture and will modify their services with respect to these evaluations, *unless discouraged from doing so by the organizational arrangements under which they work.*" While the organization may indeed discourage such evaluation, it cannot eliminate it. More important, however, the organization develops its own views which are then used to evaluate the client's moral character. These views are firmly anchored in the political economy of the organization, in the sense that they are used to manage both external and internal political and economic exigencies.

The Organizational Functions of Typification

The use of a typification scheme to manage organizational exigencies, other than those related to strictly technological matters, can be seen in several areas. First, as noted in the previous section, the typification scheme is a major tool for implementing cooling-out and tracking strategies. Working stereotypes are developed, incorporating organizational ideas about desirable and undesirable clients, and these serve as guides for differential staff responses. For example, for emergency room personnel, these working stereotypes include not only the client's medical problems, but also his or her age, sex, race, personal appearance, and self-presentation—all relevant for constructing an image of the client's moral character (Roth, 1972). Similarly, schoolteachers develop working stereotypes of "good" and "bad" students on the basis of their personal appearance, self-expression, demeanor, and industry. These stereotypes are, of course, self-reifying precisely because of the staff and client responses they evoke. When teachers lower their expectations and minimize the attention they give to students judged to be poor learners, they reinforce the students' poor performance, which, in turn, confirms the validity of their stereotypes (Rist, 1970).

Second, typification enables the organization to funnel diverse and multiple client needs and demands to its limited set of services. By focusing on certain client attributes and excluding others, the staff can fit the client into existing service categories rather than being pressured to search for service options that are not readily available. Moreover, typification can serve as a device to manage the traffic of clients to various services; it can thus ensure that certain services are not over- or underused. Both patterns were observed in a study of employment placement services (Hasenfeld, 1975). Because of the limited supply of job opportunities, mostly in low-skill occupations, the staff obtained only minimal information about the applicants' occupational backgrounds and aptitudes, since extensive knowledge could only undermine the justification for the referral. Moreover, applicants for whom employment opportunities were not available were typically categorized as needing testing and counselling. On the other hand, applicants were often retyped as needing a certain training program to fill in the available slots. McCleary (1975), in a study of a state parole agency, found that in order to have a sufficient number of parolees in a federally funded treatment program, parole officers were under pressure to type some of their cases as needing such treatment.

Third, typification can be used to increase efficiency by reducing uncertainty and increasing predictability. By fitting the client attributes into a typical case, practitioners narrow the variations considerably, and rely more heavily on a set of familiar and known diagnostic units. This enables them to reduce the potentially vast variations and idiosyncracies among clients by ignoring or discarding information deemed irrelevant to "normal" cases. Sudnow (1965) noted that public defenders, in questioning defendants, were less interested in obtaining detailed information about the particular situation and predicament than in ascertaining how well they fit typical crimes. As a result, efficiency is introduced into the service technology by reducing the time and energy spent on gathering and processing client information. Indeed, it has been suggested that the greater the volume of clients for staff to process, the fewer, more global, and less precise the diagnostic units will be.

Finally, staff may use typification to control their working conditions, to enhance positive evaluations of their performance, and, in general, to protect their positions or reputations. Prottas (1979) found that directors of housing projects developed a typification scheme of desirable and undesirable tenants on the basis of their experiences with tenants who gave them difficulties, such as defaulting on rent, failing to keep their dwellings in good condition, or complaining frequently. Through such typification, they attempted to control the type of tenants they accepted. McCleary (1977), in his study of parole officers, noted that they typified parolees essentially on the basis of how much trouble they might cause or their degree of uncontrollability, because parole officers were evaluated primarily on the amount of trouble they had with their caseloads. Finally, Scheff (1966) suggested that physicians are more likely to typify patients as ill rather than well because their positions and reputations suffer more when they categorize patients as well when they are, in fact, ill than when they categorize patients as ill when they are, in fact, well.

Clients also attempt to influence the typification process and seek to acquire a label and a moral character that will optimize their benefits and minimize their costs. The ability of the clients to do so depends on the amount of power and resources they possess vis-à-vis the organization. As Scheff (1968) has suggested, whose definition of the situation will be accepted is based on the power relations between staff and clients. Hence, in general, the greater the amount of power clients possess, the greater their ability to negotiate a favorable typing. This is most evident, for example, in the criminal justice system. Defendants from higher socioeconomic levels, who can post bail and can obtain expert legal counsel, are less likely to be convicted, and if convicted, are more likely to receive lighter sentences (Lizotte, 1978). Similarly, Rushing (1978) found that contolling for psychiatric disorders, patients with more status resources (i.e., education) are better able to control their fate and resist involuntary hospitalization.

In these and other instances, clients use their status resources to signify their social worth. Several tactics may be employed. First, clients may use their resources to absorb the costs of searching and accessing service providers who will accord them high social worth. Ability to pay for services can readily buy respectability. Second, status resources can be used to mobilize professional advocates to negotiate and confirm a client's social worth. The use of professional referrals to gain entry into specialized services, the reliance on references from known experts for educational or occupational advancement, and the retainment of legal experts to defend one's position exemplify this tactic. Third, high-status clients can use their resources to obtain the necessary knowledge and the bureaucratic competence to negotiate favorably with officials. Comprehension of organizational policies and practices gives the client a clear advantage in knowing how to deal with officials and what steps to take to obtain favorable outcomes. Gordon (1975), for example, found that clients with bureaucratic experience were more likely to obtain favorable decisions from their welfare workers. In this context, high-status clients can use their resources to redress perceived mistreatment by the organization. Threatening to challenge officials should they fail to respond to the client may serve as an inducement to respond more favorably to high-status clients. Fourth, high-status clients rely on their own self-presentation to elicit favorable evaluations. By language, appearance, mode of conduct, and expression of values and attitudes, such clients provide cues that attest to high social worth. Moreover, through appearance, clients may attempt to demonstrate normative and behavioral affinity with the officials. Lorion (1973), for example, noted that a major factor contributing to the failure of individual psychotherapy with clients of low social status was their sociocultural incompatibility with the psychotherapists.

Effects of Typification

The organizationally constructed moral character of the client has a profound impact on the attitudes, expectations, and behaviors of the staff because it prescribes a mode of conduct to both staff and clients. By shaping the pattern and content of staff-client relations—a critical determinant of the *quality* of the service delivery process—the constructed moral character predetermines the client's experience in the organization. This has been dramatically demonstrated through an experiment conducted by Rosenhan (1973). A group of eight supposedly normal persons—a psychiatrist, a pediatrician, a painter, a housewife, a psychology graduate student, and three psychology professors—sought admission to several mental hospitals by feigning schizophrenia. All were admitted, but despite reverting to their usual normal behavior, the hospital staff continued to view and treat them as patients and denied their normality. (Interestingly, the "real" patients were quick to detect them as imposters.) Casting the moral character of the pseudo-patients as schizophrenic led the staff to perceive them as objects lacking credibility and having low social worth. Thus the subsequent denial of illness was interpreted as one of its symptoms. Rist (1970), in his study of teacher-student relations, noted that children cast by the teacher as "failures" received much less attention; their requests were often ignored, and they were more often disciplined and penalized. The "failures" responded as expected by withdrawing from interaction with the teacher, losing interest in the learning process, and expressing verbal and physical hostility. Similarly, parolees defined as "clients" rather than "dangerous men" were accorded a different treatment by parole officers (McCleary, 1977). They were counseled and supported more frequently, the quality of the relationship was high, and the officers were more willing to bend the rules and regulations to assist them.

One need not conclude, however, that client typing is capricious, for it is obviously based on cues and information received from the client. Nor should it be assumed that typing has necessarily deleterious consequences for the client. Quite the contrary: Typification ensures that the client obtains valuable services that are *specifically designed* to respond to the client's problems and needs. For the client, the attainment of an appropriate and valid typification may mean the difference between remaining in a state of ill-being or escaping it. Moreover, in many instances, the tendency by human service practitioners to assume deviancy rather than normalcy reduces the risk that a client's problems and needs will go unanswered. The risk of harm may be greater when a client's illness remains undetected than when the client is assumed to be ill but is in fact well. What is important to emphasize is, first, the selectivity and partiality of the process, which is often dictated by organizational rather than client interests; second, once the client's moral character is cast, it shapes the relationship between staff and client and often results in the reification of constructed client character.

QUALITY OF THE STAFF-CLIENT RELATIONSHIP

The relationship between the staff and the client serves a dual function. First, it is the vehicle through which services are actually provided. Second, it is a mechanism through which the staff gains sufficient control over the client to ensure compliance with the intervention procedures. At the core of this relationship is the degree of *trust* that emerges between a client and a staff person (Hasenfeld, 1978), for trust represents willingness to put one's fate and welfare into the hands of the other person—a cornerstone of the helping process. The client's trust represents a belief in the quality and desirability of the services of the staff and confidence in their skills, methods, and mode of conduct (Bidwell, 1970). Concomitantly, the trust of the staff reflects their confidence that the client will not abuse the relationship and exploit it for illegitimate purposes. Clearly without trust, the client cannot hope to gain the moral commitment of the staff to respond to his or her needs, and the staff cannot hope to gain access to the client's private domain to administer intervention techniques.

A trusting relationship is predicated, first and foremost, on the compatibility between the clients' personal goals and the aims and interests of the staff. For clients, such compatibility ensures that the outcomes of the organizational intervention will serve their needs, and this provides them with the impetus to put themselves in the hands of the staff. Similarly, the staff will be less concerned that the clients might use the relationship for dubious purposes. It is partly for this reason that clients express greater satisfaction with fee-for-service medical practice, since in this system physicians are more motivated to foster congruency between the patient's personal goals and the treatment objectives (Freidson, 1970: 305–6). In contrast, forming a trusting relationship between staff and clients is exceedingly difficult in settings where clients have no choice or control over their entry or exit (Bidwell, 1970). The burden falls on staff to demonstrate to clients a mutuality of interests; and unless the organization provides inducements to do so, they are more likely to assume a custodial posture. That is, they will invest little in developing a positive relationship with clients.

In this context, the reputation of the organization will significantly influence the clients' trust. In general, the greater the prestige and reputation of the organization for providing quality services, the greater the confidence of the clients in the competence of its personnel—the major ingredient in the establishment of trust (Bidwell, 1970). However, much of the potency of the organization's reputation is based on the dissemination of diffused and selective knowledge about itself. Hence, the reputation of the organization is more effective in gaining the trust of a naïve rather than a sophisticated client. The latter is more likely to withhold judgment until concrete actions by staff attest to their trustworthiness.

The ratio of client volume to available resources will also be a determinant of the quality of relations between staff and clients. Having to serve many clients without sufficient resources to meet their needs is likely to have deleterious effects on both staff and clients. Staff will be under pressure to process as many clients as possible while being frustrated by their inability to meet the service requests. Clients will feel that they are not receiving adequate individual attention and that the organization is not sufficiently responsive to their needs. Each will view the other with suspicion. The lack of sufficient resources to meet client needs is probably the chief factor in generating hostility between staff and clients. Staff find themselves in a position of having to deny services and then justifying the denial by resorting to bureaucratic procedures. Clients are likely to lay the blame on the staff persons themselves rather than on some abstract and unfamiliar rules and regulations.

In the same vein, the degree of staff commitment to, or alienation from, their work will significantly affect the quality of relationships with clients. When staff feel positively toward their work, have a sense of control over it, and feel able to express themselves through it, they are more likely to impart these attitudes to their clients who constitute the most important component of the job. When staff members feel alienated from their work, they are also likely to feel alienated from their clients and to regard relationships with them as unrewarding.

The construction of the client's moral character plays a crucial role in determining the degree of trust that will emerge between staff and client. Clearly, a client perceived to be morally responsible for his or her predicaments is more likely to be mistrusted, and the surveillance aspect of the relationship will be emphasized over the helping aspect. Similarly, a client judged to have low social worth is also more likely to be mistrusted for trying to get more than he or she really deserves. In both instances, the burden falls on the client to demonstrate trustworthiness. Doing so may be too costly for some clients, who may then opt for a more manipulative relationship, further reinforcing staff mistrust (Fontana, 1971).

When staff treat clients as subjects—as persons capable of participating in making decisions about their own fate—rather than as objects, clients' trust is likely to increase, because they are more likely to feel that their interests and wishes are being taken into account. Several studies of physician-patient relationships have noted that a trusting relationship emerges when the patient is actively involved in the treatment process and participates in decisions about its course (Howard, 1975; Freidson, 1970; David, 1968). Similarly, studies of teacher-student interaction patterns, although not measuring trust directly, suggest that when teachers encourage students to participate in decision making and to make choices in curricular matters, students accept teachers to a greater degree, and classroom morale improves (Larkin, 1975; Bossert, 1979).

As indicated in Chapter 5, the quality of staff-client relations (i.e., trust) is also affected by the mechanisms of client control used by the organization, especially its overt control mechanisms—persuasion, promises, and threats. Clients may enter the organization with a positive, neutral, or negative attitude toward it. The interaction between clients' initial orientations and the overt control mechanisms they experience will influence their subsequent levels of trust. It is clear that trust relations cannot be established by threats; they require promises and persuasion. In principle, the movement from coercion to persuasion increases trust (Gamson, 1968). Yet, the relative impact of these mechanisms depends on the clients' initial orientation as indicated in Table 7.2.

TABLE 7.2 Effects of client's initial orientation and organization's means of control on client trust

CLIENT'S INITIAL ORIENTATION	ORGANIZATION'S MEANS OF CONTROL		
	Persuasion	Promises	Threats
Positive	M[a]	−	−
Neutral	+	M	−
Negative	+	+	M

[a]M = Maintained current level of trust
+ = Increased level of trust
− = Decreased level of trust

When the correspondence between the client's inital orientation and the organization's means of control is along the diagonal, the initial level of trust will remain unchanged. That is, when the client's initial orientation is positive and the organization's means of control is persuasion, the client's initial trust will not change. Similarly, when the client's initial orientation is negative and the organization relies on threats, the client's initial mistrust will remain unchanged. The interaction between the two dimensions below the diagonal will *increase* the client's trust; namely, when the client enters the organization with a negative or neutral orientation, and the organization responds with persuasion, the client's trust will increase. In contrast, the interaction between the two dimensions above the diagonal will *decrease* the client's trust.

DIFFERENTIAL CLIENT CAREERS

The processes through which people are linked to human service organizations, become their clients, and establish relations with their staff generate an unintended consequence of inequalities in the allocation of services. These are manifested in the differential careers that classes of clients have between and within human service organizations. The differentiation of clients by the quantity and quality of services they obtain need not produce inequalities if their distribution is based on acceptable universalistic criteria of need. As Lipsky (1980) points out, an appropriate system for differentiating clients could be the *triage*. This refers to a medical scheme in battlefield situations in which wounded soldiers are classified into three categories: (1) the mortally wounded, who have little hope of recovery; (2) the seriously wounded, who can be saved by prompt attention; and (3) the lightly wounded, who do not need immediate attention. Theoretically, such a scheme applied to all human services might ensure optimum benefits from limited resources; and undoubtedly it is implemented, albeit imperfectly, in many settings.

Nonetheless, as much of the previous discussion has demonstrated, other forces enter into the determination of client careers, and these can easily mitigate or distort the purpose of triaging. Specifically, three sets of such interrelated forces can be identified; (1) the power-dependence relations between clients and the organization, (2) the cultural and normative context of the organization and its staff, and (3) the political and economic needs of the organization and its staff.

The dynamics of the power-dependence relations between the organization and its clients are such that clients who possess resources valued by the organization can more effectively negotiate favorable organizational responses, independent of their need. This is manifested in several ways.

First, as pointed out earlier, powerful clients have greater choice and control over the organizations they choose to deal with. They can more readily absorb the costs of searching and obtaining the services of organizations judged to provide high-quality services. As a result, high-status clients are more likely to interact with human service organizations characterized by a high degree of professionalization and expertise, a favorable ratio of resources per client, and trusting and humane relations between staff and clients. In contrast, low-status clients are more likely to interact with service organizations that score poorly on these dimensions. This is amply demonstrated in the markedly different choice of schools, medical care facilities, and social service agencies by high- and low-status clients. For example, of all persons requiring psychiatric hospitalization in 1971, 36 percent of whites were admitted to private inpatient psychiatric facilities, compared to 11 percent of nonwhites (Gruber, 1980: 65). Similarly, persons of low socioeconomic status are more likely to be admitted to public rather than private psychiatric facilities, although the disparity has narrowed in the past decade (Rosen, 1977).

Second, as discussed before, even within the same organization, higher-status clients can use their resources and power to obtain better services through differential tracking systems: private rather than ward accommodations and expert physicians rather than residents and interns in hospitals (Duff and Hollingshead, 1968); academic rather than vocational tracks in public schools (Schafer and Olexa, 1971); and bail and better legal counsel in courts (Lizotte, 1978).

The organization cannot effectively insulate itself from the prevailing norms and values that sustain and justify existing patterns of social inequality. Nor can it buffer itself from prejudices and discriminatory attitudes toward certain social groups. In fact, these values and attitudes find their expression in how the staff constructs the clients' moral characters. Consequently, lower-class clients and clients from ethnic and racial minorities, among other devalued social groups, face a greater risk of being ascribed low social worth, which, in turn, limits their access to valued services. For example, youth from minority groups are more likely to be committed to juvenile correctional institutions than Anglos, when controlling for previous offenses and seriousness of the offense (Arnold, 1971). Psychiatric outpatient services are more likely to view black females as not amenable to extensive psychotherapy and assign them, therefore, to brief crisis intervention (Krebs, 1971). Racial and class biases are frequently ingrained in the professional judgments of the service providers, In an experiment on clinical judgments, Fischer and Miller (1973) found that when given hypothetical cases in which only social class and racial labels were changed, workers' clinical judgments were significantly affected. Lower-class clients were judged more negatively, as less attractive, and as having less capacity to improve.

Moreover, in many instances, human service organizations are charged with the very task of upholding values and norms that differentially ascribe social worth to various social groups. A welfare department may find itself denying services to needy but able bodied persons because they are viewed as "undeserving poor." In the same vein, when the organization is seeking to improve or protect its economic resources, it may give preference to clients whose attributes enhance its economic position, as in the preference for young blind over older blind persons (Scott, 1967a). When resources begin to shrink and the organization is forced to curtail services, it may do so less on the basis of need than on the basis of the political power of various client constituencies and the fiscal resources that can be mobilized on their behalf.

While the effectiveness of the service technologies is predicated on the differential handling of clients, organizational efforts to demonstrate success and to uphold practice ideologies may also generate inequities. As was pointed out earlier, the ideal patient, in the eyes of most psychotherapists, is youthful, attractive, verbal, intelligent, and successful—known by the acronym YAVIS (Schofield, 1964). A recent study by Link and Milcarek (1980) on dispensation of individual and group therapies in New York State hospitals found that after controlling for the psychiatric diagnosis, those who were the youngest, most competent, most communicative, and most motivated received the most therapeutic attention. As noted earlier, school officials do, in fact, use the triage argument—allocating limited resources to those with the greatest potential to succeed academically—to justify tracking. However, the criteria used to track students—ability, effort, and achievement—are of dubious validity and reliability, yet justified by the ideologies of the teachers (Rosenbaum, 1976). Once students are placed in a vocational track, their overall level of performance (i.e., GPA) persistently declines even when controlling for ability, while that of the academic track rises. This suggests that the initial biases in tracking may be reinforced through the behaviors and attitudes of the teachers toward the students (Schafer and Olexa, 1971). The differential consequences of the students' careers then reaffirm the teachers' ideologies.

Working conditions in the organization also play a role here. Clients may be differentiated on the basis of ease or difficulty in handling, with the former being preferred over the latter. For example, ward attendants tend to aggregate their patients into groups along a continuum that ranges from "inability to care for oneself" to "ability to help in running the ward." They do so for two reasons. "First, the better the condition of the patient, the less work and worry he occasions. Second, aides not only want to cut down on their own work, but, if possible, to make the patient more useful" (Strauss et al., 1964: 122). Similarly, Lorber (1975) found that patients who did not assume a submissive, uncomplaining, and undemanding role were more likely to be defined as problem patients, which might lead to their neglect, rejection, and early discharge.

It should not be implied from this discussion that inequalities in the allocation of services are inevitable in human service organizations. In several sectors of human services, such as medical care, inequality has probably declined in the past decade due to such programs as Medicare and Medicaid. Rather, it suggests that unless systematically controlled and checked, conditions outside and inside human service organizations tend to make them vulnerable and susceptible to inequitable allocations of services. In the final analysis, such vulnerability exists because human service organizations are an integral part of the larger social stratification system, and they both reflect it as well as contribute to its maintenance.

CONCLUSION

A basic characteristic of client-organization relations is the power advantage the organization holds over the client. This pattern is inevitable when individuals delegate the responsibility for caring for their needs to corporate actors (i.e., organizations), thus becoming dependent on them (Coleman, 1973). Consequently, clients of human service organizations find themselves in a power disadvantage, depending greatly on the values, norms, and policies of the organization to protect them.

It need not follow that because clients are highly dependent on human service organizations that their needs are likely to be ignored or be subjugated to organizational interests. Most studies, albeit methodologically problematic, suggest that recipients of human services tend to be satisfied with the ways they are treated (Nelson, 1981; Katz et al., 1975). This results mostly from the fact that powerful internal and external social control mechanisms limit the exercise of power by human service practitioners. Nonetheless, the protection of the clients' welfare and well-being has now become dependent on the effectiveness of these control mechanisms. Yet, ironically, the efficacy of these controls is determined to a significant extent by the ability and power of clients and their advocates to mobilize and enforce them.

The loss of client power vis-à-vis human service organizations is not distributed equally; rather, it reflects the overall social stratification system. High-status clients can mobilize more power and use it more effectively when dealing with human service organizations. Thus, client-organization relations are sensitive to status differences, and human service organizations tend to be more responsive to higher-status clients.

8

ASSESSMENT
OF ORGANIZATIONAL
PERFORMANCE

Every organization, and human services are no exception, is frequently assessed both by its task environment and by various internal groups. The
results affect the long-term survival of the organization in two critical ways:
First, a steady flow of resources and legitimation is contingent on a favorable
evaluation by those controlling them. Providers of legitimation and other
resources will continue to invest in the organization as long as it can demonstrate that its performance is congruent with their interests. Second, the
power of key groups in the organization, such as the dominant coalition, is
also dependent on a favorable assessment of the organization's performance. As noted in Chapter 6, the source of such power rests in the ability
of these groups to demonstrate that they can effectively cope with the major
issues facing the organization. Hence, the political and economic viability of
the organization, both externally and internally, is critically affected by measurements of its effectiveness and efficiency.

For the human services, assessment of performance typically probes
the following issues (Rossi, 1978): (1) is the organization reaching its target
population?; (2) is it providing its mandated services?; (3) are the services
effective?; (4) are they being provided efficiently? Clearly, the capacity to
respond to these questions varies widely among human service organizations. Nonetheless, all must address them in some fashion lest they jeopar-

dize their viability. Indeed, in recent years, with the escalating costs of human services, these organizations have been increasingly pressed to demonstrate their effectiveness and efficiency and to be accountable for their activities. An entire industry of "program evaluation" has emerged, supported largely by government agencies, dedicated to the assessment of human services. Most publicly funded programs are now required to have their services evaluated as a prerequisite for continued support.

Paradoxically, the dramatic increase in these efforts to assess the performance of human service organizations has heightened public condemnation for their failure to demonstrate their effectiveness and efficiency. To quote Rossi (1978: 236): "most programs, when properly evaluated, turn out to be ineffective or at best marginally accomplishing their set aims." Several factors pertaining to the evaluation process itself contribute to the dismal results. First, the objectives of human services are multiple and complex and cannot be readily summarized into simple performance criteria. Second, the indeterminacy of the service technologies precludes accurate measurement. Third, isolating the effects of the services on the clients from extraneous factors is exceedingly difficult to accomplish. Fourth, the effects of the services on clients are not readily quantifiable. Finally, the results of the assessment are seldom unequivocal and, therefore, are open to conflicting interpretations.

Thus it may be argued that human service organizations encounter problems in evaluating effectiveness and efficiency that are not commonly found in other types of organizations. This theme will be explored in this chapter.

DEFINITIONS OF ORGANIZATIONAL EFFECTIVENESS AND EFFICIENCY

Despite the popularity of the concepts of effectiveness and efficiency in theories of organization and management, there is no consensus about their meaning, let alone about their measurement (Steers, 1975; Campbell, 1977). Several factors account for the ambiguity of these concepts: First, organizations have their own widely different conceptions of effectiveness and efficiency, and these may change over time. Second, even when comparable concepts are available, they are often measured differently by each organization. Third, organizations use multiple measures and assign them differential weights. Fourth, the unit of analysis often refers both to subunits as well as to the organization as a whole. For the researcher interested in the comparative study of organizations, this situation is exasperating because both the meaning and the measurement of the concepts lack convergence.

Following a rational model, it can be argued that an organization's *effectiveness* refers to the degree to which it is achieving its goals (Campbell, 1977). For example, if we assume that the goal of correctional programs is to reduce future criminal behavior, then effectiveness can be measured by recidivism rates. Similarly, if the goals of schools are to improve reading, writing, and arithmetic, then their effectiveness can be measured by the improvement in students' achievement scores. *Efficiency*, in this context, refers to the ratio of outputs (i.e., goal attainment) to inputs (i.e., costs, efforts). In the case of correctional programs, one can calculate for each program the costs of achieving a certain reduction in the recidivism rate. This is often referred to as *cost-effectiveness analysis* (Gray et al., 1978).

The rational model recognizes that the organization may have multiple goals; but as long as these can be explicitly defined and ranked, the definition and measurement of effectiveness and efficiency remain unambiguous. Indeed, most program evaluations assume such a model. The first step in program evaluation always consists of defining the program's goals or objectives. To quote Rossi, Freeman, and Wright (1979: 63): "... [the] first task for the evaluator is to develop clear and consistent statements of goals in consultation with planners, project managers, and policy makers. It bears emphasis that unless goals can be clarified and objectives operationalized, it is unlikely that an adequate evaluation can be attempted."

The objections to the rational model are well known (see Chapter 2), particularly, the discrepancy between official and operative goals, the multiplicity and instability of goals, and the conflict and lack of consensus about them (see also Chapter 4). Deutscher (1976) argues that, as a result, program evaluation falls into a "goal trap." As he puts it: "It is a foolish evaluator indeed who attempts to study a program in terms of the goals which it proposed in order to get funded. Such an evaluation is most likely to show no effects as well as alienate all parties involved" (p. 252). Hannan and Freeman (1977b) conclude that because of the difficulties in defining and measuring organizational goals, the concept of effectiveness is not useful to the general study of organizations, although they acknowledge its importance to administrators.

To overcome the difficulties of the rational model, organizational theorists have proposed that the concept be viewed from a *systems perspective* (e.g., Yuchtman and Seashore, 1967). From this perspective, all organizational activities are seen as directed toward survival and growth. Consequently, effectiveness is defined as "the ability of the organization, in either absolute or relative terms, to exploit its environment in the acquisition of scarce and valued resources" (Yuchtman and Seashore, 1967: 898). This definition implies that organizations can be compared in terms of their relative capacity to mobilize resources, and that those with greater capacity are more effective. A systems perspective requires that we concentrate on identifying those organizational processes and activities that contribute directly to its survival, growth, and bargaining position in the environment. Seashore and Yuchtman (1967), in their study of insurance agencies, identify such factors as business volume, production costs, new members' productivity, youthfulness of members, business mix, manpower growth, management emphasis, maintenance costs, member productivity, and market penetration. These become, in fact, the operationalization and measurement factors of organizational effectiveness. Other researchers, with the same perspective, employ such criteria as adaptability-flexibility, productivity, satisfaction, profitability, resource acquisition, absence of strain, and the like (Steers, 1975). Applied to hospitals, for example, criteria of effectiveness include quality of patient care, staff satisfaction, availability of resources and their allocation, degree of internal coordination, social-normative integration, organizational strain and conflict resolution, and adaptation to the community (Georgopoulos and Matejko, 1967). Hospitals receiving positive ratings on these criteria are said to be effective.

The difficulties with such an approach are apparent. First, practically every organizational activity can serve as a criterion of effectiveness. It is not surprising, therefore, that Campbell (1977) can identify thirty such factors, ranging from productivity to training and emphasis on development. Second, normative assumptions must be made as to the desirable direction of these activities. Does a high degree of staff satisfaction indeed represent effectiveness? Third, as Hall (1977) points out, the capacity of the organization to survive, grow, and acquire resources *is* related to its outputs—namely, its goals. In the case of hospitals, quality of patient care is obviously of at least some importance to its survival.

A Political Economy Perspective

It may be preferable to view organizational effectiveness from a *political economy perspective*. This is based on the assumption that the organization's capacity to acquire resources depends on its ability to score well on the evaluation criteria used by those who control access to these resources. Organizational effectiveness is thus defined from the perspective of the organization's resource providers. The greater the capacity of the organization to meet *their* evaluation criteria, the greater its effectiveness. For example, when the funding of a welfare department is contingent on its ability to reduce its error rate when processing applicants, then its effectiveness is defined and measured on that basis. Similarly, when the ability of academic departments to procure resources from the university's administrators depends on the reputation and research productivity of their faculty, the latter become, in effect, measures of effectiveness.

Effectiveness, from this perspective, is still linked to resource acquisition. A comparative study of organizations will measure relative effectiveness by the capacity of each organization to acquire resources over a given period (e.g., total revenues per client in the last five years). However, if we wish to understand the dynamics through which each organization affects its own effectiveness, or how it is influenced by the environment, we must explore the definition and measurement of the concept in the *political and economic context* of the organization. From the organization's vantage point, the definition of effectiveness that has meaning for its decision-making processes is the one determined by its resource providers. Hence, the organization may well adopt multiple and often conflicting criteria to satisfy its various resource providers. Moreover, these criteria may change over time as the organization's resource needs shift, or as environmental conditions alter. It should be emphasized that members of the organization will actively participate in shaping the criteria of effectiveness as they negotiate with various resource providers. The dynamics of these negotiations will be detailed below. Efficiency, in this context, refers to the costs to the organization in meeting these criteria.

TYPES OF ASSESSMENT

If criteria of effectiveness are politically determined, it follows that some criteria will have greater importance to the organization than others. Two factors will determine the relative importance of each criterion: (1) the relative power of those upholding it, and (2) the degree of its observability or measurement. For a criterion to be elevated in importance, it must be supported by key resource providers. This is a necessary but not a sufficient condition. If a criterion cannot be observed or measured, it cannot be enforced. For example, all the providers of resources to a mental hospital will probably agree that quality of patient care is a primary criterion of effectiveness. Yet, because it cannot be explicated and specified in unambiguous terms, let alone be reliably measured, this criterion loses its potency. Units in the hospital can justify a variety of activities by claiming they improve the quality of patient care.

These two factors will determine the type of assessment performed by an organization. When the power of the resource providers is concentrated, or when there is consensus among them, the criteria of effectiveness will be crystallized. But when their power is diffused, or they fail to reach consensus, the criteria themselves will be diffused. In either instance, the observability of the criteria may range from high to low. The cross-classification of these two dimensions generates four major types of assessments, as shown in Table 8.1 (for a similar typology, see Thompson, 1967: 86).

The rational and systems types of assessment have already been discussed. The rational type can be found in organizations where highly observable criteria are imposed or agreed upon by the most powerful resource providers. For example, a university's central administration may determine

TABLE 8.1   A Typology of Assessment Patterns

CRITERIA OF EVALUATION	OBSERVABILITY OF CRITERIA	
	HIGH	LOW
Crystallized	Rational	Satisficing
Diffused	Systems	Symbolic

that the effectiveness of its admissions office be assessed by the test scores and grade point averages of the admitted students. The effectiveness of a mental hospital may be evaluated by its key funders on the basis of the rate of patients released within a specified time after admission and remaining in the community for a minimum set time period (Ullman, 1967). Similarly, one key criterion of effectiveness used by funders for vocational rehabilitation programs has been the rate of placing patients in the labor market for at least a specified time period.

When the criteria imposed or agreed to by the dominant resource providers cannot be readily observed or measured, a *satisficing* pattern will emerge (Thompson, 1967). That is, they will settle for some proximate or indirect measures. For example, because quality of care cannot be explicitly measured, mortality or fatality rates, restoration of functioning, or the extensiveness of treatment may serve as proximate measures (Donabedian, 1966). A board of education wanting "quality education" may settle on achievement test scores, number of graduates entering college, and testimonials by parents and teachers.

When resource providers pursue observable criteria but fail to agree on their relative importance, a *systems* pattern will emerge: Various and often disparate components and activities of the organization, important to different providers, will be assessed simultaneously. This can be noted, for instance, in the assessment of employment services that must account to multiple constituent groups. On the one hand, these agencies are assessed according to their productivity—that is, by the number of clients placed per staff member. On the other hand, they are also assessed by the number of disadvantaged individuals they have served and placed. In addition, they are further assessed by the types of jobs filled, wages earned, and duration of employment of clients. Clearly, some of these measures may be incompatible with others. Improvement in productivity could conflict with serving the disadvantaged. Pursuing only those placements that provide better jobs and higher wages may negatively affect productivity or the ability to serve the disadvantaged.

Finally, when the organization faces competing evaluation criteria that cannot be readily measured or observed, it will opt for symbolic evaluation. It will select symbols that portray the organization in the best possible light to the various resource providers. While these symbols have only an oblique relationship to the organization's actual activities and performance, they will evoke certain images. Put differently, the organization will adopt a myriad of extrinsic measures related to various components and activities, but which reveal little about what it is actually doing or accomplishing. As I will note below, community mental health agencies generate voluminous reports about the sociodemographic characteristics of their clients, expenditures per client, staff contact with clients, patterns of use of various services, ratings of client satisfaction, and various staff testimonials about their programs. These, however, say little about the quality of the services provided or their appropriateness or relative effectiveness. Symbolic evaluation also occurs when measures of efficiency, such as costs per client or contact hours, are substituted for measures of effectiveness.

ASSESSMENT DILEMMAS IN
THE HUMAN SERVICES

It should come as no surprise to the reader that human service organizations tend to employ satisficing or symbolic patterns of assessment. The litany of difficulties in assessing human services, a favorite topic in the literature on program evaluation, attests to the predominance of these patterns. Both structural and methodological factors contribute to this state of affairs.

Nay and associates (1976), after reviewing evaluation studies of social programs, conclude that the difficulties in assessing them derive from three key attributes of these programs: "[1] the program lacks specific, measurable objectives related to program goals; [2] the program lacks plausible, testable assumptions linking program activities to the achievement of program goals; or [3] managers lack the motivation, ability, or authority to manage" (p. 98). Much of our discussion on the structural characteristics of human service organizations indeed confirms their conclusion. To reiterate them briefly: first, human service organizations encounter competing values and interests to which they must accommodate, resulting in ambiguous and conflicting goals. Even when the dominant coalition crystallizes certain interests, these interests do not remain stable over time because of a second factor—a turbulent environment. That is, human service organizations experience frequent changes in environmental conditions, both political and economic, which necessitate program adjustments. As Weiss and Rein (1970) emphasize, social programs cannot control the situations in which they operate. Third, service technologies tend to be indeterminate and cannot provide satisfactory information about cause-effect relations. Fourth, the loose coupling of the internal structure of human services diffuses and obscures the contributions of various units to the organization's total performance.

Working on people also generates methodological problems in developing valid and reliable assessment criteria (Campbell, 1969). First, the complex and usually unknown interrelations among human attributes make it difficult to isolate and measure those subject to intervention and change. Second, extraneous factors other than the services, influence the clients and may account for the service outcomes. Moreover, people mature over time, resulting in changes that cannot be accounted for by the services. Third, an organization can rarely control the entry and exit of its clients, and as a result, biases are introduced that affect the outcomes. Lerman (1968) found that the much-acclaimed success of a treatment program for juvenile offenders dissipated when those who failed to complete the program were included in the evaluation. Because the effectiveness of the service technology is so dependent on clients' attributes, who enters and who leaves has an overwhelming impact on outcomes. Moreover, the conditions of the clients at entry also affect results quite dramatically. Finally, biases are introduced by the very instruments used to measure a program's impact. People react to these instruments in ways that jeopardize their reliability. This is not to imply that some of these methodological problems cannot be overcome, but to do so would exact high costs that the human services cannot absorb.

Displacement of the Criteria of Evaluation

One consequence of these structural and methodological difficulties is the often-noted phenomenon of organizational displacement of the criteria of evaluation. Measurable criteria of efficiency and other testimonials of performance are substituted for criteria of effectiveness (Thompson, 1967). This pattern has already been noted in the discussion on monitoring staff performance (see Chapter 6). That is, the organization follows a twofold course of action: First, it seeks measurable criteria, typically of efficiency, irrespective of their relevance to effectiveness. Second, it relies on various testimonials by clients, staff, and external experts whose impressions constitute the evaluation of the organization's effectiveness. These patterns are noted, for example, in the evaluation system developed for community mental health centers. The system has two components: The first consists of a series of thirteen performance indicators ranging from "significant" minority admission rates, under eighteen and over sixty-five admission rates, fee-for-service payments as percent of total receipts, collections as a percent of amount billed to total expenditures per patient care hour, and face-to-face patient care hours as percent of total patient care hours (NIMH, 1980). The second component includes on-site visits by teams of experts who review descriptive reports on the various programs of the center, conduct interviews with staff, review sample case records, and observe the various operations. These sources of information then serve as the basis for the performance and effectiveness ratings of the center (U.S. Dept. of HEW, 1977). Similar patterns can be readily noted in other human services. Academic departments, for example, are often evaluated on the basis of the number of Ph.D.'s they grant; the length of time it takes for students to obtain the degree; their success in securing employment; and the number of publications by the faculty, their reputation, and testimonials by peers.

One critical result of such displacement is the tendency by the organization to reify these measures as true indicators of effectiveness. The organization allocates its resources and concentrates its efforts to score well on these criteria. The mental health center will attempt to boost the admission of "desirable" clients, reduce the costs of services, and increase face-to-face contact hours. The academic department will try to recruit prestigious faculty, reward publications, and push for faster completion of students' training. While, in several instances, such displacement may actually benefit the clients (for example, by making the program more accessible to ethnic minorities), in many other instances the results can be deleterious. Schools that emphasize college placement as a measure of effectiveness are likely to neglect students in nonacademic tracks. Social service agencies that stress productivity and efficiency may compromise on quality of services or "cool-out" difficult clients.

THE POLITICS OF EVALUATION

If the assessment of an organization by its key resource providers significantly affects its future survival and growth, the definition and measurement of its effectiveness and efficiency become a matter of political contest (Cohen, 1972; Weiss, 1975). Interest groups, external and internal, attempt to influence the assessment of the organization so that the resulting resource allocations buttress their respective interests. That is, the political strategy for each interest group consists of: identifying those organizational activities and performances that support its interests, requiring the evaluation of just these activities and performances, and linking the desired outcome of the evaluation with the ability of the organization to attain and allocate resources. For example, interest groups advocating help for oppressed minorities attempt to force the organization to adopt assessment criteria that measure services to these minorities, and link the results of such measurements to the organization's ability to obtain future funding. In general, interest groups attempt to influence the following components of the assessment process: the determination of the assessment criteria, the selection of the client population to be assessed, the determination of the measurement instruments and procedures, and the interpretation of the findings.

Determination of the Assessment Criteria

Resource providers attempt to define the assessment criteria in order to *control* critical organizational activities so that such activities will conform to providers' interests. When federal funding of public assistance is contingent on the evaluation of the error rate in processing applicants, the funders clearly intend to induce the agency to uphold the norm of deservingness as defined by *them*. In contrast, welfare rights advocates, aiming to replace the norm of deservingness by a norm of entitlement, attempt to force the agency to adopt different criteria of effectiveness—such as fairness and lower rejection rates—through court challenges. Similarly, consumer advocacy groups attempt to force human service organizations to include indicators of client satisfaction in their evaluation criteria. The conflicts, bargains, and compromises that mark political negotiations among these groups generate criteria of assessment that reflect the relative power and influence of each. Therefore, human service organizations encounter multiple and conflicting criteria, some of which are aimed at appeasing contesting groups. The dominant coalition also attempts to influence these criteria to buttress its position and uphold its interests. It mobilizes the resources of its constituent members and becomes an active participant in the political contest. Finally, internal groups also attempt to influence these criteria to challenge the dominant coalition and win concessions. For example, students and faculty who believe that the quality of teaching is as important as faculty research and publications may push for the adoption of student ratings of faculty instruction as one criterion of assessment. Similarly, nursing staff will push to include specific criteria about the quality of the nursing care in order to highlight the staff's importance in the hospital.

These contests over assessment criteria are well exemplified in the evaluation of the Head Start program (Williams and Evans, 1969). The idea of Head Start originated with the notion that early childhood training could significantly boost later cognitive and affective development. The program, once started, gained rapid and wide-ranging popularity and became a showcase program for the fledgling Office of Economic Opportunity. The evaluation of the program, contracted to the Westinghouse Learning Corporation, concluded, however, that the program appeared to be ineffective in producing any cognitive and affective gains that persisted into the early elementary grades. Leaving methodological issues aside, the controversy surrounding the findings centered on the fact that the evaluation failed to assess other goals of the program not stated in its original conception, such as health, nutrition, and community involvement. Those who wished to eliminate or curtail the program pushed the criteria of cognitive and affective development; those who wanted to maintain it pushed for the other criteria.

Selection of the Client Population

Which client population will be assessed has obvious effects on the results of any evaluation. In general, an organization attempts to focus on those clients who can generate favorable outcomes on the dominant assessment criteria. For example, as mentioned earlier, when a treatment program for juvenile offenders tries to demonstrate its effectiveness, it may "conveniently" exclude from the evaluation those who have failed to complete the program (Lerman, 1968).

The phenomenon of "creaming"—selecting the clients most amenable to improvement—is clearly related to the desire of an organization to demonstrate its effectiveness. This is noted, for instance, in the selection of patients for psychotherapy, or in the tracking of students into academic and vocational courses (see Chapter 7). Likewise, police departments, when pressed to demonstrate their effectiveness as measured by crimes cleared through arrest, tend to focus their attention on crimes committed in public places, such as prostitution, gambling, and narcotics peddling, and to publicize successful prosecution of violent crimes such as homicide, even though the latter accounts for only a small proportion of the crimes known to them (Reiss and Bordua, 1967). Similarly, to demonstrate its cost-effectiveness, an organization may focus on those clients who need fewer resources, as in the case of manpower training programs. Critics of an organization, on the other hand, push for a definition of the client population that will expose its vulnerability. For example, by requesting that an organization indicate the scope of its services to oppressed minorities, they hope to ensure that the organization does not ignore them. In short, the selection of the client population to be assessed becomes a political decision by means of which various interest groups attempt to influence the service delivery patterns of the organization.

Determination of Measurement Instruments and Procedures

Similarly, the selection of methods and instruments to assess an organization is also politically motivated. The sources and content of information used to evaluate an organization affect its scores on assessment criteria. In general, human service organizations prefer to rely on their own records as sources of information because they can control the content. By means of its recordkeeping system, an organization can select the type and content of information on its various activities. In this sense, the record is not a neutral instrument. The facts contained in the record are organizationally determined because they are shaped by its information gathering, processing, and interpreting schemata (Zimmerman, 1969b; Wilensky, 1967). In my study of employment placement services (1975), for example, I found that the staff failed to record some critical employment background information on applicants because it would complicate their placement decisions. On the other hand, they tended to overstate applicants' handicaps to justify their decisions. Similarly, McLeary (1977) noted how parole officers manipulate the records of their parolees to meet organizational expectations. In other words, records can provide the *justification* for the actions taken by various members of an organization.

When the criteria of effectiveness are not readily observable, human service organizations prefer to rely on the judgments of their own staff and to resist independent appraisals. In particular, organizations dominated by professionals insist on the right to self- or peer evaluation. Various rating scales and protocols by which staff record the progress of their clients exemplify such tactics. As in the case of records, an organization can control the values of these ratings. This is not to imply that the staff will deliberately distort their judgments; rather it implies that the yardsticks being used and the information gathered and interpreted are organizationally determined, and hence biased. For example, a commonly used rating device in community mental health centers is the Goal Attainment Scaling by which staff estimate anticipated and actual client progress toward agreed-upon treatment goals (Kiresuk and Lund, 1978). Yet a careful review of the research indicates that both the validity and reliability of the instrument are questionable because it is susceptible to organizational and individual biases (Cytrynbaum et al., 1979). Similar concerns can be raised about the efficacy of such popular peer evaluation procedures as Professional Standards Review Organizations (PSRO) or the quality assurance assessment (e.g., Morehead, 1976). While these procedures may detect gross violations of professional standards, their effectiveness in enhancing quality of care is doubtful, exactly because of their self-evaluating, self-policing features.

In a more general way, the production of data for assessment purposes is also wrought with inherent biases because it is used to measure performance. Cochran (1978) has identified four sources of data corruption: (1) data acquire an aura of authenticity even when they are false; (2) a larger volume of data will be produced around services subject to review, thus giving them the appearance of greater importance; (3) when minimum or maximum standards of performance are set, they are often reversed in actuality; and (4) when a quantifiable standard is set, meeting it becomes its own end.

Interpretation of Findings

Finally, assessment results can seldom be unequivocally interpreted and are therefore subject to competing political influences. The metaphor of whether the cup is half full or half empty epitomizes this issue. Those wishing to maintain the status quo emphasize the positive; those trying to discredit the organization point to the negative findings. Neubeck and Roach (1981) point out how ambiguous results from various income maintenance experiments, particularly their effects on work efforts and marital dissolution, were seized by opponents to buttress their position. As they put it: "Political elites are likely to see as significant and useful those research results that fit well their already formed ideological predispositions, and ignore or challenge those that conflict with them" (p. 315). The same holds true at the organizational level, as exemplified by a case study of a well-known educational innovation (Levine and Levine, 1977). At the turn of the century, Gary, Indiana, had acquired a reputation for possessing one of the most effective and efficient school systems in the country. The Gary system, developed by William Wirt, gained national and international recognition and was adopted by many school districts. "Gary's fame rested on its efficient combination of 'work, study and play.' The children were divided into 'platoons,' rotating through a schedule emphasizing vocational, physical, and expressive education, as well as the usual school subjects" (p. 517). Late in 1913, prominent groups in New York City pressed the newly elected mayor to introduce the Gary system in the New York schools, which were suffering from large debts and overcrowded conditions. The innovation was resisted, however, by the school superintendent and certain members of the Board of Education. The associate superintendent, who was sent to Gary to evaluate the system, wrote a highly critical report that was vehemently attacked by Wirt and his supporters. The plan was ultimately implemented in several schools and was subsequently evaluated by the district's research department. The results showed that the achievement scores of students in these schools were lower than those of students in the traditional schools. Again, the evaluation was challenged both in the press and in professional journals, and the plan continued to have the support of the mayor. One of the key supporters of the plan sponsored a new study of the Gary schools, while at the same time advocating his own educational plan. The findings of this later study were also negative, and were published just prior to the mayoral election in which the plan was one of the campaign issues. Shortly after the election, the new mayor who campaigned against the plan, began to dismantle it.

It is clear that, in general, a considerable amount of performance data is ignored by human service organizations (Weiss, 1981). First, dominant ideologies and values tend to screen out potentially challenging or threatening information. Second, as will be shown in Chapter 9, an organization faces formidable constraints in its efforts to change. Hence, its decision makers tend to devalue performance data that challenge the status quo. Third, given the characteristics of human services, particularly the ambiguity of cause-effect relations, the information may fail to point to any effective solutions. Finally, the usefulness of the information will be judged, as indicated above, in political terms. Information that is not seen to be of political value will be discarded.

Furthermore, performance data about an organization's responsiveness to clients often come to naught. Clients lack the political influence to make their criteria important to the organization. Nor does the organization have the knowledge or capability to change its service delivery system in response to performance data. Organizations often find it more expeditious to ascribe various client benefits to existing patterns.

Organizations respond to performance data only when the data have gained enough importance to break through the barriers noted above. This is most likely to occur when the consequences of a performance assessment threaten the survival and growth of an organization.

CONCLUSION

Because human service organizations rely mostly on satisficing and symbolic assessment patterns, they are deprived of accurate, sensitive feedback about their modes of operation. Information feedback, particularly of a negative kind, enables an organization to correct operational deficiencies and is thus vital to survival. As Miller (1955) has proposed, "When a system's negative feedback discontinues, its steady state vanishes, and at the same time its boundary disappears and the system terminates" (p. 529). Hence, an assessment system of dubious validity and reliability, as is the case in many human services, jeopardizes an organization's capacity to change and adapt.

Human service organizations face particularly acute problems as they encounter an increasingly turbulent environment whose political institutions demand greater accountability and demonstrated effectiveness. Recognizing that criteria of effectiveness and efficiency are politically determined, they shape their assessment systems to be responsive to the power wielders, but in the process face the danger of becoming captive to them. An assessment system is not merely an instrument to appease powerful interest groups. It can also serve as a tool for an organization to mobilize power by means of the information it controls and uses. A multifaceted or a systems assessment approach appealing to multiple constituencies can potentially broaden the political support base of the organization. Put differently, an organization's autonomy hinges on its ability to take an active stance in formulating its evaluation criteria.

In the final analysis, human services are caught in the dialectical dilemma in defining their assessment systems. On the one hand, the quest for valid and reliable measures is likely to expose their weaknesses and vulnerabilities. On the other hand, it is only through such measures that they can ultimately provide effective services to clients.

9

CHANGING
HUMAN SERVICE
ORGANIZATIONS

To increase its responsiveness to clients, an organization must have the capacity to change both its programs and its structure. Human service organizations have been widely criticized for their seeming inability to change. For example, many innovations for providing quality education to the poor sprang up in the 1960s. Nonetheless, when the dust settled, the result was, according to Janowitz (1969) "a great deal of innovation and very little change." Most schools, after experimenting with numerous innovations, ultimately discarded most of them and returned to "business as usual." Efforts to reform public assistance experienced a similar fate. In reviewing these efforts, Street, Martin, and Gordon (1979: 117–18) concluded that "over a decade of efforts at a basic change . . . came to nought, and the fundamental operating principles of public assistance were little changed even by the activities of the War on Poverty period." Similar assertions have been made about mental hospitals and correctional programs.

Several factors that inhibit change in human services have been suggested. First, as public bureaucracies, human service organizations are controlled by powerful interest groups who seek to maintain the status quo. Second, since clients are so powerless, their needs and interests are likely to be ignored, and thus do not stimulate change. Third, the bureaucratic structure of these organizations is rigid and inflexible, making change very costly.

Fourth, professionals and bureaucrats working in these organizations attempt to promote their own interests and resist any change that affects their status.

Despite these arguments, however, other evidence suggests that human service organizations are capable of—and do—change. Ohlin and associates (1977) have documented dramatic reforms in juvenile corrections in Massachusetts. Zald (1970b) has traced the radical changes in YMCA services and programs, and Milio (1971) has studied a new way of delivering health care by neighborhood health care centers. Clearly, then, human service organizations are capable of changing.

This chapter examines the dynamics of change in human service organizations, and particularly the conditions which inhibit change and the forces which promote innovation.

ORGANIZATIONAL INNOVATION AND CHANGE

Organizational *innovation* has been defined as "any idea, practice, or material artifact perceived to be new by the relevant unit of adoption" (Zaltman, Duncan, and Holbek, 1971: 10). Such a definition is very broad and encompasses new ideas and practices related to the product, technology, structure, and interpersonal relations of the organization. The emphasis is on newness as *perceived by the organization*, even though the idea itself may have long existed in another form and may have been known to other organizations. This point is particularly stressed by Downs and Mohr (1979: 385), who define innovation as "the earliness or extent of use by a given organization of a given new idea, where 'new' means only new to the adopting agent, and not necessarily to the world in general." However, I prefer a more limited concept. Innovation here is defined as the adoption of a product, service, or technology perceived to be new by the organization (Hage, 1980). By thus limiting the definition of innovation, we can avoid the confusion between innovation and other changes that may occur in an organization, particularly those related to internal structure.

In contrast to innovation, organizational *change* refers to alterations in the allocation of resources, distribution of power, and the internal structure of an organization. For example, a redirection in an organization's mission that involves shifts in the allocation of resources from one set of activities to another, or the ascendancy to power of hitherto uninfluential groups, constitutes organizational changes. Similarly, the establishment of a new program that necessitates investment of resources and internal restructuring of the division of labor will be referred to as organizational change. Note that executive succession may not constitute change unless it involves a significant recomposition of the organization's dominant coalition, reflecting changes in the distribution of power. Hence, organizational change refers to the transformation of *both* the internal polity and the economy of the organization, while innovation is limited to alterations in the product and technology components of the internal economy.

The *attributes* of an innovation are important variables that help explain organizational responses to it. Zaltman, Duncan, and Holbek (1971) reviewed much of the literature on the attributes of innovation and identified such dimensions as costs, return on investment, efficiency, risk and uncertainty, communicability, compatibility, complexity, perceived relative advantage, impact on interpersonal relations, and the like. Yet, as Downs and Mohr (1979) point out, such a list may be expanded infinitely. Rather, the various attributes of an innovation can be reduced to one basic issue: the costs and benefits, both political and economic, an organization expects to accrue from an innovation. As we shall see, this calculation is the key determinant in the adoption of an innovation.

From this perspective, an innovation becomes *radical* when its implementation requires changes in the allocations of resources, the distribution of power, and the internal structure of an organization. For example, when a family service agency adopts a new treatment technology based on behavior modification resulting in significant decline of the previously powerful psychoanalytically trained workers, shifts in the distribution of resources to support the new technology, and alterations in the internal division of labor, a radical innovation (and, hence, organizational change) has occurred.

It is important, in this context, to distinguish between *symbolic* and *real change*. When an organization reorganizes its internal structure—shifts positions around, establishes new channels of communication and coordination, creates new groupings of work units—but does not reallocate resources and power, it has undergone only a symbolic change. That is, such a reorganization may affect the style of work but not its content or importance. For example, when an agency groups workers into teams without altering the power relations among its members, it has undergone no real change. Similarly, when an agency amalgamates services into one division to promote coordination, but does not significantly alter the patterns of supervision and authority, it has undergone only a symbolic change. Such tactics are sometimes used by the executive leadership to give an aura of change and responsiveness to pressures from line staff or clients, without affecting existing power relations.

Organizational "adjustment" should be distinguished from organizational change. Adjustment refers to a set of processes aimed at preserving an organization's homeostasis by balancing the relations between the input of clients and resources, their transformation internally, and an organization's outputs. For example, an increase in the number of clients applying for services increases the pressure on an organization. To maintain its basic mode of operation and structure, it may resort to waiting lists or reduce the time spent on each client. It may even hire additional staff. Such processes do not alter internal polity and economy, but rather constitute adjustments to fluctuations in the flow of resources, the operations of service technologies, and the disposition of outputs. Of course, should these fluctuations pose a serious threat that cannot be resolved by adjustments, there will be an impetus to innovate new service patterns or to undergo internal changes.

SOURCE OF STABILITY
AND CHANGE

The general tendency of organizations—and human services are no exception—is toward stability and maintainance of the status quo. Kaufman (1971: 39–40) has put it succinctly:

> A host of forces thus tend to keep organizations doing the things they have been doing in the recent past, and doing them in just the way they have been doing them. The generally recognized collective benefits of stability and the opposition to change based on calculations of prevailing advantages, protection of quality, and the costs of modification furnish a thought-out foundation for resisting all efforts to reshape organizations or alter their behavior . . . . So formidable is the collection of forces holding organizations in their familiar paths that it is surprising that any changes ever manage to run the gauntlet successfully.

What are some of the external and internal forces that promote stability and inertia?

Locations in a Network

To ensure the legitimation of its domain and the steady flow of resources, a human service organization establishes a "niche" for itself in the environment. It does so by developing exchange relations with various key elements in its task environment, as noted in Chapter 3. The predictability and stability of the flow of these resources to an organization depends on its establishing and maintaining mutually acceptable and desirable relations with these elements. That is, it is to the advantage of an organization to have stable, steady, and predictable relations with its key providers of legitimation and resources. Therefore, an organization negotiates exchange relations that are based on understandings and agreements beneficial to both parties and avoids actions that might jeopardize them. For example, a community mental health center may establish formal and informal contractual relations with the state department of mental health, which funds the bulk of its services; with the local county government, which provides political legitimation; with the regional state hospital from which discharged patients are referred; with various local agencies providing complementary services to its clients; and with the local psychiatric establishment, which provides consultation and professional legitimation. To stabilize these relations, the agency works out various agreements and understandings with each of these elements that are reflected in its modes of operation. For example, to obtain professional legitimation from the psychiatric establishment, the agency may hire psychiatrists for dominant positions and adopt a psychoanalytic treatment technology. To facilitate its rapport with the state agency and the regional state hospital, the center will develop a substantial after-care program. It is to the agency's advantage to continue its established modes of operation and not to disrupt these relations and risk loss of support.

Moreover, members of the interorganizational network may use their own resources to threaten and even penalize an organization for attempting to alter its programs in a way that conflicts with their interests. Warren, Rose, and Bergunder (1974) found that when Model Cities agencies attempted to develop programs that conflicted with the interests of the key elements in their environment, such as the public school board, the health department, the urban renewal agency, and the mental health planning agency, these organizations used their power and resources to threaten and ultimately withdraw their support of the Model Cities agencies. Similarly, public schools find it more advantageous to maintain the status quo lest they raise the ire of dominant political groups in the community (Rogers, 1969).

Lack of Resources and Sunk Costs

Invariably, an innovation incurs costs to an organization. These may include the costs of purchasing equipment, expertise, and personnel; the costs of disrupting modes of services; additional administrative costs; the investment of time and manpower in implementation; and the ongoing costs of maintaining the innovation. Similar costs are associated with organizational change. Consequently, the reluctance of organizations to innovate and change hinges on resource limitations (Kaufman, 1971). This is particularly evident in the human services. First, since most human service organizations lack the capacity to generate profit, they are constantly searching for funding sources and grants to cover the ever-increasing costs of their services, which typically outstrip available resources. This is particularly true for agencies serving the poor. Consequently, they are reluctant to introduce innovations and changes that might prove costly. Second, the resources allocated to these organizations are accompanied by numerous restrictions and regulations on their use, which greatly limit the organizations' fiscal autonomy. Organizations must go through a protracted process to overcome these constraints to fund innovations.

Even when an organization does not experience serious resource limitations, it may still opt to maintain the status quo because of the sunk costs associated with its existing programs. *Sunk costs* are investments of resources that cannot be readily recovered and converted to other purposes. For example, a correctional program that has invested in a big facility with a large custodial staff will find it difficult to shift to a community-based, group home program because it cannot readily dispose of its facility or retrain or dismiss the custodial staff. Both represent sunk costs to the organization. The hindrance of sunk costs to innovation has been long recognized. Scull (1977: 125) quotes the *Edinburgh Review* of 1870 about the difficulties in closing insane asylums: "The amount of capital sunk in the costly palaces of the insane is becoming a growing impediment. So much money sunk creates a conservatism in their builders ... which resists a change."

Sunk costs are manifested in an organization's service technologies, particularly in the technical specialization and expertise of the staff. The greater the level of specialization and the narrower the technical expertise of the staff, the higher the sunk costs because of the greater difficulty in retraining them to perform other activities. Concomitantly, a high degree of specialization tends to generate a complex and rigid division of labor, which in itself contributes to sunk costs. Not surprisingly, many an innovation fails because an organization cannot effectively shift its staff to new roles, let alone overcome their resistance to change.

It is interesting to note that the juvenile correctional reform plan in Massachussetts attempted initially to transform existing training schools into therapeutic communities and retrain their custodial staff. After these efforts to reduce the sunk costs failed, the reformers recognized that their only alternative was to close the schools altogether (Ohlin et al., 1977). Similarly, the closing of state mental hospitals typically begins with those facilities that have deteriorated to a point where renovation would incur considerable costs (Scull, 1977; Segal and Aviram, 1978). These facilities represent lower sunk costs than those in good repair. Indeed, a major strategy to reduce sunk costs consists of allowing facilities and equipment to deteriorate and personnel to leave and retire without replacement before embarking on an innovation.

Hence, the greater the amount of sunk costs associated with programs and services, the greater the incentive to maintain stability. In contrast, when resources can be readily shifted from one purpose to another, the greater an organization's openness to innovation and change.

Organizational Ideologies

The centrality of ideologies in shaping the character of human service organizations has been repeatedly emphasized. These ideologies, in turn, serve as a powerful source of organizational stability. Ideologies provide a normative basis for justifying and rationalizing service delivery practices, thus lending credence to the interests of the dominant coalition. In addition, they provide coherence to service technologies and particularly invaluable guidance to practitioners in selecting courses of action, thus reducing uncertainty. As such, ideologies serve as filters through which events and information that might threaten an organization's stability are screened out, or are interpreted so as to justify existing service modalities.

Moreover, ideologies enable the members of an organization to justify inconsistencies and discrepancies in their practice patterns and to minimize the gaps between what they profess and what they actually do. Thus the pressures to change, emanating from these contradictions, are significantly reduced. This is amply shown in Scott's study (1967b) of sheltered workshops for the blind. Discarding their original mission of integrating the blind in the regular labor market because of the need to preserve the economic viability of the workshops, the managers developed an ideology that supported the view that blind persons were better off in a protected work environment. Moreover, the managers argued that the feelings of sighted persons toward the blind presented insurmountable barriers to their integration in commercial industry. As Scott points out, "such beliefs served to minimize the strains which accompanied the discrepancies between official and operative goals" (p.173), and, I might add, reduced the pressure to change.

In the same vein, ideologies tenaciously held by practitioners in an organization represent a serious obstacle to innovation and change. As we have noted, the self-reifying features of these ideologies reinforce practitioners' adherence to the practices they justify, thus hindering considerations of alternative service technologies. For example, in a case study of clinical innovation in mental health, Graziano (1969) noted that the professional staff in a clinic for autistic children were totally committed to "the true and tried methods of psychoanalysis" and vehemently rejected any notions of experimenting with a treatment technology based on behavior modification principles.

Internal Power Balances

As was noted in Chapter 6, organizations develop, over time, a structure that reflects the power relations among their internal groups. These power relations become balanced in the sense that each group obtains benefits commensurate with its relative power. A balance is maintained by the reward system in the organization. Organizational change, as I have defined it, inevitably threatens such a balance. To the extent to which various groups are relatively satisfied with the existing reward system, they will have little incentive to support organizational change. For the dominant coalition, in particular, the existing internal structural arrangements maintain and reinforce its power position; hence, its members are motivated to preserve them. McCleery (1966), in his study of prison reform, documented how the dominant coalition, composed of the warden, his deputy, and the senior captain of the guard force, established an internal structure through which they monopolized all channels of communication and coopted the leaders of the inmate system to maintain control over the prisoners. Attempts to reform the prison by elevating the importance of treatment and work skills were met by stiff resistance from the "old guard"; the dominant group deliberately manipulated the inmate system, resulting in an eruption of violence that allowed it to regain its monopoly. The greater the longevity of the dominant coalition, the firmer the motivation of its members to maintain internal stability. It is not surprising, therefore, that organizational change is stimulated by the rise of new executive leadership that does not represent the old guard (Carlson, 1961).

Recognizing that change is likely to upset the balance of power in an organization, individuals and groups become concerned about the unpredictable and uncertain consequences of shifting alliances and coalitions, and specifically, their inability to control the ultimate outcomes of these processes. Consequently, they are more apt to sustain the status quo, unless they can foresee visible payoffs from the proposed change and innovation. In general, staff members are, typically, more concerned with the potential losses they may incur from innovation and change than with the potential payoffs, mostly because the former are more apparent than the latter. For example, the costs of introducing a computerized client information system into an agency are much more apparent to the staff, in terms of loss of autonomy, increased monitoring, and threats to confidentiality, than the potential payoffs in efficiency (Albrecht, 1979).

Although human service organizations are reluctant to change, they cannot always insulate themselves from forces and conditions that undermine their stability and induce them to alter programs and services. Because of the generally high degree of dependency of human service organizations on their task environments, the primary sources for change emanate from their external polity and economy (e.g., Zald, 1970b; Ohlin et al., 1977; Baldridge and Burnham, 1975). In particular, these forces include shifts in political sentiments, legislative and governmental policies, funding patterns, client characteristics and needs, and service technologies.

Shifts in Political Sentiments

Because the core activities of human service organizations express the moral and value systems of the dominant interest groups controlling the flow of power and legitimation, these organizations are particularly sensitive to shifts in political sentiments. Changes in the composition of interest groups or in their norms and values will destabilize the legitimation of the organization and spur corrective actions.

Human services are affected in no small measure by "moral entrepreneurs" who crusade to uphold or transform certain moral values. For example, the child-saving movement of the late nineteenth century, whose members included Jane Addams and Julia Lathrop, was largely responsible for the creation of the juvenile court. As Platt (1969) points out, this movement was activated not only by humanitarian concerns for children, but also by a desire to uphold and protect Anglo-Saxon middle-class values threatened by the waves of low-class immigrants. The emerging juvenile courts, as a result, were founded on the *parens patriae* doctrine, which ascribed to the state overall responsibility over children deemed lacking effective parental controls. Thus, the courts could exercise considerable discretion over such children, with few legal restrictions. In the 1960s with the rise of the civil rights movement and the changing life style of youth, a "children's rights" movement emerged; this movement was composed mostly of legal experts, public interest lawyers, and social scientists who were critical of the juvenile justice system. They advocated increased legal restrictions and greater emphasis on due process in juvenile courts, as exemplified in the Supreme Court decision *In re Gault* in 1967.

The 1970s witnessed further changes in public sentiments about juvenile offenders. Fear of violent crime and disillusionment with rehabilitation brought about a call for punishment and retribution. Several states amended their juvenile codes to require mandatory sentencing for certain crimes. Both conservative and radical critics of juvenile courts have called for their abolition. Under these pressures, juvenile courts in several states have come to resemble adult criminal courts (Rubin, 1979).

Similar patterns can be seen in such areas as adoption, where changing attitudes toward illegitimate children and abortion have greatly reduced the number of children available for adoption; in domestic violence, where the women's rights movement has significantly altered the approaches of social service agencies to the issue; and in the education of the developmentally disabled, where such children are being "mainstreamed" into regular classrooms through the efforts of parents' associations. In these and other instances, interest groups arise and mobilize sufficient resources to challenge the organization and dispute its legitimacy unless it accepts and adopts some of their cherished values. At the same time, existing interest groups upon whom the organization relies for social support may lose some of their political dominance, or may themselves adopt the new values to retain their dominant position. Moreover, moral entrepreneurship often results in new legislative enactments and governmental policies that, in themselves, provide a powerful impetus for change.

Shifts in Legislative and Governmental Policies

Publicly controlled or assisted human service organizations, which most are, are particularly sensitive to legislative enactments and changes in governmental policies pertaining to their domain and mandate, even when these are not directly accompanied by funding pressures. For example, several states have enacted laws that require local school districts to mainstream handicapped children into regular classrooms. The Massachusetts Comprehensive Special Education Law, passed in 1972, made local school districts responsible for the education of all handicapped persons, aged three to twenty-one, regardless of the nature and severity of the handicap, and required the greatest possible integration of such children into regular classrooms. Compliance with the law forced the public schools to undertake significant program changes (Weatherley and Lipsky, 1977). Similarly, several states have passed legislation that prohibits juvenile courts from detaining status offenders or from committing them to institutions, forcing the courts to alter long-held service patterns (Hellum, 1979). Frequent changes in the regulations pertaining to the administration of welfare or public employment and training programs cause much consternation to their administrators and staff because they create pressures to change service delivery patterns and procedures.

In general, legislative and governmental policies stimulate organizational innovation and change in several ways. First, they may identify certain client cohorts for the organization to serve that hitherto were not within its domain, as in the case of handicapped children. Second, they may define the nature of the services and the service delivery procedures the organization must adopt. For example, policies may enunciate the conditions under which the mentally ill may be assigned to community-based sheltered facilities and the nature of care they must receive (Segal and Aviram, 1978). Third, these policies may specify organizational characteristics that must be met in serving certain types of clients, such as levels of staff expertise, ratios of staff to clients, and supervision and accountability requirements. It is clear, for example, that much of the impetus for the introduction of computerized client record systems has come from ever-increasing governmental requirements for accountability.

Because human service organizations work with and on people, they encounter a vast array of regulations that govern and control their responses to clients. At the same time, these regulations are seldom static; they change to reflect the ever-shifting, and frequently contested, belief systems and norms about human welfare and well-being. Consequently, human service organizations function in a relatively unstable normative system whose legitimation of organizational activities are never fully assured. The organization can never take its bases of legitimation for granted, and is under periodic pressure to redefine its domain and mission.

Changing Funding Patterns

The fortunes of human services rise and fall with funding exigencies, particularly because most services depend on donors (private and public) for revenues. Three sources of instability affect the acquisition of funds (Brager and Holloway, 1978): (1) the shifting availability of funds (2) the conditions associated with their use, and (3) the dependence of the organization on funding sources. As the availability of funds shifts from one program to another, the organization's incentives and disincentives to embark on program changes alter. Certain programs or services become more attractive because of potential financial benefits, while others become unattractive. The movement toward deinstitutionalization of the mentally ill and the establishment of community-based sheltered care well illustrates this. Changes in the Social Security Act, making former mental patients eligible for financial assistance and for Medicare and Medicaid, provided the economic incentives to establish local care facilities, where the costs per patient were considerably lower than in state mental hospitals (Scull, 1977; Segal and Aviram, 1978). Similarly, the rapid expansion of the nursing home industry in the 1960s is attributed directly to the passage of Medicare and Medicaid legislation, coupled with a federal program of low-interest financing for nursing home construction (Vladeck, 1980). In both instances, the opportunities to "harvest the money tree" provided powerful inducements to undertake program innovations, although, as several studies have noted, these innovations were often more symbolic than substantive (e.g., Donicht and Everhart, 1976).

The contraction of available funds may threaten the survival of an organization or service components within it, thus generating pressures for change. For example, in the case of Mobilization for Youth—a pioneering agency in serving the poor—a decline in funds for community action and development coupled with increased concentration of funds in manpower training forced the agency to shift its goals from social advocacy to amelioration of "personal pathology" (Helfgot, 1974).

The search for alternative funding sources is likely to transform the task environment of an organization by altering the network of external units providing fiscal resources. This, in turn, results in new exchange relations, which may force the organization to change its domain to accommodate the contingencies raised by the new donors. In his study of transformation of the YMCA in the late nineteenth century, Zald (1970b) noted that, as the contributions from church organizations became precarious, the YMCA sought to diversify its sources of support. It did so by developing gymnasiums (for which membership dues were charged), constructing residences, and establishing other services for fees. As a result, the YMCA gradually moved into an "enrollment economy," in which most of its fiscal resources were obtained from membership fees, thus elevating the importance of members in shaping programs.

Hence, as an organization encounters different contingencies and constraints from existing or new funding sources, it will need to renegotiate or develop new exchange relations with them. Doing so may necessitate significant program and structural transformations. For example, federal funds for manpower training may be accompanied by stipulations about the target population to be served, the range of services that must or can be provided, and required personnel policies. Likewise, hospitals that accept Medicare and Medicaid payments are subjected to various cost containment regulations and to quality control through peer review.

Finally, the greater an organization's dependence on external funding sources, the greater the pressures on it to change when these sources become unstable or alter their conditions. Because of its high dependency, an organization cannot buffer itself from the vicissitudes of funders. Thus, for example, declining federal and state funding for mental health services forces community mental health agencies to concentrate their services on after-care patients for whom the funds are earmarked, while curtailing other programs.

Transformations in Client Characteristics and Needs

The characteristics and composition of the client population under an organization's jurisdiction determines the aggregate demand patterns for its services. Consequently, changing sociodemographic characteristics are typically accompanied by changing demands for services. For example, Zald (1977: 116) noted recent and continuing increases in the following populations at risk: "divorced and widowed women, mothers with illegitimate children, and the elderly out of the work force [who] increasingly live in separate households." Social service agencies are thus faced with new service demands such as day care for children, employment opportunities and training for women, income support for one-parent families, and medical and home care services for the elderly. Hospitals find that they need to develop special service arrangements for the increasing volume of elderly patients. Rehabilitation agencies are under greater pressure to serve the rising number of chronically ill patients referred to them. Family service agencies are faced with the demand to develop services more relevant and appropriate to single parents. Such trends, therefore, affect both the volume and the nature of service demands. Some human service organizations discover that there may be an increasing incongruency between the services offered and the services demanded, thus forcing them to contemplate innovation and change.

The settlement house movement is a case in point. Started at the end of the nineteenth century in response to the waves of immigrants settling in the large cities, their purpose was to socialize and educate immigrants to the "American way of life." The centers developed extensive informal educational and other neighborhood activities to provide a smooth cultural transition. As neighborhoods stabilized demographically with the decline of immigration, the settlement houses deemphasized their educational activities and shifted more toward recreation and socialization, particularly for youth, and toward family counselling and social casework. The education programs shifted their focus toward cultural enrichment. However, after World War II, the rapid infux of nonwhites into the central cities and the exodus of the established white ethnic groups generated a serious crisis for the settlement houses. They now encountered a new population whose sociodemographic characteristics and welfare needs were incongruent with their service patterns. The centers were forced to become more active in obtaining basic social welfare services, to offer child care services, and to engage in community action such as welfare-rights work, visits to the police, and negotiations with city hall to protect the rights of their clients (Switzer, 1973).

New Developments in Service Technologies

As indicated earlier, a major source of innovation is the invention of new service technologies and programs. Organizations generally compare themselves to others in their "industry." The adoption of new technologies by equivalent organizations tends to create a perception of a "performance gap" (Zaltman, Duncan, and Holbek, 1973), and key decision makers become aware that their own organization is lagging behind its peers technologically. This perception may evoke concern about the reputation of their organization and its competitive posture in attracting clients, personnel, and funds. This is particularly evident in the medical care industry, where hospital administrators respond readily to the latest technological advances because most of the reimbursement for the costs of such innovations comes from third parties or from the patients directly (Grossman, 1974). Moreover, in many instances, technological and service innovations become "standards" for the industry; and all organizations are expected to follow suit to be accredited, licensed, or approved.

Technological innovations can pressure organizations to change their service delivery system radically. The discovery and use of psychoactive drugs, first introduced in 1952, was heralded as one of the most important innovations in the mental health field. It provided a new means of controlling patient behavior that facilitated deinstitutionalization of the mentally ill. Though much less dramatic, the development of the therapeutic community as a more humane patient management system has put considerable pressure on mental hospitals to alter their ward structure and patterns of interaction between staff and patients. A similar example can be noted in the rapid adoption of methadone maintenance as the predominant mode of care for heroin addicts.

Fads and fashion also significantly stimulate innovation in the human services. Because many existing service technologies are indeterminate and of questionable effectiveness, human service organizations are attracted to technological entrepreneurs who market seemingly new service technologies that promise to overcome difficulties in existing ones. Promise of success attracts beleaguered organizational decision makers, particularly if the new technologies are endorsed by opinion leaders in the industry. The rise of milieu therapy, paraded as the paragon of psychiatric treatment, is a good example of this. Despite the inconclusive evidence about its effectiveness and its circumscribed applicability, many hospitals rushed to adopt it only to discover that in a few years the fad had passed, and its reputation had become tarnished. In a similar fashion, behavior modification techniques, especially the token economy, caught the imagination of administrators of total institutions such as prisons, mental hospitals, and training schools because of their promised effectiveness in inmate management. However, costs and difficulties of implementation, adverse effects on staff-inmate relations, and the legal issues they raise have diminished some of the enthusiasm that initially accompanied them.

ORGANIZATIONAL CAPACITY TO INNOVATE

Although human service organizations may encounter similar pressures and opportunities to innovate, some will have a greater capacity to do so than others. The capacity to innovate is clearly a critical determinant of the long-term survival of the organization. It has particular significance for human service organizations because in many instances the innovation and change they are asked to implement is mandated by external funders and regulatory units, and lack of capacity to respond can jeopardize their viability and vitality.

According to Mohr (1969: 114), the capacity to innovate is a function of the motivation to do so, the strength of the obstacles to innovation, and the availability of resources to overcome the obstacles. These are affected by a series of structural factors, both external and internal to the organization. Specifically, the motivation to innovate will be determined by the values of the executive leadership and the proactive stance they take toward their environment. The obstacles to innovation will be affected by the receptivity or hostility of the environment toward the organization, and by the flexibility or rigidity of its internal structure. The availability of resources will be influenced by the organization's ability to exploit its environment, and by its internal capacity to shift resources from one area to another.

Environmental Factors

Organizations located in a heterogeneous environment rich in resources have a greater potential for innovation (Baldridge and Burnham, 1975), because they can more readily mobilize these resources and obtain support for the innovation. Turk (1977) found that human services in communities rich in economic activities and diverse in voluntary associations and governmental agencies have a greater capacity to innovate.

However, the ability of an organization to exploit its environment or to overcome its obstacles depends on the effectiveness of its interorganizational relations, specifically its boundary-spanning activities (Corwin, 1972). These activities allow an organization to process strategically important information and to negotiate relations and resource transactions with important external units (Aldrich, 1979). In many respects, personnel involved in boundary spanning serve as change agents for an organization. They increase its motivation to innovate by bringing in information about new opportunities and ideas, and also help overcome obstacles by facilitating relations with the environment. Corwin (1972) found that the rate of educational innovation by schools participating in the Teacher Corps program—a joint project between inner-city schools and universities—was determined by the quality and interdependence of the boundary-spanning personnel, which was composed of both university faculty and teachers in the program.

Executive Leadership Values

No matter how supportive the environment, the motivation for innovation is critically influenced by the values of an organization's dominant coalition (Hage, 1980). Executives who are committed to maintain and enhance an organization's high standards of performance and who are dissatisfied with the status quo, will direct energy and resources toward importing new ideas and programs (Daft and Becker, 1978). They thus enhance the capacity of the organization to innovate by lending both legitimation and power to such activities. Hage and Dewar (1973), in their study of health and welfare agencies, found that the commitment of executives toward change was the key predictor of the rate of program innovation. Similarly, Kaluzney, Veney, and Gentry (1974) found that hospitals and health departments with administrators who had a strong cosmopolitan orientation had a higher rate of innovation. Two important implications are apparent from these and other studies. First, by upholding such values, executives encourage acceptance by other members of an organization. In particular, the incentive and reward structure, reflecting the influence of these values, would favor innovative members. Second, these elite values are likely to be translated into the actual commitment of resources for innovative ideas and programs.

Resources

In general, organizations rich in resources, often indicated by their size, have a greater capacity to innovate. In particular, as noted earlier, the availability of slack resources enables an organization to overcome resistance to innovation by minimizing its potential costs to various units. Nonetheless, resource richness per se is no guarantee of innovation. Specifically, the capacity of the organization to innovate is enhanced when resources are allocated for professional and support staff and services (Daft and Becker, 1978). For innovation is promoted through the skills and expertise of staff and the resources and support given them to pursue new ideas and programs. This explains why large organizations, despite their extensive resources, sometimes lack this innovative capacity: They have not invested sufficiently in staff with diverse skills and expertise or in necessary support personnel and services. Put differently, the capacity of the organization to innovate is directly related to the proportion of its resources allocated for experimentation and development.

The ability of human service organizations to invest in experimentation and development is often constrained. First, agencies dependent on external donors are not usually able to allocate such funds to experimentation and development without prior approval from the donors, who may often be hard to convince about their importance. Second, because such funds are typically controlled by external units, human service organizations must compete for them, which, in turn, requires commitment of internal resources not readily available. It is not surprising, therefore, that spurts of innovation in human services have occurred during periods of expansion of federal funding for new programs. Third, because services to clients often require additional appeals for outside support or curtailment of other services the organization finds it difficult to justify diverting resources to experimentation and development.

Internal Structure

It is generally assumed that organizations characterized by an internal structure that is decentralized, low in formalization, with highly diverse skills and knowledge have a greater capacity to innovate (Hage, 1980). Nonetheless, empirical studies offer rather contradictory findings (e.g., Corwin, 1972; Zaltman, Duncan, and Holbek, 1973). It seems that the appropriate internal structure is contingent on the *radicalness* of the innovation; namely, the degree to which it is costly and requires significant organizational changes. An internal structure that is decentralized, low in formalization, and highly complex seems most conducive to nonradical innovations. These types of innovations, mostly technological and incremental, are best promoted when staff are given flexibility and autonomy in meeting the service objectives through reliance on their knowledge and skills and through experimentation with new ideas. In contrast, radical innovations cannot be effectively adopted in such a structure because of their overwhelming impact on the entire organization. The decentralization and diffuseness of power will actually erect barriers to the acceptance of such innovations because each unit will have an independent voice about their desirability. To quote Hage (1980: 193), "Decentralization is a stabilizing force, which while it encourages higher rates of innovation, is much less likely to be associated with either radical departures or with large bursts of change." Rather, radical innovations require unity and concentration of power in the organization. Consequently, a centralized and formal internal structure is more conducive to the adoption of such innovations (Corwin, 1972; Daft and Becker, 1978).

THE DECISION PROCESS
FOR CHANGE

The adoption of an innovation, particularly a radical one, is typically a complex process involving numerous participants over a long time. It is a process that calls for *decision making* about such issues as the need to innovate, the participants in the process, the attractiveness of new ideas and programs, the receptivity and resistance of various members of the organization, the costs and payoffs associated with each alternative, and the ease or difficulty of implementation.

Various stages of the innovation process have been proposed. Zaltman, Duncan, and Holbek (1972), for example, suggest that there are two primary stages—initiation and implementation. The initiation stage has three subcomponents: (1) knowledge-awareness; (2) formation of attitudes toward the innovation; and (3) decision. The implementation stage is composed of: (1) initial implementation; and (2) continued-sustained implementation. Similarly, Hage (1980) has suggested four stages: (1) evaluation; (2) initiation; (3) implementation; and (4) routinization. These and other formulations of the stages of change are based on the assumption that the innovation decision process is rational and follows a logical sequence of steps—namely, from problem recognition, to assessment of alternatives, to adoption of a solution. However, empirical studies of change processes in human services suggest that this may not be the case, particularly for radical innovations. The turbulence that characterizes these innovations and the seeming repetition of many of the same steps defy the logic proposed by the authors cited. For example, juvenile correctional reforms (Ohlin et al., 1977) or educational reforms (March and Olsen, 1976) often involve disorganized decision-making processes of innovation and change.

These two contrasting images of change processes suggest that each may pertain to a particular organizational context. The rational model seems most appropriate to organizations in which both the output goals and the technology are unambiguous and determinate. Under these conditions, a clear causal relationship exists between the performance of the service technology and the outputs of the organization. The organization can thus reliably evaluate its outputs, compare them to some set norms or goals, and identify the needed changes in its technology should there be a gap between the actual and the desired outputs. Having identified a performance gap (Zaltman, Duncan, and Holbek, 1973), such an organization can begin to assess its magnitude and potential impact on the organization's future. For example, a hospital can evaluate the rate of tonsillectomies performed on children admitted to the hospital and compare it to established national or regional norms. Should the hospital's rate be significantly higher than these norms, a performance gap will be noted, and remedial action called for. The information about the performance gap is then processed by the key decison makers, who can then explore its causes. They may find that either physicians are not adhering to the acceptable norms for tonsillectomy, or that they are not aware of new medical advances and procedures. In both instances, the performance gap initiates an awareness of the problem, which leads to a search for causes and alternative solutions. Once these alternatives are identified, the organization can make a choice on the basis of cost-payoff calculations. The hospital, for example, may decide to purchase new diagnostic equipment or to conduct an in-house seminar on the latest developments in the field. Or, it may conclude that special circumstances justify its deviation from established norms. Should a decision be made to introduce a certain innovation or change, the organization will set up mechanisms to implement it.

This "rational" process is possible, of course, because the knowledge of cause and effect relations both within the service technology and between it and the output goals of the organization is complete. Nonetheless, even in such a process numerous political and economic factors influence its unfolding and ultimate outcome. For example, although output measures may be readily available, key decision-makers may choose to ignore them because they could threaten and undermine their position and status (Wilensky, 1967). Similarly, lack of resources or commitment to invest in boundary-spanning activities will diminish the awareness of the organization about new developments in the field. Moreover, should the organization have a monopoly for its services, it may lack the incentive to perceive performance gaps. Even when a performance gap is noted, the initiation of the change process may be hampered. First, the organization may not have sufficient slack resources to allocate to the change process. Second, those who wish to initiate the change may not have sufficient influence to obtain the commitment of the dominant coalition. Third, others in the organization may resist the initiation of a change process because they perceive a potential threat to their position. For example, in the case of the hospital, the affected physicians may resist any attempt to alter their pattern of practice on the grounds that it would encroach on their professional autonomy.

Recognizing these obstacles, Delbecq (1978) has identified the following conditions for the successful introduction of change in an organization:

1. Attainment of a mandate from the organizational elite about the general objectives of the innovation, and agreement about the planning process.
2. Careful documentation of the performance gap.
3. A broad and technically sound search for data on potential solutions and their relative effectiveness.
4. Development of a proposal that can mobilize the support of a strong coalition in the organization.
5. Capacity to develop a pilot test of the innovation to demonstrate its effectiveness.

The purpose of these strategies is to obtain, on the one hand, the support of the organizational elite, and on the other, to counteract sources of resistance. Indeed, much of the concern in this model of the change process is exactly that: to identify strategies and techniques for mobilizing support for the innovation and for overcoming resistance to it.

When, however, an organization's output goals and service technology are ambiguous and indeterminate, the change decision process is more likely to resemble the "garbage can" model (Cohen, March, and Olsen, 1972; Daft and Becker, 1978; see also Chapter 2). That is, the perception of performance gaps, the presentation of new ideas and programs, the occasions for making decisions, and patterns of participation by various decision makers are loosely connected to each other and do not occur in any specific order or pattern. As stressed throughout, many human service organizations are indeed characterized by ambiguous goals and indeterminant service technologies. Moreover, their internal structures are so loosely coupled that activities in one work unit are only weakly coordinated with those in other units. Consequently, the innovation and change decision-making process takes on its own distinct character. First, different units and individuals in the organization initiate multiple processes of change quite independently of each other, reflecting the loose coupling of its internal structure. Second, the decision-making patterns characterizing these processes indeed resemble a "garbage can" model, reflecting the ambiguities, inconsistencies, and lack of determinancy in the goals and technology of the organization. Third, these processes, nonetheless, are bounded and influenced by the external and internal political economies of the organization, reflecting the constraints and contingencies posed by the external environment, and by the internal allocation of power and resources.

The perception of a performance gap is highly problematic and fragmented in these organizations. The lack of reliable and valid measures of performance, the existence of multiple and often conflicting measures, and the intermittent frequency of measurement make it difficult for the organization to register a performance gap (Hage, 1980). Moreover, different units in the organization have their own views about the effectiveness of their own performance, quite independently of other units. Each unit also has its own set of relations with relevant components in the environment, and is especially sensitive to new developments and innovations pertaining to its own activities. For example, a community mental health center will have several competing measures of effectiveness including client satisfaction, rates of readmission to hospitals, global ratings of clients' clinical progress, and numerous cost-effectiveness measures (Attkisson et al., 1978). Because the various service components of the center are loosely coupled, the clinical services unit, for instance, may be quite satisfied with its performance, while the after-care unit may be under pressure to reduce the readmission rate. Moreover, clinical staff are attuned to ideas and development in clinical practice, while after-care staff are attuned to issues and practices in the management of chronic patients. The top administrators, on the other hand, are sensitive to cost per unit of service in each component and to new ideas about cost containment. As a result, the awareness of the need to change may differentially arise from various segments of the agency and relate to totally different aspects of the organization's activities.

As different and somewhat discrete stimuli for change arise in the organization, they evoke a decision-making process tenuous in content and structure, and subject to unpredictable twists and turns—for several reasons. First, it is not clear who should participate in the process since links among units are weak. Second, the causes of the problem are unknown, and it is not apparent who would benefit from the new ideas. Third, there is no determinate causal relationship between problems and proposed solutions; several different problems may attract the same solution and vice versa. Finally, numerous potential organizational areas could be appropriate for making a decision on the problem or proposed new idea. That is, the problem may be seen to be under the purview of budgeting, personnel, program development, or direct services.

As a result, some problems and performance gaps do not attract any particular interest in the search for solutions (Daft and Becker, 1980). Others may attract the interest of certain staff because they present an opportunity for them to raise their own agenda. Similarly, individuals and units may have ideas and solutions they would like to advance, but are waiting for the opportunity to attach them to other problems that may arise. Members of the organization may use various decision situations as opportunities to present either problems or innovative ideas and solutions. Participants in the decision-making process will drift in and out on the basis of their interests, available time, and attitude toward other participants. March and Olsen (1976) analyzed several case studies of innovation and change within a university, including the elimination of a department, transfer of an academic program, changes in a grading system, and the development of a new doctoral program. In all instances, they point out, the impetus for the change shifted several times and reflected different interests, such as strengthening the reputation of the university, saving money, getting rid of nonproductive faculty, promoting personal ideologies, and the like. Moreover, in each instance the cast of characters in the decision-making process kept changing, and some persons who might be directly affected by the change participated only minimally. In each case, several agendas were pursued by different participants, who used the occasion to promote their own interests. The ultimate decisions, however, were not totally unpredictable or unexpected because the whole process was bounded by the political economy of the university—namely, its resource distribution, dominant ideologies, and its internal power distribution.

The environmental constraints and the distribution of power and resources inside the organization do provide some predictable directions for the decision-making process. First, whatever changes are contemplated, they must be congruent with external commitments and obligations; otherwise the external obligations will have to be renegotiated. Nor can the proposed changes jeopardize the organization's critical sources of legitimation. Internally, the change process must take into account the relative power and influence of the various participants, simply because those who have more power typically have the wherewithal to stay with the process, invest their energies in it, and influence it in accordance with their interests. Furthermore, the change process is also bounded by the organization's dominant ideologies and by its history. These serve as filters through which problems and new ideas are interpreted.

The constraints of the organization's political economy therefore tend to favor incremental rather than radical innovations and changes. Derthick (1979) demonstrates this eloquently in her study of program changes in Social Security. Over several decades the agency pursued an incremental strategy, because of the need of its leadership to adapt to the political realities of Congress and the Executive Branch. Agency executives "learned not to ask for everything at once. They asked for a piece at a time, and then trimmed the pieces. They forwent goals that were not urgent or immediately feasible. . . . They assimilated program changes that Congress valued even at the costs of doctrinal consistency. . . . Executive leaders conceived proposals and presented them in a way that enhanced acceptabilty to the public in general, the public's elected representatives, and diverse private interests" (Derthick, 1979: 206-7).

The adoption of a radical innovation, hence, almost always necessitates a shift in the external political economy of the organization, a change in its executive leadership, and the unfreezing of key resources (Hage, 1980). The juvenile correctional reform in Massachusetts (Ohlin et al., 1977) met all three conditions. The reform was initiated when the state switched to a Republican governor who appointed a new director for the juvenile correctional agency. The director, in turn, mobilized a new supporting coalition and used funds available through the Law Enforcement Assistance Administration, coupled with the closure of several institutions, to push through the reform.

The unique character of the innovation and change decision-making process in the human services also stems from its frequently involuntary causation, having been imposed on the agency by external funding and regulatory organizations. The mainstreaming of the developmentally disabled into regular classrooms or the deinstitutionalization of the mentally ill into community-based sheltered care are cases in point. To members of the organization, these changes may bear no relationship to their perceptions of performance gaps or their awareness of new ideas and innovations. Consequently, such changes tend to cause bewilderment and evoke resentment. For some members, however, the forced change presents an opportunity to enlarge their agendas and to push for their own ideas in its wake. For example, the cutoff of external funds to one or more programs in an agency may prompt the executive leadership to launch their own changes, such as getting rid of undesirable services or staff, restructuring various work units, or instituting a new monitoring and accountability system. Other members of the organization may also take advantage of the occasion to jockey for position or to push for their own pet ideas and interests. For example, when New York University was forced to undergo drastic changes because of declining enrollment and increasing deficits, central administrators and several academic units used the occasion to pursue their own interests. The Graduate School of Business, which wanted to become a nationally recognized research and education center, joined forces with the central administration to reduce the importance of the undergraduate School of Commerce by eliminating faculty, changing admission standards, and revamping its curriculum (Baldridge, 1975). Thus, while mandated changes can force an organization to pursue specific courses of action, at the same time they unfreeze the status quo, allowing relatively independent streams of problems, solutions, participants, and occasions for decisions to pour into the "garbage can" of decision making.

IMPLEMENTATION OF CHANGE[1]

Having decided to adopt an innovation or to undergo change, the organization enters the *implementation phase*. There is no reason to assume that once the decision has been made its implementation is assured. Quite the contrary. It is during the implementation phase that political and economic realities are acutely felt. These may lead to consequences not envisioned or anticipated in the decision phase. This is most evident for radical innovations, which, as it will be recalled, necessitate significant modification of the resource allocation rules in the organization. It is only during the implementation phase that the true magnitude of these shifts becomes apparent.

Focusing, then, on radical innovations and change, successful implementation requires the deployment of strategies that enhance the power of the change advocates and their access to needed resources. At the political

[1]This section is adapted from Hasenfeld (1980).

level, strategies for the mobilization of power may include bargaining, forming coalitions, coopting elites, and disruption (Wilson, 1973; Benson, 1975). At the economic level, mobilization of resources may depend on documenting demand for the new program, minimizing the costs of change, increasing the competitiveness of the organization through the change, opening up new fiscal resources, and providing incentives for the change. Yet successful deployment of these strategies may result in deviations from the original change objectives. Unless the change advocates have ample access to power and fiscal resources, modification and even abandonment of certain change objectives is almost inevitable, because to attract resources controlled by other interest groups, the advocates must accommodate their values.

It is not surprising, therefore, that in many instances the ultimate outcomes of change efforts only vaguely resemble the original objectives. Pressman and Wildavsky (1973) point out that the probability of successful change implementation is quite low. For example, assuming that change advocates need the agreement of only four key decision makers and the probability of obtaining the agreement of each is .80, then the probability of successful implementation is .40. With six decision makers, the probability of successful implementation declines to .26.

The effectiveness of implementation efforts depends on: the ability of the change advocates to mobilize external resources and legitimation to counteract internal and external resistance to the change, their possession of sufficient technical expertise and knowledge to operationalize the proposed change, their occupying a position of functional centrality in the organizational division of labor, and their offering of sufficient inducements to overcome internal resistance. Therefore, change advocates must address themselves to three clusters of organizational variables: (1) organization-environment relations, (2) technological factors, and (3) internal power and inducement patterns[2] (see Figure 9.1).

Organization-Environment Relations

Program changes that modify an organization's domain inevitably affect the relations between it and its environment. Therefore, the reaction of different elements in the environment to the proposed change and the organization's responses to them will influence the implementation process and outcome.

The effectiveness of change efforts is, in part, contingent on the mobilization of two key environmental resources: legitimation and money. While the impetus for change may arise from the potential availability of new external fiscal resources, mobilizing them and securing their steady flow are major challenges to successful implementation. First, the utilization

---

[2]As noted earlier, these variables also affect the *capacity* of the organization to innovate.

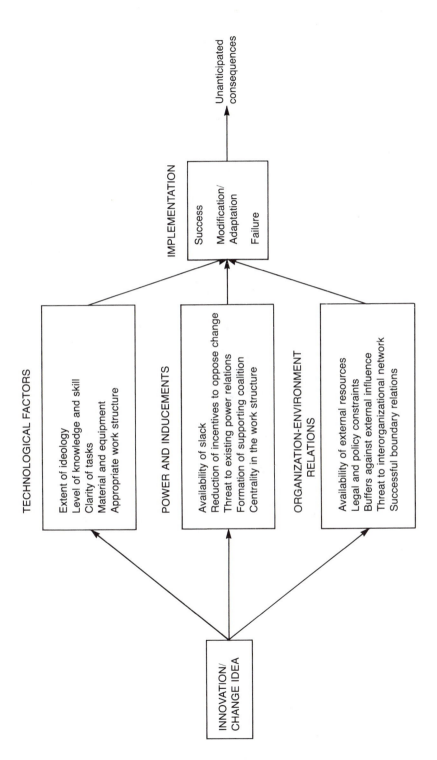

FIGURE 9.1 Determinants of successful implementation of change in human service organizations

of such resources may be constrained by legal and policy regulations, which will make the costs of utilization too high for the organization, particularly if they limit its autonomy or threaten the power position of its key groups. Second, ensuring a steady flow of fiscal resources may increase the organization's dependence on external funding agencies, making the implementation and continuation of the program innovation vulnerable to their vagaries. For example, while the deinstitutionalization of juvenile offenders in Massachusetts was made possible by mobilizing federal grants, the grants created serious barriers and obstacles to the reform process. Reimbursements to contracting agencies that provided community care were delayed, threatening their existence; and grant stipulations and accounting procedures severely hampered efforts of the Department of Youth Services to develop sufficient alternatives to institutionalization. With the decline in federal funding, the Department of Youth Services became increasingly dependent on state resources, whose appropriations were made contingent on extensive auditing and reduced autonomy for the agency; the department was also urged to develop some secure closed facilities, contrary to the spirit of the reform (Ohlin et al., 1977).

Another major precondition for successful implementation of change is the ability of its advocates to mobilize external sources of legitimation. The greater the external support for change, the greater the capacity to neutralize resistance to it. Studies of juvenile correctional reforms, for example, demonstrate that the success of a reform is usually contingent on the ability of the reformers to enlist the support of child interest groups, liberal political coalitions, and the mass media (Empey and Erickson, 1972). Legitimation provides change advocates with effective weapons to ward off attacks against the validity and value of the proposed change. Yet to enlist such legitimation, advocates may have to modify the change objectives to make them congruent with the values and interests of the legitimators.

Program changes that alter an organization's domain also disturb the balance of relations in the interorganizational network. The change may be such that it challenges the domain of other human service organizations, or calls for modifications in the flow of resources in the network. Consequently, the success of change efforts will depend on the ability of their supporters to demonstrate to the interorganizational network that it will accrue benefits from the new program with no serious threat to its domain. Alternatively, change advocates must be able to link themselves to a different organizational network that can neutralize threats from other organizations. For example, a new drug rehabilitation program may try to link up with the criminal justice system rather than seem to threaten the mental health network; but in so doing it may have to compromise its change objectives.

Interorganizational relations are, therefore, a critical factor in the successful implementation of change. This factor loomed large in a study by Corwin (1972) of the promotion of educational innovations in low-income schools through the Teacher Corps program. The most salient predictor of the degree of change in the schools was the quality of the relations and degree of cooperation between them and the colleges who supplied the interns. The importance of effective boundary relations cannot be underestimated. It is through such relations that change advocates can alleviate the fears of other organizations, negotiate exchange arrangements that will enlist their support, and forecast the directions from which resistance might arise. Moreover, successful boundary relations can help an organization buffer a change from external influences by controlling the information disseminated to other organizations.

Technological Factors

The improvement of service delivery to clients lies at the heart of any important organizational change. In the final analysis, this objective is the raison d'etre for all change efforts in human services. Substantively, it means that change efforts will, at least in part, modify or augment the service technology of the organization with new and different service procedures. Therefore, the successful implementation of planned change also depends on the ability of its advocates to operationalize effectively the technological components identified in the plan (Gross, Giacquinta, and Bernstein, 1971).

Yet to do so may pose serious difficulties to the planners because, not infrequently in human services, ideologies are paraded as viable service technologies. That is, the ideas and belief systems defining new modes of service cannot be readily translated, if at all, into explicit and specific sets of techniques and procedures. It will be recalled, for example, that the new technology encapsulated in the therapeutic community considered democratization, permissiveness, communalism, and reality confrontation as the key principles underlying staff-patient relations. The operationalization of these principles, however, proved to be exceedingly problematic because their abstraction and vagueness generated conflicting interpretations, and they failed to address and respond to many issues arising from the daily management of the patients (Rapoport, 1960). Moreover, the loftiness of these new service ideologies, coupled with their ambiguous meanings, may actually enable practitioners to justify the very techniques and procedures they aim to replace.

When a planned change is laden with ideology, it fails to provide specific and clear guides for action, permitting members of the organization to cling to old, familiar procedures while maintaining the illusion of innovation. Furthermore, the lack of a well-defined technology results in uncertainty, confusion, and ambiguity in the tasks to be performed. This measurably raises the costs of change efforts and reinforces resistance to it. In their study of educational innovations, Gross, Giacquinta, and Bernstein (1971) suggest that three basic technological prerequisites are necessary to implement a new program successfully: (1) availability of a sufficient level of expertise and knowledge about the technological components of the new program, (2) clarity and specificity of the new tasks staff will be asked to perform, and (3) availability of necessary equipment, materials, and supplies. Similar conclusions were reached by Fairweather, Sanders, and Tornatzky (1974) in their study of mental health innovations, and by Bogdan and associates (1974) in their study of program innovation in institutions for the mentally retarded. These and other studies demonstrate that a major cause of failure in changing programs arises from the difficulty of articulating concrete and specifically defined sets of skills and tasks from broad ideological statements and belief systems.

In this context, when a planned change requires new tasks and shifts in role definitions, correspondent changes must occur in the divisions of labor. These may include modifications in authority and supervisory relations and in patterns of communication and mechanisms of coordination. Successful implementation of new programs calls for the establishment of appropriate work structures congruent with the requirements of the new tasks. For example, if a new program calls for highly complex and variable tasks, the staff cannot function adequately if their work is structured by hierarchical authority, vertical communication patterns, and rigid coordination mechanisms (Van de Ven, Delbecq, and Koenig, 1976; Litwak, 1978).

Internal Power and Inducement Patterns

A major source of resistance arises from those in the organization who fear losing rewards or being denied access to the inducements of the new program. Change planners must, therefore, engage in strategies that reduce this type of resistance (Kaufman, 1971). These strategies may include assurances that no staff person will lose income or suffer from adverse working conditions; that staff will have a strong voice in the implementation of the change; or that the change will reinforce and strengthen professional values and norms. Most often, the success of a new program hinges on the compliance of lower-level staff in direct contact with clients. As street-level bureaucrats, lower-level staff may have considerable discretion over encounters with clients and be capable of circumventing effective supervision. They can often undermine a new program, even when it has been sanctioned by the executive leadership. Therefore, at the very least, change planners must demonstrate to these staff that they will not be adversely affected by the new program. When their active compliance is needed, they must be provided with direct incentives to support it. Clearly, reducing resistance to the change may necessitate significant modifications and compromises in the change objectives.

Organizational change also disturbs existing power relations, which leads to resistance to its implementation. The more likely that a planned change will threaten existing relations, the greater the need to enlist the support of power sources. Consistently, studies of organizational change point to the importance of executive support as a major precondition for the successful implementation of change (Delbecq, 1978; Hage and Dewar, 1973). Executive support is often achieved by cooptation—providing executives with formal participatory roles in the decision-making processes for the new program.

Nevertheless, cooptation is not the only strategy for mobilizing sources of power. Indeed, it may be ill-advised if the proposed change conflicts with the interests and values of the executive group. Rather, change advocates may have to form coalitions with other key groups in the organization in order to wield sufficient power to neutralize resistance to the change. Forming coalitions, however, entails some risks. First, to forge a coalition, change advocates may have to modify the change objectives substantially in order to offer diverse inducements to the coalition members. Second, the coalition may be unstable, and at crucial points important members may desert it. Finally, one coalition may encourage the formation of countercoalitions.

In an alternative strategy to acquire power in an organization, actors move into areas of high uncertainty and successfully cope with them (Hinings et al., 1974). For example, in an agency facing serious budget uncertainties, those with effective solutions to the fiscal problems are likely to rise in power if no one in power has equal skills and talents. Similarly, an agency worried about a decline in demand for its services will accord power to those who can offer new, effective ways to recruit clients. Thus the successful implementation of a new program will be enhanced if its promoters can demonstrate—as no one else in the organization can—its effectiveness in areas of high uncertainty. Also, change advocates who have acquired power by such a strategy can use their newly acquired prestige and credibility to neutralize resistance to their change efforts.

Human service practitioners eager to make changes must keep in mind the complexity of implementing change. Their ability to influence all the variables involved in implementation may be quite limited. Most important, they will undoubtedly have to compromise and modify their change objectives, and the changes ultimately implemented may only vaguely resemble those originally intended.

CONCLUSION

While many individual human service practitioners may be change oriented and ready to intervene on behalf of clients, their organizations are often likely to resist change and innovation. On balance, the forces that promote stability outweigh those that push for innovation and change. Human service organizations seem to change only when under duress—that is, when external conditions have reached a point at which they cannot be ignored. Rare indeed are the instances when the organization has the foresight, the motivation, and the wherewithal to undertake innovation and change without external pressures. Yet the long-range survival and vitality of an organization depend on its capacity to change before it encounters crises. A crisis period may be the worst time to initiate innovation because the organization's capacity to change is often at a low ebb. The environment may be inhospitable; the executive leadership may cling to old ideas; resources may be strained; and the internal structure too entrenched in old patterns.

Human services are entering an era of high uncertainty in which the pressures for change will be ever present. The rising costs of human services coupled with the decline in public funding will put these organizations under serious fiscal constraints. Efforts by governments—federal, state, and local—to reduce operating costs and the resources allocated to human services will undermine the survival of these organizations unless they undertake radical changes in their service delivery systems. At the same time, demands for human services will continue to rise for two reasons: First, as noted by Zald (1977), sociodemographic changes, such as the aging of the population and the continued increase in single-parent households, will create a greater need for human services. Second, many more citizens will come to view their need for human services as a matter of right.

Squeezed between rising demands and declining resources, human service organizations will be forced, on the one hand, to direct their efforts to desperately needy members of the population, and on the other hand, to increase service costs to the less needy. As a result, human services face the danger of increased bifurcation of their services by social class. Moreover, concentrating public human services on the very needy will actually raise the costs of services per client and diminish their effectiveness. Yet, the public demand for accountability and demonstrated effectiveness and efficiency will become more persistent.

The future also holds some exciting opportunities for the human services. New advances in service technologies will be made as our knowledge about human functioning continues to expand. For example, our rapidly increasing knowledge in such diverse fields as human biology, learning and cognition, life-cycle changes, and aging will generate new and more effective service technologies. Moreover, as needs change, new arenas for the human services will open, for example, in genetic counselling, industrial social work, and the care of the chronically disabled. In addition, the revolutionary developments in information technology will have a dramatic impact on the administration and management of human services.

An effective organization must, therefore, develop a capacity to innovate and change *regularly*, and be particularly responsive to new developments and trends in the environment (Hedberg, Nystrom, and Starbuck,

1976). An organization needs to be free from entrenched ideologies, inflexible goals, and rigid structures. Paradoxically, human service organizations by their very nature possess characteristics that potentially can enhance their capacity to change. That is, they have multiple, conflicting goals; they operate with indeterminate technologies; and they have loosely coupled internal structures. Yet in their quest for stability, certainty, and control, they, like other types of organizations, establish mechanisms, such as dominant ideologies, routine technologies, and bureaucratic controls, that reduce their capacity to innovate. As Hedberg, Nystrom, and Starbuck put it (1976: 45): "Residents of changing environments need a tent. An organizational tent places greater emphasis on flexibility, creativity, immediacy, and initiative than on authority, clarity, decisiveness, or responsiveness." To enhance its capacity to innovate and change they propose that an organization: (1) encourage diversity of opinions and objectives based on minimal consensus; (2) promote sufficient satisfaction for staff to remain in the organization, but not enough to make them happy with the status quo; (3) maintain enough unrestricted resources to absorb the costs of experimentation, but not excessive affluence, which discourages searches for new and better ideas; (4) be willing to replace long-term plans in the face of new environmental developments; and (5) maintain a loosely coupled structure. In the long run, an organization's responsiveness to the needs of its clients will depend on developing and improving its capacity to innovate and change.

REFERENCES

Ackoff, R. L., and P. Rivett. *A Manager's Guide to Operations Research.* New York: Wiley, 1963.

Adrian, C. R., and C. Press. "Decision Costs in Coalition Formulation," *American Political Science Review,* 62 (1968), 556–63.

Aiken, M., R. Dewar, N. Di Tomaso, J. Hage, and G. Zeitz. *Coordinating Human Services.* San Francisco: Jossey-Bass, 1975.

Albrecht, G. L. "Defusing Technological Change in Juvenile Courts: The Probation Officer's Struggle for Professional Autonomy," *Sociology of Work and Occupations,* 6 (1979), 259–82.

Aldrich, H. "Cooperation and Conflict Between Organizations in the Manpower Training System: An Organization-Environment Perspective," In *Conflict and Power in Complex Organizations,* ed. A. R. Negandhi. Kent, Ohio: Center for Business and Economic Research, Kent State University, 1972. Pp. 11–27.

——. *Organizations and Environments.* Englewood Cliffs, N.J.: Prentice-Hall, 1979.

Aldrich, H. E., and J. Pfeffer. "Environments of Organizations," In *The Annual Review of Sociology,* ed. A. Inkeles. Palo Alto: Annual Reviews, Inc., 1976. II: 79–105.

Alford, R. R. *Health Care Politics.* Chicago: University of Chicago Press, 1975.

Allen, M. P. "The Structure of Interorganizational Elite Cooptation: Interlocking Corporate Directorates," *American Sociological Review,* 39 (1974), 393–496.

Alvarez, R., K. G. Lutterman, and associates. *Discrimination in Organizations.* San Francisco: Jossey-Bass, 1979.

Arnold, W. R. "Race and Ethnicity Relative to Other Factors in Juvenile Court Dispositions," *American Journal of Sociology,* 77 (1971), 211–27.

ASTRACHAN, B. M. "Changing Institutional Direction: The Connecticut Mental Health Center." In *Innovation and Implementation in Public Organizations*, eds. R. Nelson and D. Yates. Lexington, Mass.: Lexington Books, 1978. Pp 1–18.

ATTKISSON, C. C., W. HARGRAVES, M. J. HOROWITZ, and J. E. SORENSEN, eds. *Evaluation of Human Service Programs*. New York: Academic Press, 1979.

AVIRAM, U., and S. SEGAL. "Exclusion of the Mentally Ill: Reflections on an Old Problem in a New Context," *Archives of General Psychiatry*, 29 (1973), 120–31.

AVNET, H. H. *Psychiatric Insurance: Financing Short-Term Ambulatory Treatment*. New York: Group Health Insurance, 1962.

BALDRIDGE, V. J. "Organizational Change: Institutional Sagas, External Challenges, and Internal Politics." In *Managing Change in Educational Organizations*, eds. J. V. Baldridge and T. E. Deal. Berkeley, Calif.: McCutcham, 1975. Pp. 427–48.

————, and R. A. BURNHAM. "Organizational Innovation: Individual, Organizational, and Environmental Impacts," *Administrative Science Quarterly*, 20 (1975), 165–76.

BALINT, M. *The Doctor, His Patient, and the Illness*. London: Pitman, 1964.

BARKER, L., and D. JANSIEWICZ. "Coalitions in the Civil Rights Movement." In *The Study of Coalition Behavior*, eds. S. Groennings, E. W. Kelley, and M. Leiserson. New York: Holt, Rinehart and Winston, 1970. Pp. 192–208.

BARNARD, C. *The Functions of the Executive*. Cambridge, Mass.: Harvard University Press, 1938.

BECKHARD, A. R. *Strategies of Organizational Development*. Reading, Mass.: Addison-Wesley, 1969.

BELKNAP I. *Human Problems of a State Mental Hospital*. New York: McGraw-Hill, 1956.

BENDIX, R. *Work and Authority in Industry*. New York: Wiley, 1956.

BENSON, J. K. "The Interorganizational Network as a Political Economy," *Administrative Science Quarterly*, 20 (1975), 229–49.

————. "Organizations: A Dialectic View," *Administrative Science Quarterly*, 22 (1977), 1–21.

BERGIN, A., and M. LAMBERT. "The Evaluation of Therapeutic Outcomes." In *Handbook of Psychotherapy and Behavior Change*, 2nd ed., eds. S. Garfield and A. Bergin. New York: Wiley, 1978. Pp. 139–89.

BERKANOVIC, E., and L. G. REEDER. "Can Money Buy the Appropriate Use of Services?" *Journal of Health and Social Behavior*, 15 (1974), 93–99.

BERNARD, S., E. KURTAGH, and H. JOHNSON. "The Neighborhood Service Organization: Specialist in Social Welfare Innovation," *Social Work*, 13 (1968), 76–84.

BIDWELL, C. "Students and Schools: Some Observations on Client Trust in Client-Serving Organizations." In *Organizations and Clients*, eds. W. Rosengren and R. Lefton. Columbus, Ohio: Charles E. Merrill, 1970. Pp. 37–70.

————. "The Social Psychology of Teaching." In *Second Handbook of Research on Teaching*, ed. R. Travers. Chicago: Rand McNally, 1973. Pp. 413–49.

BIGELOW, R. "Changing Classroom Interaction Through Organizational Development." In *Organizational Development in Schools*, eds. R. A. Schmuck and M. B. Miles. Palo Alto: National Press Books, 1971. Pp. 71–85.

BLAKE, R. R., and J. S. MOUTON. *The Management Grid*. Houston: Gulf, 1964.

BLAU, P. M. *The Dynamics of Bureaucracy*. Chicago: University of Chicago Press, 1955.

————. *Exchange and Power in Social Life*. New York: Wiley, 1964.

————, and R. SCHOENHERR. *The Structure of Organizations*. New York: Basic Books, 1971.

BOGDAN, R., S. TAYLOR, B. DE GRANDPRE, and S. HAYNES. "Let Them Eat Programs: Attendants' Perspectives and Programming on Wards in State Schools," *Journal of Health and Social Behavior,*   15 (1974), 142–51.

BOSSERT, S. T. *Tasks and Social Relations in Classrooms*   (The Arnold and Caroline Rose Monograph Series of the American Sociological Association). Cambridge, Eng.: Cambridge University Press, 1979.

BOWLES, S., and H. GINTIS. *Schooling in Capitalist America.*   New York: Basic Books, 1976.

BRAGER, G., and S. HOLLOWAY. *Changing Human Service Organizations.*   New York: Free Press, 1978.

BRAGINSKY, B., D. BRAGINSKY, and K. RING. *Methods of Madness: The Mental Hospital as Last Resort.*   New York: Holt, Rinehart and Winston, 1969.

BRENNER, H. *Mental Illness and the Economy.*   Cambridge, Mass.: Harvard University Press, 1973.

BRIAR, S., and H. MILLER. *Problems and Issues in Social Casework.*   New York: Columbia University Press, 1971.

CAMPBELL, D. "Reform as Experiments," *American Psychologist,*   24 (1969), 409–29.

CAMPBELL, J. "On the Nature of Organizational Effectiveness." In *New Perspectives on Organizational Effectiveness,* eds. P. S. Goodman, J. M. Pennings, and associates. San Francisco: Jossey-Bass, 1977. Pp. 13–55.

CARLSON, R. O. "Succession and Performance Among School Superintendents," *Administrative Science Quarterly,* 6 (1961), 210–27.

————. "Environmental Constraints and Organizational Consequences: The Public School and Its Clients." In *Behavioral Science and Educational Administration,*   Chicago: National Society for the Study of Education, 1964. Pp. 262–76.

CAUDILL, W. *The Psychiatric Hospital as a Small Society.*   Cambridge, Mass.: Harvard University Press, 1958.

CHILD, J. "Organizational Structure, Environment, and Performance: The Role of Strategic Choices," *Sociology,*   6 (1972), 2–22.

————. "Predicting and Understanding Organizational Structure," *Administrative Science Quarterly,*   18 (1973), 168–85.

CHU, F., and S. TROTTER. *The Madness Establishment.*   New York: Grossman, 1974.

CLARK, B. R. *Adult Education in Transition.*   Berkeley: University of California Press, 1956.

————. "The Cooling-out Function in Higher Education," *American Journal of Sociology,* 65 (1960), 569–76.

————. *The Distinctive College: Antioch, Reed, and Swarthmore.*   Chicago: Aldine, 1970.

CLOWARD, R., and I. EPSTEIN. "Private Social Welfare's Disengagement from the Poor: The Case of Family Adjustment Agencies." In *Social Welfare Institutions,*   ed. M. N. Zald. New York: Wiley, 1965. Pp. 623–45.

COCH, L., and J. R. P. FRENCH, Jr. "Overcoming Resistance to Change," *Human Relations,*   1 (1948), 512–32.

COCHRAN, N. "Grandma Moses and the 'Corruption' of Data," *Evaluation Quarterly,* 2 (1978), 363–73.

COE, R. *Sociology of Medicine.*   New York: McGraw-Hill, 1970.

COHEN, D. K. "Politics and Research: Evaluation of Social Action Programs in Education." In *Evaluating Action Programs,* ed. C. H. Weiss. Boston: Allyn and Bacon, 1972. Pp. 137–65.

COHEN, M. D., J. G. MARCH, AND J. P. OLSEN. "A Garbage-Can Model of Organizational Choice," *Administrative Science Quarterly,*   17 (1972), 1–25.

COLEMAN, J. "Loss of Power," *American Sociological Review,*   38 (1973), 1–17.

CONNERY, R. H. *The Politics of Mental Health.* New York: Columbia University Press, 1968.

COOK, K. S. "Exchange and Power in Networks of Interorganizational Relations," *The Sociological Quarterly,* 18 (1977), 62–82.

―――, and R. H. EMERSON. "Power, Equity, Commitment in Exchange Networks," *American Sociological Review,* 43 (1978), 721–39.

CORWIN, R. *Militant Professionalism.* New York: Appleton-Century-Crofts, 1970.

―――. "Strategies for Organizational Innovation: An Empirical Comparison," *American Sociological Review,* 37 (1972), 441–54.

COSER, L. R. "Authority and Decision Making in a Hospital," *American Sociological Review,* 23 (1958), 56–64.

―――. "Alienation and the Social Structure: Case Analysis of a Hospital." In *The Hospital in Modern Society,* ed. E. Freidson, New York: Free Press, 1963. Pp. 231–65.

CRAIN, R. L. *The Politics of School Desegregation.* Chicago: Aldine, 1968.

CRESSEY, D. "Prison Organizations." In *Handbook of Organizations,* ed. J. G. March. Chicago: Rand McNally. Pp. 1023–70.

CUMMING, E., and J. CUMMING. *Closed Ranks: An Experiment in Mental Health Education.* Cambridge, Mass.: Harvard University Press, 1957.

CYERT, R. M. *The Management of the Nonprofit Organization.* Lexington, Mass.: D. C. Heath, 1975.

―――, and J. G. MARCH. *The Behavioral Theory of the Firm.* Englewood Cliffs, N.J.: Prentice-Hall, 1963.

CYTRYNBAUM, S., Y. GINOTH, J. BIRDWELL, and L. BRANDT. "Goal Attainment Scaling: A Critical Review." *Evaluation Quarterly,* 31 (1979), 5–40.

DAFT, R., and S. BECKER. *Innovation in Organizations.* New York: Elsevier, 1978.

DANET, B. "Giving the Underdog a Break: Latent Particularism Among Custom Officials." In *Bureaucracy and the Public,* eds. E. Katz and B. Danet. New York: Basic Books, 1973. Pp. 329–37.

DAVID, M. S. "Variations in Patients' Compliance with Doctors' Advice: An Empirical Analysis of Patterns of Communication," *American Journal of Public Health,* 58 (1968), 279–86.

DELBECQ, A. L. "The Social Political Process of Introducing Innovation in Human Services." In *The Management of Human Services,* eds. R. C. Sarri and Y. Hasenfeld. New York: Columbia University Press, 1978. Pp. 309–39.

DERTHICK, M. *Uncontrollable Spending for Social Services Grants.* Washington, D.C.: The Brookings Institution, 1975.

―――. *Policymaking for Social Security.* Washington, D.C.: The Brookings Institution, 1979.

DEUTSCH, A. *The Shame of the States.* New York: Harcourt, Brace, 1948.

DEUTSCHER, I. "Toward Avoiding the Goal-trap in Evaluation Research." In *The Evaluation of Social Programs,* ed. C. C. Abt. Beverly Hills, Calif.: Sage, 1976. Pp. 249–68.

DICKSON, D. T. "Bureaucracy and Morality: An Organizational Perspective on a Moral Crusade," *Social Problems,* 16 (1968), 143–56.

DIEHR, P., K. O. JACKSON, and M. V. BOSCHA. "Access to Medical Care: The Impact of Outreach Services on Enrollees of Prepaid Health Insurance Program," *Journal of Health and Social Behavior,* 16 (1975), 326–340.

DINGWALL, R. "Problems of Teamwork in Primary Care." In *Social Services and Health Care,* eds. S. Lonsdale, A. Webb, and T. L. Briggs. Syracuse, N.Y.: Syracuse University School of Social Work, 1980. Pp. 111–37.

DOHRENWEND, B. P. "Sociocultural and Social-psychological Factors in the Genesis of Mental Disorders," *Journal of Health and Social Behavior,* 16 (1975), 365–92.

DONABEDIAN, A. "Evaluating the Quality of Medical Care." *The Milbank Memorial Fund Quarterly,* 44 (1966), 166–88.

DONICHT, T. L., and R. B. EVERHART. "Harvesting the Money Tree: Educational Innovations as Revenue Sharing," *Social Problems,* 24 (1976), 247–58.

DORNBUSCH, S., and W. R. SCOTT. *Evaluation and the Exercise of Authority.* San Francisco: Jossey-Bass, 1975.

DOWNEY, H. K., D. HELLRIEGEL, and J. W. SLOCUM, Jr. "Environmental Uncertainty: The Construct and Its Application," *Administrative Science Quarterly,* 20 (1975), 613–29.

DOWNS, G. *Bureaucracy, Innovation, and Public Policy.* Lexington, Mass.: D.C. Heath, 1976.

——, and L. MOHR. "Toward a Theory of Innovation," *Administration and Society,* 10 (1979), 379–408.

DRUCKER, P. F. *The Practice of Management.* New York: Harper, 1954.

DUFF, R. S., and A. B. HOLLINGSHEAD. *Sickness and Society,* New York: Harper & Row, 1968,

DUNHAM, H. W., and S. K. WEINBERG. *The Culture of the State Mental Hospital.* Detroit: Wayne State University, 1960.

DURMAN, E. "Have the Poor Been Regulated? Toward a Multivariate Understanding of Welfare Growth," *Social Service Review,* 47 (1973), 339–59.

DUTTON, D. "The Use of Health Services by the Poor," *American Sociological Review,* 43 (1978), 348–67.

ELESH, D. "Organization Sets and the Structure of Competition for New Members," *Sociology of Education,* 46 (1973), 371–95.

——, and P. T. SCHOLLAERT. "Race and Urban Medicine: Factors Affecting the Distribution of Physicians in Chicago," *Journal of Health and Social Behavior,* 13 (1972), 236–30.

EMERSON, R. M. "Power-dependence Relations," *American Sociological Review,* 27 (1962), 31–41.

——. "Exchange Theory, Part II: Exchange Relations and Network Structures." In *Sociological Theories in Progress,* eds. J. Berger, M. Zelditch, and B. Anderson. Boston: Houghton Mifflin, 1972. II: 58–87.

——. "Social Exchange Theory." In *The Annual Review of Sociology,* ed. A. Inkeles. Palo Alto, Calif.: Annual Reviews Inc., 1975. I: 335–62.

EMERSON, R. M. *Judging Juvenile Delinquents.* Chicago: Aldine, 1969.

——, and M. POLLNER. "Dirty Work Designations: Their Features and Consequences in a Psychiatric Setting," *Social Problems,* 23 (1976), 243–54.

EMPEY, L., and M. ERICKSON. *The Provo Experiment.* Lexington, Mass.: Lexington Press, 1972.

EPSTEIN, I. "Professionalization, Professionalism, and Social Work Radicalism," *Journal of Health and Social Behavior* 11, (1970), 67–77.

ETZIONI, A., ed. *The Semi-professions and Their Organization.* New York: Free Press, 1969.

FAIRWEATHER, G. W., D. H. SANDERS, and L. G. TORNATZKY. *Creating Change in Mental Health Organizations.* New York: Pergamon Press, 1974.

FISCHER, J. *The Effectiveness of Casework.* Springfield, Ill.: Charles C. Thomas, 1976.

——, and H. MILLER. "The Effects of Client Race and Social Class on Clinical Judgments," *Clinical Social Work Journal,* 1 (1973), 100–109.

FONTANA, A. F. "Machiavellianism and Manipulation in the Mental Patient Role," *Journal of Personality,* 39 (1971), 252–63.

FOX, R. C. "Advanced Medical Technology—Social and Ethical Implications." In *Annual Review of Sociology,* ed. A. Inkeles. Palo Alto, Calif.: Annual Reviews, inc., 1976. Pp. 231–68.

FRANKE, R. H., and J. D. KAUL. "The Hawthorn Experiments: First Statistical Interpretation," *American Sociological Review,* 43 (1978), 623–42.

FREIDSON, E. *Patients' Views of Medical Practice.* New York: Russell Sage Foundation, 1961.

———. "Disability as Social Deviance." In *Sociology and Rehabilitation,* ed. M. Sussman. Washington, D.C.: American Sociological Association, 1965. Pp. 71–99.

———. *Profession of Medicine.* New York: Dodd, Mead Co., 1970.

———. "Professions and the Occupational Principle." In *The Professions and Their Prospects,* ed. E. Freidson. Beverly Hills, Calif.: Sage, 1973. Pp. 19–38.

FRENCH, W. B., and G. H. BELL. *Organizational Development.* Englewood Cliffs, N.J.: Prentice-Hall, 1973.

GALBRAITH, J. R. *Organization Design.* Reading, Mass.: Addison-Wesley, 1977.

GALPER, J. H. *The Politics of Social Services.* Englewood Cliffs, N.J.: Prentice-Hall, 1975.

GAMBRILL, E. D. *Behavior Modification: Handbook of Assessment, Intervention, and Evaluation.* San Francisco: Jossey-Bass, 1977.

GAMSON, W. A. *Power and Discontent.* Homewood, Ill.: Dorsey Press, 1968.

GEORGIOU, P. "The Goal Paradigm and Notes Toward A Counter Paradigm," *Administrative Science Quarterly,* 18 (1973), 291–310.

GEORGOPOULOS, B. S., and A. MATEJKO, "The American General Hospital as a Complex Social System," *Health Services Research,* 2 (1967), 76–112.

GILBERT, N. "The Transformation of Social Services," *Social Service Review,* 51 (1977), 624–41.

———, and H. SPECHT. *Dimensions of Social Welfare Policy.* Englewood Cliffs, N.J.: Prentice-Hall, 1974.

GLASSER, I. "Prisoners of Benevolence: Power Versus Liberty in the Welfare State." In *Doing Good,* eds. W. Gaylin, I. Glasser, S. Marcus, and D. Rothman. New York: Pantheon, 1978. Pp. 97–168.

GOFFMAN, E. *Asylums.* Garden City, N.Y.: Anchor Books, 1961.

GORDON, L. K. "Bureaucratic Competence and Success in Dealing with Public Bureaucracies," *Social Problems,* 23 (1975), 197–208.

GOSS, M. "Patterns of Bureaucracy Among Hospital Staff Physicians." In *The Hospital in Modern Society,* ed. E. Freidson, New York: Free Press, 1963. Pp. 170–94.

GOULDNER, A. W., "Organizational Analysis." In *Sociology Today,* eds. R. K. Merton, L. Broom, and L. S. Cottrell, Jr. New York: Basic Books, 1959. Pp. 400–428.

GRAY, C. M., C. J. CONOVER, and T. M. HENNESSEY. "Cost-effectiveness of Residential Community Corrections: An Analytical Prototype," *Evaluation Quarterly,* 2 (1978), 375–400.

GRAZIANO, A. "A Clinical Innovation and the Mental Health Power Structure," *American Psychologist,* 24 (1969), 10–18.

GREENBLATT, M., D. LEVINSON, and R. WILLIAMS, eds. *The Patient and the Mental Hospital.* Glencoe, Ill.: Free Press, 1957.

GREENLEY, J. R., and S. A. KIRK. "Organizational Characteristics of Agencies and the Distribution of Services to Applicants," *Journal of Health and Social Behavior,* 14 (1973), 70–79.

GREENWOOD, E. *The Practice of Science and the Science of Practice.* Papers in Social Welfare No. 1 Waltham, Mass.: Brandeis University, Florence Heller School for Advanced Studies in Social Welfare, 1960.

GRIFFIN, L., and K. L. ALEXANDER. "Schooling and Socioeconomic Attainment: High

School and College Influences" *American Journal of Sociology,*   84 (1978), 319–47.

GROSS, N., J. B. GIACQUINTA, and M. BERNSTEIN. *Implementing Organizational Innovation.*   New York: Basic Books, 1971.

GROSSMAN, J. "Shifting Patterns in the Nature of Technological Innovations in Health Care Delivery." In *The Management of Health Care,*   eds. W. J. Abernathy, A. Sheldon, and C. K. Prahalad. Cambridge, Mass: Ballinger, 1974. Pp. 63–66.

GRUBER, M. "Inequality in the Social Services." *Social Service Review,*   54 (1980), 59–75.

GUMMER, B. "On Helping and Helplessness: The Structure of Discretion in the American Welfare System," *Social Service Review,* 53 (1979), 214–28.

GUSFIELD, J. R. "Moral Passage: The Symbolic Process in Public Designations of Deviance," *Social Problems,* 15 (1967), 175–88.

HAGE, J. *Communication and Organizational Control.*   New York: Wiley, 1974.

———. *Theories of Organizations.*   New York: Wiley, 1980.

———, and M. AIKEN. "Routine Technology, Social Structure, and Organizational Goals," *Administrative Science Quarterly,* 14 (1969), 366–77.

———. "Relationship of Centralization to Other Structural Properties," *Administrative Science Quarterly,* 12 (1967), 72–91.

———, and R. DEWAR. "Elite Values vs. Organizational Structure in Predicting Innovation, *Administrative Science Quarterly,* 18 (1973), 279–90.

HALL, R. H. "Professionalization and Bureaucratization," *American Sociological Review,* 33 (1968), 94–104.

———. *Organizations: Structure and Process,*   2nd ed. Englewood Cliffs, N.J.: Prentice-Hall, 1977.

HALL, S. *The Point of Entry: A Study of Client Reception in the Social Services.*   London: George Allen and Unwin, 1974.

HAMPSON, D. "Curriculum Change at the Local Level: A Case Study." In *Managing Change in Educational Organizations,*   eds. J. V. Baldridge and T. E. Deal. Berkeley, Calif.: McCutchan Publishing Co., 1975. Pp. 355–77.

HANDLER, J. F. *Reforming the Poor.*   New York: Basic Books, 1972.

———. *The Coercive Social Worker.*   Chicago: Markham, 1973.

———. *Protecting the Social Service Client: Legal and Structural Controls on Official Discretion.*   New York: Academic Press, 1979.

HANNAN, H. T., and J. FREEMAN. "The Population Ecology of Organizations," *American Journal of Sociology,* 82 (1977a), 929–64.

———. "Obstacles to Comparative Studies." In *New Perspectives on Organizational Effectiveness,* eds. P. S. Goodman, J. M. Penning, and associates. San Francisco: Jossey-Bass, 1977b. Pp. 106–31.

HASENFELD, Y. "Organizational Dilemmas in Innovating Social Services: The Case of Community Action Centers," *Journal of Health and Social Behavior,*   12 (1971), 208–16.

———. "People-Processing Organizations: An Exchange Approach," *American Sociological Review,* 37 (1972), 256–63.

———. "Organizational Factors in Services to Groups." In *Individual Change Through Groups,* eds. P. Glasser, R. C. Sarri, and R. D. Vinter. New York: Free Press, 1974, Pp. 307–22.

———. "The Role of Employment Placement Services in Maintaining Poverty." *Social Service Review,*   49 (1975), 569–87.

———. "The Juvenile Court and Its Environment." In *Brought to Justice? Juveniles, the Courts, and the Law,*   eds. R. C. Sarri and Y. Hasenfeld. Ann Arbor, Mich.: National Assessment of Juvenile Corrections, 1976. Pp. 72–95.

————. "Client-Organization Relations. A Systems Perspective." In *The Management of Human Services*, eds. R. C. Sarri and Y. Hasenfeld. New York: Columbia University Press, 1978. Pp. 184–206.

————. "Implementation of Change in Human Service Organizations: A Political Economy Perspective," *Social Service Review*, 54 (1980), 508–20.

————, and R. A. ENGLISH. EDS. *Human Service Organizations*. Ann Arbor, Mich.: University of Michigan Press, 1974.

————, and D. STEINMETZ. "Client-Official Encounters in Social Service Agencies." In *The Public Encounter*, ed. C. T. Goodsell. Bloomington: Indiana University Press, 1981. Pp. 83–101.

HEDBERG, B. L., P. C. NYSTROM, and W. H. STARBUCK. "Camping on Seesaws: Prescriptions for a Self-designing Organization," *Administrative Science Quarterly*, 21 (1976), 41–65.

HELFGOT, J. "Professional Reform Organizations and the Symbolic Representation of the Poor," *American Sociological Review*, 39 (1974), 475–91.

HELLUM, F. "Juvenile Justice: The Second Revolution," *Crime and Delinquency*, 25 (1979), 299–317.

HENRY, J. "Types of Institutional Structure." In *The Patient and the Mental Hospital*, eds. M. Greenblatt, D. Levinson, and R. Williams. Glencoe, Ill: Free Press, 1957. Pp. 73–90.

HERRIOTT, R. E., and B. J. HODGKINS. *The Environment of Schooling: Formal Education as an Open Social System*. Englewood Cliffs, N.J.: Prentice-Hall, 1973.

HICKSON, D. J., D. S. PUGH, and D. C. PHEYSEY. "Operations Technology and Organizational Structure: An Empirical Appraisal," *Administrative Science Quarterly*, 14 (1969), 378–97.

HININGS, C. R., D. J. HICKSON, J. M. PENNING, and R. E. SCHNECK. "Structural Conditions of Intraorganizational Power," *Administrative Science Quarterly*, 19 (1974), 22–44.

HIRSCHMAN, A. O. *Exit, Voice, and Loyalty*. Cambridge, Mass.: Harvard University Press, 1970.

HOOS, I. R. *Systems Analysis in Public Policy*. Berkeley: University of California Press, 1972.

HOWARD, J. "Humanization and Dehumanization of Health Care." In *Humanizing Health Care*, eds. J. Howard and A. Strauss. New York: Wiley, 1975. Pp. 57–102.

HUGHES, E. C. *The Sociological Eye: Selected Papers*. Chicago: Aldine, 1971.

INDIK, B. P. "Organization Size and Member Participation: Some Empirical Tests of Alternative Explanations," *Human Relations*, 18 (1965), 339–50.

JACKSON, L. R., and W. A. JOHNSON. *Protest by the Poor*. Lexington, Mass.: D. C. Heath, 1974.

JACOBS, D. "Dependency and Vulnerability: An Exchange Approach to the Control of Organizations," *Administrative Science Quarterly*, 19 (1974), 45–59.

JACOBS, J. B. *Stateville: The Penitentiary in Mass Society*. Chicago: University of Chicago Press, 1977.

JANOWITZ, M. *Institution Building in Urban Education*. New York: Russell Sage Foundation, 1969.

————. *Social Control of the Welfare State*. New York: Elsevier, 1976.

————. *The Last Half-Century*. Chicago: University of Chicago Press, 1978.

JOHNS, R. L., and R. B. KIMBROUGH, *The Relationship of Socioeconomic Factors, Educational Leadership Patterns, and Elements of Community Power Structure to Local School Fiscal Policy*. Washington, D.C.: Bureau of Research, Office of Education, 1968.

JOHNSON, T. *Professions and Power*. London: Macmillan, 1972.

KADUSHIN, C. *Why People Go to Psychiatrists.* New York: Atherton Press, 1969.

KALUZNY, A., J. VENEY, and J. GENTRY. "Innovations of Health Services: Hospitals and Health Departments," *Milbank Memorial Fund Quarterly,* 52 (1974), 51–82.

KANTER, R. M. *Men and Women of the Corporation.* New York: Basic Books, 1977.

KAPLAN, H. R., and C. TAUSKY. "Humanism in Organizations: A Critical Appraisal," *Public Administration Review,* 37 (1977), 171–80.

KASSENBAUM, G., D. WARD, and D. WILNER. *Prison Treatment and Parole Survival.* New York: Wiley, 1971.

KATZ, D., B. A. GUTEK, R. L. KAHN, and E. BARTON. *Bureaucratic Encounters.* Ann Arbor, Mich.: Survey Research Center, Institute for Social Research, The University of Michigan, 1975.

————, and R. L. KAHN. *The Social Psychology of Organizations,* 2nd. ed. New York: Wiley, 1978.

KATZ, E., and B. DANET, EDS. *Bureaucracy and the Public.* New York: Basic Books, 1973.

KAUFMAN, H. *The Limits of Organizational Change.* University, Ala.: University of Alabama Press, 1971.

KIRESUK, T., and S. H. LUND. "Goal Attainment Scaling." In *Evaluation of Human Service Programs,* eds. C. C. Attkisson, W. A. Hargreaves, M. J. Horowitz, and J. Sorensen. New York: Academic Press, 1978. Pp. 341–70.

KLATSKY, S. R. "Organizational Inequality: The Case of the Public Employment Agencies," *American Journal of Sociology,* 76 (1970), 474–91.

KOONTZ, H., and C. O'DONNELL. *Principles of Management.* New York: Knopf, 1959.

KOSBERG, J. I. "Differences in Proprietary Institutions Care for Affluent and Non-affluent Elderly," *Gerontologist,* 13 (1973), 299–304.

KRAMER, R. M. "Public Fiscal Policy and Voluntary Agencies in the Welfare State," *Social Service Review,* 53 (1979), 1–14.

KRAUSE, E. A. "After the Rehabilitation Center," *Social Problems,* 14 (1966), 197–206.

————. *Power and Illness: The Political Sociology of Health and Medical Care.* New York: Elsevier, 1977.

KREBS, R. L. "Some Effects of a White Institution on Black Psychiatric Outpatients," *American Journal of Orthopsychiatry,* 41 (1971), 589–97.

KROEGER, N. "Bureaucracy, Social Exchange, and Benefits Received in a Public Assistance Agency," *Social Problems,* 23 (1975), 182–96.

LARKIN, R. W. "Social Exchange in the Elementary School Classroom: The Problem of Teacher Legitimation of Social Power," *Sociology of Education,* 48 (1975), 400–410.

LAWRENCE, P. R., and J. W. LORSCH. *Organization and Environment.* Boston: Harvard Business School, Division of Research, 1967.

LEE, S. M., and L. J. MOORE. "Multicriteria School Busing Models," *Management Science,* 23 (1977), 703–18.

LEFTON, M. "Client Characteristics and Structural Outcomes." In *Organizations and Clients,* eds. W. R. Rosengren and M. Lefton. Columbus, Ohio: Charles E. Merrill, 1970. Pp. 17–36.

————, and W. R. ROSENGREN. "Organizations and Clients: Lateral and Longitudinal Dimensions," *American Sociological Review,* 31 (1966), 802–10.

LEONARD, P. "Toward a Paradigm for Radical Practice." In *Radical Social Work,* eds. P. Bailey and M. Brake. New York: Pantheon, 1975, Pp. 46–61.

LERMAN, P. "Evaluative Studies of Institutions for Delinquents: Implications for Research and Social Policy," *Social Work,* 13 (1968), 55–64.

———. *Community Treatment and Social Control.* Chicago: University of Chicago Press, 1975.

LERNER, B., and D. W. FISK. "Client Attributes and the Eyes of the Beholder," *Journal of Consulting and Clinical Psychology,* 40 (1973), 272–77.

LEVINE, A., and M. LEVINE. "The Social Context of Evaluative Research," *Evaluation Quarterly,* 1 (1977), 515–42.

LEVINE, S., and P. E. WHITE. "Exchange as a Conceptual Framework for the Study of Interorganizational Relationships," *Administrative Science Quarterly,* 5 (1961), 583–601.

LIKERT, R. *New Patterns of Management.* New York: McGraw-Hill, 1961.

———. *The Human Organization.* New York: McGraw-Hill, 1967.

LINK, B., and B. MILCAREK. "Selection Factors in the Dispensation of Therapy: The Matthew Effect in the Allocation of Mental Health Resources," *Journal of Health and Social Behavior,* 21 (1980), 279–90.

LIPSKY, M. *Protest in City Politics.* Chicago: Rand McNally, 1970.

———. "Toward a Theory of Street-level Bureaucracy." In *Theoretical Perspectives on Urban Politics,* eds. W. D. Hawley and M. Lipsky. Englewood Cliffs, N.J.: Prentice-Hall, 1976. Pp. 196–213.

———. *Street-level Bureaucracy.* New York: Russell Sage Foundation, 1980.

LIPTON, D., R. MARTINSON, and J. WILKS. *The Effectiveness of Correctional Treatment.* New York: Praeger Publishers, 1975.

LITWAK, E. "Models of Bureaucracy which Permit Conflict," *American Journal of Sociology,* 67 (1961), 177–84.

———. "Organizational Constructs and Mega Bureaucracy." In *The Management of Human Services,* eds. R. C. Sarri and Y. Hasenfeld. New York: Columbia University Press, 1978. Pp. 123–62.

LIZOTTE, A. J. "Extra-legal Factors in Chicago's Criminal Courts," *Social Problems,* 25 (1978), 564–80.

LORBER, J. "Good Patients and Problem Patients: Conformity and Deviance in a General Hospital," *Journal of Health and Social Behavior,* 16 (1975), 213–25.

———, and R. SATOW. "Creating a Company of Equals: Sources of Occupational Stratification in a Ghetto Community Mental Health Center," *Sociology of Work and Occupations,* 4 (1977), 281–302.

LORION, R. P. "Socioeconomic Status and Traditional Treatment Approaches Reconsidered," *Psychological Bulletin,* 79 (1973), 263–70.

LORTI, D. *School-Teacher.* Chicago: University of Chicago Press, 1975.

LUDWIG, E. G., and S. D. ADAMS. "Patient Cooperation in a Rehabilitation Center: Assumption of the Client Role," *Journal of Health and Social Behavior,* 9 (1968), 328–36.

LYNCH, B. P. "An Empirical Assessment of Perrow's Technology Construct," *Administrative Science Quarterly,* 19 (1974), 338–56.

MANDELL, B. "Welfare and Totalitarianism. Part I: Theoretical Issues," *Social Work,* 16 (1971), 17–26.

MANNING, N. "Values and Practice in the Therapeutic Community," *Human Relations,* 29 (1976), 125–38.

MANSER, E. "Further Thoughts on Purchase of Service," *Social Casework,* 55 (1974), 421–74.

———, J. JONES, and S. ORTOF. "An Overview of Project Enable," *Social Casework,* 48 (1967), 609–17.

MARCH, J. G., and H. SIMON. *Organizations.* New York: Wiley, 1958.

———, and J. P. OLSEN. *Ambiguity and Choice in Organizations.* Bergen, Norway: Universitetsforlaget, 1976.

MARRIS, P., and M. REIN. *Dilemmas of Social Reform.* New York: Atherton Press, 1967.

MARTINSON, R. "What Works? Questions and Answers about Prison Reform," *Public Interest*, 35 (1974), 22–54.

MASSIE, J. L. "Management Theory." In *Handbook of Organizations,* ed. J. G. March. Chicago: Rand McNally, 1965. Pp. 387–422.

MAYER, R., R. MORONEY, and R. MORRIS. *Centrally Planned Change.* Urbana, Ill.: University of Illinois Press, 1974.

MCCLEARY, R. "How Structural Variables Constrain the Parole Officer's Use of Discretionary Power," *Social Problems*, 23 (1975), 209–25.

———. "How Parole Officers Use Records," *Social Problems,* 24 (1977), 576–89.

MCCLEERY, R. "Policy Change in Prison Management." In *Complex Organizations,* ed. A. Etzioni. New York: Holt, Rinehart and Winston, 1966. Pp. 376–400.

MCGREGOR, D. *The Human Side of Enterprise.* New York: McGraw-Hill, 1960.

MCKINLAY, J. "Some Approaches and Problems in the Study of the Use of Services—An Overview," *Journal of Health and Social Behavior*, 13 (1972), 115–52.

———, and S. M. MCKINLAY. "Some Social Characteristics of Lower Working-Class Utilizers of Maternity Care Services," *Journal of Health and Social Behavior,* 13 (1972), 369–81.

MCNEIL J., and W. J. POPHAM. "The Assessment of Teacher Competence." In *Second Handbook of Research on Teaching,* ed. R. Travers. Chicago: Rand McNally, 1973. Pp. 218–44.

MCNEIL, K. "Understanding Organizational Power: Building on the Weberian Legacy," *Administrative Science Quarterly,* 23 (1978), 65–90.

MECHANIC, D. *Mental Health and Social Policy,* 2nd. ed. Englewood Cliffs, N.J.: Prentice-Hall, 1980.

MERTON, R. K. "Bureaucratic Structure and Personality," *Social Forces,* 18 (1940), 560–68.

———. *Social Theory and Social Structure,* rev. ed. New York: Free Press, 1957.

MEYER, J., and B. ROWAN. "Institutionalized Organizations: Formal Structure as Myth and Ceremony," *American Journal of Sociology* 83 (1977), 340–63.

———. "The Structure of Educational Organizations." In *Environments and Organizations,* eds. M. Meyer and Associates. San Francisco: Jossey-Bass, 1978. Pp. 78–109.

MILLER, J. G. "Toward a General Theory for the Behavioral Sciences." *American Psychologist*, 10 (1955), 513–31.

MILIO, N. "Health Care Organizations and Innovation," *Journal of Health and Social Behavior*, 12 (1971), 163–73.

MILTON, O., and J. W. EDGERLY. *The Testing and Grading of Students,* U.S.A.: Change Magazine and Educational Change, 1976.

MISHLER, E. G., and N. E. WAXLER. "Decision Process in Psychiatric Hospitalization: Patients Referred, Accepted and Admitted to a Psychiatric Hospital," *American Sociological Review*, 28 (1963), 576–87.

MOHR, L. "Determinants of Innovation in Organizations," *American Political Science Review,* 63 (1969), 111–26.

———. "Organizational Technology and Organizational Structure," *Administrative Science Quarterly,* 16 (1971), 444–59.

———. "The Concept of Organizational Goal," *American Political Science Review,* 67 (1973), 470–81.

MOONEY, J. D., and A. C. REILEY. *The Principles of Organization.* New York: Harper, 1939.

MOREHEAD, M. A. "P.S.R.O.—Problems and Possibilities," *Man and Medicine,* 1 (1976) 113–32.

MORRIS, R., and I. HIRSCH LESCOHIER. "Service Integration: Real Versus Illusory Solution to Welfare Dilemmas." In *The Management of Human Services,* eds. R. C. Sarri, and Y. Hasenfeld. New York: Columbia University Press, 1978. Pp. 23–50.

MOUZELIS, N. P. *Organization and Bureaucracy.* Chicago: Aldine, 1968.

MURASKIN, W. "Review of Piven and Cloward: Regulating the Poor," *Contemporary Sociology,* 4 (1975), 607–13.

MURPHY, R. D. *Political Entrepreneurs and Urban Poverty.* Lexington, Mass.: D. C. Heath, 1971.

NATIONAL INSTITUTE of MENTAL HEALTH. "A Description of the Revised 1981 Management System for Federally Funded Community Mental Health Centers." Rockville, Md.: Division of Biometry and Epidemiology, 1980.

NAY, J. N., J. W. SCALON, R. E. SCHMIDT, and J. WHOLEY. "If You Don't Care Where You Get To, Then It Doesn't Matter Which Way You Go." In *The Evaluation of Social Programs,* ed. C. C. Abt. Beverly Hills: Sage, 1976. Pp. 97–120.

NELSON, B. J. "Client Evaluations of Social Programs." In *The Public Encounter,* ed. C. Goodsell. Bloomington: Indiana University Press, 1981. Pp. 42–74.

NEUBECK K., and J. L. ROACH. "Income Maintenance Experiments, Politics, and the Perpetuation of Poverty," *Social Problems,* 28 (1981), 308-320.

NILSON, L. B. "The Application of the Occupational 'Uncertainty Principle' to the Professions," *Social Problems,* 26 (1979), 570-81.

NUTHALL, G., and I. SNOOK. "Contemporary Models of Teaching." In *Second Handbook of Research on Teaching,* ed. R. Travers. Chicago: Rand McNally, 1973. Pg. 47-76.

OHLIN, L. E., A. D. MILLER, and R. A. COATES. *Juvenile Correctional Reform in Massachusetts.* Washington D.C.: National Institute of Juvenile Justice and Delinquency Prevention, 1977.

ORLINSKY, D. E., and K.I. HOWARD. "The Relation of Process to Outcome in Psychotherapy." In *Handbook of Psychotherapy and Behavior Change,* 2nd ed., eds. S. Garfield and A. Bergin. New York: Wiley, 1978. Pp. 283–329.

OUCHI, W. "Relationship between Organizational Structure and Organizational Control," *Administrative Science Quarterly,* 22 (1977), 95–113.

OVERTON, P., R. SCHNECK, and C. B. HAZLETT. "An Empirical Study of the Technology of Nursing Subunits," *Administrative Science Quarterly,* 22 (1977), 203–19.

PARLOFF, M., I. E. WASKOW, and B. E. WOLFE. "Research on Therapist Variables in Relation to Process and Outcome." In *Handbook of Psychotherapy and Behavior Change,* 2nd ed., eds. S. Garfield and A. Bergin. New York: Wiley, 1978. Pp. 233–82.

PARSONS, T. "The Mental Hospital as a Type of Organization." In *The Patient and the Mental Hospital,* eds. M. Greenblatt, D. J. Levinson, and R. Williams. Glencoe, Ill.: Free Press, 1957. Pp. 108–29.

———. "How Are Clients Integrated Into Service Organizations." In *Organizations and Clients,* eds. W. Rosengren and M. Lefton. Columbus, Ohio: Charles E. Merrill, 1970. Pp. 1–16.

PATTON, M. Q. *Utilization-Focused Evaluation.* Beverly Hills, Calif.: Sage, 1978.

PEABODY, R. L. *Organizational Authority.* New York: Atherton Press, 1964.

PEARL, G., and D. H. BARR. "Agencies Advocating Together," *Social Casework*,   57 (1976), 611–18.

PERLMAN, R. *Consumers and Social Services*.   New York: Wiley, 1975.

PERROW, C. "The Analysis of Goals in Complex Organizations," *American Sociological Review*,   26 (1961), 856–66.

――――. "Goals and Power Structures." In *The Hospital in Modern Society*,   ed. E. Freidson. New York: Free Press, 1963. Pp. 112–46.

――――. "Hospitals: Technology, Structure and Goals." In *Handbook of Organizations*,   ed. J. G. March. Chicago: Rand McNally, 1965, Pp. 910–71.

――――."A Framework for the Comparative Analysis of Organizations," *American Sociological Review*,   32 (1967), 194–208.

――――. *Organizational Analysis: A Sociological View*.   Belmont, Calif.: Wadsworth Publishing Co., 1970.

――――. *Complex Organizations: A Critical Essay*.   Chicago: Scott Foresman, 1972.

PFEFFER, J. "The Micropolitics of Organizations." In *Environments and Organizations*,   eds. M. Meyer and associates. San Francisco: Jossey-Bass, 1978, Pp. 29–50.

――――, and A. LONG. "Resource Allocations in United Funds: Examination of Power and Dependence," *Social Forces*, 55 (1977), 775–90.

PILIAVIN, I. "Organizational Factors Involved in the Processing of AFDC Eligibility and Budgetary Decisions." Paper given at the 75th annual program meeting of the American Sociological Association,   New York, 1980.

――――, and A. E. GROSS. "The Effects of Separation of Services and Income Maintenance on AFDC Recipients," *Social Service Review*, 51 (1977), 389–405.

PIVEN, F. F., and R. A. CLOWARD. *Regulating the Poor*.   New York: Pantheon Books, 1971.

――――. *Poor People's Movements*.   New York: Pantheon Books, 1977.

PLATT, A. M. *The Child Savers*.   Chicago: University of Chicago Press, 1969.

POLK, K., and W. SCHAFER. *Schools and Delinquency*.   Englewood Cliffs, N. J.: Prentice-Hall, 1972.

PORTER, L. W., E. E. LAWLER, III, and J. R. HACKMAN. *Behavior in Organizations*.   New York: McGraw-Hill, 1975.

PRESSMAN, J., and A WILDAVSKY. *Implementation*.   Berkeley: University of California Press, 1973.

PROTTAS, J. M. *People-Processing*.   Lexington, Mass.: D. C. Heath, 1979.

RANSON, S., B. HININGS, and R. GREENWOOD. "The Structuring of Organizational Structure," *Administrative Science Quarterly*,   25 (1980), 1–17.

RAPOPORT, R. *Community as a Doctor*.   London: Tavistock Publications, 1960.

REEDER, S. J., and H. MAUKSCH. "Nursing: Continuing Change" In *Handbook of Medical Sociology*,   3rd ed. eds. H. E. Freeman, S. Levine, and L. G. Reeder. Englewood Cliffs, N.J.: Prentice-Hall, 1979. Pp. 209–29.

REIN, M., T. E. NUTT, and H. WEISS. "Foster Family Care: Myth and Reality." In *Children and Decent People*, ed. A. L. Schorr. New York: Basic Books, 1974. Pp. 24–52.

REISS, A.J., JR. *The Police and the Public*.   New Haven: Yale University Press, 1971.

――――, and D. J. BORDUA. "Environment and Organization: A Perspective on the Police." In *The Police*,   ed. D. Bordua. New York: Wiley, 1967. Pp. 25–55.

RIST, R. C. "Student Social Class and Teacher Expectations: The Self-fulfilling Prophecy in Ghetto Education," *Harvard Educational Review*, 40 (1970), 411–51.

RITTI, R. R., and D. W. HYMAN. "The Administration of Poverty: Lessons from the Welfare Explosion 1967–1973," *Social Problems*,   25 (1977), 157–75.

ROETHLISBERGER, F. J., and W. J. DICKSON. *Management and the Worker.* Cambridge, Mass.: Harvard University Press, 1939.

ROGERS, D. *110 Livingston Street: Politics and Bureaucracy in the New York School System.* New York: Vintage Books, 1969.

ROSEN, B. M. "Mental Health of the Poor: Has the Gap Between the Poor and the 'Nonpoor' Narrowed in the Last Decade?" *Medical Care,*   15 (1977), 647–61.

ROSENBAUM, J. E. *Making Inequality.* New York: Wiley, 1976.

ROSENBERG, M., and L. I. PEARLIN. "Power-Orientations in the Mental Hospital," *Human Relations,*   15 (1962), 335–50.

ROSENHAN, D. L. "On Being Sane in Insane Places," *Science,* 179 (1973),   250–58.

ROSSI, P. H. "Some Issues in the Evaluation of Human Services Delivery." In *The Management of Human Services,*   eds. R. C. Sarri and Y. Hasenfeld. New York: Columbia University Press, 1978. Pp. 235–61.

———, H. E. FREEMAN, and S. R. WRIGHT. *Evaluation.*   Beverly Hills, Calif.: Sage, 1979.

ROTH, J. A. "Some Contingencies of the Moral Evaluation and Control of Clientele: The Case of the Hospital Emergency Service," *American Journal of Sociology,*   77 (1972), 839–56.

———, and E. EDDY. *Rehabilitation of the Unwanted.*   New York: Atherton, 1967.

ROTHMAN, D. *The Discovery of the Asylum.*   Boston: Little, Brown, 1971.

RUBIN, H. T. "Retain the Juvenile Court?" *Crime and Delinquency,*   25 (1979), 281–98.

RUSHING, W. A. "Status Resources, Societal Reactions, and Mental Hospital Admissions," *American Sociological Review,*   43 (1978), 521–33.

RUZEK, S. K. "Making Social Work Accountable." In *The Professions and their Prospects,*   ed. E. Freidson. Beverly Hills, Calif.: Sage, 1973. Pp. 217–43.

SALANCIK, G. R., and J. PFEFFER. "The Bases and Uses of Power in Organizational Decision Making: The Case of a University," *Administrative Science Quarterly,*   19 (1974), 453–73.

SARASON, S. B., C. F. CARROLL, K. MATON, S. COHEN, and E. LORENTZ. *Human Services and Resource Networks.*   San Francisco: Jossey-Bass, 1977.

SARRI, R. C., and Y. HASENFELD, EDS. *Brought to Justice? Juveniles, the Courts and the Law.*   Ann Arbor, Mich.: National Assessment of Juvenile Corrections, 1976.

SCHAFER, W., and C. OLEXA. *Tracking and Opportunity.*   Scranton, Pa.: Chandler, 1971.

SCHEFF, T. J. "Typification in the Diagnostic Practices of Rehabilitation Agencies" In *Sociology and Rehabilitation,*   ed. M. Sussman. Washington, D.C.: American Sociological Association, 1965. Pg. 139–47.

———. *Being Mentally Ill: A Sociological Theory.*   Chicago: Aldine, 1966.

———. "Negotiating Reality: Notes on Power in the Assessment of Responsibility," *Social Problems,*   16 (1968), 3–17.

SCHMUCK, R. H., P. RUNKEL and D. LONGMEYER. "Using Group Problem Solving Procedures," In *Organization Development in the School,*   eds. Schmuck, R. A. and M. B. Miles. Palo Alto, Calif.: National Press Books, 1971. Pp. 51–69.

———, and M. B. MILES, EDS. *Organization Development in the Schools.*   Palo Alto, Calif.: National Press Book, 1971.

SCHOFIELD, W. *Psychotherapy: The Purchase of Friendship.*   Englewood Cliffs, N. J.: Prentice-Hall, 1964.

SCHULBERG, H., and F. BAKER. *The Mental Hospital and Human Services.*   New York: Behavioral Publications, 1975.

SCHWARTZ, B. *Queuing and Waiting: Studies in the Social Organization of Access and Delay.*   Chicago: University of Chicago Press, 1975.

Scott, R. A. "The Selection of Clients by Social Welfare Agencies: The Case of the Blind," *Social Problems*, 14 (1967a), 248–57.

————. "The Factory as a Social Service Organization: Goal Displacement in Workshops for the Blind," *Social Problems*, 15 (1967b), 160–75.

————. *The Making of Blind Men*. New York: Russell Sage Foundation, 1969.

Scott, W. R. "Effectiveness of Organizational Effectiveness Studies." In *Perspectives on Organizational Effectiveness*, eds. P. S. Goodman, J. M. Penning, and associates. San Francisco: Jossey-Bass, 1977. Pp. 63–95.

Scull, A. T. *Decarceration*. Englewood Cliffs, N.J.: Prentice-Hall, 1977.

Seashore, S. E., and E. Yuchtman. "Factorial Analysis of Organizational Performance," *Administrative Science Quarterly*, 12 (1967), 377–95.

Seeley, J. R., B. H. Junker, R. W. Jones, Jr. *Community Chest*. Toronto: University of Toronto Press, 1957.

Segal, S. P., and U. Aviram. *The Mentally Ill in Community-based Sheltered Care*. New York: Wiley, 1978.

Selznick, P. "Foundation for the Theory of Organization," *American Sociological Review* 13 (1948), 25–35.

————. *TVA and the Grass Roots*. Berkeley: University of California Press, 1949.

————. *Leadership in Administration*. New York: Harper & Row, 1957.

Sexton, P. *Education and Income*. New York: Viking Press, 1961.

Sills, D. L. *The Volunteers*. New York: Free Press, 1957.

Simon H. A. "On the Concept of Organizational Goal," *Administrative Science Quarterly*, 9 (1964), 1–22.

Smith, C. G., and J. A. King. *Mental Hospitals*. Lexington, Mass.: D. C. Heath, 1975.

Smith, D. E. "The Logic of Custodial Organizations," *Psychiatry*, 28 (1965), 311–23.

————. "Front-line Organization of the State Mental Hospital," *Administrative Science Quarterly*, 10 (1965), 381–99.

————. *Administrative Behavior*, 3rd ed. New York: Free Press, 1976.

Steers, R. M. "Problems in the Measurement of Organizational Effectiveness," *Administrative Science Quarterly*, 20 (1975), 546–58.

Stimson, H. D., and R. H. Stimson. *Operations Research in Hospitals: Diagnosis and Prognosis*. Chicago: Hospital Research and Educational Trust, 1972.

————, and R. P. Thompson. "The Importance of 'Weltanschauung' in Operations Research: The Case of the School Busing Problem," *Management Science*, 21 (1975), 1123–31.

Stinchcombe, A. L. "Social Structure and Organizations" In *Handbook of Organizations*, ed. J. G. March. Chicago: Rand McNally, 1965. Pp. 142–93.

Stogdill, R. M. "Dimensions of Organizational Theory." In *Organizational Design and Research*, eds. J. D. Thompson and V. Vroom. Pittsburg: University of Pittsburgh Press, 1971. Pp. 1–52.

————. *Handbook of Leadership: A Survey of Theory and Research*. New York: Free Press, 1974.

Stolz, S., and associates. *Ethical Issues in Behavioral Modification*. San Francisco: Jossey-Bass, 1978.

Strauss, A., L. Schatzman, R. Bucher, D. Ehrlich, and M. Sabshin. *Psychiatric Ideologies and Institutions*. New York: Free Press, 1967.

Strauss, G. "Human Relations— 1968 Style," *Industrial Relations*, 7 (1968), 262–76.

————. "Organization Development." In *Handbook of Work, Organization, and Society*, ed. R. Dubin. Chicago: Rand McNally, 1976. Pp. 617–85.

STREET, D., G. T. MARTIN and L. K. GORDON. *The Welfare Industry.* Beverly Hills, Calif.: Sage, 1979.

_____, R. D. VINTER, and C. PERROW. *Organization for Treatment.* New York: Free Press, 1966.

STRUP, H. "Psychotherapy Research and Practice: An Overview." In *Handbook of Psychotherapy and Behavior Change,* 2nd ed., eds. S. Garfield and A. Bergin. New York: Wiley, 1978. Pp. 3–22.

SUDNOW, D. "Normal Crimes: Sociological Features of the Penal Code in a Public Defender's Office," *Social Problems,* 12 (1965), 255–76.

_____. *Passing On.* Englewood Cliffs, N. J.: Prentice-Hall, 1967.

SWITZER, E. "Chicago Settlements, 1972: An Overview," *Social Service Review,* 47 (1973), 581–92.

SZASZ, T. S., and M. H. HOLLENDER. "The Basic Models of the Doctor-Patient Relationship," *Archives in Internal Medicine,* 97 (1956), 582–92.

TABER, L. R., and R. H. TABER. "Social Casework." In *The Field of Social Work,* ed. A. E. Fink. New York: Holt, Rinehart and Winston, 1978. Pp. 135–57.

TANNENBAUM, A. S. *Hierarchy in Organizations.* San Francisco: Jossey-Bass, 1974.

TEDESCHI, J., B. R. SCHLENKER, and S. LINDSKOLD. "The Exercise of Power and Influence: The Sources of Influence." In *The Social Influence Process,* ed. J. Tedeschi. Chicago: Aldine, 1972. Pp. 287–345.

TEELE, J. E., and S. LEVINE. "The Acceptance of Emotionally Disturbed Children by Psychiatric Agencies." In *Controlling Delinquents,* ed. S. Wheeler. New York: Wiley, 1968. Pp. 103–26.

THOMPSON, J. D. "Organizations and Output Transactions," *American Journal of Sociology,* 68 (1962), 309–24.

_____. *Organizations in Action.* New York: McGraw-Hill, 1967.

TOREN, N. *Social Work: The Case of a Semi-profession.* Beverly Hills, Calif.: Sage, 1972.

TOWNSEND, C. *Old Age: The Last Segregation.* New York: Grossman, 1971.

TROPMAN, J. E. "The Welfare Calculus: Allocation and Utilization Within the American States," *Journal of Sociology and Social Welfare,* 2 (1975), 416–35.

TURK, H. *Organizations in Modern Life.* San Francisco: Jossey-Bass, 1977.

TUSSING, A. D. *Poverty in a Dual Economy.* New York: St. Martin's Press, 1975.

ULLMAN, L. P. *Institution and Outcome.* Oxford, Eng.: Pergamon Press, 1967.

URWICK, L. F. *The Elements of Administration.* New York: Harper & Row 1943.

U.S. DEPARTMENT OF COMMERCE, BUREAU OF THE CENSUS. *Statistical Abstracts of the U.S.: 1980.* Washington, D.C.: U.S. Government Printing Office, 1980.

U.S. DEPARTMENT OF HEALTH, EDUCATION, and WELFARE. *Community Mental Health Centers Monitoring Package.* Washington, D.C.: Public Health Service; A. D. M. H. A., 1977.

VAN DE VEN, A., A. DELBECQ, and R. KOENIG. "Determinants of Coordination: Models Within Organizations," *American Sociological Review,* 41 (1976), 322–38.

VINTER, R. "Analysis of Treatment Organizations," *Social Work,* 8 (1963), 3–15.

_____, R. C. SARRI, and Y. HASENFELD. *Federal Correctional Programs for Young Offenders: A Comparative Study* (Research Report). Washington, D.C.: Bureau of Prisons, U.S. Department of Justice, 1974.

_____, R. KISH, and T. NEWCOMB, EDS. *Time Out: A Comparative Study of Juvenile Correctional Institutions.* Ann Arbor, Mich.: National Assessment of Juvenile Corrections, 1976.

VLADECK, B. C. *Unloving Care: The Nursing Home Tragedy.* New York: Basic Books, 1980.

WALSH, J. L., and R. H. ELLING. "Professionalization and the Poor: Structural Effects and Professional Behavior," *Journal of Health and Social Behavior,* 9 (1968), 16–28.

WAMSLEY, G. L., and M. N. ZALD. *The Political Economy of Public Organizations.* Bloomington: Indiana University Press, 1976.

WARREN, R., S. M. ROSE, and A. F. BERGUNDER. *The Structure of Urban Reform.* Lexington, Mass.: D. C. Heath, 1974.

WEATHERLEY, R., and M. LIPSKY. "Street-level Bureaucrats and Institutional Innovation: Implementing Special-education Reform," *Harvard Educational Review,* 47 (1977), 171–97.

WEBER, M. *From Max Weber: Essays in Sociology,* eds. H. Gerth, and C. W. Mills. New York: Oxford University Press, 1946.

———. *The Theory of Social and Economic Organizations,* trans. A. M. Henderson and T. Parsons. New York: Free Press, 1947.

———. *Basic Concepts in Sociology,* trans. H. A. Secher. New York: The Cidatel Press, 1962.

WEDEL, K. R. "Government Contracting for Purchase of Service," *Social Work,* 21 (1976), 101–5.

WEICK, K. "Educational Organizations as Loosely Coupled Systems," *Administrative Science Quarterly,* 21 (1976), 1–19.

WEISS, C. "Evaluation Research in the Political Context." In *Handbook of Evaluation Research,* eds. E. L. Struening and M. Guttentag. Beverly Hills, Calif.: Sage, 1975, Pp. 13–26.

———. "Use of Social Science Research in Organizations: The Constrained Repertoire Theory." In *Organization and the Human Services,* ed. H. Stein. Philadelphia: Temple University Press, 1981. Pp. 180–204.

WEISS, R., and M. REIN. "The Evaluation of Broad-aim Programs," *Administrative Science Quarterly,* 16 (1970), 97–109.

WHEELER, S., ED. *On Record.* New York: Russell Sage Foundation, 1969.

WHITE, P. E. "Resources as Determinants of Organizational Behavior," *Administrative Science Quarterly,* 19 (1974), 366–76.

WHITE, R. K., and R. LIPPIT. *Autocracy and Democracy: An Experimental Inquiry.* New York: Harper & Row 1960.

WILENSKY, H. *Organizational Intelligence.* New York: Basic Books, 1967.

———. *The Welfare State and Equality.* Berkeley: University of California Press, 1975.

WILLIAMS, V. L., and M. FISH. *Convicts, Codes, and Contraband.* Cambridge, Mass.: Ballinger, 1974.

WILLIAMS, W., and J. W. EVANS. "The Politics of Evaluation: The Case of Head Start," *Annals of the American Academy of Political and Social Science,* 385 (1969), 118–32.

WILSON J. Q. *Political Organizations.* New York: Basic Books, 1973.

WIRT, F.M. and M. W. KIRST. *The Political Web of American Schools.* Boston: Little, Brown, 1972.

YUCHTMAN, E., and S. E. SEASHORE. "A System Resource Approach to Organizational Effectiveness," *American Sociological Review,* 32 (1967), 891–903.

ZALD, M. N. "Organizational Control Structures in Five Correctional Institutions," *American Journal of Sociology,* 68 (1962), 335–45.

———. "The Power and Function of Boards of Directors: A Theoretical Synthesis," *American Journal of Sociology,* 75 (1969), 97–111.

_____ . "Political Economy: A Framework for Comparative Analysis." In *Power in Organizations,* ed. M. N. Zald. Nashville, Tenn.: Vanderbilt University Press, 1970a. Pp. 221–61.

_____ . *Organizational Change: The Political Economy of the YMCA.* Chicago: University of Chicago Press, 1970b.

_____ . "Demographics, Politics, and the Future of the Welfare State," *Social Service Review,* 51 (1977), 110–24.

_____ , and P. DENTON. "From Evangelism to General Service: The Transformation of the YMCA," *Administrative Science Quarterly,* 8 (1963), 214–34.

ZALTMAN, G., R. DUNCAN, and J. HOLBEK. *Innovation and Organization.* New York: Wiley, 1973.

ZEIGLER, N., and K. F. JOHNSON. *The Politics of Education in the States.* Indianapolis: The Bobbs-Merrill Co., 1972.

ZEITZ, G. "Hierarchical Authority and Decision Making in Professional Organizations," *Administration and Society,* 12 (1980), 277–300.

ZEY-FERRELL, M. *Dimensions of Organizations.* Santa Monica, Calif.: Goodyear, 1979.

ZIMMERMAN, D. "The Practical Basis of Work Activities in a Public Assistance Organization." In *Exploration in Sociology and Counseling,* ed. D. Hansen. Boston: Houghton Mifflin Co., 1969a. Pp. 237—66.

_____ . "Record Keeping and the Intake Process in a Public Welfare Agency." In *On Record,* ed. S. Wheeler. New York: Russell Sage Foundation, 1969b. Pp. 319-54.

Author Index

Subject Index

Judicial bodies, 45. *See also* Juvenile courts
Juvenile corrections: agencies, 38, 71, 160, 185, 188; deinstitutionalization battle in, 97–98; institutions, staff-inmate relations in, 101; reforms in, 219, 223, 238, 242; technologies, 146
Juvenile courts, 227; admissions to, 187; and child-saving movements, 226; "cooling out" tactics in, 189; establishment of, 225–26; interest groups competing for, 9, 44, 91; legitimation of, 45; official vs. operative goals of, 86; processing vs. treatment in, 5; referral rates, 54; social labelling by, 135; task environment of, 63, 64
Juvenile offenders, 5, 214; attitudes toward, 9; custody vs. rehabiliation of, 97–98, 242; minority, 201

Knowledge: of casual relations, 112, 116–17, 128, 133, 235; incomplete vs. complete, 128, 235; new, 230–31, 246–47, scientific vs. moral values, 118–19; as technological base, 127–28

Labor unions, 80, 181
Law enforcement agencies, 1, 3, 71, 157, 214. *See also* Police
Leadership, executive. *See also* Authority; Decision-making; Dominant coalition, interests of, 60, 65, 79, 140–41, 143, 234; new, as force for change, 225, 238–39, 245; and productivity, 27; style, 23, 27; succession in, 47, 144, 219–20; tactics, 220; values of, 231, 232
Legislative agencies, 45; enactments of, as stimulus to change, 226–27; regulations and constraints by, 58, 74
Legitimation, 8, 51, 60–61, 63, 104, 151–52, 204; acquisition, 44–45, 60, 180; for change, 104, 108, 240–43; of domain, 62, 221–22; as key resource, 97, 180; by local community, 50, 104; and monitoring, 61, 99–100, 204; official goals and, 87; as power tool, 70, 97, 159–60, 242; of profession, 163; professional, 141, 162–64, 222; providers of, 44, 61, 204; as structural determinant, 151–52, 240; threats to, 63, 225, 227
Line staff. *See also* Staff-client relations; Staff, control of; autonomy of, 10, 121; control of information by, 157, 170; difficulties of monitoring, 121–22, 149, 155, 156–57, 167, 169–70; discretion of, 10, 121, 137, 151, 157, 158, 167–70, 172, 173; indoctrination of, 17, 167, 172; interests of, 157–158, 180; rule evasion by, 170; as street-level bureaucrats, 10, 121, 156–58, 160, 167, 244–45
Loosely coupled systems, 150–58, 175; advantages of, 155–56, 158; decision-making process in, 236–39; defined, 150; evolution of, 154–55; and multiple goals and interests, 152–53; quality of services in, 158–59; and resource-dependence, 151–52; staff-client relations as key in, 156–57

Management information systems, 21
Managerial theories, 13. *See also* Organizational theories; and "good administration," 19
Manpower training programs: funds for, 228–29; goals and assumptions, 89, 214
Medicaid and Medicare, 45
Mental health agencies, 3. *See also* Community mental health centers; Mental hospitals; Psychotherapy
Mental hospitals: assessing quality of care in, 208; and deinstitutionalization, 229, 230, 239; invol-

untary commitment to, 4; official vs. operative goals, 85–86; open systems approach, 14; patient control in, 131; patient-labeling in, 135; patient treatment in, 25, 28, 102, 158; practice ideologies disparate in, 90, 102, 158; psychoactive drugs in, 13; staff, 8, 102; state, 190; systems approach to, 36; therapeutic community in, 13, 25, 31
Monitoring. *See also* Performance evaluation; Staff, control of; administrative costs of, 157, 169; by bureaucratic review, 170–71; constraints on, 162, 167; contracted services, 75–76; criteria, goals as, 99–100; and forms, 168; mutual, by staff, 173–74; of other organizations, 70–71; of professionals, 174. *See also* Professional autonomy; staff-client encounters, 170; staff performance, difficulties of, 149, 155–57, 167, 169–70; by supervision, 171–72

Natural systems theory, 35–39, 44, 48; concept of effectiveness, 206–7; and exposé tradition, 37–38; vs. rational model, 35–36, 206
Need(s), 3, 39; diagnostic units of, 192, 194; and economic change, 53, 103; goal adaptation to changing, 105–6, 108–9; ideologies interpreting, 100; and sociodemographic change, 229–30
Neo-Marxian perspective, 39–44; contribution of, 42; on public welfare, 41–43; on schools, 41–42
Network, human services. *See* Interorganizational relations
Normative choices, 9, 22, 39; service technologies as, 115–16; typing of clients as, 192–93, 196
Nurses, 21, 126, 131, 163, 212; dual accountability of, 151, 164
Nursing homes, 5, 71, 138, 187–88; conflict of interests in, 183; goals of, 99

Organizational change: vs. adjustment, 220–21; attributes of, 220; capacity for. *See* Innovation, capacity for; client role in, 219; coalition for, 245; conditions for implementing, 240–45; cooptation of leaders for, 245; costs of, 222–23, 243; in decentralized systems, 233–34, 236–39; decision process, 234–35, 236–37, 239; defined, 219; fads, 231–32; failure of, 218, 244; and funding patterns, 227–29; hindrances to implementing, 243–44; initiating, strategies for, 235–36; vs. innovation, 219–20; involuntary, 80, 239, 245–46; legitimation for, 104, 108, 240–43; mobilization of resources for, 240–43, 245; new leadership required for, 225, 238–39, 245; objectives, displacement of, 240, 245; obstacles to, 10, 218–19, 221–25, 245. *See also* Organizational stability; and performance gap, perceived, 235–36, 237, 239; political shifts and, 225–26; public policy shifts and, 226–27; radical vs. nonradical, 220, 222, 233, 238, 239; skills needed for implementing, 241, 243–44; and sociodemographic shifts, 229–30; staff resistance to, 225, 232, 240, 244; symbolic vs. real, 220–21, 228, 243; technological innovations and, 230–31, 247
Organizational control, 16–17, 150–52, 162–75. *See also* Client, control of; Staff, control of
Organizational development, 23–24, 26, 28
Organizational effectiveness, 14, 22; concepts of, 205–7; criteria. *See* Evaluation criteria of; vs. efficiency, 174, 206, 210, 211–12; human relations approach to, 25–27; measures of, 10, 93, 205–10; official claims to, 141; political-economic view of, 207–8;

Organizational effectiveness (cont.)
rational model, 13, 206, 208–9; and resource acquisition, 207–8; structural determinants of, 149; systems view of, 206–7, 208

Organizational stability: decentralization and, 233–34; and existing rewards, 224–25, 232; forces of, 221–25; ideological, 223–24; and internal balance of power, 224–25; and network of exchange, 221–22; and resource limitations, 222–23; and sunk costs, 223; tendency toward, 221

Organizational structure, 8. *See also* Division of labor; Loosely coupled systems; Organizational theories; bureaucratic, 14–18, 49, 160–62; capacity for change, 233–34. *See also* Innovation, capacity for centralized, 33, 151, 160–62, 233; and clarity of task perceptions, 154–55; and control, 154–58; decentralized, 13, 16, 33, 150–51, 173, 233; differentiation within, 33–35. *See also* Division of labor; and distribution of power, 165–66. *See also* Power, distribution of; "front line," 156–58; and goal succession, 104; and homogeneity of environment, 34; as key to effectiveness, 25; "linking pin" concept, 23; in loosely coupled systems, 150–58; and multiple goals and interests, 152–54; and political economy, 47; position of professionals in, 164–65; as rational, 16, 149–50; and resource dependence, 151–52; and service technology, 46, 148–52; shifts in, 219–20, 224–25; stability of. *See* Organizational stability; and stability of environment, 34, 149, 152–54; uncoupling of: prison study, 152–54

Organizational technology, 9–10, 34–35, 110–12. *See also* Service technologies

Organizational theories, 1–49, 148–49. *See also* Bureaucracy: Weberian model of; Contingency theory; Decision-making theory; Human relations theory; Natural systems theory; Neo-Marxian perspective; Political economy perspective; Scientific management; assumptions underlying, 14; of design, 33; evolution of, 13; prerequisites for complete, 43; prescriptive, 18, 23; proliferation of, 12; of service technologies, 111–12

Organization-environment relations, 7, 43, 50–83. *See also* Task environment; changes in, 53, 103, 219, 225–31; cultural, 55–56, 57, 82, 103; economic, 52–53, 225–27. *See also* Funding; local community, 52–53, 58, 103; political-economic, 44–48; political-legal, 57–58, 225–27; power-dependence, 68–69, 82. *See also* Exchange relations; and service delivery, 82. *See also* Service technologies; sociodemographic, 53–55, 229–30; technological, 59, 230–31

Paraprofessionals, 163; alienation of, 164; emergence of, 164; low status of, 165, 166

Parole officers, 194–96

People-changing technologies, 5–7, 134–35, 143; administrative concerns in, 140–41, 143; assumed worth of client in, 140; client control in, 142; effectiveness of, 7; mutual participation in, 141–42; role of professionals in, 141; staff-control in, 142–43

People-processing technologies, 5–7, 134–37, 143; accountability of, 6–7; boundary relations of, 135–36; classification-disposition in, 5, 135–36; client control in, 136–37

People-sustaining technologies, 5–7, 134–35, 137–40, 143; assumption of, 137; control in, 139–40; core activities in, 138; dehumanization in, 139;

eligibility, 7; formalization of activities in, 138–39; level of care in, 7, 138–39; and social status of client, 137–38

Performance evaluation, 141; and changing environment, 210–11; circumvention of, 155, 215–17; "creaming," 214; criteria. *See* Evaluation, criteria of, and data corruption, 215–17; feedback, 20–21, 217; and goal displacement, 211–12; interest-group politics of, 204, 212–16, 217; need for valid, 149, 167; process, failure of, 205, 217; in public schools, 216; rating devices, 212, 214–15; and resistance to change, 10, 216–17; by resource providers, 204–5; self- or peer, 155, 174, 215; by self-selected measures, 214–15; of service outcomes, 11; symbolic, 209–10, 217; target population for, 204, 214

Physicians, 7, 72; hospital, dual control system, 17, 164. *See also* Hospitals; Professionals; as interest group, 96; professional power of, 166; typing of patients by, 115, 142, 191, 193

Police, 9, 71, 157, 214

Political economy perspective, 43–47; defined, 44; on effectiveness, 207–8; on goal determination, 95–99

Political-legal environment, 45–47, 82; changes in, 103, 225–27; community power structure, 58; and funding, 57–58, 227–29; "hospitality" of, 58

Poverty. *See also* Antipoverty programs; ideologies of, 81, 88, 106–7; sociodemographics of, 54

Power attainment: by formal authority, 160–62; and outside connections, 159–60; by possession of skills, 160; by professionalization, 162–65

Power-dependence relations. *See also* Exchange relations; conditions for dependence, 67–68; constraints on power, 183–84; countervailing powers, 67–68; formula for, 66, 179–80; organization-client, 178–85; and resource control vs. availability, 44, 66–69, 159; strategies for changing, 66–69, 79–82, 159; as structural determinant, 165–66; task environment-organization, 178–85

Power, distribution of: differential, 30; and division of labor, 165–66; dominant coalition as key to, 47, 96, 180, 219–20; equalized, 27–28; vs. formal authority, 161–62; and individual freedom, 17–18; relation of, to goals, 46; and resource acquisition, 46; shifts in, 219–20, 223

Power strategies, organizational. *See also* Authority; Coalition; Contracting for Services; Cooperation; Cooptation; Interorganizational competition; choice of, 70; disruptive, 79–82

Practice ideologies, 11, 106, 243; as barriers to innovation, 120, 173, 224; defined, 119; as self-fulfilling, 120, 202; in social work, 119–20; and sponsorship, 173

Prestige, 37, 186, 187, 202, 214. *See also* Legitimation

Prisons, 190; custody vs. rehabilitation in, 84; efforts to reform, 225; segregation of inmates in, 191; transformation of: study, 152–54

Private practice, 72, 185–87

Probation officers, 171–72

Professional associations, 45, 61, 91, 98

Professional autonomy. *See also* Professionals; attainment of, 163; vs. bureaucratic authority, 16–17, 163–64; and evaluation criteria, 174; threats to, 235

Professionalization, 122, 162–65; definition, 162; degrees of, 163; process, 162–63

Professionals, 16, 186, 187, 202, 214; aspiring, and "desirable" clients, 165, 180; legitimating role of,

141; norms of, 16, 24, 164, 183; power of, 162–63; recruitment of, 172–73; training and socialization of, 90, 172–73

Program evaluation. *See also* Evaluation, criteria of; Organizational effectiveness; Performance evaluation; "goal trap," 206; industry, 205; literature on, 210

Protest: by client, 181–82, 188, 191; by organization, 79–82

Psychotherapy, 5, 119, 140, 142; vs. behavior modification, 129; client biographies in, 126; and client status, 196; and desirable clients, 186, 202, 214; effectiveness, 7, 11, 121; referral network, 186; spontaneous remission in, 117; techniques, proliferation of, 117; technologies, 111

Public assistance, 1, 180; efforts to reform, 218; eligibility for, 7, 82; entitlement, 7, 137; grants, allocation of, 52, 81, 82; workers, 184

Public welfare: vs. charity, 2, 3; and civil disorders, 41, 54, 180; expenditures for, 2, 51–52; explosion, in 1960's, 41–43, 54; as "safety valve" for elite, 40–41; and unemployment, 40–41; and urban economy, 54

Referral: vs. steering, systems of, 61, 185–86, 188;189

Resource allocation, 20–21; and acquisition, 44, 227; as goal-commitment, 87, 92–93, 108. *See also* Funding; Legitimation; decisions, 43, 108; for innovation, 219–21, 223, 233, 235, 239–40; *See also* Operative goals; and performance evaluation, 204, 207–8, 213–14; and restrictions, 222–23; as value commitment, 92–93, 116

Resources, availability of: and access to, 61; for change, 226–29, 231, 232–33, 241–42; and economic conditions, 53; and goal transformation, 103; vs. need. *See* Power-dependence relations; and organizational domain, 60; and technology selection, 145

Role expectations, 25, 140, 142, 192, 194, 196. *See also* Typification of clients

Routinization, 138, 160, 163, 167–68. *See also* Standard operating procedures

Rules and regulations: and "bureaucratic personality," 16, 35–36, as control mechanisms, 29–30, 39, 167–68; dehumanization by, 16, 35, 40; operative vs. regulative, 164; vs. professional autonomy, 16–17

Sanctions. *See also* Clients, control of; Staff, control of; against other organizations, 70; power of, and authority 161–62; staff, 167, 174–75

Satisficing, 29, 209–10

School integration, 181; and racial balance, 19; scientific management approach to, 19, 21; symbolic compliance to, 71

Schools, public. *See also* Education; Teachers; Teaching technologies; and capitalism, 41–42; classroom climate in, 24; contracting by, 74; curriculum, 41, 150; effectiveness in, 26; evaluation of, 216; experimental, 31–32; innovation in, 218, 242–43; low income, 53; mainstreaming in, 226, 227, 239; meritocracy in, 41; political climate, 58; vs. private schools, 67; tracking in, 111, 116, 189, 214

Scientific management, 13, 18–22; applied to human services, 19–20; assumptions, 21; cooperation and productivity, 18; critique of, 21–22, 49; and executive cadre, 21; goals, 20; in hospitals, 21–22; tools, 19

Self-actualization: in workplace, 22

Semiprofessionals: buffer role of, 163, 164; delegation of tasks to, 164, 165, 166; upward mobility by, 165

Sensitivity training, 23

Service costs: for needy vs. less needy, 246; rising, 20, 222

Service delivery, 16; choices, 32; control of, by bureaucratic elite, 17–18; and domain consensus, 82; and dominant ideologies, 100–101; effects of competition on, 72–73; innovation, and improvement of, 243; lack of coordination in, 101–2, 109, 158, 170; and multiple goals, 101, 102, 109; patterns, 32, 39, 68, 99; and resource-dependence, 68–69; shaped by official goals, 89, 99–100; structure of, and evaluation, 99–100

Service technologies, 29. *See also* Organizational technology; adoption of, 11, 59, 145; attributes of, 114–24; available, 82; as client control systems, 122–24; components of, 133; craft, 34; defined, 111–12; and dependence on environment, 59; dilemmas of, 110–11; educational, 111–12; engineering, 34; and face-to-face interactions, 10, 120–22. *See also* Staff-client relations; functions, typology of, 134–43. *See also* People-changing technologies; People-processing technologies; People-sustaining technologies; and goal succession, 104–5; indeterminacy of, 9, 33, 59, 91, 116–18, 146, 154–56; innovations in. *See* Organizational change; and internal structure, 46, 150; and level of knowledge, 9–10, 117–18, 127–28, 211; and moral values, 9, 59, 120; operationalization of, 10, 46, 124–34, 146; operations component, 132, 133; people as raw material of, 114; politics of selection of, 46, 48, 111, 144–46; as practice ideologies, 118–20; processing phases of, 113, 114; role of social context, 117–18; routinization of, 34–35, 160; and staff control, 122; summary of components of, 133; and sunk costs, 223; and task perceptions, 154–55; in theory vs. practice, 146–47; transformation, types of, 5–7; typification process, 192–97

Shelter care facilities, 74–75, 106

Social exchange theory, 66. *See also* Exchange relations

Social Security, 45; changes in, 238

Social service agencies, 186; private, client selection in, 55

Social welfare. *See also* Public assistance; Public welfare; Welfare departments; expenditures, 2; programs, 57–58

Social work: radical, 119–20; casework, 30

Social workers: advocacy by, 146; family service, 179; as an interest group, 44; lack of autonomy, 164–66; psychiatric, 102

Staff. *See also* Line staff; Professionals; Staff, control of; alienation, 40, 164, 198; commitment, 24, 198; lower status, 10, 39, 165–66; motivation, 23–24, 28, 94; personal goals of, 94; socialization of, 17, 18, 167, 175; well-being, 26–27

Staff, control of, 17, 111, 122, 166–75. *See also* Practice ideologies; behavior, 167–70, 172; for change, 244; and flow of information to, 17, 168–70; ideological, 17, 18, 167, 175; by incentives and rewards, 46–47, 224–25, 232, 244; indirect, 167–70; and low task visibility, 167; and monitoring, 121–22, 149, 166–67, 169–70; output, 167, 172–75; overt, 17, 167, 170–72, 174; by reducing decision alternatives, 29, 167–70, 172; role of values and commitments, 142–43

Staff-client relations. *See also* Client, control of; Client

Staff-client relations (cont.)
power; Staff; asymmetry of power in, 121–22, 138–39, 142; and client attributes, 125–27, 135–37; communication patterns in, 130–31; and confidentiality, 121–22, 156; and dominant ideologies, 100–101; dual purpose in, 123; as exchange-based, 10; face-to-face interactions, 120–22; goal compatibility in, 197; importance of, 120–21; and intervention techniques, 128; limited visibility of, 156–57; mutual trust in, 197–200; in paraprofessional settings, 165; quality of, 197–99; and ratio of resources per client, 198, 201; role of client biographies in, 126; and role expectations, 129, 130, 142; and staff-staff relations, 24; and success or failure of organization, 10, 155, and typification process, 196–97; ubiquitousness of, 156; and use of forms, 168

Standard operating procedures, 8, 31, 167–70; and reduced decision alternatives, 29, 167–70; and uncertainty avoidance, 31

Street-level bureaucrats. *See* Line staff

Structural-functional approach, 36, 38, 85

Survey feedback, 23

Survival, 152; and capacity for change, 218, 231; goal adaptation for, 105–6; goal displacement for, 106–7, 211–12; and member goals, 94; and providers' assessment, 212; resource certainty and, 65; and self-maintenance, 36–37; and service effectiveness, 185, 212; from systems perspective, 206–7

System 4, 23–28

Task environment, 59–66. *See also* Organization-environment relations; composition of, 61–63; control of resources by, 60–61; defined, 51, 61; exchange relations with, 63–65; homogeneous vs. heterogeneous, 34, 65–66, 232; increasing dependence on, 152, 225; and internal differentiation, 33–34, 38; mapping of, 62–63; relevant, 60; stable vs. unstable, 34, 65–66; turbulent vs. placid, 9, 65–66, 149, 152–54

Tasks, organizational, 8, 46; formalization of, 3, 8,

167–68; interdependence of, 132, 157; nonroutine, 16–17, 34, 155; nonuniform, 27, 34; perception of, 154–55; routine, 16, 160

Taylor: time and motion study, 18, 22

Teachers. *See also* Schools, public; typing of students by, 3, 4, 116, 140, 194, 196

Teaching technologies, 111, 112, 140; recitation vs. multitask, 132–34

Tracking, 193; cost-benefit function, 191; in domesticated organizations, 190–91; in schools, 100, 116, 189, 202, 214

Trust, client, 197–200

Typification of clients, 192–97; as differential treatment guide, 193–94; favorable, 195–96; of high status clients, 195–96; and moral decisions, 192–93, 196; self-, 195–96; staff interest in, 195; usefulness of, 197

Uncertainty: avoidance, 31; degree of, 34, 116–17; and power attainment, 159, 162–63; reduction of, 83, 194; of results, 115–16

Unemployment, 40–41, 53

Universities, 3, 4; administrative decisions, 33, 208–9

Welfare departments, 67, 73, 178–79, 188, 190, 202; alienation in, 41; contracting by, 74; discretion of line staff in, 157; error rate, 207; multiple goals of, 5, 102; protest against, 81

Welfare rights organizations, 81–82

Welfare state: bureaucratization, of, 2–3, 14; and client loss of power, 4; services guaranteed by, 1–2

Work flow, types of, 132

Working conditions, 195, 202–3; and performance, 22–23

Work units. *See also* Division of labor; Organizaitonal structure; differentiation of, 33, 36; structure of, 33–35

YMCA: transformation of, 46–47, 98, 104, 228